ARD

D0894146

Infectious Ideas

JENNIFER BRIER

Infectious Ideas

U.S. Political Responses to the AIDS *Crisis*

THE UNIVERSITY OF NORTH CAROLINA PRESS Chapel Hill

©2009 Jennifer Brier
All rights reserved

Designed and set
by Rebecca Evans
in Minion Pro

Manufactured
in the United
States of America

The paper in this book meets the guidelines for permanence
and durability of the Committee on Production Guidelines
for Book Longevity of the Council on Library Resources.

The University of North Carolina Press has been a member
of the Green Press Initiative since 2003.

Library of Congress Cataloging-in-Publication Data
Brier, Jennifer.

Infectious ideas : U.S. political responses to the AIDS crisis /
by Jennifer Brier.
    p. ; cm.
Includes bibliographical references and index.
ISBN 978-0-8078-3314-8 (cloth : alk. paper)
1. AIDS (Disease) — Political aspects — United States — History.
2. AIDS (Disease) — Government policy — United States —
History. I. Title.
[DNLM: 1. Acquired Immunodeficiency Syndrome —
epidemiology — United States. 2. Federal Government —
United States. 3. History, 20th Century — United States.
4. History, 21st Century — United States. 5. Public Policy —
United States. 6. Social Conditions — United States.
WC 503.4 AA1 B853i 2009]
RA643.83.B75 2009
362.196′9792 — dc22   2009011632

Parts of Chapter 1 were originally printed in *wsq: Women's
Studies Quarterly* 35, nos. 1 and 2, published by the Feminist Press
at the City University of New York. Reprinted with permission.

cloth   13 12 11 10 09   5 4 3 2 1

For *Oliver* and *Kathryn*

Contents

Illustrations

Acknowledgments

WHILE I HAVE LONG IMAGINED what it would be like to write the acknowledgments for a book I completed, I had no idea how difficult it would be to actually write them. In part, that's because there are so many people and institutions that have helped me. Over the last decade, I have been unbelievably fortunate to receive support, guidance, and assistance from more people than I can count and probably mention here. I hope my forgetfulness does not diminish my profound appreciation for their efforts on my behalf. Without them, this book surely would not have come to fruition.

This book began in the archives. Each chapter required numerous trips to different libraries and historical societies, where I always found people committed to preserving queer history and the history of AIDS. I would like to thank Karen Sendziak at the Gerber/Hart Library and Archives in Chicago; Valerie Wheat from Special Collections at the University of California at San Francisco, who retired in 2002 and still managed to send me a huge package of photocopies during her last week of service; Tim Wilson at the San Francisco Public Library, who graciously sent images to me several times; Shelley Jacobs, the most diligent and committed Freedom of Information Act librarian at the Ronald Reagan Presidential Library in Simi Valley, California; Alan Divack and Anthony Maloney at the Ford Foundations Archives in New York, each of whom has an encyclopedic knowledge of Ford and helped me navigate the institution's collection; and Sarah Schulman for undertaking the ACT UP Oral History Project and making the archive available online. I also owe Bill Walker, of the GLBT Historical Society in San Francisco, a special debt, as he cataloged all the archival collections related to AIDS in the Bay Area and was immensely helpful when I began my research at the historical society in the summer of 1998. While Walker did not live long enough to see the book; I hope I have done justice to his archival legacy. Finally, I would like to thank the librarians at UIC's Daley Library, particularly Ana Ortiz, the interlibrary loan librarian, who has made it possible for me to do the transnational research for this book, often without leaving campus.

As a first-time book author, I cannot believe my good fortune to have worked with UNC Press. The staff, most notably my editor Sian Hunter, are truly first rate. For several years before I signed a contract with the press, Sian built a relationship with me and encouraged me to write the book I wanted to write. She has supported me as a scholar and person with tremendous kindness and wit. Beyond her individual attention, Sian secured two incredibly thoughtful readers, one of whom, Leisa Meyer, provided me with the kind of generous critique that any author would be lucky to receive. I am sure this is a better book because of Leisa's suggestions. The book received expert copyediting from Stephanie Wenzel.

As a graduate student at Rutgers University, I was lucky to learn in a vital intellectual environment, where history and women's studies came alive in the work of numerous colleagues and friends. I would like to thank Karen Balcom, Miriam Bartha, Herman Bennett, Ethyl Brooks, Chris Brown, Wesley Brown, Cheryl Clarke, William Cobb, Ed Cohen, Sarah Dubow, Noah Elkin, Tiffany Gill, Sarah Gronim, Matt Guterel, Nancy Hewitt, Beth Hutchison, Rick Jobs, Dan Katz, Melissa Klapper, James Levy, Jan Lewis, Hilary Mason, Patrick McDeavitt, Lucia McMahon, Jennifer Milligan, Khalil Muhammad, Jennifer Nelson, Mary Poole, Jasbir Puar, Scott Sandage, Chris Stacey, Martin Summers, Deborah Gray White, Jenny Worley, and Serena Zabin. I particularly would like to acknowledge the support I received from Kim Brodkin, who read more of this book in draft form than I care to admit having written and has been a caring and committed friend for fifteen years; Barbara Balliet, who taught me how to teach and think in women's studies; Jennifer Morgan, who has been a giving friend and reader; and finally, Jim Reed, Evelynn Hammonds, Mia Bay, Bonnie Smith, and Alice Kessler-Harris, all of whom served on my dissertation committee. As I have told her many times, and will never tire of telling her, Alice is a tremendous advisor, mentor, and colleague. I hope, one day, to be half the advisor to my students that she was, and continues to be, to me.

At the University of Illinois at Chicago, I am surrounded by some of the greatest colleagues and friends that I can imagine. I would like to thank my comrades across the campus: Frances Aparicio, Eric Arnesen, Cynthia Blair, Michelle Boyd, Chris Boyer, Mark Canuel, Elspeth Carruthers, Leon Fink, Javier Villa Flores, Lisa Freeman, Lorena Garcia, Judith Gardiner,

Helen Gary, Anna Guevarra, Sharon Holland, Kirk Hoppe, Stacy Horn, Lynette Jackson, Johari Jabir, Geri James, Robert Johnston, Jennifer Langdon, Maureen Madden, Alicia Matthews, Dwight McBride, Norma Moruzzi, Jay Mueller, Brian Mustanski, Barbara Ransby, Stephanie Riger, Beth Ritchie, Jim Sack, Laurie Schaffner, Katrin Shultheiss, Laura Stempel, Peg Strobel, Astrida Tantillo, Cassandra Veney, and Paul Zeleza for supporting me as I completed the manuscript, sometimes by reading and commenting on work, sometimes by helping me get things done when the book needed to be put on hold. UIC's Great Cities Institute gave me a year off to think and write. I would like to thank David Perry, Joe Hoereth, Marilyn Ruiz, and Joy Pamintuan, as well as the other staff at GCI, for all their incredible help that year. I also want to thank my fellow faculty scholars, especially Ed Trickett, Dick Simpson, Kim Gomez, and Elena Gutiérrez for their continued support. Although not at UIC, Linda Gordon and Marc Stein both read early versions of chapters and gave me insightful and supportive comments for improvement.

I have worked with some amazing undergraduates and graduate students at UIC: Cat Jacquet, Anne Parsons, Rohan Barrett, Brian Kelly, Mike Speilman, Stephen Seely, Ariella Rotramel, Alanah Ryding, Tara Theobald, Gabrielle Anderson, Tania Unzueta, Nadia Unzueta, and Nicole Moret. I would like to thank them for engaging me in classes and seminars as well as making me think about how to communicate beyond a circle of academic historians. I would also like to acknowledge Johnanna Ganz, my mentee from the Point Foundation, who has been a pleasure to work with over the last two years. I save special thanks for Katie Batza, my most incredible research assistant. Katie did research for me, helped me traverse the maze of government documents, and worked on endnotes, permissions, and the bibliography. Beyond her attention to detail, I have benefited from her inquisitiveness, her wonderful sense of humor, and her patience.

I want to acknowledge a handful of people at UIC who really went above and beyond the call of duty to help me finish this project. In the process they have made me a better historian, feminist, and queer scholar. Elena Gutiérrez and Gayatri Reddy, my fellow musketeers/mouseketeers, not only read whole sections of the book and helped me make the prose and argument stronger but, more importantly, provided me with the kind of support that I had only ever gotten from family and my fellow graduate school comrades. They have become the core of my Chicago girls, and for that I am grateful. Corey Capers arrived at UIC a few years after me and in a very short time has become an amazing intellectual and political support, a critical and constructive sounding board, and a truly dear friend. I still pinch myself when I realize that John D'Emilio is not only my colleague but uses an office only three doors down from mine. Before I arrived at UIC, John's work shaped how I thought about, wrote about, and taught gay and lesbian history. Since arriving at UIC five years ago, John has become a mentor and friend. I have benefited from his historical knowledge, but more importantly, I have been the recipient of John's incredible intellectual generosity and what I believe is the best giggle of all time. Finally, Sue Levine, whom I have known since I was five, has been the kind of senior colleague that I hope to be someday. She not only read the entire manuscript twice but, in the final moments, when I was out of gas, helped me get it out the door. Sue and Leon are the center of my Chicago family, and I am thankful to them in more ways than I can articulate.

My friends in Chicago, some of whom are fellow academics and many of whom are not, deserve special thanks for supporting my work with great conversations, delicious food, and a few too many drinks. I am grateful to count among them Veronda J. Pitchford, Angel Ysaguirrue, Bob Webb, Angela Carini, Becky Streifler, Kerri Ellis, Lane Fenrich, Jay Grossman, Jeffrey Matsen, Jennifer Brody, Sharon Holland, Lisa Freeman, Heather Schmucker, Kristina Del Pino, Rand Harris, Tom Schroeder, E. Patrick Johnson, Missy Bradshaw, Jaime Hovey, Robert Kohl, Evette Cardona, Nancy MacLean, Jane Saks, and Rebecca Wellish. I am lucky to add them to my New York crew, a group that has been a vital part of my life even though I no longer live there. I thank J. Bob Alotta, Ed Cohen, Barbara Krauthammer, Lisa Furst, Ben Doren, Mariah Doren, Toshi Reagon, David Hogg, Nick Fagella, Julie List, Danny Greenburg, and Karen Nelson.

Roxanne Panchasi, my dear friend of over a decade and comrade from Rutgers, has been my extraordinary reader and writing partner throughout. We have read each other's work, sometimes in the middle of the night; had intense, often daily conversations about writing history; and sustained an intimate and intellectual connection through some very difficult times. I have become a better writer, historian, and teacher because of her intellectual munificence and abiding friendship.

Finally, I am indebted to my family. My stepfather, Peter Aschkenasy, has been an ardent supporter of my work since the moment he came into my life. As an avid reader and participant in the world of politics, Peter is the person I hope to write for. My mother, Pam Brier, has been inspirational to me not only because she works harder than almost anyone I know, but more importantly because she has a fierce commitment to public health and caring for those who are disenfranchised by the health care system. Quite simply, she is a fierce advocate for the kind of political commitment I have tried to describe in this book. My father, Steve Brier, has supported my evolution as a scholar in more ways than I can spell out here. He is the best editor I have ever had the pleasure of working with: he read and edited the entire manuscript, sometimes going over problematic sections more than once. But his greatest gift to me has been his sustained commitment to documenting the history of ordinary people and detailing the ways they have changed their worlds and ours. Because of that, I am a better historian and daughter. I save my final thanks for Kathryn Hindmand, my partner of more than eleven years (all of which coincide with the researching, writing, and revising of this book). Kat has supported me through some of the most joyous and painful moments of my life. She is, without a doubt, the most caring person I know, despite her protestations to the contrary, and has given me the strength to complete this book. Her love and affection sustain me.

Abbreviations and Acronyms

AAPHR	American Association of Physicians for Human Rights
ABIA	Associação Brasileira Interdisciplinar de AIDS (Brazilian Interdisciplinary AIDS Association)
ACT UP	AIDS Coalition to Unleash Power
AIDS	Acquired Immune Deficiency Syndrome
ARC	AIDS Related Complex
ARV	antiretroviral drug
ASO	AIDS service organization
AZT	azidothymidine
BAR	*Bay Area Reporter*
BWMT	Black and White Men Together
CCG	Community Constituency Group
CDC	Centers for Disease Control
COSATU	Congress of South African Trade Unions
CPFO	Centre de Promotion des Femmes Ouvrières (Center for the Promotion of Women Factory Workers)
DPC	Domestic Policy Council
EMPOWER	Education Means Empowerment of Women Engaged in Recreation
FDA	Food and Drug Administration
GAPA—Rio	Support Groups for the Prevention of AIDS, Rio de Janeiro
GAPA—São Paulo	Support Groups for the Prevention of AIDS, São Paulo
GATT	General Agreement on Tariffs and Trade

GCN	*Gay Community News*
GMHC	Gay Men's Health Crisis
GPA	Global Programme on AIDS
HHS	Health and Human Services
HIV	Human Immunodeficiency Virus
IMPACT	Implementing Agency for Cooperation and Training
INS	Immigration and Naturalization Service
KS	Kaposi's sarcoma
MAC	Majority Action Committee, ACT UP
NGO	nongovernmental organization
NGTF	National Gay Task Force
NIAID	National Institute of Allergies and Infectious Diseases
NYN	*New York Native*
OPL	White House Office of Public Liaison
PATH	Program for Appropriate Technology in Health
PDA	Population and Community Development Association
PHS	Public Health Service
POCC	People of Color Caucus, San Francisco AIDS Foundation
PWAC	People with AIDS Coalition
R and D	Research and Decisions Corporation
SFAF	San Francisco AIDS Foundation
SPA	Special Programme on AIDS
STD	sexually transmitted disease
SWAA	Society for Women and AIDS in Africa
TAC	Treatment Action Campaign
T&D	Treatment and Data Committee, ACT UP
TWAATF	Third World AIDS Advisory Task Force
USAID	U.S. Agency for International Development
WGHP	Working Group on Health Policy
WHO	World Health Organization

Infectious Ideas

Prologue

IT IS NOW AXIOMATIC that the AIDS epidemic was, and continues to be, political. We know less, however, about how that axiom came to be. *Infectious Ideas* argues that AIDS became political over the course of the 1980s, not only because more and more people were infected with what came to be known as Human Immunodeficiency Virus (HIV) as the state failed to respond adequately to the health problem created as more people became ill, but also because a wide range of actors articulated a multifaceted set of ideas in response to the AIDS epidemic. Those actions, which evolved over the course of the decade, existed in opposition to the state's initial intransigence and reframed AIDS in a larger political and economic context.[1]

People reacting to the emergent AIDS epidemic in the early 1980s inserted sexuality into the public sphere at a moment when the state did everything it could to avoid the subject. AIDS workers — I use this term to identify people who were expressly committed to addressing the effects of AIDS — and people with AIDS insisted that AIDS required a return to, not a departure from, the explicitly political tenets of gay liberation. While they talked in graphic detail about sexual practices and how those acts could be "safe," deploying explicit sexual images in AIDS prevention posters, they also understood that sexuality had a political dimension.[2] Part of that political ethos, won in battles for gay liberation in the 1970s, held that gays and lesbians had the power to create healthy communities. By the 1980s, an era when the state was in a process of political and cultural retrenchment manifested most dramatically by the dismantling of the welfare state and attempts to surveil the moral content of federal directives, AIDS workers used their historical vision and political commitments to carve out important spaces in which sexuality figured in new models of care.

Over the course of the 1980s, however, this model of sexual politics became increasingly problematic. The definition of sexual politics inherited from the 1970s held an unspoken assumption about race. The very idea that an open discussion of sexuality was universally good ignored the historical context that linked people of color to hypersexuality. By the mid-1980s, a new group, including gay men of color as well as women and lesbians of color, began to expand, even in the face of significant opposition, the discussion about how best to prevent the spread of AIDS. Rather than promote "safe sex" exclusively, these AIDS workers connected AIDS to struggles around incarceration, immigration, and poverty.[3]

By mid-decade, as the scope of AIDS politics in the United States slowly expanded to include more than a discussion of sexuality, AIDS approached pandemic proportions in the global South. Where most American observers looked on in despair, alongside multiple nation-states that delayed responding to the medical and political crisis, AIDS workers across the global South demonstrated that solutions existed. AIDS workers in Brazil and Thailand, in particular, responded by insisting that the only way to sustain AIDS prevention was to incorporate economic and social analysis into public health models.[4] By linking AIDS to larger issues of economic disempowerment, southern AIDS workers made it clear that treatment models that did not include attention to affordability and access were doomed to failure. In the face of what was constantly reported as an unstoppable and unending global crisis, they developed effective models for treatment and social change. The models they created subsequently influenced how AIDS workers in the United States thought about, and dealt with, the national epidemic.

Despite evidence of people developing arguments about the political nature of AIDS throughout the 1980s and early 1990s, AIDS, and the response to it, have been all but left out of most political historical narratives of the 1980s. Instead, political historians of the postwar period detail the 1980s as a decade that witnessed the triumphant march of conservatism, embodied in the election of Ronald Reagan, the rise of the New Right/Moral Majority, the evisceration of the welfare state, the expansion of the Cold War with the Soviet Union, and the rise of neoliberalism.[5] More specifically, since the mid- to late 1980s, historians have pushed the periodization of the rise of conservatism back to the immediate aftermath of World War II. According to this narrative, locally based activists, grounded in postwar suburban expansion, began to organize in opposition to the post–New Deal state that seemed intent on implementing some kind of racial integration.[6] This nascent social movement picked up steam in the 1960s as people — from campus Republicans to Goldwater supporters in Orange County, California — began to react to the social movements of the 1960s and 1970s. By

1980, so this argument goes, the election of Ronald Reagan seemed all but inevitable.[7] Beyond the lengthening of conservatism's historical trajectory, historical accounts have told how postwar conservatism continued to expand its power base through its ability to bring together people who had once been ideological adversaries — social and economic conservatives. Analysts of 1980s conservatism also have underscored that opposition to changes in sexual and gender relations in the postwar era — especially increasing numbers of women working outside the home, the expansion of gay and lesbian visibility and demands for rights, the legalization of abortion, and the incorporation of depictions of the sexual revolution into mainstream media and culture — fueled the consolidation of conservative social movements.[8] AIDS rarely, if ever, appears in this work, but when it does, AIDS exists either as a catalyst for coalescence among social and economic conservatives or as an example of the effects of a welfare state in retrenchment.[9] *Infectious Ideas* counters the narrative of coalescence by highlighting how AIDS produced different fissures in the conservative movement. Players ranging from the surgeon general to State Department officials resisted the welfare state retrenchment in their efforts to confront the AIDS pandemic head on, even if they did not consistently succeed in having their demands met.

Accounts of the devolution of the Left-liberal coalition of the 1960s exist alongside assessments of the rise of the Right in political narratives of the postwar period and also tend to elide the significance of AIDS work. There are two major interpretative strands in this body of literature. First, scholars such as Todd Gitlin and Walter Benn Michaels see the Left's obsession with the language of multiculturalism and diversity as the reason that a unified progressive movement was no longer possible in the United States in the late twentieth century.[10] Arguing that attention to identities of race, gender, and sexuality fractured the Left and made it unable to appeal to the wide range of people and groups that constituted the backbone of the original New Deal coalition, scholars suggest that progressives need to return to an analysis that centers on how class functions in the late twentieth century. In *The Trouble with Diversity*, Michaels argues that "we love race — we love identity — because we don't love class."[11] Alternatively, in *Infectious Ideas* I argue that when AIDS workers acknowledged the racial implications of the AIDS epidemic, whether in the domestic or the international arena, they opened up a larger discussion of economic inequality and the role it played in the local and global spread of AIDS.

Another cohort of scholars, who see themselves as fundamentally at odds with critiques of identity politics outlined above, argue that over the course of the 1980s the Left's problem was less a move toward identity politics and instead a descent into "neoliberalism." According to historian Lisa Duggan, "The New Deal consensus was dismantled in the creation of a new vision of national and world order, a vision of competition, inequality, market 'discipline,' public austerity, and 'law and order' known as *neoliberalism*."[12] For Duggan, this neoliberal ideology problematically embraced "a stripped down, nonredistributive form of 'equality' designed for global consumption during the twenty-first century, and compatible with continued upward redistribution of resources."[13] While she sees AIDS activism as a model that resisted neoliberalism, in part because of her focus on the internal battles between "liberal" and "radical" factions, Duggan's account of AIDS activists is limited. By considering the evolution of AIDS work while paying particular attention to the AIDS workers who made arguments within a political economic framework, *Infectious Ideas* highlights the people who refused neoliberal models and became some of the first to insist that economic redistribution was the only way to make people healthy.

While the political historiography of the 1980s fails to address AIDS, the interdisciplinary literature on AIDS itself is voluminous. Its expansive nature makes it almost impossible to characterize, but from the perspective of political history (as opposed to medical history), two critical issues emerge.[14] First, most narratives of AIDS draw a sharp distinction between "AIDS activism," defined as direct action targeted against the state and industry in hopes of producing dramatic change in AIDS policy, treatment, and prevention, and "AIDS service," defined as the entities that developed to provide the actual "services" people with AIDS needed as well as to produce the material necessary to prevent the further spread of AIDS.[15] By using the terms "AIDS work" and "AIDS workers," my intention is to deemphasize the distinction between these two categories — activism and service. Detailing the historical evolution of AIDS work gives me access to a wide range of people who worked to fundamentally change both the state's response to AIDS and the response to AIDS produced by white AIDS service providers. This holds true in both the United States and the global South. People working with the most disenfranchised, at the grass roots, whether in the United States or Nigeria, saw little purpose in distinguishing between service and activism.

My desire to address another limit in the AIDS literature — the practice that treats the domestic AIDS epidemic as a phenomenon entirely separate and different from the experience of the disease in the global South — has also shaped the scope of this book.[16] When scholars do discuss the U.S. AIDS epidemic alongside the global pandemic, the movement of ideas and resources is often from North to South. That is, AIDS service and activism developed in the United States and Europe and was imported into the global South, where "developing countries" with recalcitrant state governments were unable and unwilling to address AIDS. Here, I question this model and look for moments when AIDS workers across the global South produced arguments about the link between physical health and economic health, and in effect spearheaded the focus on economic disenfranchisement and AIDS in the United States.

Infectious Ideas treats the struggle to develop a response to AIDS over the course of the 1980s and 1990s as a mirror on American political transformations in the post-1960s era. AIDS workers inspired structural and political changes in municipal, federal, and international governments that shaped institutional and political possibilities in health care, community development, and foreign policy priorities. I detail five distinct yet interrelated case studies of AIDS work, each of which combines gay history, medical history, and the history of sexuality, to suggest that AIDS belongs at the center of recent political history.

The presence of a persistent debate among fledgling AIDS activists over the meanings and uses of sexual liberation provides one of the clearest cases of AIDS work functioning as a political response to conservatism. This is the subject of Chapter 1. Writing in the gay press in direct response to reports of the first cases of the disease that would soon be known as AIDS, gays *and* lesbians turned to lessons learned in the gay liberation movement, explicitly rejecting what they perceived as homophobic silence by the national media and political establishment. As early as 1982, they spoke and wrote about the ways same-sex desire and sex might need to change in the age of AIDS and what the relationship among love, sex, and power should look like in the late twentieth century.

The press coverage was littered with disagreements over the practical meaning of gay liberation, however. I take the presence of such enthusiastic debate about gay liberation to revise the chronology of the ideology's supposed demise. As an idea and driving concept, gay liberation remained central to gay and lesbian life into the 1980s. This continued centrality forces a reconsideration of the dominant narrative of gay liberation's transformation from a radical social movement in the early 1970s to a more conformist civil rights movement by the 1980s.

Chapter 2 shifts from what is largely a national story to the local level, where AIDS workers designed ways to mass-produce gay liberationist arguments in hopes of curbing the spread of AIDS. I detail what happened when the San Francisco AIDS Foundation (SFAF), the first and largest AIDS service organization (ASO) in San Francisco, embraced a particular strand of the gay liberation discussion to address AIDS.[17] By marketing the model of safe sex to gay men, SFAF advanced the argument that open and frank discussions of sex were necessary for effective AIDS prevention education. SFAF created partnerships with a wide range of commercial institutions — from gay bars and bathhouses to gay marketing firms that specialized in tapping into what was increasingly defined as a "gay market." The outreach to community-based businesses gave SFAF access to many gay-identified men living in San Francisco.

While this strategy had dramatic effects on "gay-identified men [who] tend to be disproportionately highly-educated, Caucasian, and upscale in occupation," by marking that very specific group (white, gay-identified, wealthy) as its main target audience, SFAF effectively reified the equation between whiteness and gay identity.[18] This meant that the desires of "out" white gay men came to represent most gay men, regardless of race, while all non-gay-identified homosexual men, that is, men with same-sex attraction, were understood as either African American or Latino. Rather than seeing racial identity and sexual orientation as mutually productive of each other, this model ensured that the production of prevention material that targeted both gay men and communities of color existed at cross-purposes and made it difficult for SFAF to fully address either group's needs.[19]

The Third World AIDS Advisory Task Force (TWAATF) was among the first groups on the West Coast to suggest an alternative model to the one employed by SFAF. When AIDS service providers of color from across San Francisco formed TWAATF in 1986, they intended for the organization to expand the nature of AIDS prevention. TWAATF argued that gay institutions alone would not effectively reach the wide range of people with same-sex desire, nor would it attend to the needs of heterosexuals of color, a group increasingly at risk for AIDS over the course of the 1980s. At the same time, TWAATF refused to desexualize AIDS prevention. While it expanded beyond sex to include discussions of prisons, immigration, and drug use, the volunteer-led organization recognized that discussions of sexual practices needed to be included to ensure that gay-identified people of color were recognized.

The central arguments of the first two chapters — that AIDS provided an opportunity, sometimes realized, sometimes not, for AIDS workers to articulate an alternative communal and political vision to the Reagan administration's inaction — begs the question of how the Reagan administration actually responded to AIDS.[20] Given that Reagan did not mention the term "AIDS" in public until 1987, I expected to find very little on AIDS in Reagan's official papers. I was wrong. The Reagan archive was full of information on AIDS, an analysis of which forms the basis of Chapter 3. Contrary to standard historical narratives of conservatism that argue AIDS served as a rallying point for conservative activists, just as feminism and gay rights had, the evidence in Chapter 3 suggests that AIDS divided conservatives in three areas: questions of sexual morality and where it fit in education, the need for increased social services for people with AIDS, and Cold War foreign policy objectives. In the domestic sphere, political appointees battled over the federal response to AIDS. Gary Bauer — a political and social conservative who had worked his way up the administrative ladder over the course of the early 1980s to run the administration's AIDS effort — tried to enact a three-pronged strategy to deal with AIDS: a national testing program that would detail exactly how many people had AIDS and where they lived; an education policy that emphasized personal, moral responsibility as the best way to enforce necessary behavior changes; and policies based on local community control because of its ability to enforce moral standards more effectively than the federal government and therefore comport better with conservative ideology. The president's longtime conservative ally Surgeon General C. Everett Koop directly contradicted Bauer's ideas, arguing that widespread testing would do little to curb AIDS and that condoms and frank conversations about sexual practices were the best way to change people's behavior. Koop's position found support from the Presidential Commission on HIV/AIDS, established at Bauer's behest to rubber-stamp the administration's domestic AIDS policy. The commission refused to reiterate blindly the administration's position on drugs ("Just Say No") as a response to AIDS and proposed instead a dramatic expansion of the welfare state, most notably drug treatment, as the best way to address the U.S. AIDS epidemic.

The disagreement among administration conservatives became even more visible as the Reagan administration entered the global AIDS arena in the late 1980s, the subject of the second half of the third chapter. Some conservative policymakers hoped to contain AIDS by testing for it at the U.S. border, but the U.S. State Department and the Central Intelligence Agency recommended against it, arguing that this policy of containment would anger elites in the developing world. Although a coalition of conservatives in the administration and Congress were successful in closing U.S. borders to people with AIDS, the State Department and its affiliate, the U.S. Agency for International Development (USAID), adopted AIDS as a centerpiece of its diplomatic strategy, making it possible not only for people with AIDS to seek asylum in the United States but also to encourage discussion of sexual practices and distribution of millions of condoms in the global South. U.S. State Department officials hoped that this policy would strengthen America's image in the eyes of the world.

While the State Department launched some of the first U.S.-funded AIDS programs in the global South, the Ford Foundation, the focus of Chapter 4, explicitly looked to its feminist history when entering AIDS work. Ford, the largest private philanthropy in the world, awarded its first grants to organizations undertaking AIDS work in 1987. Defining its effort as a response to both the growing AIDS pandemic and the limited reach of federal action, the Ford Foundation was the first U.S.-based institution to implement a global AIDS program that not only dealt with the particular effects the epidemic had on women but, more specifically, saw AIDS work as integral to its programs in reproductive health and justice. With an explicitly feminist perspective on AIDS beginning in the late 1980s, the Ford Foundation funded dozens of locally based initiatives in countries ranging from Brazil to Thailand to Senegal, the majority of which worked in the area of reproductive health. This meant that the foundation supported AIDS workers who argued that the best way to initiate and sustain individual behavior change was to incorporate the struggle for women's empowerment and economic empowerment into its AIDS programs.

Chapter 4 returns to the themes of the first two chapters, most notably that AIDS work became a central site for building an opposition to conservatism and conservative policies in the 1980s. Ford saw its AIDS work as a response to what it defined as the uneven policies of the conservative-controlled federal government. With an unequivocal focus on the ideas of feminists from the global South, Ford's work demonstrated that consistent and practical attention to the impact of gender and economic inequality on AIDS circulated in the global South at the same time that it did in the North.

By assessing the state of feminist responses to AIDS in the global South before I narrate the rise and fall of what has come to be known as the first instance of radical AIDS activism in the form of the AIDS Coalition to Unleash Power (ACT UP), I am able to situate the "coalition of activists united in their anger" in a larger historical context. In Chapter 5, I detail the proliferation of various contingents within ACT UP, some formed around identity (e.g., people of color and women), others formed around issues (e.g., treatment and housing). In the beginning, the contingents coexisted in ways that allowed for the execution of dramatic protests that changed the tenor of AIDS work and served as a political critique of the state in all its myriad forms. The coalition did not last long, however. Within five years, ACT UP members were no longer united around a common set of missions. One contingent wanted to see the group work on drug access (defined as the availability of new treatment protocols created through scientific advancements), while another faction insisted that availability of new treatments would not be sufficient to guarantee all people with AIDS access to drugs. For the latter, ACT UP's mission needed to include a commitment to affordable treatment and universal health care, a point that proved prescient when set against the development of protease inhibitors in 1996 and the inability to distribute them.

Paradoxically, the discovery of protease inhibitors produced the conditions for a major surge in AIDS activism outside the United States. The Epilogue shifts the focus of the book to South Africa, one of the global centers of AIDS activism in the twenty-first century. This allows me to end the book with an investigation of the combined efforts of South Africa's Treatment Action Campaign (TAC), an activist organization formed to provide treatment for South Africans with AIDS, and the Congress of South African Trade Unions (COSATU), the largest federation of trade unions in the country. The South African coalition between AIDS activists and trade unionists developed a strategy that allowed it to combine arguments about treatment development, treatment distribution, and general economic security/stability. The class analysis at the heart of COSATU's mission was critical to the success of this strategy and supported TAC's development of systems for effective service delivery, particularly in the face of a state apparatus that was hostile to drug treatment for HIV/AIDS.

Scholars have become so convinced that the 1980s were the most conservative era of the postwar period after the 1950s that they often fail to see how opponents of conservatism were invigorated by what they saw as an ineffective, at best, and immoral, at worst, conservative response to AIDS. In the 1980s, the federal government's AIDS policy produced the conditions that made it possible to defy conservatism and build an alternative to it. Even though the Reagan administration and conservative lobbyists tried to restrict the use of federal money for projects that "promoted" homosexuality and instead argued for a new kind of "federalism" that made local and state governments more central to the development and distribution of AIDS prevention materials, they were never fully able to control the shape and content of AIDS work. In part this resulted from the federal government's supposed disinterest in AIDS, which paradoxically produced a sense of empowerment among the very people trying to cope with the epidemic. AIDS workers did not stop working because the political environment told them what they were doing was wrong or immoral. Rather, they tried to form, albeit imperfectly, a new model for thinking about the state's responsibility to its citizens as well as people beyond its borders.

The historical understanding of the 1980s as a period of unrelenting conservatism also has much to do with how people who considered themselves opponents of the Right experienced the decade. With the election of Ronald Reagan and expansion of the Religious Right's visibility and influence, opponents on the Left, not including most AIDS workers, became increasingly disheartened, fearing they could no longer muster effective opposition to the dominant political culture they witnessed. This, coupled with profound disagreements within the Left over the significance of key identities such as gender, race, and sexuality, made production of a unified oppositional political culture difficult. This pessimistic position has been read back into our historical accounts of the 1980s, so much so that historians and other analysts have failed to acknowledge that political alternatives existed side by side with conservatism throughout the decade.[21] *Infectious Ideas* begins with the premise that a fuller picture of all the ideas associated with AIDS — the sexual, the political, and the transnational — will show how AIDS transformed the political landscape it inhabited. Ultimately, I argue that AIDS work that began as a critique of the policies of indifferent nation-states and greedy industries became an alternative vision of what progressive politics should and could start to look like at the turn of the twenty-first century.

1 | Affection Is Our Best Protection

Early AIDS Activism and the Legacy of Gay Liberation

ON JUNE 18, 1983, almost two years to the day after the Centers for Disease Control (CDC) reported in its *Morbidity and Mortality Weekly Report* the first cases of the disease that would be called Acquired Immune Deficiency Syndrome (AIDS), Boston's weekly gay newspaper, *Gay Community News* (GCN), published a discussion between writer-activists Cindy Patton and Bob Andrews about the personal and political implications of what had become the AIDS epidemic. Patton, who in 1983 served as the managing editor of GCN and would go on to be a prolific social theorist of AIDS, was one of the first women to publish commentary on AIDS.[1] In this early article she made a political argument about how gays and lesbians should respond to AIDS:

> What we are experiencing in the gay community right now is "It's not political until it's personal." . . . In dealing with the government agencies and the health industry regarding AIDS, we can channel our anger outside of our community. Turning our anger inward and toward others in our community divides us unnecessarily. Gays are worn down by our oppression. We worry about our jobs, our lovers, about coming out. Straight society has said to us, "You lead this terrible lifestyle and your punishment is to be sick all of the time," and on some level we've accepted that. We have to turn that around now, and say: This society is not going to kill us any more.[2]

Patton's analysis illustrated a particular moment in both the early history of AIDS and the epidemic's place in the larger political history of the 1980s. First, Patton connected AIDS to feminism, albeit in a somewhat altered form. By reversing the feminist proverb "the personal is political," a phrase that had acquired meaning in the feminist movement of the previous decades, she suggested that lesbians and gay men needed to see their collective health as a political problem, even if only some of them were actually sick or personally affected by illness. Second, Patton's words echoed the language of the gay and lesbian liberation movement. By rejecting individual solutions and instead calling for the end to "straight" oppression, Patton imagined a response to AIDS that would reinvigorate gays and lesbians in a struggle for more systemic liberation. By combining gay and lesbian liberation with feminism, Patton provided an alternative to her contemporaries who suggested that controlling AIDS required, first and foremost, individual behavior change, in the form of gay men altering the way they had sex. Instead, Patton suggested that mobilizing against homophobic oppression was the only way to address the roots of the AIDS epidemic. A few months after GCN published the Andrews/Patton interview, Patton wrote, "I have developed a personal obsession to understand AIDS in the broad context of gay liberation."[3]

Patton's response to the epidemic does not jibe with much that has been written about the early response to AIDS on three counts. First, we assume that lesbians were largely absent from nascent political conversations about the epidemic, in part because public health officials refused to consider how lesbians might be at risk for AIDS, and in part because they served in caretaking roles for gay men with AIDS rather than as political spokespeople for ways to address the AIDS epidemic. Their support role included organizing blood drives when men were banned from donating blood and serving as buddies in the volunteer programs started by new ASOs.[4] Second, historical accounts of AIDS have told us that the gay press, except New York's gay paper the *Native*, did little to warn gay communities about AIDS.[5] In his widely republished article about the AIDS epidemic, "1,112 and Counting," originally published in the *Native* in March 1983, writer-activist Larry Kramer wrote, "With the exception of the New York *Native*, and a few, very few, other gay publications, the gay press has been useless."[6] Finally, and arguably most significantly, we have come to the conclusion that the earliest gay attacks on AIDS figured the disease as the end to gay liberation. Again, Kramer contributed to this model. In his published essays and plays, Kramer encouraged gay men to stop having sex in the ways they had in the 1970s. Kramer demanded of gay men, "Get your head out of the sand, you turkeys! I am sick of guys who moan that giving up careless sex until this blows over is worse than death. . . . I am sick of guys who think that all being gay means is sex in the first place. I am sick of guys who can only think with their cocks."[7] Kramer's contemporary, reporter Randy Shilts, joined in his effort to effect sexual transformation. A gay man writing for the *San Francisco Chronicle*, Shilts became one of the most prolific popular writers investigating AIDS in the early 1980s. In his best-selling book, *And the Band Played On*, published in 1987, Shilts represented Kramer as one of the heroes of the book: "Larry Kramer was growing more militant in this stance . . . [to] tell people that, if they wanted to survive, they should just stop having sex."[8] Beyond his defense of Kramer, Shilts coined the term "AIDSspeak" as "a new language forged by public health officials, anxious gay politicians, and the burgeoning ranks of 'AIDS activists.'"[9] In the process, he characterized attempts to reinvent gay liberation in the age of AIDS as dangerous pipe dreams. "For the past decade, spokespeople of the gay rights movement had held endless press conferences to argue against the stereotype that gay men were sex fiends wholly preoccupied with getting their rocks off. With AIDSspeak, however, many of these same spokespeople were now arguing that bathhouses must stay open because gay men were such sex fiends that they would be screwing behind every bush if they didn't have their sex clubs."[10] Together, the two most infamous proponents of the position that the end to AIDS would come from the abandonment of what they defined as the legacy of gay liberation continue to shape our historical understanding of the epidemic.

Patton's writing suggests the limits of all three historical claims: that lesbians did not play a role in theorizing how to contain AIDS through politics, that the gay press did nothing about AIDS, and that people who embraced the healthy potential of gay liberation just wanted an excuse to have sex in irresponsible ways. Lesbians not only theorized and wrote about how sexuality would change in the age of AIDS, but they also worked with gay men to chart an alternative response to the emerging AIDS epidemic, one based explicitly on gay liberation and implicitly on feminism. In the pages of gay newspapers across the country, but particularly at GCN, the only gay paper that explicitly combined feminism and gay liberation, gays and lesbians who had lived through the liberation movement of the 1970s participated in a vociferous debate about the meanings and practices of health and liberation as well as the role gender politics might play in that discussion.[11] In effect, these feminist writers, both male and female, shaped their response to AIDS around both their personal experiences with AIDS and their role as activists in the social movements of the postwar era, particularly feminism, the women's health movement, and gay and lesbian liberation.

In this chapter I explore the arguments made by these earliest AIDS activists who used the medium of the gay press to communicate a message that AIDS provided a moment in which to return to gay liberation, not run away from it. They struggled with, and argued over, the meaning of key terms, including "gay liberation," "health," "behavior," "fulfillment," and "promiscuity." They asked if gay liberation required complete sexual freedom, often described by critics and defenders alike as promiscuity; what role love and affection should play in liberated behavior; and how communities could be empowered by coalition building around sexual health. Taken together, these questions signaled that writer-activists struggled with how to develop complete and long-term sexual health for gay and lesbian citizens. Instead of calling on men to curtail sexually liberated behavior, they sought to reinvigorate gays and lesbians in the fight for political and cultural recognition as well as to push for equality of diverse sexual practices. These women and men argued that sexual expression itself held the potential for containing the spread of AIDS. Numerous gay and lesbian periodicals echoed the theme and struggled to describe a new disease to their readership. In the process, these writers created a conversation about the possibilities for queer community and queer politics among people thinking about and studying AIDS.

Looking at this evolving community-based AIDS work provides an opportunity to see beyond the unfolding of scientific events and toward the kinds of conversations made possible by the scientific unknown. In a period of medical uncertainty, there was room for a far-reaching conversation among a more diverse group of people, in particular laypeople trained not in science but in the intricacies of grassroots political struggle.[12] Community members could talk about AIDS without being trumped by doctors and health professionals. This, when coupled with the legacy of the feminist health movement of the 1970s, which argued that women should participate in their own health care, produced a moment where a community approach to knowledge was possible.[13]

This chapter ultimately argues for a reconsideration of the periodization of both the gay and lesbian liberation movement and the AIDS activist movement. While historians have paid considerable and productive attention to finding the roots of gay liberation earlier in the postwar period, the same kind of inquiry has not been applied to the other end of the period.[14] Few, if any, accounts of gay and lesbian liberation see it continuing into the 1980s. Instead, a multidisciplinary field of scholars has argued that by the 1980s gay and lesbian activism became increasingly concerned with liberal civil rights and abandoned calls for radical, liberationist political change.[15] I do not disagree with accounts that ultimately explain how fights for gay liberation became fights for gay marriage over the course of the 1980s and 1990s, but the material cited in this chapter suggests that AIDS actually allowed liberation politics to define the gay and lesbian social movement well into the 1980s. In a 1983 speech to a Boston community center, delivered a few month after Kramer's "1,112 and Counting," activist Diane Feinberg forcefully exclaimed that "AIDS is not just a medical crisis. The intransigence of the U.S. government, . . . the stepped-up violence against lesbians and gay men, violently racist scapegoating of Haitian immigrants . . . all this has made AIDS a profoundly political crisis as well."[16]

Before AIDS

The AIDS epidemic was not the first time gays and lesbians thought about sexually transmitted diseases (STDs) or speculated about the connection between the frequency of sexual acts and sexual health or the link between sexual health and physical health more generally. Before the appearance of AIDS in the early 1980s, gay men experienced the effects of other STDs, including hepatitis B, syphilis, and gonorrhea.[17] At the time, some gay men argued that this was a predictable, even acceptable, consequence of gay liberation. In his memoir about AIDS, Richard Berkowitz writes that "coming of age in the 1970s, many young gay men outside cities had no concept of sex without danger — of being found out, disgraced, arrested, beaten up, etc. STIs [sexually transmitted infections] were just one more thing to be added to a long list."[18]

Without access to competent and sensitive medical care in established institutions, many gay men sought treatment for STDs with the handful of gay doctors whose client roster was almost entirely gay. In New York City, Joseph Sonnabend was one of those doctors. A white South African immigrant trained in infectious disease, Sonnabend embodied this role as a doctor with a large gay practice in the gay neighborhood of Greenwich Village. Known as a "clap doctor," he regularly prescribed antibiotics and other treatments for STDs to hundreds of clients, many of whom returned to Sonnabend's clinic often.[19]

Sonnabend was not alone in his efforts. Beginning in 1979, Robert K. Bolan, a gay doctor with a private practice in San Francisco, helped form the National Coalition of Gay Sexually Transmitted Disease Services, a network for the just over fifty service groups and individuals addressing STDs in gay men across the country. The organization advocated infusing an understanding of gay life into health services. Writing as a member of the coalition in 1981, Bolan explained that "knowledge of specific Gay sexual activities, and the ability to be supportive of Gay sexual expression while discussing health and avoidance of disease is absolutely essential if individual health education is to be effective."[20] Bolan strongly urged fellow health care providers to reiterate that gay sexuality was, in and of itself, healthy. In an article published in the *Bay Area Reporter* (BAR), one of San Francisco's main gay newspapers, Bolan expanded the definition of healthy sexual behavior to "expression of one's natural sex drives in satisfying, disease-free ways. Guarding your health and respecting the health of your partners means, for one thing, being aware of your body and the messages it may be giving you."[21] The reciprocation implied in Bolan's model came from his commitment to one of the central arguments of gay liberation, that gay sex was healthy.

At the same time that Bolan devised the guidelines for healthful gay sex, other members of the gay community took a number of steps, both formal and informal, to promote gay sexual health. Small groups of gay doctors and health professionals established community health care clinics in several cities, including Boston, Chicago, New York, and Los Angeles, throughout the 1970s.[22] In Boston, a city with a long history of women's health activism embodied by the Boston Women's Health Book Collective, author of *Our Bodies, Ourselves*, gay and lesbian health activists took over a community health center called the Fenway Clinic. In 1975 a group of health care providers formed the Gay Health Collective and began to offer a free VD clinic at the Fenway one night a week. Over the course of the next several years, with the hard work of many collective members, gay and lesbian health became an "integral part of the function of the health center."[23]

Ron Vachon, a physician's assistant in Boston, was a founding member of Boston's Gay Health Collective and a member of the National Coalition of Gay Sexually Transmitted Disease Services. Vachon worked at the Fenway until 1980, when he moved to New York to work at a health clinic in Chelsea, an increasingly gay and gentrified neighborhood in Manhattan.[24] As was the case with Bolan, Vachon expressed a desire to connect sexual health with the forms of intimacy between men that had been at least partly destigmatized by gay liberation. In March 1981 he wrote "Care for Your Rectum," explaining that anal intercourse had the ability to produce a "bond that other sexual positions can't approach."[25] Written a few months before the first cases of AIDS would be reported, Vachon's discussion of "bonds" suggested not only his stance as a gay liberationist but also his comprehensive view that gay sexual health encompassed mind, body, and spirit. He concluded the piece by explaining, "Most medical people who don't enjoy [anal intercourse] will tell you that it's hazardous and painful. A lot of gay medical people see the damage that is done subsequent to no relaxation, bad lube, and excessive drugs to help 'get into it.' But the pleasure is real . . . trust me!"[26] Anal sex thus served as a metaphor for a commitment between men to the intimate bonding as well as the reality of what could bring a community of interest together for gay men. Nothing could be forced: sexual liberation required both healthful behavior and sexual pleasure. A few months later, Vachon wrote, "Getting in touch with myself means getting in touch with my sexual needs. Staying physically healthy is intimately connected to self-love."[27]

Not as explicitly liberationist, gay medical students in Chicago opened the Howard Brown Health Center in 1974. Almost immediately, Howard Brown became a "hub of the research that's going on in gay health."[28] In addition to major research studies, Howard Brown employed outreach strategies to reach gay men. A drag queen/nurse known as Wanda Lust staffed a "VD van" that traveled to bathhouses and bars in gay neighborhoods to test gay men for STDs and suggest methods for maintaining sexual health.[29] While this method had a real impact on men who defined bar life as central to their sexual liberation, it had less of an effect on men who were either excluded from this world, such as men of color or poorer men, or those who chose to avoid such obviously "gay" places and figures.

Beyond those who provided pro–gay liberationist health care, informal sexual health networks created by non–health professionals addressed gay health needs as well. The work of an organization called Meridian typified this strategy. In 1980, a full year before the first cases of AIDS appeared, Richard Edwards, a gay New Yorker, created Meridian to address the spread of STDs among sexually active gay men. Meridian members agreed to disease screening as a condition of belonging to the organization. After being issued a clean bill of health signed and dated by a doctor, members received an "identification card and an official membership signal pin."[30] The circular pin, gray with a white stripe through the center, designed "so it could go with everything," would then be worn in one of two ways. If the stripe was horizontal, the man fell into the Status 1 group, which indicated he had had sex with non-Meridian members. When a man wore the stripe vertically, he was Status 2, which meant that he had sex only with other Meridian men in the Status 2 category.[31]

Edwards envisioned Meridian as a "further step out of the closet" because it stood on the shoulders of liberation and at the same time disciplined its unintentional consequences for men's health.[32] Membership in this type of gay community was not secured simply by becoming visible to others. Instead, men had to be willing to change sexual practices learned in the closet to achieve membership in a community of identity. A fraternal worldview explicitly shaped this enterprise. Edwards explained, "Meridian is a privately established, discreet, fraternity of men who want to alleviate the problem of V.D. infection through a consensual gentlemen's agreement, and open and honest communication."[33] Meridian tried to make bathhouse use less dangerous and more fulfilling. While bathhouses could be dangerous because some men "knowingly [spread] disease with the attitude of let the other guy take care of himself," the bathhouse would be vital to the "social evolution" of Meridian members.[34]

Redefining gay liberation as a kind of "camaraderie," Meridian promised to allow men sexual freedom while protecting them from exposure to disease. Men had the power to reshape the sexual market as a healthier location without reducing the frequency of their contacts, the kinds of sex acts they preferred, or, importantly, necessarily discussing what they did with each other. In mid-1982 Edwards argued that "we must find new ways to meet the substantial responsibilities of sexual freedom."[35] Rather than relying on governmental health efforts, this model emphasized men's responsibility to their "brothers." Rejecting top-down surveillance, Edwards (or "Mr. Rick," as he signed his letters to the Native) explained, "When it comes to disease we are all related. Buddies care about buddies; it is naturally masculine."[36] In this case, he refused to link nonmonogamy and irresponsibility and suggested that it was possible for gay men to protect and to trust one another while continuing to lead sexually liberated lifestyles.

But Edwards's rhetoric did not necessarily reach all gay men; in fact, it implied activating existing friendship and commercial networks that were themselves shaped by racial and class segregation. Even though he talked about the needs of "straight, bisexual, and gay men and women who are not monogamous," he more regularly deployed an image of a homogenous fraternity.[37] By imagining themselves as "a discreet fraternity," Meridian members attempted to elevate themselves above the out-of-control, uneducated gay men they imagined surrounded them.[38] As "gentlemen" they took part in a social contract that entitled them to certain privileges not accorded to the larger gay public. The "naturally masculine" nature of the "gentlemen's agreement" resonated with a long tradition of male chivalry and republican values accorded to specific racial and class fractions. Gentlemen would protect the entire society if only they were allowed to do what they thought best for themselves and provide a model on which others might pattern their own behavior. This masculine language reflected an older American tradition of individual responsibility — one could only belong to a community after having become a moral individual. In this model, the individual had a part to play in health reform efforts. Meridian members argued that gay men needed to create their own safety net, one based on the love "buddies" have for one another. But the rhetoric of love, despite its communal implications, could not hide the group's exclusionary foundations.

Over the course of the 1970s, the efforts undertaken by people like Bolan and Vachon made gay physical health more central to the definition of healthy gay sexual expression. They were driven to make these changes by a strong desire to expel all vestiges of the homophobic pathologizing of gay desire. They combined their medical prescriptions with ideas that had roots in gay liberation, particularly that pleasure was a step toward health. At the same time, however, these examples of gay health activism before AIDS betrayed the potential for the exclusion of people who did not identify as gay or use their sexual behavior as a way of organizing their lives, a problem that would grow over the course of the next decade and is explored in more detail in the next chapter.

AIDS: The Makings of a Crisis

Even the presence of preexisting community-based health models could not prevent fear and confusion when the first published reports of a "rare cancer" affecting "homosexuals" appeared in newspapers in July 1981.

Dr. Lawrence Altman, the medical reporter for the *New York Times*, suggested that "cancer [specifically, Kaposi's sarcoma (KS)] is not believed to be contagious, but conditions that might precipitate it, such as particular viruses or environmental factors, might account for an outbreak among a single group."[39] But the brevity of the article, combined with the sense that public health entities were unlikely to address something considered a gay disease, produced uncertainty and fear. In direct response to Altman, Lawrence Mass, a gay doctor living in New York, tried to calm people with the first substantive article on the cancer to appear in the gay press, "Cancer in the Gay Community." The article ran in the *New York Native*, New York City's most widely circulated gay periodical and one of the nation's major gay newspapers. In the article, Mass cautioned against panic, a theme he returned to again and again over the course of the next half decade as he became the *Native*'s main medical reporter and doctor-in-residence. But Mass asked more questions than he answered. "The most immediately seductive environmental explanation of 'the gay cancer' is that it is being caused by an infectious or otherwise cancerous agent. . . . If the cause is infectious, why is KS being seen only among certain gay men?"[40] Mass ended the article with what he intended to be a balanced discussion of sexual practices. He wrote, "Sexual frequency with a multiplicity of partners — what some would call promiscuity — is the single overriding risk factor for developing infectious diseases and KS. This is not to say that sexually responsible individuals can't get the same diseases, nor does it imply that sexually active individuals are going to contract these conditions because of immorality."[41] While the quote implied that promiscuity did not necessarily cause KS, Mass emphasized the argument that all gay men were at risk. Larry Kramer followed up on his friend's article with his own missive in the form of a "personal appeal" to the gay community for money and support. In August 1981 Kramer exclaimed, "It's difficult to write this without sounding alarmist or too emotional or just plain scared. . . . It's easy to become frightened that one of the many things we've done or taken over the past years may be all that it takes for a cancer to grow from a tiny something-or-other that got in there who knows when from doing who knows what."[42]

The positions articulated by Mass and Kramer aggravated other gay men as well as other health professionals. Kramer's appeal elicited pointed reactions from Robert Chesley, a fellow gay New Yorker, and Edmund White, coauthor of *The Joy of Gay Sex*. In a letter to the editor following

Kramer's appeal, Chesley wrote that for Kramer, "the wages of gay sin are death."[43] White's commentary grouped Mass and Kramer together, suggesting that "some moralists are using the appearance of Kaposi's sarcoma as a pretext for preaching against gay promiscuity under the guise of giving sound medical advice."[44] Finally, some health professionals cautioned against panic, suggesting that AIDS was not yet an epidemic. Writing in GCN, J. B. Molaghan, a nurse practitioner from the Fenway Clinic, argued that the 169 cases since 1980 "justified serious concern," but that gay men should be more concerned with the "22 sexually transmitted diseases that exist, [and] substance abuse and alcoholism."[45] Molaghan wanted men to understand AIDS in relation to the other medical problems they faced and not let it blind them to how to become sexually healthy in general.

The debate over how best to respond to AIDS in the context of gay liberation continued. In March 1982, Mass followed up on his first article with "The Epidemic Continues: Facing a New Case Every Day, Researchers Are Still Bewildered." Implicitly rejecting Molaghan's caution about the use of the term "epidemic," Mass described a "disorder of immunity" that some public health officials referred to as Gay Related, or GRID, Immunodeficiency and others called Acquired Immunodeficiency Disease. He explained that "most of the victims have been characterized as sexually active, otherwise healthy, 'homosexual or bisexual men' in their twenties and thirties."[46] Jokingly, Mass explained that "on the superficial basis of numbers alone, of course, wearing handkerchiefed Levi's and having Judy Garland records in one's collection might also seem risky."[47] Anticipating the argument that gay institutions that provided space for public sex should be shuttered, Mass cautioned against the rush to close the institutions. "It's probably that *some* sexually transmitted diseases that *may* be related to the current epidemic are being spread at the baths, but not because of the baths per se."[48]

Lending support to Mass's position on the baths, an arresting photograph appeared just to the left of Mass's lead article. Directly under the bold headline "The Epidemic Continues," a black-and-white image of a naked man bound by a leather harness appeared with a teaser for an article on page 11: "My Weekend in Hell, a Bottom's First Time." The article promised readers a titillating tale of two nights spent at a New York City gay bathhouse. (See ill. 1.1.) The juxtaposition of these stories — one on the disease that would become AIDS, one detailing various forms of sexual expression in New York's gay community in the early 1980s — foreshadowed the

1.1 | *New York Native* cover, March 29–April 11, 1982. Courtesy of Gerber Hart Library.

argument Mass would make on the last page of his article: "Within the gay community, a . . . crisis of ideology is threatening to explode. With much confusion on all sides, advocates of sexual 'fulfillment' are being opposed to critics of 'promiscuity.'"[49]

The debate was, in fact, multisided and involved disagreements over the meanings of words that had become part of a liberationist lexicon in the 1970s. During the next three years, gay men and lesbians, health professionals and laypeople, argued about the best way to change the course of the AIDS epidemic and, in the process, articulated and embraced a wide range of responses to what was still a medical mystery. Disagreement about the best way to proceed existed among medical professionals, many of whom were veterans of the work described in the preceding section. Laypeople, too, articulated myriad reactions. Some looked to the legacy of gay liberation as defined by a kind of brotherhood among gay men, while others reminded gay men that their diverse sexual practices did not have to involve the exchange of bodily fluids; still others called for a drastic change to gay sexual culture. At the time, these differences produced animosity between community members, but in retrospect, it is possible to see commonalities among the perspectives.

Medical Questions and Answers

Beginning in 1982, just months after the first reported cases, doctors across the country used community forums and the gay press to inculcate gay men with the message of having fewer sex partners. New York City physician Dan William, a cofounder of New York's Gay Men's Health Project, told attendees at a 1982 community meeting held in a 500-seat auditorium at New York University, "'Don't have less sex — just have it with fewer people.'"[50] In a pamphlet originally written for Gay Men's Health Crisis (GMHC) in late 1982 and reproduced in both the *BAR* and *GCN*, Larry Mass called on men to limit their partners: "A number of physicians, many of them Gay as well, have advised their Gay patients to moderate their sexual activity with fewer partners who are in good health. It is the number of different sexual encounters that may increase the risk, not sex itself."[51] In one of the first articles to appear in Chicago's *Gay Life*, reporter Chris Heim interviewed Dr. Paul Paroski of the National Gay Health Education Foundation, the same group Ron Vachon headed, after which the reporter suggested that "without knowing the cause, it is hard to determine preventive measures. It has been suggested that reduction of drug use and limitation of the number of sexual partners may help reduce risk."[52] Boston's Fenway Community Health Center communicated a similar message to Bostonians with pieces in *GCN*: "So far, no one has been able to further define other risk factors that are specific for AIDS. . . . Once again, be aware that the frequency of sexual activity does not appear to be a factor in acquiring AIDS, but instead it is the number of different sexual partners that may be relevant."[53]

Many gay men heard the call to limit sexual partners as a message infused with moralism. In a report on one of the community forums, the *Advocate*'s reporter Stephen Greco commented, "One couldn't help thinking that with the voices of the Moral Majority ringing in our ears, it is hard for some of us to hear . . . that we should cramp our own style."[54] Fear that gay doctors would unwittingly join forces with the Right was put in sharp relief by Dr. Joseph Sonnabend. Sonnabend advocated the position that gay liberation, and its promotion of sexual freedom, was inherently unhealthy. In a 1982 article published in the *Native* Sonnabend wrote, "Promiscuity is a considerable health hazard; this is not a moralistic judgment, but a clear statement of the devastating effect of repeated infections. If we are truly to serve our patients, we must admit that our desire to be non-judgmental has interfered with our primary commitment. With this understanding, we can move on to provide the care that our patients deserve."[55] Sonnabend made similar arguments in mainstream journals. In a 1983 article in the *Journal of the American Medical Association* Sonnabend stated, "The question is, 'Why now?' We propose that an unprecedented level of promiscuity has developed during the past decade in large urban areas such as Greenwich Village."[56] Sonnabend's word choice had an effect on what people heard when he spoke or wrote, allowing them to dismiss his theories as ineffective at best and antigay at worst.[57]

Not all gay doctors rejected "promiscuity" or embraced the position that men should limit their sexual partners. Tom Smith, director of the Alcohol Treatment Center at San Francisco General Hospital, spoke forcefully on the possibility of combining sexual liberation and sexual safety.

> Sexual abandonment and "animal" sexuality are often cherished aspects of sexuality. These important aspects of sexuality seem to be in conflict with sexually safe limits. But not necessarily. At each level of sexual risk taking (no risk, minimal risk, moderate risk, high risk), a person can enter deep (or high) states of altered consciousness with or without high level of "letting go" automatic physical activities on orgasmic control. Sexual abandonment is not necessarily the same as very unsafe sexual practices. . . . I strongly feel that sexuality should be part of the solution. I feel that we should appeal to the majority of Gay men that are interested in positive change and not focus as heavily on the careless (plan for them but not focus on them).[58]

Smith refused to assume that gay men were essentially careless and instead believed that a highly conscious sexual freedom could be safe. In so doing, Smith resisted the idea that gay men were unwilling to adjust to AIDS at the same time that he recognized that "sexual abandonment" needed to play a role in helping people change their actions. In the end, Smith emphasized that men could redefine what positive sexual expression meant.

Ron Vachon, the former member of Boston's Gay Health Collective, agreed with Smith and continued to write about sexual health in ways that gay men could understand and appreciate. In an article Vachon wrote for the *Native* in 1982 titled "Risks and Responsibilities of Recreational Sex," he extended his liberationist analysis by questioning the relationship between consenting partners and health. He asked men to consider their partner's risk when having sex. Vachon wanted every gay man "to stimulate self-evaluation of [his] sexual lifestyle; and to encourage responsibility for [his] health and the health of others."[59] This would signal a gay man's commitment to the larger community of gay men. Vachon concluded his article with a call to individual action that would ultimately serve the larger community by encouraging men to think of one another and foster a "healthy STD attitude." He claimed that men needed to imagine "a genuine affection for [their] gay brothers." Addressing his fellows in the gay community, Vachon claimed, "The pleasure we give each other through sex is directly proportional to our sense of responsibility for each other."[60] In other words, prevention would only be effective if an ethic of caring and a fraternal model of community was tied to sexual pleasure.

The American Association of Physicians for Human Rights (AAPHR) adapted Smith and Vachon's positions, combining them with the earlier model of limiting sexual partners. In the spring of 1983 the association published recommendations for "healthful" sex:

> Healthful sexual behavior is an expression of one's natural sexual drive in a satisfying, disease-free way. We are supportive of gay sexual expression. As health educators, we believe that knowledge of specific gay sexual practices and their implications for health and disease are essential for a safe and satisfying sexual life. . . . Decrease the *number* of *different* men with whom you have sex, and particularly with those men who also have many different sex partners. This does *not* mean to reduce the frequency of sex with any *one* partner, but only the number of different partners.[61]

Signaling its commitment to gay liberation by mentioning "gay sexual expression" and the need for a "satisfying sexual life," the AAPHR's rhetoric suggested an inclusivity not necessarily implied by earlier medical accounts. The language not in the statement also highlighted the lack of consensus on what constituted effective AIDS prevention. At no point in the document did the AAPHR discourage men from practicing specific sexual acts, most notably anal intercourse, nor did it suggest that men use condoms. Rather, the recommendation asked men to limit the number of men they had sex with in a context of gay sexual expression. The AAPHR saw its role as an advocate for sexual freedom and sexual health and re-fused the idea that gay sex was essentially dangerous.

These varying accounts among health care professionals suggest that no consensus yet existed about how to deal with AIDS. Despite the disagree-ments, a majority of health professionals recalled several of the principles of gay liberation, namely the need for gay sexual expression and the ability of gay men to act with concern for their own health as well as the health of their partners. In this respect, most of the medical professionals writ-ing between 1981 and 1983, except Sonnabend, represented gay men not as selfish but, rather, as capable of healthy sexual behavior.

Gay Communities Respond

Community activists, few of whom had medical or health training, began to articulate myriad stances on AIDS and gay life, but the nature of the de-bate was different from those among medical professionals. Embracing the "gay liberationist" moniker, the debate among these men and women re-volved around how they defined the term. Some writer-activists cautioned against homophobic panic, seeing it as a reiteration of the pathologizing of gay desire that permeated an earlier era; others criticized "promiscuity" by name, specifically railed against the commercialization of gay life, and refused to see their position as the antithesis of advocacy of sexual fulfill-ment. Still others thought AIDS provided an opportunity to combine the struggle for sexual freedom with the struggle for gender freedom. Because most of the writer-activists defined themselves as gay liberationists, the disagreements became even more vociferous, even though most of the po-sitions were compatible.

The first community actors to develop information to help gay men cope with AIDS using the tenets of gay liberation were the Sisters of Perpetual Indulgence, a group of gender-queer gay men in San Francisco. Started in 1979 by several gay men who wanted to resist the overt masculinity of the gay scene in the Castro, San Francisco's gay neighborhood, the Sisters used their form of performance activism to fight for free sexual expression.[62] In the summer of 1982, the Sisters, led by their members who worked as nurses — Sister Florence Nightmare (aka Bobbi Campbell, who also wrote a column about AIDS under the nom de plume the "KS Poster Boy") and Sister Roz Erection — created *Play Fair!* a brochure that talked about AIDS with sex-positive language for distribution at the June Gay Pride parade.

1.2 | *Play Fair!* First edition, © 1982, The Sisters of Perpetual Indulgence, Inc. Reprinted with permission.

(See ill. 1.2.) Funded by half a dozen bathhouses and the San Francisco chapter of the North American Man Boy Love Association, the brochure used a combination of humor and the language of gay liberation to effect change. The Sisters told men that "if you know — or even suspect — that you have a Sexually Transmitted Disease, don't put other people at risk by engaging in sexual activity. Wait until you KNOW you can cum clean." As the group's leader, Mother Superior, counseled, "We are giving these diseases [referring to a range of conditions from gonorrhea to crabs to KS to guilt] to ourselves and each other through selfishness and ignorance. We are destroying ourselves."[63]

Few authors could harness the comedic and liberatory potential of the Sisters of Perpetual Indulgence. Instead, people emphasized the seriousness of AIDS at the same time that they demanded that gay liberation be front and center. In October 1982 GCN published its first two feature-length articles on AIDS, each of which tried to strike a balance between the need for both concern and free sexual expression. In pieces written by two of the paper's regular contributors, Michael Bronski and Gordon Murray, GCN began to sketch out a response to AIDS that refused to blame individual sexual practice for the spread of the disease. In "AIDS Mystery" Murray explained that AIDS was a public health crisis threatening gay communities across the country. Murray cited statistics that AIDS was spreading quickly and seemed to be quite deadly. Murray's position in "AIDS Mystery" differed from doctors' demands to reduce sexual partners. The piece informed readers that, while some "AIDS victims" had more than 1,000 sexual partners over their lifetimes, others "have long histories of monogamy."[64] Murray refused to blame sexually active men for behaving in ways that brought on disease and ended with a call to action that invoked the struggles of gay liberation of the 1970s: "The challenge of AIDS [is] enormous. The personal toll is tragic and immeasurable. Yet there is a potential in the AIDS crisis to catalyze the gay movement to new levels of consciousness, organization and loving bondedness."[65] Echoing the words Ron Vachon wrote in the same paper two years earlier, Murray reiterated the idea that gay liberation provided for a political solution to a health problem.

Bronski, in his "AIDing Our Guilt and Fear," shared Murray's political sentiment but went beyond his fellow writer's analysis to attack the AIDS coverage of other gay periodicals and suggest that certain gay sexual practices typical of gay liberation had the potential to contain AIDS. In a specific reference to the *Native*'s and the *Advocate*'s coverage, Bronski commented on what he saw as a problematic model of going back and forth on the causes of AIDS. The effect of this was fear: "The constant reader would waver from thinking that they knew everything to knowing almost nothing, while getting more paranoid all the time."[66] This, when coupled with the representation of AIDS as a "GAY PLAGUE," even though each publication "mentioned other groups that have been afflicted (heterosexual Haitians, hemophiliacs, and intravenous drug users)," convinced men that a "gay" cancer actually existed.[67] Bronski also took aim at those who called on gay men to drastically modify their sexual practices, and in the process he specifically linked Mass and Sonnabend to "new-right-middle-America notions of right and wrong."[68]

Alternatively, Bronski refused to overgeneralize about how gay men should have sex. He reasoned that certain sexual practices were safer than others, noting, "certainly bondage and flagellation would be safer than kissing. But the connection between 'bad' sex and disease has been made and it is a hard combination to strike down."[69] By maintaining a pro-sex argument that had its roots in the gay liberation movement of the 1970s, Bronski suggested that sexual liberation allowed people to have sex in ways that were, in fact, healthy.

Bronski's article infuriated Mass, who felt wrongly accused as a "critic of promiscuity." Two weeks after Bronski's article appeared, Mass penned an angry response. In the letter, Mass answered Bronski's charges of sexual policing by framing his position as the earnest belief in "sex revolutionary ideals." He explained that AIDS made changing behavior vital, but that this had to be done in a way that allowed "sexual freedom and sexual health . . . to complement rather than conflict with each other."[70] Mass concluded with an accusation that GCN waited a year to feature an article on AIDS; "hindsight is easier if not better than foresight."[71]

Before Bronski could respond to Mass, Toronto-based gay activists and academics Michael Lynch and Bill Lewis wrote to defend the idea that AIDS should not necessitate a rejection of gay liberation. Contrary to Mass's rhetoric, Lynch and Lewis argued that gay men were capable of making their own decisions about how to maintain sexual freedom and health at the same time. In their letter to GCN, Lynch and Lewis wrote, "Gay men are quite accustomed to accepting various risks of contracting STDs, and to weighing them carefully against the pleasure and nourishment we gain from multiple sexual partners."[72] At the same time that Lynch and Lewis wrote to GCN, they also published feature-length articles on AIDS in the Canadian gay periodical *The Body Politic*. Each article attacked health professionals for promoting fear among gay men. Lynch criticized Dan William, the doctor who had held forums on gay sex, explaining that "Dr. William and his followers . . . seek to rip apart the very promiscuous fabric that knits the gay male community together and that, in its democratic anarchism, defies state regulation of our sexuality. . . . The thrust of gay liberation, even if the term does feel nostalgic in 1982, remains that we make our own lives, that we do not give ourselves over to the panic mongering journalists and doctors."[73]

That this journalistic sparring over the particulars of gay liberation took place in GCN made sense, given the periodical's historical connection to the gay liberation movement. Founded in 1973 and run by a collective of reporters, GCN's mission was not to be "objective"; rather, according to former collective member Amy Hoffman, the goal "was explicitly activist. . . .

We supported the most radical expressions of the gay liberation movement. We believed in upsetting the social order and in creating alternatives to traditional gender roles, definitions of sexuality, and hierarchical power structures of all kinds."[74] Former collective member Richard Burns, who went on to run New York's Gay and Lesbian Community Center, agreed with Hoffman's assessment, arguing that at GCN "feminism and gay liberation were closely connected."[75] By the 1980s, GCN provided a space for self-defined progressive or Left-leaning gays and lesbians to debate how to continue the political and cultural gains of the 1970s. Beyond that, as will be clear later in the chapter, GCN also encouraged lesbians to write about AIDS, a decision shared by no other gay periodical.

Not all gay men praised gay liberation's attachment to a "promiscuous fabric." One month after the GCN exchange among Bronski, Mass, Lynch, and Lewis, the New York Native published an article written by two New York gay men, Michael Callen and Richard Berkowitz. Titled "We Know Who We Are: Two Gay Men Declare War on Promiscuity," Callen and Berkowitz described themselves as "both 27 years old, have both been excessively promiscuous, and are both victims of AIDS."[76] The authors made a clarion call against promiscuity: "We could continue to deny overwhelming evidence that the present health crisis is a direct result of the unprecedented promiscuity that has occurred since Stonewall, but such denial is killing us. Denial will continue to kill us until we begin the difficult task of changing the ways in which we have sex."[77] Their decision to attack the "promiscuity" that occurred after Stonewall mimicked the position articulated by their doctor, Joseph Sonnabend. Sonnabend, who had treated each man for STDs in his Greenwich Village office, introduced Callen and Berkowitz, hoping that they would work together to write a document about AIDS with widespread appeal.[78]

Callen and Berkowitz's attack on promiscuity by name potentially blinded readers to their equally substantive argument about gay liberation in the age of AIDS. The authors reasoned that the commercialization of gay sexual life in the 1970s and 1980s, a situation made possible by the devolution of gay liberation into gay markets, produced the conditions for gay men to develop AIDS. Callen and Berkowitz argued that the commercialization of gay life amplified the lack of concern anonymous sexual contacts had for each other. In hypothesizing that the market had made itself part of gay male sexuality, Callen and Berkowitz marked the limits of a gay liberation understood as the proliferation of places to have sex: "The commercialization of promiscuity and the explosion of establishments such as the bathhouses, bookstores, and backrooms is unique in western history. It has been mass participation in this lifestyle that has led to the creation of an increasingly disease-polluted pool of sexual partners — which has in turn very likely led to the epidemic of AIDS."[79] The market, in fact, tainted the production of sexual freedom and dimmed its revolutionary aura.[80]

Rather than blaming individual gay men, a point that often followed in other attacks on promiscuity, Callen and Berkowitz reasoned that gay men had experienced the effects of multiple STDs for so long that their systems gave out and produced AIDS. They described their experience with infections increasingly common in parts of the gay community, like cytomegalovirus, hepatitis, herpes, and amebiasis. The combination of these infections ultimately produced a collapse of the immune system from which men could not recover. In an interview that appeared in the *Native* a month after the article on promiscuity ran, Berkowitz said, "We both came to understand early in the game that it was promiscuity that made us sick and not some new mutant virus from Mars. But most of gay men are still being told that they have AIDS because they came into contact with a mysterious killer virus — by other gay men, no less — so they don't feel that it makes any difference for them to stop being promiscuous."[81] This theory also allowed Callen and Berkowitz to connect the needs of gay men and lesbians to those of other disenfranchised groups and ultimately to argue that social and political inequality made AIDS more likely.

In refusing the viral explanation, Callen and Berkowitz's argument resisted a very common image in 1982, one that continues to this day, that AIDS came from somewhere outside the United States. In 1982 that place was thought to be Haiti. Callen and Berkowitz looked for a less exotic and racist explanation: "But to go even further and imply that 'we' got 'it' from the Haitians is a particularly ugly example of the Western tradition of blaming calamity on the Third World. And it's bad science. . . . What promiscuous urban gay men, intravenous drug abusers, hemophiliacs, and Haitians all have in common is a pattern of accumulation of risk through re-infection with common viruses."[82] In a 2005 interview Berkowitz confirmed this link when he replied to a question about how the overload theory applied to AIDS in South Africa: he said that sex without prophylaxis created an overloaded immune system and caused AIDS in gay men, and the chronic poor health associated with poverty caused AIDS in South Africa.[83]

The solution, for Callen and Berkowitz, was to return to gay liberation, not run away from it. Callen and Berkowitz argued that this would not entail more sex but, rather, required encouraging people to behave ethically and to consider their partners' health in addition to their own. Callen and Berkowitz called on gay men to act "as individuals, [who] must care enough about ourselves to begin this re-evaluation. As a community we must initiate and control this process ourselves." They continued:

> We are not suggesting legislating an end to promiscuity. Ultimately, it may be more important to let people die in the pursuit of their own happiness than to limit personal freedom by regulating risk. . . . The motto of the promiscuous gay man has been "So many men, so little time." In the '70s we worried about so many men; in the '80s we will have to worry about so little time. For us, the party that was the '70s is over. For some, perhaps, homosexuality will always mean promiscuity. They may very well die for that belief. The 13 years since Stonewall have demonstrated tremendous change. So must the next 13 years.[84]

While many readers cringed at their reiteration of the attack on promiscuity and feared that the authors wanted to see the end to gay liberation, Callen and Berkowitz embraced a libertarian argument about choice. Gay men needed to be free to change without regulation.

As soon as Callen and Berkowitz's article appeared, critics began to compose responses to what they saw as a moralistic piece of journalism. Criticisms of the manifesto appeared in many forms, ranging from articles and letters to the editor that suggested the authors were puritanical, to pieces in other gay newspapers that presented a defense of unfettered sexuality as critical to maintaining gay liberation.[85] In a direct attack on Callen and Berkowitz, Charles Jurrist, a regular contributor to the Native's arts page, posited that promiscuity, a word the author used proudly, needed defense. In his essay "In Defense of Promiscuity," Jurrist relied on the unknown etiology of AIDS to argue for "promiscuous" sexual practice. Using his authority as a GMHC volunteer, which although it was a new organization was certainly recognized as critical to AIDS work in New York, Jurrist called for an end to what he deemed unnecessary "hysteria." He then launched into a critique of Callen and Berkowitz's version of gay liberation, and in so doing, he voiced a perspective that was prevalent in the gay community in 1982, one that encouraged men to weigh the risks of anonymous sex and its potential health consequences against the eradication of the sexual ethic that was foundational to modern gay identity. "The fact is that no one yet knows what causes AIDS. . . . It therefore seems a little premature to be calling for an end to sexual freedom in the name of physical health. . . . [Callen and Berkowitz] are not merely calling on us to forego that type of orgiastic unselectivity. They seem to be saying that anything other than monogamy or sex restricted to two or three ongoing, tightly controlled relationships constitutes promiscuity and ought to be avoided."[86] Jurrist wanted gay men to have "sexual freedom," the same "freedom" that Callen and Berkowitz claimed was "unique in western history." Jurrist warned men to hold on to their sexuality and not fall prey to the rampant fear produced by the likes of Callen and Berkowitz.

Writers in Boston echoed Jurrist's attacks on Callen and Berkowitz. In March 1983 GCN published Tom Reeves's essay "On Backlash, Closets, and Sexual Liberation," in which the author suggested that Callen and Berkowitz were attacking gay men's lifestyles without cause.

> The question should be why are we dying, not why are we killing
> ourselves. Our own media are full of self-hate and sex-fear in their
> coverage of AIDS. The New York *Native* article by two sufferers of the
> disease said it all in its title, "We Know Who We Are." In other words,
> we are the unclean; our blood is contaminated; we live in a "disease
> pool" of sexuality. The solution is monogamy, possibly celibacy,
> for who can tell who is the carrier? One gay reporter asked shyly if
> masturbation were ok. "Sure," said a doctor, "you can even sleep with
> people are far as we know, just avoid any fluids — semen, piss, saliva."
> Don't suck, don't fuck, don't kiss. What a relief! No crusade yet against
> jerking off.[87]

That other gay men agreed with Jurrist and Reeves was confirmed by a new but fast-growing field of social scientific study, the psychology of AIDS. In November 1983 the AIDS Behavioral Research Project conducted a survey that seemed to confirm their position that many gay men had no intention of limiting their sexual contacts. Interviews with 1,550 gay men in the San Francisco Bay Area documented how the emerging AIDS crisis had and had not changed sexual behavior.[88] Researchers found that while changes in men's behavior depended on their "pre-AIDS" sexual practices, such as being in open relationships, going to bars, and regularly using the bathhouses, "sixty-nine per cent of the men having three or more sexual partners the previous month agreed with the statement, 'It is hard to change my sexual behavior because being gay means doing what I want sexually.'"[89]

For all these men the most lasting effect of gay liberation meant that they could and should act on individual sex desires. In his conclusion Jurrist wrote, "Tell us how this blessed and healthy state is to be attained; and how, until it is, a man with ordinary sex drives is supposed to satisfy them. . . . I will continue to be 'promiscuous.' I won't be scared out of seeking fulfillment. Nor will I consider my behavior in any way as self-destructive. I see it as life-affirming. I refuse to blight my life in order — supposedly — to preserve it."[90] Sexual liberation for Jurrist, and for the men his conclusions spoke to, meant the possibility of a sexual practice that was the antithesis of heterosexuality and represented complete freedom from heterosexist domination. Homosexuality provided men with a unique sexual outlet: They did not have to participate in a culture that considered only marital, monogamous sex acceptable. Jurrist believed that this kind of individualistic behavior continued the struggles of gay liberation, allowing men the possibility of real desire. His individualist, laissez-faire claims resonated with a tradition of male heterosexual privilege at the same time that he called attention to the positive health consequences of sexual liberation.

Callen and Berkowitz responded to their critics in a cowritten book, *How to Have Sex in an Epidemic*. Published in 1983, Callen and Berkowitz's second collaborative writing project was a forty-page manifesto that sold out its initial 5,000 print run. The new project allowed Callen and Berkowitz to expand the ideas presented in their controversial article and temper the use of the term "promiscuous." The writers provided readers with practical ideas for how men could have sex in new ways. Callen and Berkowitz cautioned readers to ask not simply "Will this pose a health risk to me?" but also "Will this pose a risk to my partner?"[91] By resisting the tendency to separate the two, Callen and Berkowitz challenged what they saw as a central tenet of gay liberation as practiced in the 1970s and 1980s, the belief that an individual's erotic life was more about his own pleasure than anything else. Individuals had not only the ability but also the obligation to control their sexual actions for the sake of their gay brothers. Instead of simply rejecting unfettered sexuality (what they called promiscuity), Callen and Berkowitz worked to reclaim other aspects of gay liberation such as the idea that love could be fleeting and still healthful.

Callen and Berkowitz were well aware of the resistance in gay communities to sexual restraint as a form of AIDS prevention. They doubted that men would completely stop attending the baths and so presented what they called a "scientific approach to the bathhouse." Men needed to practice "talking, washing, light and rubbers" in bathhouses.[92] As one of the first published documents to call for the use of condoms as a form of AIDS prevention, *How to Have Sex in an Epidemic* was the first safe-sex manual. In reimagining liberatory practices, Callen and Berkowitz elucidated a form of eroticized safe sex. If limiting sexual contacts to a few men at the baths failed to satisfy you, Callen and Berkowitz suggested forming a "Closed Circle of Fuck Buddies," which required complete trust among a small group of close friends. They also suggested that sexual contact was not necessary for sexual expression, recommending that some men might enjoy forming a "Jerk-Off Club," an association similar to one employed by Meridian years earlier where mutual masturbation meant that no fluid contact occurred.[93]

In their conclusion, Callen and Berkowitz argued that a solution to AIDS would come from rewriting the relationship between love and sex. They argued that gay liberation in particular, and sexual liberation as generally practiced in the 1960s and 1970s, decoupled sex from love. Consenting people could and should have sex regardless of whether or not they loved each other. However, in the 1980s, Callen and Berkowitz claimed that by putting love back into sex, even if the love was entirely fleeting and lasted for the time it took to have sex, a different kind of liberation would be possible.

> Sex and "promiscuity" have become the dogma of gay male liberation. Have we modified the belief that we could dance our way to liberation into the belief that we could somehow fuck our way there? If sex is liberating, is more sex necessarily more liberating? . . . Men *loving* men was the basis of gay male liberation, but we have now created "cultural institutions" in which love or even affection can be totally avoided. If you love the person you are fucking with — even for one night — you will not want to make them sick.[94]

Callen and Berkowitz's addition of the word "with" after "fucking" changed the sentence's meaning. While "fucking" someone usually meant that you were having sex without intimacy, "fucking with" suggested that intimacy could be fleeting, temporary, and substantial at the same time. The "with" implied a shared responsibility based not on morality but, rather, on a desire to care for other gay men. Callen and Berkowitz concluded that "maybe affection is our best protection."[95]

A strategy that emphasized communal responsibility had the potential to preempt possible reactionary and homophobic state action, something that seemed increasingly likely as public discussions of sex became more conservative in the early 1980s. In a 1983 gay cable television show, Michael Callen suggested, "What is over isn't sex — just sex without responsibility. . . . As long as we continue to selfishly ask, 'Is that man a health risk to me,' without first asking, 'Am I a health risk to him,' we will never be free from the tyranny of AIDS. Our challenge is to figure out how to have gay, life-affirming sex, satisfy our emotional needs, and stay alive. Hard questions for hard times, but whatever happened to our great gay imagination."[96] Echoing the concerns of Mother Superior from the Sisters of Perpetual Indulgence, Callen considered his position as emerging directly out of his experience as a gay liberationist. In a speech Richard Berkowitz gave at the National AIDS Vigil held in Washington, D.C., on October 8, 1983, he articulated this position by asking, "What better way to honor the dead than to live and prosper — to get on with the business of gay liberation by taking responsibility for our own health and the health of our community?"[97] This vision provided a broader and more systemic solution for AIDS prevention because it looked at AIDS in relation to the political construction of what it meant to be a gay man.[98] Callen and Berkowitz argued that sexual transformation was far from merely personal. Rather, it was an explicitly political act.

While Callen and Berkowitz's approach suggested a fraternal model of community, it was not the same as Meridian's ideas about brotherhood of a few years earlier. Emphasizing inclusion rather than exclusion, the authors claimed that their manifesto spoke to the particular needs of economically disenfranchised gay men. They argued that disseminating "information about how diseases are transmitted" would allow all gay men to make decisions about their health even if they were not "well-educated and well-off" or did not have access to "proper health care."[99]

Throughout 1983, Callen and Berkowitz's manifesto received an equal measure of praise and contempt. In Randy Alfred's copy of How to Have Sex in an Epidemic held at the Gay, Lesbian, Bisexual, Transgender Historical Society in San Francisco, the gay radio journalist wrote all over the margins of the text as if he were in a conversation with the authors.

In reaction to sections of the text on promiscuity and disease, he wrote "judgmental" and "disease the men have, not the men themselves." Alfred responded more positively to the sections that called for redefining love and responsibility. When Callen and Berkowitz talked about the need to attend to a partner's health risk, he exclaimed, "YES!!!" and underlined the phrase "plan ahead."[100]

Some gay writers were even more supportive, expanding on Callen and Berkowitz's analysis that gay men had become alienated from one another through commercialism. Writing in the August 13, 1983, "Speaking Out" section of GCN, a section of the paper designed to give community members a chance to voice their opinions in more developed form than letters to the editors, Richard Royal explained that members of the gay community needed to promote the use of "condoms and the development of erotically stimulating prophylactics. . . . We don't have to give up sexual enjoyment. We do have to give up irresponsibility and the failure to understand ourselves physically."[101] He concluded, "What started out as liberating (the escape from the claustrophobic phoniness of traditional monogamy) often arrives at a different place, where objectification reigns supreme and the delicacy of our desire is reduced to the easily satisfied but insatiable appetite characteristic of a commodity-saturated society."[102] In a letter to the editor of the BAR, the "Red Queen," an otherwise unidentified reader of the San Francisco paper, wrote that "unless we build new and nurturing Gay institutions — ones based on our ability to love rather than on profit-making, butch posturing, and competition for sex — we will die."[103]

All of these writers, Callen, Berkowitz, Royal, and the Red Queen, sought to decouple gay sex from materialism and recalled the powerful rhetoric of the Gay Liberation Front, an organization formed in the wake of the 1969 Stonewall Riots. The front hypothesized that open and honest gay sexuality was revolutionary, and that gay liberation had the potential to free society from what historians John D'Emilio and Estelle Freedman have called "the manipulative images of consumer capitalism."[104] Ten years later, in response to the sexual excess they saw around them, these writers suggested that the truly liberationist move would be to expel as much of the capitalist impulse from gay life as possible. In 1972, gay liberation meant that an individual was free to act as he chose in a gay sexual environment. In 1982, he had to think about how his actions affected the larger gay community. With a sense of responsibility and duty to fellow gay citizens, this early idea about AIDS prevention valorized gay sex because of its potential to resist individualism, rejecting what these writers identified as a selfish potential of gay liberation.

While some praised Callen and Berkowitz's position on anticommercialism, a group of women writers responded to the call to revise the connections between love and sex. In one of the first "Speaking Out" articles on AIDS written by a woman, Marie Goodwin, a GCN reader, explained, "Our love and our sexuality are not mutually exclusive. We cannot embrace one and deny the other out of fear. . . . We have nothing to be sorry for. Yes, people are dying. Yes, we need to review, and in many cases change, our sexual behavior. But we must not do this out of confusion and hysteria. Whatever changes we make, we must make for reasons of health, not morality. . . . We may have at times been careless, but we were never immoral."[105]

Amy Hoffman, who served as GCN's features editor from 1978 to 1980 and the managing editor from 1980 to 1982, echoed Goodwin's concerns about sex, love, and morality in a speech at the 1983 Boston Lesbian and Gay Pride March in front of almost 20,000 people:

> One of the gay men's achievements over the past decade — which I as a lesbian and the entire lesbian movement have been challenged by and learned much from — has been the exploration of the experience and meaning of gay sex and pleasure and love. We must resist the feeling that AIDS means that this exploration, this path to liberation, was *wrong*, and we now have to abandon it. This feeling comes from homophobia: haven't they always told us we are sick, sinful and disposable people. Instead, it is more important than ever that we continue to explore our particular sexualities — our bodies, our lives.[106]

GCN reprinted the text of Hoffman's speech for those who did not hear it live. Regular contributor Sue Hyde, who later worked at the National Gay and Lesbian Task Force, argued that gay men and lesbians needed to act for themselves: "Whether or how we regulate the sexual practices of members of our community is a decision for *our* community. We have been stereotyped as 'self-destructive' because of our excessive sexuality, but any tendency toward recalcitrance is borne out of years of having our sex lives scrutinized for immorality, psychosis, and disease."[107]

Goodwin, Hoffman, and Hyde all argued that separating sex from love needed not to have an amoral effect. In fact, were gays and lesbians to return to the "path to liberation," people would more likely change their sexual behaviors, not because lesbians would show men how to be committed, monogamous beings but, rather, because together they would produce a larger, political context in which to consider their actions. In a description of one of the first AIDS forums held in Denver, Colorado, in 1983, GCN reporter Debi Law explained, "There is sentiment among men for denouncing their casual-anonymous/many-partnered post-Stonewall sex in reaction to the AIDS crisis, setting the stage for polarization of the men's community as well. A gay and/or feminist moral minority is not what is needed, but rather an expansion of a continuum of many sexual styles and habits."[108] Or as Callen and Berkowitz and the Sisters of Perpetual Indulgence had suggested a few months earlier, men needed to think about their partners as much as themselves and would then have access to a whole new range of sexually pleasurable acts.

While the women's arguments about health and pleasure outlined the beginning of a position that implied a reinterpretation of masculinity mattered in the AIDS crisis, some men complemented their argument by reiterating the need to develop an inclusive model of gay brotherhood. In 1983, Kevin Gordon, a regular contributor to GCN, articulated a version of brotherhood similar to Callen and Berkowitz's, as well as Ron Vachon's from the Fenway Clinic. This was sometimes articulated as fraternity and, more frequently over time, as "friendship." "A concerted focus on fraternal friendship by the gay male community, especially at this time of AIDS, might provide us a relational context to creatively see what we can come up with, that is not necessarily monogamy on the one hand, nor genital anonymity on the other."[109] The author reiterated a significant debate among gay liberationists about the effect of liberation on sexual practices — he resisted a bifurcated model of either monogamy (often meaning heterosexual marriage) or anonymous sex. With a call for "creativity," he implied that solutions were possible in a community connected through "friendship," a friendship that was sexual and platonic at the same time.

The language of brotherhood also invoked a communal responsibility for AIDS that provided the grounds for men not blaming one another for diseases that they had transmitted, knowingly, unknowingly, or in ignorance of the ultimate consequences. Across the country in San Francisco, bathhouse owner Hal Slate echoed the themes and metaphors Gordon used in his description of the changes taking place in the bathhouses.

Even the Caldron itself, long the epitome of the uninhibited, abandoned, "sleazy" sex club, has undergone radical changes in a short period of time, yet by almost any standards is still "hot." Don't underestimate the creativity of our Gay brothers. And these are times that demand creativity, rather than panic, repression, or recrimination. . . . Hysterical anti-sex rhetoric will go unheeded because it lacks credibility. Gay men are eager to hear the truth, *and they will listen*. We must also bear in mind that we are talking about major changes in deeply conditioned patterns of behavior. . . . *We must view the actions of our brothers and ourselves with great compassion*. Recriminations are unfair; they are products of prejudice; and they only result in guilt and defensiveness.[110]

Here Slate rejected the idea that gay men were resistant to calls for changing sexual behavior, but he did so in a way that refused to pathologize gay men and abandon sexual freedom. Instead, Slate called for an ethical approach to behavior change.

Gordon and Slate saw potential in the idea of brotherhood as a strategy for the reinforcement of community and empowerment, two of the most basic goals of gay liberation. In so doing, they both relied on an older understanding of brotherhood that signified a familial bond that went beyond bloodlines and altered the meaning of the term by removing it from a heterosexual context. This stance mirrored the liberationist literature of the preceding decade where gay and lesbian activists echoed the language of black power. The gay liberationist rhetoric of brotherhood held radical cooperative potential as well as the possibility for exclusion.[111]

Callen and Berkowitz's prose sparked the creation of AIDS prevention designed specifically for gay men. In 1983, both the People with AIDS Coalition (PWAC) and GMHC produced prevention materials that echoed Callen and Berkowitz's ideas about changing sexual behavior. As a founding member of PWAC, Callen helped shape its "Safe Sex Guidelines," which described what men could do in bathhouses to make them more responsible places, such as exchanging phone numbers with sex partners and using condoms.[112] In 1984, GMHC designed a poster that featured the slogan "Great Sex is Healthy Sex," an image by the gay cartoonist Howard Cruse, and Callen and Berkowitz's rhetoric. It pictured two men, one white, one black, eyeing each other in a locker room. "Affection is our best protection" was printed on the right side of the poster, which did not mention the use

1.3 | "Great Sex is Healthy Sex" poster. Howard Cruse, 1984. Reprinted with permission.

of condoms (ill. 1.3). By creating a community of practice where everyone could become an insider, both PWAC and GMHC resisted identifying some gay men as permanently dangerous outsiders who spread AIDS, a strategy that appeared in many of the initial public statements about AIDS to appear in the popular press.

Why did self-proclaimed gay liberationists disagree so vehemently? While they shared the desire to allow men to make their own decisions about how to have sex, as well as the idea that gay sex could and did encompass a wide range of activities that gave men pleasure, they saw one another as ideological adversaries. According to Nathan Fain, the *Advocate*'s AIDS reporter, who also served as one of the founding members of GMHC, the debate between AIDS activists was generational:

> But the style of gay answers to the issues of AIDS has a familiar ring from the old political days. It is hard and plangent and awash with rage. While many gay men find themselves swept into new community bonds for the first time in their lives, veterans of the struggle for liberation have been waiting for their renaissance. The parvenues

generally seem to want to concentrate on helping AIDS patients and on cooperating with established authority, making friends wherever possible. The old guard wants blood.[113]

Fain's rhetoric illustrated the power of a new guard/old guard analysis that becomes less clear when we look at the historical sources. While he asserted that liberation veterans waited to no avail while a new generation of service providers ignored their elders' political analysis, the distinction between service and activism did not appear so sharp in the historical sources.

Unlike Fain, Cindy Patton, then managing editor at GCN, saw the disagreement over the look of sex in the age of AIDS, rooted in unresolved debates about gay men's masculinity. By 1984 Patton incorporated a gender analysis into her discussion of AIDS prevention. She reasoned that solutions for AIDS required talking about sexual practices but doing so in ways that made a critique of misogyny. In her article "Illness as a Weapon," Patton called on gays and lesbians to challenge, politically, "sex-roles and gender-identities":

In our minds, men are still "active" whether fucking or being fucked; and women are still "passive" whether they engage in "vanilla" sex, or s/m, in which case the top is sick or *imitating men*. In this context, when you ask gay men to shift to "safe sex," which is usually described as touching, hugging, less genital, you are in essence asking them to have sex like women, to be "passive." This comes as a direct blow to men who have never really thought about the stereotypes about sexuality. But it comes as a profound sense of loss, or disconnection from the roots of sexual desire, even for men who have intricate analysis about their sexuality.[114]

Here Patton provided an argument that countered the gender dynamics of certain gay male cultures she observed and participated in. Perhaps Patton saw problems with clone culture, defined by anthropologist Martin Levine as a place where "gay men enacted a hypermasculine sexuality as a way to challenge their stigmatization as failed men, as 'sissies.'"[115] Patton's contemporary, gay author Edmund White, hypothesized similar concerns. He told one reporter that "'given how conformist gay life has become, one could just as easily single out any other feature of a clone's existence as being carcinogenic — wearing button-fly jeans, perhaps, or weightlifting or excessive disco dancing.'"[116] For Patton the best way to address hyper-masculinity was to include lesbians in a conversation about the relation-ship between gay liberation and gender liberation: "Both lesbians and gay men are grappling with the relationship between sexual desire and sexual practice, although we seem to be moving in different directions. This is an excellent time for lesbians and gay men to talk with one another about sex, and re-ground sexual liberation in our understanding of sexual desire."[117] She suggested that gay men and lesbians needed to work together in con-sidering alternative ways of imagining sex and community together. This cooperative coalition held the potential for societal and political change in terms that would result in a healthier community: "If we can translate our fight to survive AIDS into a political agenda of cultural health, of a coalition of parts working together, then the lesbian and gay liberation movement may prove to be the driving force of the '80s."[118] In many ways, Patton's conclusion proved prescient. Over the course of the 1980s, by ar-ticulating how gays and lesbians could make themselves and each other healthy and liberated, AIDS activists consistently offered alternatives to the dominant conservative ideology of the era.

THIS CHAPTER HAS DETAILED how gays and lesbians tried to define and respond to what they experienced as an emerging medical and political crisis. Because they had so few palatable medical models, activists looked to political positions articulated in the 1970s for answers about what sex could look like. Emphasizing the need for new relational models, they re-fused to be constrained by false dichotomies between sexual fulfillment and critiques of promiscuity. Whether in the form of attacking commer-cialization, calling for brotherhood, embracing feminist partnerships, or collecting "fuck buddies," the first AIDS activists imagined and brought into being unique forms of sexual and platonic partnerships.

While men spoke more often than women, the chapter has also tried to show that lesbians carved out space for their own political voices. In addi-tion to the work they performed as caretakers, lesbians found a new kind of subjectivity in the early 1980s. While they continued to develop alternative systems for their own health care needs, in part because AIDS made it dif-ficult for clinics like Fenway to focus on the particularities of women's and lesbians' health, they brought their political experiences to AIDS work. The feminists of the GCN collective represented the first feminists to comment on AIDS, but they would not be the last or the most vociferous. Some of the most vocal feminist critics of AIDS came from the global South. As we will see in Chapter 4 on the Ford Foundation's response to AIDS in the global South, activists not only talked about why gender mattered when it came to AIDS prevention but demanded that economic changes were necessary to raise the status of women.

The discovery in 1984 that a virus (ultimately named Human Immunodeficiency Virus, or HIV) was at the root of a cluster of opportunistic infections that produced AIDS marked the end of this form of conversation about gay liberation and highlights the paradoxical potential of this early period. By the mid-1980s, most activists coalesced around the idea that condoms provided the best protection against the spread of a virus, effectively derailing the argument about how sexual freedom, variously defined, might provide a broader political solution to a health problem. Looking at this earlier moment, then, provides us with an opportunity to do more than understand in detail a contest over the meaning of gay liberation. These early debates show awareness that sexual health in particular, and physical health in general, might require more than preventing the spread of disease. As responses to AIDS moved away from these debates about the meaning of gay liberation and focused on behavior modification alone, such as condom usage, AIDS activists and their audiences left behind some important ideas, ideas that held the potential for broader social and political change, a topic that will be explored at length in the next chapter.

Marketing Safe Sex

*The Politics of Sexuality, Race, and Class
in San Francisco, 1983–1991*

"'UNTIL RECENTLY GAY MEN had as much interest in condoms as Eskimos do in air conditioning.'" With this line, Les Pappas, an AIDS prevention campaign designer at the San Francisco AIDS Foundation (SFAF), opened his speech at the CDC in Atlanta, Georgia. Invited to participate in one of the many conferences on the AIDS epidemic the CDC organized in 1987, Pappas geared his remarks specifically to an audience made up of public health officials and condom manufacturers. He described gay men as an all-but-untapped market, ripe for sales pitches to their particular needs. According to Pappas, SFAF had begun the hard work of increasing demand for condoms among gay men by creating alliances with gay department stores and gay bars to display condoms prominently and provide customers with information on how to use them. The AIDS service organization now needed partners to take the campaign out of the Castro, the "gay" neighborhood in San Francisco, and to a national audience. Growth like this would require two strategies: to create "culturally relevant" material, meaning campaigns that were "sexually explicit because the gay community is used to talking openly and frankly about sex," and to "produce materials and products that are directed to the gay condom user, the gay consumer, the gay market. There are 25 million gay consumers waiting for the government and private industry to fill this demand. They will respond if you will."[1]

This speech marked the culmination of a four-year effort undertaken by Pappas and SFAF to eroticize AIDS prevention, particularly the use of condoms, and market the strategy to gay men. SFAF pitched the eroticization of AIDS prevention as an alternative to two other public health strategies in particular: traditional public service announcements that used bland text and images to give advice to the public, and images of the ravages of AIDS in an attempt to scare people into changing their behavior. Beginning with its first AIDS prevention campaign in 1983, SFAF repeated the arguments made by the Sisters of Perpetual Indulgence and Michael Callen and Richard Berkowitz. What made SFAF different from the community activists described in the preceding chapter was that the service organization mass-produced the idea that AIDS did not need to end sexual activity and that sexual behavior could be made "safe."[2]

The new level of safety would come from gay men consistently and properly using condoms when they had sex. But barriers existed to widespread acceptance of this argument. Until the mid-1980s, condom makers and public health officials marketed condoms exclusively to heterosexuals, first and foremost as effective birth control, secondarily as barriers to the spread of STDs.[3] While heterosexual men may have been told to use condoms to maintain their sexual health, as was the case with soldiers in World War I, like Eskimos and air conditioning, few gay men considered the condom a necessary component of their sexual lives. Gay men rejected condom use not only because they resisted a product they identified as heterosexual but also because public health authorities did not complete the scientific study on the ability of condoms to prevent the spread of AIDS until 1985.[4] Two years later when Pappas delivered his speech, he hoped to dispense with both problems by suggesting that gay men would make condoms their own if condom manufacturers actively pursued them as customers.

Pappas's articulation of SFAF's marketing and condom mission had other consequences as well. Pappas embraced what he saw as the most important strand of gay liberation: the open and frank discussion of gay male sex would help foster AIDS prevention. In his effort to elevate that particular argument above others posed by activists ranging from broader definitions of gay liberation that called for the de-emphasis of commercial markets to the role gender analysis might play in AIDS efforts, Pappas and SFAF explained that the best way to reach gay men was to tap into their interests as consumers of sex in specialized institutional settings.

Pappas's speech on consumption assumed that the gay community was homogeneous *and* that safe sex was the only way to make AIDS prevention effective. In effect, consumerism became a solution to the epidemic and simultaneously the mechanism by which difference among "homo-sexually active men" disappeared. Pappas's speech suggested that condom producers should view the gay community as both a cohesive culture and a viable market of consumers with similar tastes. By arguing that being gay was akin to being an Eskimo, Pappas not only called attention to the "exotic" qualities of both groups, each with its unique sexual acts (nose rubbing and anal sex), but more importantly suggested that each group was a monolithic culture. Pappas marked all gay men as requiring a kind of acculturation into a gay culture of sexual liberation. In this view, gay men (25 million of them) not only enjoyed sex but also had a disposable income that allowed them to consume all sorts of products. This claim had obvious appeal to condom producers but was, in fact, rather unrealistic.

By employing a single-minded focus on the marketing of safe sex, SFAF stumbled when it tried to diversify the communities it reached. Because SFAF returned again and again to a model that focused on the gay institutions it defined as most important (bars and bathhouses with a regular clientele of self-identified gay men), it was less able to recognize the extent to which its policies implicitly and explicitly relied on a white gay identity as a universal model for gayness. When SFAF tried to increase the attention it paid to the needs of communities of color, particularly men it defined as "not-gay-identified homosexuals," who were almost always black or La-tino, it struggled to hear their voices because they could not be found in traditional gay spaces or neighborhoods. Using a consumer model to deal with racial difference did not help either; it simply increased the number of niche markets for which SFAF designed sexually explicit AIDS prevention. Looking at the evolution of AIDS prevention material in San Francisco provides us with an opportunity to understand how SFAF saw its constituents and how that vision fit into the larger historical moment in which identity politics facilitated *and* prevented effective responses to AIDS.

SFAF's inability to understand and articulate fully how race mattered in AIDS prevention work was put in sharp relief with the formation of the Third World AIDS Advisory Task Force (TWAATF), a community-based organization formed in 1985. This group focused attention on AIDS in communities of color and challenged the consumer model of prevention. TWAATF began with the idea that dealing with racial and economic dif-ference among people affected/infected by AIDS required not only talking about sex but also initiating conversations about issues such as poverty, drug use, and incarceration. With several gay men of color working at TWAATF, most notably the longtime Chicano activists who were part of the board and a group of gay-positive researchers, the organization became one of the first to insist on a simultaneous conversation about racial disparities, sexual desire, and AIDS.

To underscore a particular moment in the history of liberalism in the post-1960s era, this chapter juxtaposes the efforts undertaken by SFAF and TWAATF in the mid- to late 1980s. On one hand, SFAF existed in direct opposition to what it saw as a conservative government that refused to acknowledge the needs of people with AIDS. SFAF regularly inserted conversations about sexuality into public spaces and called for an increase in government spending and the need to care for citizens. On the other hand, SFAF often failed to reach people of color affectd by AIDS because it was unable to comprehend, and act on, how racial inequality affected both gay culture and AIDS prevention.

By ignoring the causes of inequality among groups affected by AIDS (e.g., poverty and racial segregation in housing), an argument that TWAATF regularly emphasized, SFAF placed itself in an impossible bind in terms of crafting AIDS prevention material. That is, relying on gay identity politics — defined as the articulation of needs based on particular identity — subverted the ability to consider the intersections of identity. SFAF's initial work on race became an example of what historian Lisa Duggan calls "'multicultural,' neoliberal 'equality' politics," and what social theorist Vijay Prashad describes as a "liberal doctrine to undercut the radicalism of anti-racism."[5] Focusing on identities outside a larger systemic context made it difficult to produce material that addressed the reality of AIDS *and* the effects of economic dispossession and racial inequality. When SFAF began to create AIDS prevention for gay men of color at the end of the decade, and after consultation with affected groups, it faced a different set of obstacles, most notably the censorship of images that represented gay men of color as sexual beings.

San Francisco: A Racially and Sexually Diverse City

San Francisco has been a "gay" or "queer" town since the mid-nineteenth century. According to historian Nan Boyd, the queer character of San Francisco was due as much to the large number of same-sex-loving people who have lived there as to the "queerness sewn into the city's social fabric."[6] Over the course of the twentieth century, due in part to the in-migration of people with same-sex desires, San Francisco became one of the first centers of same-sex-loving people organizing culturally and politically.

San Francisco was also an increasingly racially diverse, yet segregated, town after World War II. By the late 1960s, the city's neighborhoods were divided by race. Segregation affected African Americans more than any other racial group, such that African Americans, no matter what their socioeconomic status, lived in neighborhoods without whites.[7] Over the course of the 1980s, the Asian and Latino populations of the city grew substantially, while the African American community remained relatively stable. By the late twentieth century, San Francisco was one of several "majority-minority" cities, municipalities where whites accounted for less than half of the city's residents.[8]

The sexual and racial characteristics of the city shaped the way activists dealt with homophobia, racism, and combinations of the two. Residents built vibrant yet cantankerous gay communities. Some queer public spaces such as bars, cafeterias, and bathhouses became venues for political organizing for working-class and transgender patrons, many of whom were also people of color.[9] In 1961 José Sarria, a Chicano entertainer at San Francisco's Black Cat Bar, was the first openly gay man to run, unsuccessfully, for elected office.[10] Sarria's loss fueled the political resistance brewing in San Francisco neighborhoods. Five years after Sarria's run, a racially diverse group of transgender prostitutes fought back against police brutality and launched a riot at the Compton Cafeteria, a diner in the Tenderloin neighborhood, the red-light district of San Francisco.[11] The militancy and racial alliances among transgender activists did not stop at Compton's. Over the course of the next ten years, transgender activists working in antipoverty campaigns built alliances with other Bay Area activists, including the Black Panthers, the black liberationist group based in Oakland. In fact, historian Susan Stryker argues that race and class affinity shaped San Francisco's earliest gay organizing as much as sexual desire and gender identity did.[12]

Alongside, and sometimes in competition with, the organizing taking place in the Tenderloin, gays and lesbians in San Francisco, most of whom were white, became a driving force behind the homophile movement of the 1950s and 1960. A much more complex movement than its sometimes assimilationist propaganda suggested, activists in homophile organizations such as the Mattachine Society and the Daughters of Bilitis fought for civil rights in the decades before the gay and lesbian liberation movement.[13]

The combustible combination of political activists in both bars and civil rights organizations produced the condition under which a dramatic growth of political activism was possible in 1970s San Francisco. According to sociologist Elizabeth Armstrong, between 1964 and 1994 the number of lesbian and gay organizations in San Francisco rose exponentially, from 6 to 276.[14] By 1975, the city was home to almost 100 gay and lesbian organizations, including several gay newspapers, Democratic clubs, community-based cultural institutions, sex establishments, and gay-owned businesses. In 1977, San Franciscans elected the first openly gay public official, Harvey Milk, to the Board of Supervisors.[15]

As was the case with earlier attempts to organize on behalf of the diverse population of the Tenderloin neighborhood, gays and lesbians of color created organizations dedicated to their needs as racialized and sexualized subjects in the 1970s as well. Armstrong argues that by the 1970s, San Francisco witnessed the proliferation of organizations for "sub-identities" (e.g., Gay Asian Pacific Alliance, Gay American Indians, etc.). By 1980, eleven different organizations for gays of color existed.[16] Historian Horacio Roque-Ramirez argues that Chicano gays and lesbians, for example, struggled to balance their identities in both the Chicano movement and the gay and lesbian liberation movement, forming the Gay Latino Alliance in San Francisco in 1975 with the intention of "integrat[ing] racial, gender and sexual politics."[17] The alliance fought white racism in gay institutions and struggled for "cultural citizenship."[18]

Despite a history of organizing around both sexual and racial identities, San Francisco's image has often been one of a white gay town. Over the course of the 1970s, white, upwardly mobile gay men made their political and social demands central and universal at the same time. This prevented a wide range of people from seeing racial and class diversity among gay people and produced a culturally essentialist sense of "gayness" that actually was about "whiteness." As sociologist Armstrong argues, while gay liberation spokespeople used a language of diversity, in practice their definition of difference was limited. As a result, white gay male leadership obfuscated much of the activism initiated by gay and gender-queer people of color.[19]

From Gay Liberation to Gay Markets and Consumers

When public health officials in San Francisco first diagnosed the disease that would become AIDS, the representation of gay life in San Francisco shaped the epidemiological investigations as much as did the symptoms shared by the people who were getting sick. In her analysis of the first twenty-four cases of people retrospectively diagnosed with AIDS, medical geographer Michelle Cochrane suggests that "surveillance practices and politics jointly produced and continue to produce representations of the AIDS epidemic that overly simplify the demography of risk for acquiring the disease."[20] In three of the first nine cases, public health workers overlooked intravenous drug use as a risk factor in favor of naming homosexual identity as the likely cause of illness. Included in the first nine cases was an African American man whose bisexual behavior allowed public health workers to ignore his drug use. In addition to using gay identity to overdetermine risk, public health workers also disregarded the fact that seven of the nine men lived close to or at the poverty line, economic circumstances that severely compromised their health as well.[21]

Despite the complex reality of the first cases of AIDS, SFAF, first known as the KS Foundation (reflecting one of the primary symptoms of AIDS, a cancer called Kaposi's sarcoma, or KS), opened its doors in 1982 with the intention of serving self-identified gay men. Much like its New York counterpart, GMHC, SFAF provided some of the first, and at the time only, services for many of the gay men affected by the mysterious symptoms of a disease not yet called AIDS.[22] With a mix of health professionals, local gay politicos, and gay community members all volunteering their time, the organization's workers used whatever influence they could to procure resources in the early fight against AIDS.[23] The overwhelming majority of SFAF's initial clients were homosexual, but the agency made no reference to any difference within that group.[24]

As the organization's priorities took shape in 1982 and 1983, preventing the spread of AIDS through the dissemination of information became a main concern. In the first year of its existence, SFAF's AIDS Hotline, a telephone information and referral service, answered almost 6,500 calls. Beyond providing information to callers, SFAF also established venues for community education, including support groups "led by psychotherapists . . . [to] allow individuals to deal with lifestyle issues and risk reduction."[25]

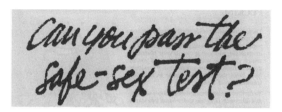

SEX I LIKE TO DO (OR MIGHT BE TALKED INTO)

Please check the boxes that apply to you.	SAFE	POSSIBLY UNSAFE	UNSAFE
☐ Being fucked without a condom			■
☐ Fucking without a condom			■
☐ Being fucked with a condom		■	
☐ Fucking with a condom		■	
☐ Sucking/getting sucked		■	
☐ Sucking to climax			■
☐ Masturbation/jacking off	■		
☐ Body rubbing	■		
☐ Hugging/kissing	■		
☐ French kissing		■	
☐ Watersports in mouth			■
☐ Watersports on unbroken skin	■		
☐ Finger fucking		■	
☐ Fisting			■
☐ Dildoes and toys, not shared	■		
☐ Fantasies	■		

If you checked boxes for sexual activities that are coded black or gray, your job is to change to activities that are coded pink. Our goal is to stay in the pink—and stay healthy!

2.1 | *Can We Talk?* Courtesy of Archives and Special Collections, Library and Center for Knowledge Management, University of California, San Francisco. Reprinted with permission from the San Francisco AIDS Foundation.

In addition to answering people's questions about AIDS, SFAF developed and distributed health education materials, some of which targeted the "high-risk gay (and homosexually active) male population," while others were for the general public.[26] One of the first examples of material for high-risk gay men was *Can We Talk?* The brochure featured two cartoon figures: at the top, a black man wearing a t-shirt that read, "so many men, so little time," and at the bottom, a white gay "everyman" wearing a leather harness, a big leather boot on one foot, and a fishnet stocking and high-heel pump on the other. These figures asked men to take a safe-sex test that determined if sexual behaviors were safe, possibly safe, or unsafe (ill. 2.1). Echoing the strategies of community activists like Michael Callen and Richard Berkowitz in New York City and Tom Smith in San Francisco, SFAF focused on convincing gay men to use condoms. *Can We Talk?* was probably one of the first mass-produced AIDS prevention materials to suggest men don condoms for sex with other men.[27] SFAF distributed 50,000 copies of *Can We Talk?* at "major gay community events"; "gay community organizations, businesses and in places where men gather"; and "health care facilities, providers and other social service agencies with gay, bisexual and homosexually active clients" by mid-1984.[28]

SFAF also led efforts to turn gay bathhouses into community education sites. In August 1983, the board authorized Ed Power, the acting executive director, to work with bathhouse owners to develop education campaigns designed for the gay baths. At one of the first gatherings of SFAF staff and bathhouse owners held in the last weeks of 1983, Power asked the owners to pass out a condom to each patron entering the bath as well as having free condoms available throughout the venue. To help men learn how to use condoms, Power called for "safe sex" parties, where men could learn about condom usage and how to negotiate with their sexual partners. He hoped to see "Concerned Porno Stars" create fun demonstrations showing men how to choose the right condom as Tom Smith's safe-sex slide show ran in the background.[29] Power wanted SFAF to create materials for owners and employees at the baths to disseminate.

SFAF sought to change the location of health education campaigns from doctors' offices to bathhouses because the agency knew that men were likely to feel more comfortable in gay spaces. In a 2001 interview, SFAF staff member Les Pappas argued that banning sexual activity in the baths, a policy that was a real possibility given the demands by many different groups to close the bathhouses in the first half of the decade, would force men to practice unsafe sexual behavior elsewhere far beyond the reach of activists and educators.[30] At least at the baths, Pappas reasoned, SFAF had the chance to effect change through the circulation of erotic safe-sex material.[31] One year into the bath project, Rick Crane, the executive director of SFAF, highlighted that the organization's "efforts to increase private clubs/bathhouse education have proven highly successful. . . . Overall sex-positive approach is being heralded nationwide, and attendance at local public forums is at an all-time high."[32]

While SFAF began to develop AIDS prevention material steeped in the language and practice of gay liberation as manifested at the baths, the limits of the message became clear. At the same meeting in which SFAF authorized Power to collaborate with bathhouse owners, the board discussed a letter from Billy S. Jones, a member of the East Bay Chapter of Black and White Men Together (BWMT), an organization formed in 1980 in an attempt to fight racism within gay communities. The letter challenged SFAF to consider the consequences of using an exclusively pro-sex argument in AIDS prevention material. Jones wrote, "Unless I am out of touch with my brothers and sisters of color, many believe that AIDS is a white gay male disease stemming from unusual, bizarre, excessive, and permissive sexual behavior practices."[33] Jones did more than suggest that SFAF's use of a white model of gay liberation to design AIDS prevention was problematic; he also called attention to SFAF's inability or unwillingness to find models that made sense for gay communities of color. Jones called for a collaboration very different from that of Power's: he wanted to see SFAF work with groups not organized exclusively around sexual practice, including BWMT and the National Coalition of Black Gays, to create campaigns for communities of color in general and gay communities of color in particular that moved away from an exclusive focus on gay liberation. His demands also called attention to a small but growing network of black gay male activists who interpreted the interconnections between race and sexuality as necessitating AIDS prevention that moved beyond sexual explicitness.[34]

Perhaps implicitly in response to Jones's concerns, but more likely an acknowledgment of interracial desire, about ten months after the meeting where Jones sought to draw the board members' attention to the importance of addressing racial difference, SFAF produced one of its first explicitly erotic posters, "You Can Have Fun (and be safe too)." The poster pictured two naked men — one white, one black — holding each other, and it explained that sexual activity was still possible, and even exciting, in the age of AIDS (ill. 2.2).[35] Even though the poster did not show a condom (as subsequent SFAF posters would), it did tell men to use both "condoms when you play" and "your imagination." The foundation printed an initial run of 2,000 copies in January 1984 and distributed them to each bathhouse in the city.[36] While there is no evidence of explicit attempts to distribute the poster to bars frequented by African American men, the representation suggests that SFAF campaign designers recognized the existence of interracial desire in gay communities. Beyond that, however, they seemed to have done little to recognize why race mattered in designing AIDS prevention campaigns. A poster that defined gay liberation as the freedom to have interracial sexual relationships did not fully address the needs of men of color who desired other men.[37]

Despite concerns about the consequences for men who did not define themselves in gay liberationist terms or use gay institutions, SFAF continued to encourage consumption in its AIDS prevention in 1984 and 1985. The changing nature of advertising in the postwar era made it possible for SFAF to consider the value of marketing for public health initiatives. In

YOU CAN HAVE FUN

(and be safe, too)

■ **Be creative.** Mutual masturbation and erotic massage are
pleasurable and safe.
■ **Use your imagination.** Fantasies
can be fun and no risk, as long as
they're by mutual consent and
don't involve exchanging semen
or blood-contaminated secre-
tions. Indulge yourself!
■ **Avoid** sexual acts which involve
the exchange of semen or blood.
Use condoms when you play.
■ **Limit** your use of recreational
drugs and DON'T share needles.

For more information, call the
San Francisco AIDS Foundation:
In SF **863-AIDS**
In Northern Calif
800-FOR-AIDS

PRODUCED AND DISTRIBUTED BY THE
SAN FRANCISCO AIDS FOUNDATION

PHOTO BY MICK HICKS

2.2 | "You Can Have Fun."
Courtesy of Archives and
Special Collections, Library
and Center for Knowledge
Management, University of
California, San Francisco.
Reprinted with permission
from the San Francisco AIDS
Foundation.

her work on postwar mass consumption, Lizbeth Cohen argues that by
the 1960s retailers no longer relied on mass marketing to gain consumers
for their products. Instead, they articulated what came to be known as seg-
mented or niche markets. This meant that more often than not, advertisers
created specific campaigns for specific demographic groups, for example,
marketing to women or African Americans. This development, when coupled with the social movements of the 1960s and 1970s, produced a "new
commercial culture that reified — at times exaggerated — social difference
in the pursuit of profits, often reincorporating disaffected groups into the
commercial marketplace. . . . [Marketers'] embrace of market segmenta-
tion [after the 1950s] lent marketplace recognition to social and cultural di-
visions among Americans, making 'countercultures' and 'identity politics'
more complex joint products of grassroots mobilization and marketers'
ambitions than is often acknowledged."[38]

While Cohen concentrates on the political implications of commercial
marketing, niche strategies also had implications in public health initiatives, particularly those organized to enact changes in sexual and repro-

Marketing Safe Sex | 55

ductive behavior. For example, population control advocates developed a technique called "social marketing" to limit population growth and used it to "sell" Third World people on the need for birth control in general and condoms in particular. According to Richard Manoff, social marketers borrowed research techniques from "anthropology, sociology, social psychology, communications theory. . . . They provided a capability for insight into group behavior and motivations, target audiences, and attributes, and for designing responsive message and media strategies."[39] In his description of the first attempts to encourage condom use in India in 1964, Philip Harvey recounts how a group of academics, government officials, local businessmen, and Ford Foundation population experts produced "Proposals for Family Planning Promotion: A Marketing Plan."[40] The document provided a blueprint for how to encourage the use of condoms and then plan for their proper distribution. Harvey claims that public health workers continued to use the marketing plan for the next several decades in birth control efforts as well as public health campaigns.

While the complex and often contradictory effects of population control as a model for AIDS prevention will be described in much fuller detail in the next two chapters, SFAF employees, including Les Pappas and Marketing Director Sam Puckett, believed that social marketing had an important role to play in AIDS prevention.[41] Puckett, a former advertising executive, spearheaded SFAF's marketing campaign in 1984. He developed public displays such as posters, flyers, and other ephemera in conjunction with focus group testing.[42] Working with Puckett, Pappas argued that he modeled his projects on birth control efforts undertaken in the developing world, a practice he learned while in the Peace Corps.[43]

The foundation increasingly incorporated frank and open sexual discussions into its AIDS prevention material. In 1984, SFAF hired Research and Decisions Corporation (R and D), a marketing firm run by gay men to research the needs of gay men. Tellingly, the form that R and D's sampling took ensured that self-defined gay men (mostly white) would be surveyed more than others.[44] As a first step, the marketing firm interviewed 500 self-identified homosexually active men on the phone. R and D chose men living in census tracks determined to be "gay" by finding the clusters of the highest number of unmarried male-headed households. R and D assumed that these men would be representative of the just over 69,000 gay or bisexual men it estimated to be living in San Francisco.[45]

With the market research under way, SFAF began a community business outreach program that leaned on gay institutions to educate patrons. R and D followed the quantitative survey of urban gay men with a series of focus group sessions that allowed it to collect quantitative information from a "cross-section of gay men recruited through street intercepts in predominantly gay locations throughout the city of San Francisco."[46] This experiment was the first time "traditional market research techniques [were utilized] to study gay male sex practices, sexual lifestyle and attitudes toward AIDS and safe sex."[47] While R and D believed this effort would allow it to reach "all strata within the gay community," it made no attempt to design intercepts that reached non-gay-identified homosexual men.[48]

Even in a limited form, however, R and D's research model located significant disparities among certain groups of gay men in San Francisco. By analyzing the responses in the quantitative survey, R and D reported that some groups tended to "lag behind" the shift to safer forms of sexual expression. The survey found that men in lower income and education groups, as well as those living in the Polk/Mission district (one of the city's poorer areas), were more reluctant to change their sexual behaviors.[49] The findings clearly suggested that prevention strategies directed specifically at established gay institutions in gay neighborhoods like the Castro would have little effect on a significant number of people R and D hoped to reach.

Instead of acknowledging these results and developing alternative approaches, SFAF advanced efforts to get traditional local gay businesses — bars, bathhouses, and retail outlets — involved in the work of AIDS prevention. Beginning in 1984, Pappas reinvigorated SFAF's project to make gay bars and bathhouses effective sites for public education. Pappas was well aware of the historical significance of bars as meeting places in the gay community. He proposed to exploit these venues for distributing literature, condoms, video commercials, posters, and flyers and to involve "employees and owners as health educators."[50] In so doing, SFAF was likely one of the first organizations to implement a plan that put condoms and AIDS prevention material in commercial venues.

Over the course of the next year, Pappas trained bartenders at more than 100 gay bars in San Francisco and oversaw the creation of Bartenders Against AIDS, an organization that highlighted the important role bartenders played in the lives of their regular customers as "models and opinion leaders" in gay communities. To call attention to the trained members, Pappas designed buttons and t-shirts to be worn on bartending shifts.[51]

He reported that some bartenders slipped condoms to customers if they thought the men were heading off to have sex.

Pappas also tried to get bar and bathhouse owners involved in AIDS prevention by creating a mass distribution chain for condoms. After researching how SFAF could obtain condoms at a "non-profit/clinic rate," Pappas tested several brands and styles and "chose some that [he] thought would be particularly well received by the community in terms of texture, smell, taste, packaging, and price."[52] To create a distribution system for the chosen condoms, Pappas sought assistance from the San Francisco Tavern Guild, an organization that had been active in city gay politics since the 1960s.[53] Using his persuasive skills, Pappas convinced the guild to purchase, and have each of its member bars distribute, "15,000 condoms, along with safe sex cards" across the city.[54] It is not clear how many bars outside the Castro actually participated. According to one assessment, people living in "general assistance hotels in the Tenderloin/Polk St. areas . . . [felt] ignored." While "bars [and] bookstores" outside the Castro were soon added to the foundation's distribution list, it seemed quite possible that further outreach would not be an immediate concern for SFAF.[55]

Pappas's commitment to a particular kind of gay institution became clear in the relationships he developed with retail outlets in the Castro. The owners of Image Leather, for example, a store specializing in sex toys and leather clothing, bought condoms from SFAF at cost and gave away a free condom with every purchase. The Obelisk, "an exclusive Castro gift shop," decided to sell "a particular condom [imported from Japan and in a very attractive box of one dozen] which they thought would fit into the philosophy of their store."[56] Mark Christofer, co-owner of Obelisk, put his "'designer' condoms" in a "predominant and classy display."[57] Finally, Headlines, a "gay" department store with locations on Castro Street and Polk Street, in the Tenderloin neighborhood, sold condoms at nonprofit prices of about ten cents apiece. Pappas estimated that between April and June, Headlines sold 50,000 condoms.[58] He hoped this strategy would eliminate some of the barriers gay men experienced when buying and using condoms. If a hip store sold the product, Pappas hoped, it would become more hip to use the product. Christofer confirmed this idea. "'Our store has a long standing commitment to do what we can during this crisis, we feel that every responsible business should respond to the concerns of its community — it's good business morals. Also, the condoms we are selling make great gift items.'"[59]

The consequences of SFAF's survey and marketing strategy were complex. On one hand, SFAF tried to listen to what gay men were saying about AIDS and design a business strategy that made condoms visible to gay men who frequented institutions like bars and gift stores in the Castro. The organization believed these institutions were important to gay men, a point confirmed by R and D's surveys. On the other hand, SFAF ignored how their research and outreach strategies slighted the historical reality of racial discrimination in gay institutions and in the city at large. While R and D acknowledged that, for example, "bisexuals having little or no contact with the gay community as such . . . cannot be reached through traditional gay communication channels," it made no allowances for changing its research plan.[60] One SFAF assessment of R and D's survey methods found that while African Americans accounted for 13 percent of San Francisco's population, only 4 percent of the people R and D reached were black.[61] This was due, at least in part, to the consistent practice of racial exclusion at bars. Throughout the 1970s, gay men of color reported that bars often denied them access by requiring multiple forms of identification.[62]

SFAF efforts in 1984 and 1985 to solicit information from gay men about how the foundation should respond to AIDS relied on a cycle of exclusion. Because R and D used the census to locate the men, it was unable to find sufficient numbers of men of color with homosexual practices to recommend actions on their behalf. The same was true for interventions. Even though R and D and SFAF recognized that only a small percentage of men of color frequented gay institutions, they continued to design prevention efforts specifically for gay venues where the overwhelming majority of patrons were white.

Race, Sexuality, and Desire

In direct response to the inability of organizations like SFAF to acknowledge how its work functioned as much to exclude as it did to include, a group of San Franciscan AIDS workers formed TWAATF (the Third World AIDS Advisory Task Force) in 1985. An outgrowth of conversations with people serving on the Human Rights Commission, TWAATF was open to representatives from all San Francisco ASOS "regardless of racial and sexual identification." Members designed the steering committee so that it had an overwhelming majority of people of color, representing a range of sexual orientations.[63] The task force's structure facilitated its mission of "assisting existing AIDS organizations with providing educational material that is relevant, culturally sensitive, and can be understood by our communities."[64]

Because the task force got its members from local ASOs, all of the members wore two or three institutional hats in addition to their work at TWAATF. They not only held jobs in San Francisco ASOs; they also served on various community groups. Hank Tavera, for instance, ran Client Services at SFAF, sat on the Latino Coalition on AIDS, and chaired TWAATF. Miguel Ramirez worked in the education department at SFAF, volunteered at the Latino Coalition on AIDS, and went to TWAATF meetings. Amanda Hamilton-Houston, a psychologist employed by the AIDS Health Project, led the Black Coalition on AIDS and participated in meetings of a researchers' group made up of other Third World San Franciscans. While this often meant that many members were overextended in their work, it facilitated communication between groups, allowed representatives from various communities to network with one another, and most importantly, highlighted the similarities and differences in the way service organizations and the state treated people with AIDS.

TWAATF members used their expertise as community leaders, as well as their knowledge of one another's activities, to force San Francisco's growing AIDS bureaucracy to recognize that people of color had special needs in the AIDS crisis. Using strategies that included "client advocacy, public testimony, lobbying, needle exchange, civil disobedience, political activism and multicultural awareness and training, along with education, information and referral," members targeted state agencies such as the AIDS Office and service organizations like SFAF to do more for people of color.[65] By design, this meant that the task force often advised ASOs on how to articulate and implement diversity plans. TWAATF cautioned against a model that "painted a broad stroke for compassion" and demanded that "ethnic and population specificity is needed" for all AIDS plans.[66] Put even more explicitly, TWAATF insisted that ASOs "avoid the jargon and seduction of 'being multicultural'" and instead implement "real change in the power structure of the organization."[67]

TWAATF members, however, did not fall into the trap of seeing race and sexuality as analogous. Instead, they insisted on articulating a connection between the two. As Houston-Hamilton argued, "Black and Latino people are found in every risk group."[68] She explained that people of color were overrepresented in AIDS cases and hypothesized that this disparity existed because of a combination of intravenous drug use and bisexuality in ethnic communities. Houston-Hamilton concluded that "education campaigns and anonymous HIV antibody test site programs should be developed by and provided to ethnic communities to guarantee sensitivity to the diversity of lifestyles, support systems, and risk behaviors found within ethnic neighborhoods."[69] Houston-Hamilton acknowledged that ethnic communities had unique needs, and she insisted that these needs could be met only if more funding was made available. Activists of color throughout the Bay Area utilized Houston-Hamilton's research to justify increasing funding for people of color, many of whom were also homosexually active.[70]

Two events symbolized TWAATF's political commitment: the 1985 production of a brochure designed exclusively for people of color and the 1986 planning and coordination of the first Western Regional Conference on AIDS and Ethnic Minorities, held at the University of California–San Francisco.[71] With both the document and the conference, TWAATF called on people of color to be more aware of AIDS and organizations to recognize the different needs of communities of color. This strategy pushed ASOs to consider what it meant to incorporate antiracism strategies into providing care for all people with AIDS.

The 1985 brochure *Information for People of Color: Asians, Blacks, Latinos, Native Americans* used words, both sexually explicit and not, to convey the need for behavior change among people of color. Once unfolded, the pamphlet opened with a bold statement: "AIDS IS STRIKING PEOPLE OF COLOR. It is not limited to gay white men. In fact, two out of five Americans with AIDS are Black, Latino, Asian, American Indian, and other people of color. Among women, half are Black and one in five are Latina." In contrast to this forceful yet mild language, the long list of how people could get AIDS used more sexually explicit language. The bullet points read,

You can get AIDS from someone who is infected with the AIDS virus:
If you have intercourse without a rubber . . . .
If you use someone else's sex toys, such as vibrators or dildoes.
If you swallow urine (piss), semen (cum), or feces (shit) or allow them in your mouth . . . .
If you shoot up drugs with someone else's needles, "works," "rigs," or tools.
If you have sex and take inside yourself the blood or cum of someone who does the things listed above.[72]

The text covered a wide range of behaviors that both men and women could perform, but it did not shy away from sexually explicit imagery. TWAATF hoped to utilize a central premise of gay liberation — the ability to have frank and open conversations about sex — in conjunction with the need to write for an audience that included gay and bisexual men but was not limited to that group. While no record exists of how many brochures the task force printed and distributed, the pamphlet remained in print into the early 1990s, and TWAATF regularly mailed copies of it to AIDS organizations across the country.[73]

The Western Regional Conference followed on the heels of the brochure and continued to address the uneven HIV infection rates among people of color. Citing national CDC statistics that 25 percent of AIDS cases were black and 14 percent were Latino, TWAATF hoped the conference would educate health care professionals about the needs of people of color, as well as allow service providers a chance to network with one another. With fourteen workshops, ranging from "The Politics of AIDS" to "AIDS and Correctional Institutions," over the course of the three-day conference, the group began conversations that had not yet taken place in formal settings. The conference expanded the focus of prevention efforts from the promotion of safe sex to risk reduction more broadly defined to include everything from substance abuse to ways to control perinatal transmission of HIV.[74] By assessing the problem of AIDS in prison, the participants specifically considered how location affected behavior and knowledge. Male and female inmates required prevention efforts that acknowledged their unsafe actions, especially because the state ignored sex and drug use in penal institutions. In a prison setting, the lack of freedom and access made prevention work very different from what could happen in a bar or a bathhouse.

TWAATF's initial efforts to expand the definition of AIDS prevention clearly had an effect on SFAF. Beginning in 1985, SFAF began a three-part initiative to address the needs of people of color more consistently. The foundation hired a more racially diverse staff, which it encouraged to join workplace caucuses based on identity and to serve as advisors to the entire organization. It reached out to communities of color to solicit their sense of what AIDS prevention needed to look like. And finally, SFAF began the process of designing AIDS prevention campaigns specifically for gay men of color. Despite these significant attempts at racial integration, by maintaining the role of focus groups and marketing firms in its data collection about homosexually active San Franciscans, SFAF often had a hard time fundamentally changing its almost single-minded focus on sexual frankness.

While SFAF had several people of color on staff within its first few years of operation, in 1985 board members expressed concern about the need for a more diverse staff to enact initiatives for communities of color. At a May 1985 meeting, the board boasted that its "commitment to 3rd world outreach" was "strong and unquestioned," but it also admitted that the agency did have not enough staff members to realize the commitment.[75] To address this lack, the foundation brought in two Chicano gay men, Ernesto Hinojos, a public health worker hired to work on campaign development, and Hank Tavera, a longtime Chicano activist and performer, who joined the staff in the Client Services Department.[76] Over the course of the next half dozen years, these men played important roles in the organization as advocates as well as functioning as activists outside SFAF.

Around the same time that SFAF hired Hinojos and Tavera, staff members began to talk about statistical evidence that called attention to the intersections of race and sexuality in the AIDS epidemic. The statistics both concerned and motivated them. Just a few months after he arrived at SFAF, Hinojos noted that between 1984 and 1986 the percentage of blacks and Latinos in San Francisco with AIDS increased from 4.3 percent to 6.5 percent and from 6.2 percent to 6.6 percent, respectively, while the number of Asian and Pacific Islanders reported to have AIDS remained at a fraction of 1 percent. Even if there was significant undercounting of women and children with AIDS, groups that were statistically more likely to be majority people of color, these numbers were quite low in comparison with the national statistics. Indeed, government figures suggested closer to 40 percent of new AIDS cases were among people of color. SFAF staff seemed sure that black and Latino men who had sex with men, despite having numbers below the national level, were likely to be at significant risk for HIV. By 1986, SFAF reported that just over 24 percent of its clients were people of color.[77]

To help develop material for clients of color, SFAF staff solicited "Third World Gay or Bisexual Men" to comment on the agency's prevention campaigns. SFAF placed advertisements in the *Bay Area Reporter* and the *Sentinel USA*, both gay newspapers in the San Francisco area, calling on "Third World Gay or Bisexual Men" to join its focus groups. SFAF did not run the advertisements in African American or Latino newspapers. Instead, staff members handed out flyers devoid of sexual content in and beyond the Castro, including the Tenderloin and the Western Addition neighborhoods, each of which had large communities of color and significant numbers of people living in poverty.[78]

These focus groups produced mixed results that both confirmed and challenged SFAF's efforts. When shown the poster "Affection is the Best Protection,"[79] the interracial group of men of color (comprised of eight men — five African Americans, one Native American, one Hispanic, and one Asian) reported ambivalence. While one participant called the poster "cartoonish and silly," another liked the use of "Third World" images.[80] One man disliked the "stereotypical notion that Third World people needed simplistic materials." The poster offended him because he believed the creators assumed that most people of color lacked education. He suggested that "maybe you just need brown/black faces — the language doesn't necessarily need to change." Others in the focus group spoke even more directly to the issue of perceived racial difference, saying that "technicality should be avoided and the text should be limited — 'white boys don't read either.'"[81] The men in this focus group seemed more interested in pushing the foundation staff to see gay men of color as similar to white gay men because of class affinity. That is, their social class status as educated people made white men like them, and vice versa.

The focus group comprised exclusively of Latino gay men expressed a set of concerns different from those of the mixed-race group. They feared that AIDS prevention created for gay-identified men would not translate for Latino communities. "They suggested that in our literature, the use of the word 'homosexual' or 'gay' would be interpreted in Hispanic communities as meaning 'white' unless we made it clear to the contrary."[82] Beyond the fear that Latino men would not pay attention to the prevention materials, the participants also worried about how straight Latinos would receive erotic safe sex. "They expressed concern that 'straight people' are learning all our 'secrets' in terms of sexual activity. They didn't want families, etc., to be aware of gay men practicing rimming and fisting, for example, and seemed to want the guidelines 'cleaned-up' if they were to be circulated to the public."[83]

Hinojos provided his fellow SFAF staff members with a summary of both discussions and, in so doing, concluded that race was not as much of a factor as education. "If there are substantial differences in the knowledge, attitudes, or behavior of gay men by demographic subset, the differences more likely relate to educational background (without regard to race) rather than relating to ethnic background. Many educated gay men of color related more to the gay community than to their ethnic communities of origin."[84] This likely made it possible for SFAF to claim it reached enough men of color without having to change how it disseminated AIDS prevention.

SFAF staff found much more resistance to their attempts to design and disseminate AIDS prevention for communities of color when they met with leaders of "minority communities" in 1986. Interviewed over the course of three days in July as part of the foundation's "overall heterosexual risk study" (perhaps assuming that people of color affected by AIDS were more likely to be heterosexual than homosexual), the twenty-eight participants provided SFAF staff and consultants with their opinions about a wide range of topics, including diversity within, and among, communities of color and what it meant to define gayness in such a way as to exclude men who did not consider same-sex desire as indicative of homosexual identity.[85]

In addition to a conversation about heterosexuality and AIDS, the "prominent community members" also tried to describe what "gayness" looked like and, in turn, raised concerns about using a historically specific representation of gay liberation to define a kind of transhistorical gay identity. Echoing the words of Billy Jones from BWMT three years earlier, participants agreed that "some minority gays deny the reality of AIDS, believing it to be associated with promiscuous white homosexuals. Many of these men perceived gay community institutions as racist, insensitive, or irrelevant to their lives. . . . Asian gays believe themselves to be less promiscuous and hence not at risk. Some even believe they are immune to AIDS." Instead of claiming a gay identity, participants drew a sharp distinction between behavioral practices and identity. "Large numbers of . . . Blacks and Latinos . . . do not even consider themselves to be homosexuals, although they frequently have same-sex partners. These men are not being reached by risk reduction programs targeted at openly gay men, because they do not read gay publications and are not integrated into the predominantly white gay male subculture."[86] The distinction the focus group participants drew between identity and behavior contained two separate arguments: first, practicing certain sexual behaviors did not necessarily mean someone identified as gay and, second, claiming a gay identity did not translate into practicing certain sexual behaviors.

Like the gay men of color, some participants at the minority leaders' session, who did not identify as openly gay, criticized SFAF for how it dealt with racial stereotypes in its prevention materials. They focused particularly harsh criticism on the sexually explicit materials and thought the campaigns failed to acknowledge "cultural taboos about sexuality [that] had to be respected if minority audiences were to be reached." Ultimately, the people interviewed found that SFAF material fed "stereotypes about who is at risk for AIDS."[87] The focus group members seemed concerned that by associating people of color with sexual imagery, SFAF bought into, and ultimately re-created, stereotypical ideas that people of color were hypersexual.[88]

Beyond the shared concerns about an attack on respectability, the community leaders were also very troubled by what they saw as a consistent link between people of color and drug use. While scholars have described the controversy that erupted in some black communities when activists attempted to implement needle exchange programs, the people in this focus group were more interested in discussing the class difference that existed among drug users and how that influenced their practices. They reasoned that poor people who used drugs on the street were more likely to benefit from needle exchange programs than middle-class users who might see themselves as immune to infection via this mode of transmission.[89]

After detailing a strong critique of SFAF's work, the focus group participants suggested an alternative method that would encourage more dialogue and grassroots response. Instead of using the marketing technique of data extraction, they called for the use of "ethnographic research methods that rely on participant observation rather than survey research techniques." The call for an ethnographic approach acknowledged that cultural norms might inhibit easy discussions of sexual behavior, particularly among older, more traditional individuals in the Asian and Latino communities.[90] By creating a space for more interpersonal communication and open channels of discussion among people with AIDS and encouraging SFAF to pay particular attention to issues of translation, community leaders hoped to provide safe spaces where people could talk about their concerns without being guided by an SFAF staff member. They imagined this "bottom up approach" would be more likely not only to change the content of AIDS prevention material but also to help the agency imagine new ways to distribute it.

SFAF responded to the ideas articulated by the community leaders by changing the way the institution related to its staff. In 1986, SFAF encouraged its staff members to join caucuses divided by identity category, forming the People of Color Caucus (POCC), the Gay Men's Caucus, the Women's Caucus, and the Support Staff Caucus.[91] This model was intended to provide a space for conversations about affirmative action for women and people of color within the organization as well as to offer a way for SFAF to expand its mission to more effectively provide for the needs of all people with AIDS. However, because the model divided workers by race, sexuality, gender, and class, it did more to fuel disagreements among SFAF staff than to generate proposals to deal with the expanding AIDS epidemic.

In January 1988 a conflict erupted between the Gay Men's Caucus and POCC. Infuriated by an article in the *San Francisco Chronicle* that discussed the complicated relationship between AIDS prevention services for gay men and people of color, the Gay Men's Caucus sent an angry memo to SFAF president Tim Wolfred. Attached to the memo were paragraphs taken directly from the article, quoting SFAF coordinator for bilingual multicultural services and POCC member Miguel Ramirez. The quote read, "'[Mayor Art Agnos needs to] shift the city's focus away from white gay men and tailor more of its education and services to minority people." Calling his language "homophobic" and a form of "verbal gay bashing," members of the Gay Men's Caucus demanded that Wolfred "send a letter to the *Chronicle* . . . making it clear . . . that we are committed to continuing programs that serve gay men while at the same time promoting needed programs for minorities. This letter should stress that some people are both gay and ethnic minority, and that they are most damaged by this kind of rhetoric. The letter should also make note of the gigantic contributions of gay men as staff of the Foundation, workers in the AIDS field generally, and the gay community at large."[92] The memo writers also wanted these opinions reinforced to foundation employees at the weekly staff meeting and expressed forcefully to the mayor's office as soon as possible.

The memo enraged Ramirez. He quickly penned a response to Wolfred pointing out that the caucus had selectively deleted part of the article's text from the photocopy sent to the entire staff. Comparing a full copy of the newspaper article to the one provided by the Gay Men's Caucus, Ramirez highlighted one sentence left out of the original attachment. "'Every day we get more and more cases of minorities with AIDS, but their understanding of the problem is about two years behind the white population.'" Ramirez went on to argue that the city's AIDS services needed to be revamped, "based on a principle of inclusion not exclusion."[93] Here his words echoed

POCC's statement of purpose: "[POCC] supports increased funding not reallocations of funds for education, prevention, etc. for ethnic minorities with AIDS/ARC [AIDS Related Complex]."[94]

The exchange between Ramirez and the Gay Men's Caucus suggested that SFAF still had a long way to go to integrate an analysis of race and sexuality into its AIDS work. In September 1988 the Long Range Planning Committee of SFAF took up the question of how to produce a multicultural workplace at the foundation, which would be the first step in creating an antiracist outreach program. In a questionnaire distributed to the entire staff, the committee asked, "How can SFAF build an anti-racist, anti-sexist, and more inclusive multiculturally sensitive organization? How can we succeed in meeting the differing needs of gay men and people of color?" and "How should the racism, sexism, and homophobia fuelling the (continual state and federal legislative) assaults be confronted?"[95] The questions showed that POCC and TWAATF had made headway into the SFAF establishment. The foundation realized that to create effective prevention, it needed to be committed to the needs, presence, and survival of all people with AIDS, but it must do so in a way that did not assume that all people experienced AIDS in the same way.

POCC met to discuss these important questions and submit its answers to the planning committee. Responding to the first question on organizational structure, the caucus members wanted people of color in "more visible, less tokenistic positions of power." They also suggested that using a "multicultural model" would help them develop client services for all communities.[96] To address the second question, about differing needs, the membership troubled the nature of the question itself. They argued that the very language of "gay men" and "people of color" perpetuated the problem. Instead, they suggested using phrases like "How do we meet the needs of all people affected by HIV?" To encourage this change, the caucus desired more communication between groups and a better sense of the agency's total services.[97] In response to the last question, the caucus's answer was quite direct: "Put together a multi-racial, multi-sexual, sexually diverse team" to help the public policy office respond to the federal assault on AIDS service providers.[98]

Jackson Peyton, SFAF's education director and a Gay Men's Caucus member, did not agree with POCC's analysis. In a response to the questionnaire, Peyton wrote, "We do NOT have as our mission the development of an anti-racist, anti-sexist organization. Our mission is to stop the

AIDS epidemic and to provide services to HIV affected people."[99] He saw no direct connection between the internal structure of the organization and the work the organization did in the world. Peyton followed his first response with a sentence that used the same words POCC had used, but in this context the answer had a very different meaning. "We are not here to meet the *needs* of gay men and people of color. We are supposed to meet the needs of people at risk for AIDS and people affected by AIDS."[100]

That POCC and Peyton used the same words to very different ends exemplified the extent to which discussions of the intersection of race and sexuality came to an impasse in the mid-1980s. While each talked about the need to care for all people affected by AIDS, they disagreed on whether that meant they needed to deal with how inequality — whether based on sexuality, race, gender, or combinations of all these categories — affected their potential clients and target populations. In that respect, the debate between POCC and Peyton not only symbolized the limits of SFAF's caucus model that split people by identity, but it also suggested that few politically feasible and salient models for alliance-based politics existed in this period.

Prevention Campaigns for Gay Men of Color

The split among SFAF staff over the relationship between race and sexuality began to heal when the organization undertook the design of AIDS prevention campaigns for gay men of color. Following the lead established internally by POCC and externally by TWAATF, SFAF's new process put the voices and concerns expressed by gay men of color much more at the center of the design and development process than they had been earlier. In 1989, working with a series of focus groups, SFAF created "Get Carried Away" for black men and "Listo para la acción" for Latinos. Both strategies sparked serious controversy for SFAF, but this time the controversy came not from communities of color but, rather, from the CDC's review board, which tried to censor the prevention campaigns. With new battle lines that pitted the entire staff — across race, sexuality, and gender — against the governmental review board, SFAF resisted governmental control of its AIDS prevention work.

The first step SFAF took toward designing new prevention materials was to change its marketing and survey methods. In 1989, SFAF made a conscious effort to reach more men of color in its fifth survey of openly gay and bisexual men in San Francisco. SFAF located 200 men to interview through random dialing of telephone numbers throughout the entire city; another 200 were found through random digit dialing of phone numbers in "those parts of the city where a greater number of gay/bisexual men were found in the first stage of interviewing."[101] With the new method, SFAF acknowledged the effects of racial segregation on gay neighborhoods by seeking half of its interviewees outside traditional gay neighborhoods that tended to be overwhelmingly white. The survey also addressed concerns of racial bias by diversifying the core of interviewers and making sure that everyone was trained to be "sensitive to cultural difference surrounding the issue of sexuality, including the issue of the bisexuality." Interviewers should, the planners cautioned, "be more sensitive to these issues, and better able to recognize respondents who might be reluctant to reveal their sexual orientation in the telephone."[102] This attempt to move beyond equating self-identified men with the adjectives "out" and "proud" made SFAF more successful at reaching a wider range of men who had sex with other men.

With the survey complete, SFAF developed spaces where black gay men could talk about safe sex in a series of open-ended focus groups. In late 1989, before producing a poster, SFAF conducted two focus groups in the Tenderloin neighborhood of San Francisco to see what kind of issues and images black men would like to see. The men at these sessions objected to the absence of blacks in safe-sex material. They also complained that the bars they frequented did not have the prevention materials posted, as they were in many white bars. Here, the racial division felt in the larger gay community played itself out in how black men viewed AIDS prevention services and whether they paid attention to the messages that were available to them in public spaces. While the men interviewed possessed some information about HIV transmission, in the end "they had a lot of confusion on safe sex."[103]

To address the ideas presented in the initial focus groups, SFAF's education department created a poster and pamphlet with images of black men. The poster showed a side-view photograph of two black men in a naked embrace. One man is standing and holds the other man, whose legs are wrapped around his waist, in his arms. The two men kiss passionately, and a condom covers the standing man's erect penis. The text above the image reads, "Get Carried Away"; "with Condoms" appears below it.*[104] The

---

*This image can be viewed at ⟨http://www.sfaf.org/aboutsfaf/gallery/get-carried-away⟩.

pamphlet featured the same models, image, and text, but it also included more text explicitly warning about how to avoid harm. The brochure told men that "you can't tell if he has AIDS by looking at him, so protect yourself, protect him, ALWAYS USE A CONDOM." It also provided a four-point guide on how to use a condom. In addition, the brochure explained how to clean needles between each use. This last section was added after the focus groups suggested that the brochure needed to include information for intravenous drug users who might, or might not, also be gay.[105] With the materials in a more definitive form, SFAF convened another focus group. The eighteen men, ranging in age from twenty-one to forty-one, liked the poster and pamphlet. They appreciated that the models "were Black and loving." They also confirmed that the information presented was accurate and useful.[106]

To help distribute the materials and ensure visibility, SFAF sought help from BMWT, the multiracial gay organization that had called for such coalitions six years earlier. Together the organizations hired an outreach worker for bars frequented by black gay men. He went to bars during peak hours and spoke with patrons about safe sex and HIV prevention. SFAF then arranged follow-up information and services for anyone who needed it. SFAF clearly tried to connect the production of knowledge to the dissemination of knowledge. SFAF's effort to build a service coalition with BWMT suggested that the foundation's board recognized why it was problematic to use safe-sex workshops intended to be universally appealing for gay men but that were actually geared toward white gay men. Contemporaneous survey data from a 1990 BMWT study of almost 1,000 black gay men confirmed that an overwhelming majority of black men objected to this practice.[107]

Despite the outreach, the project soon ran into problems. As a contract agency with the San Francisco AIDS Office, SFAF had to present any campaign receiving federal funding to a community review board for vetting. The community review board developed out of policy guidelines created by the CDC in 1986. In its initial guidance, the CDC recognized that "programs to promote a 'safer sex' risk reduction strategy may involve supporting communication of suggestions using candid terms, some of which may provoke criticism by some in society," but it refused to reject sexual content and instead called for a review board that could "consider the bounds of explicitness believed needed to communicate an effective message to those for whom it is intended."[108] While the CDC certainly placed restrictions on what AIDS workers could say if they received federal funds, actions by the Reagan administration had a much greater effect on the content of AIDS prevention material than did the CDC's initial guidelines. In February 1987, President Ronald Reagan required that all funded materials "emphasize local control and encourage responsible sexual behavior based on fidelity, commitment, and maturity, placing sexuality within the context of marriage."[109] These new presidential guidelines, which will be explored in greater detail in the next chapter, provided new censorship powers to community review boards across the country.

Five individuals volunteered to serve on the San Francisco community review board to vet AIDS prevention material: Marilyn Borovoy, a housewife and member of the Social Service Commission; Juan Cruz, a patients' rights advocate and a board member at Instituto Familiar de la Raza; Valerie Edwards, a student at the University of California at Berkeley; James Foster, a marketing consultant and city health commissioner; and Julie Tang, an assistant district attorney. The AIDS Office chose the individuals to represent what it defined as the key populations affected by AIDS: the "panel is comprised of three women and two men; one Asian, one Black, one Latino, and two Whites; one individual who is a member of a group considered at increased risk for AIDS and four whom CDC would classify as 'the general public.'"[110] While it was not clear who the "at increased risk" individual was, or even what that term meant in this case, it likely referred to a gay man on the panel (probably Cruz, but he was never named as such).

On January 31, 1990, the review board was empanelled to review SFAF's campaign for black gay men. At the meeting held in the AIDS Office, members discussed their objections to the poster. One argued that it was "too sexually explicit for a reasonable person" and that it may "land in other's hand." Another commented that the poster failed to "depict with dignity and empowerment." Three members of the panel expressed support for the poster. They argued that the crisis situation called for this approach and that "provocative" material would "start where the client is."[111] Ultimately, the board approved the poster but suggested that SFAF work on consulting more people in future campaigns.

The board's ambivalence about SFAF's campaign did not stop the foundation's education staff from designing a poster specifically for Latino men. In March and October 1989, SFAF convened focus groups of "gay and bisexual health educators from the Latin Community" in an attempt to determine the best message for, and how to disseminate it to, the community.[112] The focus group participants concluded that certain segments of San Francisco's Latino community needed more help than others. To elaborate, they ranked six groups in order of importance, defined as most in need of prevention information: injecting drug users; undocumented immigrants; Latin gay homeless; Latin transvestites; Latin gays over age fifty; and Latin gay youth.[113] The educators called for the incorporation of "family, religion, friendship and spirituality" into prevention work because "these issues are an intrinsic component of the Latin community."[114] In so doing, they resisted stereotypical notions about macho Latino men with overactive sex drives even as they embraced some essentialist notions of Latino culture.

In an attempt to continue the lively discussion, SFAF showed the group "Dress for the Occasion," a poster that SFAF had designed the year before for white men.[115] It showed a photograph of a seated naked man from nose to knees. His hands are placed on his inner thighs, providing a frame for his erect penis covered with a condom. Below the image the text reads, "Dress for the occasion."† The group, on the whole, thought that the poster was too direct and sexually explicit for Latino men. One man suggested that two men, not just one, should appear in the image for Latino men.[116] When the meeting ended, SFAF staff had several good ideas for a new prevention poster. The overwhelming majority of participants wanted to see images with two partially nude men.

Six months later, SFAF created two versions of a poster titled "Listo para la acción . . . con condón" ("Ready for action . . . with a condom"): one was a "sexually explicit erotic safe-sex" poster designed for distribution in Latino gay bars; the other was "less sexually explicit" and would appear as a newspaper advertisement.[117] Using a production strategy for this poster similar to that for "Get Carried Away," SFAF then conducted a series of focus groups with Latino gay men and showed them potential versions of the campaign. The sexually explicit poster shows a photograph of two nude young men, locked in a face-to-face embrace, seated on a stool. One man sits astride the other, who caresses his partner's back, which faces the viewer. The condom-sheathed penis of the man on the bottom is about to penetrate the anus of the man on top.‡ At a session held in March 1990,

---

† This image can be viewed at ⟨http://www.sfaf.org/aboutsfaf/gallery/dress-for-the-occasion⟩.

‡ This image can be viewed at ⟨http://www.sfaf.org/aboutsfaf/gallery/en-cualquier⟩.

Listo para la acción...
con condón.

Para más información, comuníquese con San Francisco AIDS Foundation (415) 864-4376

2.3 | "Listo para la acción . . . con condón" poster. Courtesy of San Francisco Public Library. Reprinted with permission from the San Francisco AIDS Foundation.

this poster elicited one negative and five positive responses. Those who liked the poster commented that the models were attractive and the situation was realistic. But even those who approved of the poster expressed concerns about the explicitness of the image. They felt that many people, including "Latinos recently arriving from Latin America," might find the poster offensive.[118] None of the participants objected to an alternative image that showed two men—one wearing only underwear, the other clad in jeans with a condom tucked into the waistband—holding hands (ill. 2.3). They liked the display of affection between the two men as well as the fact that this image could be shown to the larger Latino community in Spanish-speaking newspapers.[119]

With suggestions from the focus groups incorporated into the more sexually explicit poster, SFAF's education director, Ernesto Hinojos, sent both posters to the AIDS Office for review in April 1990. Several members of the review board were outraged by what they saw. Juan Cruz wrote an angry memo to the group protesting the message of the poster.

> My first reaction was "what the fuck are they doing now!" And it doesn't get any better. I won't be a "liberal" and say that due to this crisis etc, I will pass on this: The poster implies that people can only be reached through the lowest common denominator (pornography). . . . I don't read porno for edification or education, I use it for thrills. In

this case it denigrate the viewers; it's [*sic*] message implies that the viewers can only learn to save their lives through porno, I don't buy it. This is also racist. Why do the men of color have to be reached by the most in-your-face porn and that other people, white gay men and heteros, don't need to be informed and encouraged by such blatant material?[120]

There is no record of Cruz's reaction to the campaign designed for white gay men, but his opposition to these sexually explicit images was severe. Cruz would not approve the material, refusing to be considered a "liberal" enabler.

At that point, the review panel revoked the city and county funding for the "Listo para la acción" project. It not only objected to the content but also questioned the process of focus group testing that produced the posters in the first place. In a letter to Les Pappas, the campaign development director, Sandra Hernandez, director of the AIDS Office, suggested that "you take into serious consideration the cultural, as well as educational impact of an erotic poster to the target audience, and to the larger Latino community."[121] A week later, Pappas responded to Hernandez's rejection. He explained that SFAF had "rigorously" worked with "representatives from the Latino AIDS Project, Mano a Mano, and Men of All Colors Together," all key organizations in gay and bisexual Latino communities. He had confidence in "Listo para la acción" as part of a "multi-faceted campaign for the Latino gay male community." He ended the letter by adding that "the required budget transfers have been made" to produce and distribute the poster without city funds.[122]

The controversies that ensued upon completion of these campaigns suggest that attention to the intersections between race and sexuality occurred in fits and starts over the course of the first decade and a half of the AIDS epidemic. They also make clear that all of the actors in this story had a problem dealing with the reality of those intersections. The dominant (i.e., white) gay community could not imagine how racial difference was implicated in conversations about sexuality, while the dominant African American and Latino community (i.e., straight, maybe religious) refused to see sexually explicit material as anything other than the legacy of a racist sexual imagination. This is not to say that communities of color were more homophobic than white communities, or that gay white men were more racist than straight white men; rather, at this moment in the late 1980s and early 1990s it was exceptionally difficult, if not impossible, to build coalitions across these identity categories.[123]

Beyond the controversy, changes in SFAF's clientele were equally telling. Between 1986 and 1992, the racial breakdown of people seeking assistance from SFAF's Client Services Office changed dramatically. In 1986, 24 percent of SFAF's clients were people of color. Six years later, more than 79 percent of clients were African Americans or Latinos.[124] While there is no specific evidence to suggest that the campaigns for gay men of color directly had an effect on the people with AIDS who came to SFAF for assistance, the foundation's increasing willingness to listen to communities of color clearly had an impact.

SFAF, AS ONE OF THE NATION'S largest and oldest ASOs, constantly struggled with the consequences of implementing AIDS prevention using a model of gay liberation defined through the experiences of white gay men. Would events have developed differently if SFAF had chosen a broader definition of gay liberation as a starting point, as articulated in the previous chapter? Would this have allowed this agency to address the changing needs of people with AIDS as well as to work on prevention efforts with groups of people who not only refused gay identities but also regularly experienced rejection from gay institutions? Without conscious attention to the extent of racial discrimination present in San Francisco's gay institutions and the racial and class segregation of the urban space in post-1960s America, it would be difficult to reach a true cross section of homosexually active men. As Larry Bye, the head of Communications Technology, one of the marketing firms that worked with SFAF, reported, "Gay-identified men tend to be disproportionately highly-educated, Caucasian, and upscale in occupation. Homosexuals who do not identify as gay are a more diverse group in terms of race and demographic characteristics generally. Gay-identified communication channels cannot reach many of these men because they deny they are homosexuals. Minority homosexuals tend, in fact, to deny the threat of AIDS because of its negative association with homosexuality. Hence, behavior change probably lags among non-gay-identifying homosexual men."[125] When SFAF consistently reiterated its appeal to the "gay-identified" group — whether through prevention services or pitches to condom manufacturers — it reified the idea that the non-gay-identified or "minority homosexuals" were largely unreachable.

The activism undertaken by gay men of color, most notably Hank Tavera, Ernesto Hinojos, and BWMT, changed the way ASOs such as SFAF functioned. Insisting that attention to communities of color need not be totally devoid of sexually explicit language, these AIDS activists and service providers tried to balance sex-positive discussions with ones that more fully acknowledged how racial and economic inequality affected the ways people of color accessed information about AIDS prevention and treatment.

This and the preceding chapter have detailed the first responses to AIDS organized largely by people who lacked previous health care experience but who had with a strong political commitment to gay activism. Building on years of political organizing and political disagreements, the people described in these chapters, most but not all of whom were gay and lesbian, found it necessary to create a system for dealing with a disease that by 1987 had killed at least 28,000 people in the United States.[126] While these activists were far from universally successful, particularly when they had to deal with people who did not use their sexual practices as a way of identifying themselves, their sense of urgency came as much from a displeasure with the federal government's failure to mount a campaign against AIDS as it did from the scope of the problem. The next chapter turns to a discussion of how the federal government, particularly the presidential administration of Ronald Reagan, began to develop a program to address AIDS beginning in 1985, a full four years into what was increasingly being called an AIDS epidemic and a full four years after concerned individuals and ASOs had designed a medical and political response to AIDS in the absence of a state-based response.

3 | What Should the Federal Government Do to Deal with the Problem of AIDS?

The Reagan Administration's Response

WHEN A MEMO TITLED "What should the federal government do to deal with the problem of AIDS?" crossed Carl Anderson's desk, the special assistant for the Office of Public Liaison (OPL) in the Reagan White House changed the content of the text with one stroke of his pen. Initially drafted by the Working Group on Health Policy (WGHP) in September 1985, a committee with representatives from the Departments of Justice, State, and Health and Human Services (HHS), the document laid out a course of action to deal with the then four-year-old AIDS epidemic. The WGHP concluded that the White House needed to sponsor a major public education campaign that addressed AIDS as "a public health problem" but that also considered "the civil rights and needs of individuals." A month later, Anderson, the first White House staffer to edit this memo, deleted the civil rights phrase and inserted a call for the publication of a "special report on AIDS, and enhanced public information efforts."[1] Anderson sent his version of the document to the Domestic Policy Council (DPC), the presidential domestic advisory board, for vetting.

On December 19, 1985, the DPC reviewed the memo in a meeting that was both typical and atypical for that advisory body. As was usually the case with DPC meetings, about a dozen Reagan administration officials, including representatives from the Departments of Education, Labor, and HHS, participated in discussions about domestic issues. But the meeting was unusual in two ways: first, President Reagan attended the session; second, the agenda included a discussion of the AIDS epidemic. The DPC meeting held at the end of 1985 was only the fifth time the advisory body had discussed AIDS, and it was the only time, up to that point, that Reagan had attended a session with AIDS on the agenda.[2] In the middle of the meeting, President Reagan commented that "AIDS must be dealt with as a major *public* health problem," echoing the phrase in the memo and subtly eliding the civil rights approach. Most of the DPC members agreed and called on all individuals to take responsibility for their actions. Notably, the representative from the Department of Education, Gary Bauer, the undersecretary for education, flagged the lack of "emphasis on personal responsibility" in "booklets developed for students" as a problem that the federal government needed to address. The meeting ended with the DPC strongly recommending that the president sign the revised memo. Three days later he did just that: in the last days of 1985, Reagan initialed the final version of "What should the federal government do to deal with the problem of AIDS?" He authorized federal agencies and state and local governments "to take all necessary steps to lessen the risks of the spread of AIDS" and to treat AIDS as a public health problem in need of "a special report on AIDS."[3]

One month after the president called for the special report on AIDS, the Department of Health and Human Services, the agency that would ultimately oversee the writing of the report, requested that the president take an entirely different kind of action on AIDS. HHS proposed that Reagan sign Executive Order No. 12291, a rule that sought to add AIDS to the list of Dangerous Contagious Diseases. With AIDS on this list, the State Department could deny visas to applicants with AIDS and the Immigration and Naturalization Service (INS) could prevent any potential immigrant with AIDS from entering the country.[4] While the decision to adopt this policy would not take effect for another year and a half, the simultaneity of these events suggests that the Reagan administration considered the development of domestic AIDS policy in concert with AIDS policies that affected people outside the United States.

Contemporary critics of the Reagan administration's AIDS policy criticized it for failing to address the actual scope of the epidemic, particularly as it manifested itself in the United States. The most widely read of those attacks, journalist Randy Shilts's *And the Band Played On*, published in 1987, cited numerous examples of how Reagan's first-term administration refused to fund AIDS programs.[5] Shilts assigned the failure to address AIDS to the rise of the New Right, the administration's desire to shrink the welfare state, and the consistent demonization of homosexuality by modern conservatives.[6] Almost every review of the best-selling book highlighted

Shilts's argument about the administration's meager response, making it one of the central issues in public discussions of Shilts's exposé.[7]

Historical accounts of the AIDS epidemic, Ronald Reagan's presidency, and the rise of the New Right have echoed Shilts and his reviewers. These explanations would have us believe that this chapter's opening vignettes, particularly the first one, which showed how slow Reagan was to act on AIDS, typified his administration's response to AIDS. Most historians have argued that Reagan all but ignored the epidemic. Pointing to Reagan's slow start on AIDS — he did not sign a document dealing with AIDS until the end of 1985, did not mention the term "AIDS" in public until 1986, and spent very little money on researching the epidemic even though the first reported cases of AIDS coincided precisely with Reagan's first months in office — most authors writing about him omit anything but a passing reference to AIDS and Ronald Reagan.[8]

Instead of discussing AIDS, historical accounts of the politics of the 1980s describe the ways the New Right came to power, in part, through a reaction to gay rights and AIDS. According to historian Sara Diamond, "The onset of the Reagan era brought unity to the Right's disparate elements. New Right think tanks and electoral projects promoted a three-fold set of priorities: anticommunist militarism, supply-side economics, and 'traditional family values.'"[9] On this point, theorists whose work makes up the interdisciplinary history of AIDS agree, arguing that Reagan failed to act on AIDS because of his commitment to the New Right, which required a moralistic stance against gays and lesbians and drug users, the people most associated with AIDS. Ultimately, both sets of scholars argue that the administration's response to AIDS was part of its larger conservative attack on the social movements of the 1960s and 1970s, which had loosely united to extend civil rights to racial, gender, and sexual minorities.[10]

While I agree that the Reagan administration's sluggishness in responding to AIDS must be documented and reiterated for us to have a full account of the political history of the 1980s, the historical record points to a more complicated, and internally contradictory, administrative reaction to AIDS after 1985. Focusing on the administration's rhetoric, as articulated by the officials charged with plotting a course to deal with AIDS, to the exclusion of understanding what the government actually produced once it acknowledged the necessity of action prevents us from seeing that a conservative, morally driven ideology about AIDS was not all-powerful in this period. This chapter will argue that putting AIDS at the center of a historical analysis of Reagan's presidency unsettles our understanding of modern conservatism previously understood by historians and other analysts as a movement that brought together people who defended "family values" with those who called for laissez-faire economic policy and anticommunism.

Careful attention to the historical narrative of how the administration responded to AIDS suggests that the federal government's decision to design an AIDS prevention strategy produced splits and disagreements among political appointees in both the domestic and foreign policy arenas. When it came to the making of domestic AIDS education, on one hand, education and religion advisors to the president, namely, Gary Bauer, William Bennett, and Carl Anderson, steered the administration toward a morality-based AIDS initiative that shunned homosexuality and hailed abstinence and heterosexual marriage as the only forms of effective AIDS prevention. On the other hand, Surgeon General C. Everett Koop and Admiral James Watkins, the head of the Presidential Commission on the Human Immunodeficiency Virus Epidemic (Presidential Commission on HIV), fundamentally disagreed with Bauer, Bennett, and Anderson. Koop argued that to address AIDS required a commitment to rational science and Christianity as well as explicit discussions of sexual practice, drug use, and condom distribution. The presidential commission, under Watkins's leadership, presented sharp criticisms of the eviscerated welfare state, a position that put the commission in direct opposition to those who called for economic conservatism in the form of less governmental spending. While all of these men considered themselves religious and conservative, the stances of Koop and Watkins infuriated Bauer, Bennett, and Anderson, three of the leading religious conservatives in Reagan's administration.[11]

Beyond the disagreements AIDS exposed among social conservatives working on domestic policy, it also produced splits within the administration over how to incorporate a response to AIDS in a foreign policy based almost entirely on anticommunism and containment of the Soviet Union. Beginning in 1986, when the administration began to act on the foreign policy implications of AIDS by instituting an immigration policy that excluded potential immigrants with AIDS, foreign policy specialists who worked at the State Department and the Central Intelligence Agency criticized attempts to control the spread of AIDS within the United States by keeping immigrants with AIDS outside the borders as well as the administration's apprehension about condom distribution. The State Department defended the use of diplomacy instead of restricting the movement of immigrants with AIDS to win favor among nations who might otherwise align with the Soviet Union. Even though the president overrode State's concerns by suggesting that AIDS, like communism, needed to be physically prevented from entering the country, beginning in 1987 the State Department, working primarily through the U.S. Agency for International Development (USAID), created an AIDS prevention plan that was more comprehensive and sexually explicit than any program the government designed for use within the United States.

Giving weight to these three examples of disagreement within the administration illustrates that AIDS actually had the potential to disaggregate conservatives allied under the New Right umbrella. Instead of reading conservatism in the 1980s and early 1990s as a strong united front, this historical investigation of how the Reagan administration dealt with "the problem of AIDS" exposes the fragility of the conservative consensus. Social conservatives in positions of power were never able to completely censor the material produced by the federal government for domestic and international consumption. Beyond how AIDS complicates the historical narrative of conservatism in this period, this chapter also argues that the making of domestic AIDS policy must be considered in relation to the development of AIDS as a form of foreign policy. American Studies scholar Amy Kaplan argues that "cultural phenomena we think of as domestic or particularly national are forged in a crucible of foreign relations."[12] In that respect, one of the more infectious ideas of the 1980s — surprising, given the growing strength of the New Right in these years — was that frank discussions of sexuality were necessary for AIDS prevention to be effective in the global South.

First Administrative Actions

The first two recorded meetings on AIDS convened during Ronald Reagan's first term in office took place in the summer of 1983. The first session, held on June 21, brought together Judi Buckalew, special assistant to the president for public liaison; staff members from HHS; and gay activists Virginia Apuzzo and Jeff Levi of the National Gay Task Force (NGTF). Convening at HHS and not the White House, where many conferences with political organizations took place, Buckalew reported that "the meeting was an informal 'get-acquainted' meeting, where the groups shared their concerns and the HHS people responded with information about their efforts."[13] In what was, according to Apuzzo, "the first meeting between the gay/lesbian community and the Reagan Administration," the NGTF expressed a hope that Buckalew would arrange for further meetings with HHS officials.[14]

The second session seemed much more representative of how the administration hoped to respond to the AIDS epidemic. Five people attended the session; three worked for the OPL and two were conservative activists. Representing the OPL were Faith Ryan Whittlesey, who had recently left her post as ambassador to Switzerland to head the OPL, and two of her staff members, Buckalew and Morton Blackwell, special assistant to the president for public liaison for religion. The three White House staffers met with Dr. Ron Goodwin of the Moral Majority and Howard Phillips, the national director of the Conservative Caucus, who had called for the session to discuss their concerns about AIDS as a growing public health problem. Goodwin and Phillips believed that the public was not getting enough information from the administration, a stance that made the administration unresponsive to "overwhelming public concern." While they differed on whether the administration should "come out and publicly condemn homosexuality as a moral wrong and link this statement to the AIDS outbreak" (Phillips favored this strategy; Godwin did not), each man called on the OPL to encourage the administration to close the gay bathhouses, require all blood donors to fill out a detailed form about their sexual habits, and become "more visible and vocal" about its AIDS efforts.[15]

Two years would pass before the next recorded conversation about AIDS took place among White House staff. In August 1985, a full four years into the epidemic, the Public Health Service (PHS) briefed Reagan's domestic policy advisors in what appeared to be the first briefing of its kind. Staffers both provided a scientific assessment of AIDS and discussed ways that assessment might influence policymaking.[16] At the information session the DPC members were told the causes and symptoms of AIDS and were given information on who got AIDS ("sexually active homosexual and bisexual men with multiple partners; present or past abusers of intravenous drugs; persons with hemophilia or other coagulation disorders; heterosexual contacts of someone with AIDS or at risk for AIDS; and persons who have had transfusions with blood or blood products")[17] as well as the role condoms might play in preventing the spread of the epidemic.

Using language not dissimilar to contemporaneous public discourse on AIDS, the briefers gave special recommendations for "persons with positive HTLV-III [Human T-Lymphotropic Virus-III] antibody tests." Using terminology to describe the virus that causes AIDS before the term "HIV" existed, they suggested condom use for HTLV-positive people but did not extend the recommendation beyond that population. "There is a risk of infecting others by sexual intercourse, sharing of needles, and possibly, exposure of others to saliva through oral-genital contact or intimate kissing. The effectiveness of condoms in preventing infection with HTLV-III is not proved, but their consistent use may reduce transmission, since exchange of body fluids is known to increase risk." For the general population, PHS discouraged people from having "sexual contact with persons known or suspected of having AIDS" or "sex with multiple partners, or with persons who have had multiple partners." PHS concluded that "communities can help prevent AIDS by vigorous efforts to educate and inform their populations about the illness, with special emphasis on educational activities for members of high risk groups."[18]

The briefers' position on condoms assumed that only HIV-positive people needed to protect themselves, and even then the briefers did not fully embrace the idea that condoms would be effective in preventing the spread of the virus. This focus on "risk groups" was at odds with the claims of service providers, described in the first two chapters, who argued that behavior, not identity, put people at risk; that all individuals needed to protect themselves; and that condoms should be widely distributed. Despite its ambivalent position on condoms and risk groups, the PHS briefing assumed that the state and parts of the gay community had a role to play in designing and implementing AIDS prevention programs.

While the public health establishment tried to assert its authority in defining the scope of AIDS prevention material, many of Reagan's domestic advisors and aides wanted to bend what they called "AIDS education" to fit the model of social and religious conservatism that posited gay men as sick and dangerous. Staff members were flooded with material with vitriolic attacks on homosexuality. Mariam Bell, the associate director for religious affairs in the OPL, received an illustrated book titled *Homosexuality: Legitimate, Alternative Deathstyle* from its author, Dick Hafer.[19] In addition to linking homosexuality to crime, especially child molestation, the document justified discriminating against people with AIDS to protect "normal people" from the disease.[20]

Attacks on gay men for the spread of AIDS appeared in other, less explicit forms as well. In a letter to the president, several members of Congress argued that health agencies had overstepped their boundaries by applying political solutions to a health problem. Nine Republican congressmen, including William Dannemeyer and Robert Dornan, both from California, and Newt Gingrich from Georgia, all of whom were conservative Republicans, accused the administration of mounting an overly liberal approach to AIDS. "AIDS should have been handled like any other health threat of epidemic proportions, with prompt, common sense guidelines that address the problem and ignore the politics." They concluded that "the choice for your administration is either seek solution aimed principally at protecting the public health and secondarily protecting the sensitivities of those tragic victims of AIDS, or to continue pursuing a reversal of these goals, which is the apparent course of your administration at this time."[21] The letter writers had particular contempt for PHS and the CDC, a sister agency of PHS housed in HHS, charged with investigating infectious diseases, as the two agencies in charge of the medical response to AIDS. These offices had "failed to take any prudent steps to ensure that AIDS will not spread to the population at large. In addition to closing the bathhouses, we feel that steps such as encouraging direct donation of blood, mandating reporting of AIDS and ARC to CDC, and encouraging local public health services to notify partners of AIDS victims as is done with other venereal diseases, would be positive steps to discourage the spread of this deadly disease."[22] Gingrich made a point of emphasizing his displeasure with the CDC when he wrote a separate letter to Dr. James Mason, the assistant secretary of HHS, cautioning him against "temper[ing] your medical advice with political problems."[23]

What "political" meant for the congressmen was quite different from what it meant for the activists described in the previous chapters as well as the members of ACT UP, the subject of the final chapter. When Gingrich used the term "political," he used it as an epithet to attack government officials he believed were overly liberal as well as activists he believed put politics over health. Gingrich implied that Mason's actions were overly complicated and, in effect, not medical enough. This construction would become quite common within the administration, where senior advisors labeled opponents, most often Democratic congresspeople, "political" as opposed to "scientific," or wrongly concerned with civil rights instead of public health.

Gingrich's argument went beyond questioning the claim that health was in and of itself political to include a call for "commonsense" responses to

AIDS. In this case, Gingrich argued that closing bathhouses or mandating reporting of AIDS was a more reasonable policy than trying to provide sex education in bathhouses or keeping the names of people who tested positive for HIV anonymous. Here, the commonsense arguments betrayed a particular stance on AIDS, one that sought to make the public healthy by restricting the civil rights of those believed to be sick. This approach flew in the face of the arguments of AIDS activists, who insisted that the only way to deal with the AIDS epidemic was to imagine state-based solutions that acknowledged people's civil rights.

The Reagan administration was persuaded by Gingrich's articulated position rather than that of AIDS activists, and it set out to develop a plan to address AIDS with a three-pronged strategy that looked quite different from the one called for initially by PHS. First, in September 1985 the DPC formed the WGHP, a subcommittee headed by William Roper of the Health Care Financing Administration. If it worked properly, this advisory body would lessen the role of PHS in advising the administration. Despite representation from various agencies in the federal government, including the Veterans' Administration and the Departments of Defense, State, Education, and Justice, the higher levels of the administration often did not take the group's advice. Beginning with the revisions to the memo (that opens this chapter) on what the federal government should do to deal with AIDS and continuing with the DPC's dismissal of the WGHP's arguments in DPC meetings, the WGHP did not have as much power as its name implied.

Second, the administration began to talk about its AIDS budget in whole numbers so that it could temper the perception that it was in the process of shrinking the social welfare budget.[24] Because senior advisors to the president, including the HHS secretary, Margaret Heckler, knew that some constituents were concerned that the federal government was dragging its feet on AIDS, whenever they commented on the state of the AIDS budget, they talked about the total amount of money the federal government spent or planned to spend. For example, PHS pointed out that in 1986, $126 million had been allocated for HHS's AIDS efforts.[25] While this seemed like a significant amount of money, considering it as a percentage of HHS's total budget changes its meaning. In 1986, $126 million appropriated for AIDS was approximately .08 percent of HHS's total $1.5 billion budget. The entire budget for the CDC was only four times as much, accounting for .32 percent of the total HHS budget.[26] Clearly, using whole numbers made actions seem more significant than the actual percentages revealed. Beyond the numbers game, because the administration ordered HHS to reshuffle the money instead of giving the agency new resources, HHS's budget did not increase. Its percentage of the total federal budget remained relatively constant at about 13 percent from 1983 to 1985, only going up to 14.5 percent in 1986–87 when the administration sponsored AIDS actions by name.[27]

The third and ultimately most important part of the administration's strategy made William Bennett and Gary Bauer, secretary and undersecretary of education, respectively, the administration's key AIDS spokesmen. Bennett — who ran the National Endowment for the Humanities between 1981 and 1985, served as the secretary of education from 1985 to 1988, and worked as President George H. W. Bush's drug czar from 1989 to 1990 — embodied the social conservative ideology, with a strong emphasis on moral training and family values that were presumed to underpin the education of the nation's children. Bauer, too, had powerful connections to the growing Religious Right, particularly in terms of his work as one of President Reagan's main advisors on "the family." Bauer used his post as aide to the president to promote heterosexual marriage and traditional gender roles throughout the 1980s.[28]

Working together, Bennett and Bauer tried to build AIDS prevention from a conservative model that emphasized morality, local control, and a strong executive branch. Bennett and Bauer used their credentials as educators to control the content of educational responses to AIDS, shaping material for both children and adults. They called attention to how federal programs focused on protecting children from unseemly discussion of sexuality outside heterosexual marriage and pushed a commitment to heterosexual sex within marriage and individual responsibility as central to national policy. In a 1987 memo, Bauer explained that the Department of Education needed to emphasize the idea that "heterosexual sex within marriage is what most Americans, our laws and our traditions consider the proper focus of human sexuality."[29]

In addition to calling on the government to embrace traditional values and action in developing AIDS prevention strategy, Bennett and Bauer also championed the need for local control over content as well as a strong executive branch to provide guidance. Using these three tenets of modern conservative ideology, Bauer and Bennett developed what they hoped was a well-rounded strategy to address AIDS that claimed to put health before politics but ultimately relied on a conservative political approach instead of a public health program. In the process, they shaped the administration's fight against AIDS and helped quell conservative fears that the administration's response would be weak.

The Surgeon General's Report on AIDS

Despite their role as AIDS spokesmen, Bauer and Bennett were not the first people, nor the first social conservatives, in the federal government to produce a document on AIDS for the American people. That job fell to Surgeon General C. Everett Koop, whom Reagan empowered to write a special report on AIDS in December 1985. Koop became surgeon general at the beginning of Reagan's first term, but not without a very contentious nomination fight. Democrats fiercely opposed Koop, particularly because of his antichoice stance on abortion, which grew out of his religious convictions as a Christian. Four years later, in the minds of the upper-administration officials, Koop's beliefs made him the perfect candidate to write a special report on AIDS that would emphasize morality, defined as a commitment to heterosexual marriage as the key institution of the American family and nation, rather than condoms and sex education. Much to the disappointment of many conservatives, Koop failed to live up to their expectations.[30]

Instead of producing a document that emphasized what was increasingly becoming a kind of conservative dogma about the need to push marriage over frank conversations about sex, Koop stressed his commitment to public health and accumulated a wide range of information about the epidemic. He consulted myriad ASOs and nongovernmental organizations (NGOs), from the U.S. Catholic Conference and the National Council of Churches to the AIDS Action Council and the National Coalition of Black Lesbians and Gays, to determine their positions on AIDS prevention.[31] Koop then wrote dozens of drafts of the report over the course of six months. In the end, he and his staff presented what they considered a balanced report that detailed how to prevent the spread of AIDS.

The final surgeon general's report, released on October 22, 1986, delineated an education program for both school-age children and adults at the same time that it placed a conversation about AIDS in a larger political context. At the press conference to announce the report's release, Koop drew particular attention to the racial disparities of the epidemic, noting that African Americans accounted for 25 percent of all people with AIDS but only 12 percent of the general population, statistics that AIDS workers in

San Francisco regularly cited.[32] This statistical data allowed Koop to argue that race and racism helped shape the epidemic, a point I have not found in any other contemporaneous document created by the U.S. government.

The most contentious recommendations in Koop's report, however, were his calls for condom usage and AIDS education at a young age:

> Many people — especially our youth — are not receiving information that is vital to their future health and well-being because of our reticence in dealing with the subjects of sex, sexual practices, and homosexuality. This silence must end. We can no longer afford to sidestep frank, open discussions about sexual practices — homosexual and heterosexual. Education about AIDS should start at an early age so that children can grow up knowing the behaviors to avoid to protect themselves from exposure to the AIDS virus.[33]

Using the terms "frank" and "open" resonated with the rhetoric of contemporaneous AIDS activists, who wanted to instigate discussions about the way people actually had sex. Instead of shying away from talk of same-sex sexual practices, Koop wanted to "deal with [homosexuality, promiscuity of any kind, and prostitution], but [do] so with the intent that information and education can change individual behavior, since this is the primary way to stop the epidemic of AIDS."[34] This informational responsibility was best met by the federal government, so long as it never utilized certain forms of intervention, in particular compulsory testing and quarantine. Koop concluded that his work was a central feature of his identity as a Christian. In his memoir he writes, "My position on AIDS was dictated by scientific integrity and Christian compassion. I felt that my Christian opponents had abandoned not only their old friend [Koop himself], but also their own commitment to integrity and compassion."[35]

Koop's "commitment to integrity and compassion" pleased a wide range of AIDS workers. Gil Gerald, the executive director of the National Coalition of Black Lesbians and Gays, commended Koop

> because of your positions favoring sex education for school age children, against compulsory mass blood testing, and against quarantining persons with AIDS, ARC, or who test positive for HIV antibodies. To be quite honest the report and your statements exceeded our expectations. Please count on our support for promoting the recommendations you outline in issuing this report. We urge you to use the

prestige and influence of your office to see that the federal response to AIDS as a health concern in Black and Brown communities is adequately addressed.[36]

Koop presented his message of scientific reasoning mixed with Christian compassion to the general public. The federal government printed more than 20 million copies for distribution, while smaller organizations helped to disseminate the report; the National Parent Teacher Association, for example, sent out 55,000 copies of the report to parents and educators across the country.[37] Emboldened by his new position as an AIDS spokesman, Koop went on the road, giving speeches across the country. In an address to the California legislature in March 1987, Koop told the people assembled for the Joint Session on AIDS, "Our decisions regarding the way we pay to care for AIDS patients contaminate our entire social and political decision-making *itself*. We must not allow that to happen. Such an effect on our public life would be an 'AIDS-related complex' every bit as serious as the more recognizable A.R.C.'s like pneumonia and cancer."[38]

Koop's call for condom use and AIDS education for young people pitted him against other self-defined social conservatives who advised the president. Some conservative activists claimed that Koop had betrayed his Christian roots, including Carl Anderson from the OPL, who in 1986 ended his decades-long friendship and mentorship of Koop over his report's recommendations.[39] Bennett, too, found Koop's action particularly troubling. Bennett sent Koop's California legislature speech, along with an angry cover letter, to Bauer, who had recently left the Department of Education to work in the White House as Reagan's chief domestic policy advisor. He highlighted sections of Koop's speech in Sacramento as "straight homosexual propaganda, lifted out of their tirades: *our* reaction is a disease too! I warn you: Sooner or later, and probably sooner, [Koop] will endorse school-based clinics."[40] Robert Sweet, a senior aide for education, expressed real concerns about condoms: "To date, Dr. Koop has resisted attempts by nearly everyone to modify his promotion of condoms as a solution for the AIDS epidemic rather than to promote fidelity, chastity and sex within marriage."[41]

Bauer responded to these warnings by initiating an investigation into Koop's research. Concerned that the government was "preparing materials that [were] offensive to people concerned about their children's education," Bauer called on one of his former aides at the Department of Education,

3.1 | Safer Sex Comix #2. Courtesy of Michigan State University Special Collections. Reprinted with permission from Gay Men's Health Crisis.

John Klenk, to put together a packet of information on the organizations Koop consulted for his report.[42] Klenk found references to GMHC and was especially troubled by a series of the group's safe-sex brochures called the "Safer Sex Comix" (see ill. 3.1). He wrote that the comic books "are obscene. They also present what everybody acknowledges is high-risk behavior — namely anal sex — in an exciting and favorable light. . . . Is this the kind of AIDS information the Surgeon General wants young people to receive?"[43] Klenk sent Bauer several versions of the comics.[44] Klenk's illustrated memo convinced Bauer, who tried to keep Koop from reprinting the report unless he agreed to remove the discussion of condoms from the document. Koop refused.[45]

Presidential Responses to Koop: The Presidential Commission on the Human Immunodeficiency Virus Epidemic

Beyond his attack on Koop, Bauer used his disagreements with the surgeon general to craft an alternative AIDS agenda. Bauer's socially conservative vision, in particular his desire to emphasize personal responsibility, encourage distrust of homosexuals, and maintain presidential authority, shaped his policy ideas about AIDS. In December 1986, with Klenk's help,

Bauer drafted an education policy that focused on how school-age children should learn about AIDS. In response to efforts undertaken by PHS, Klenk and Bauer spelled out five principles for sex education directed at young people, ranging from the need for parental involvement to the belief that AIDS education "should *not* be neutral between heterosexual and homosexual sex. Homosexuals should not be persecuted — but heterosexual sex within marriage is what most Americans, our laws and our traditions consider the proper focus of human sexuality." The document ended with the claim that AIDS education "should comport with the good sense of the American people — thus the necessity of parental and community involvement." Klenk added, "The most common cause of the spread of AIDS is irresponsible sexual behavior. Anyone who engages in such behavior endangers him (her) self, his (her) partner, his (her) children, and other innocent victims — not to speak of causing enormous medical costs to taxpayers and the public. Society must show its disapproval for such behavior."[46] Despite the references to men and women, Klenk's focus remained squarely on "irresponsible" sexuality. Within a month, Bauer notified Bill Roper, the head of the WGHP, that all AIDS education should "comport with the good senses of the American people. . . . We trust that the Department of Education would be involved in the clearance of any materials for our schools."[47]

By February 1987, just four months after the release of Koop's report, Reagan approved Bauer and Klenk's language and in so doing undermined Koop's ongoing AIDS prevention efforts. Bauer and Klenk's document read, in part, that all AIDS education produced by the federal government needed to "encourage responsible sexual behavior — based on fidelity, commitment, and maturity, placing sexuality within the context of marriage."[48] It also called for local control over the development of material and applied to education designed for school-age children as well as adults. The DPC distributed the document to every federal agency and began the process of ensuring implementation of the new regulation. Eight months later, Senator Jesse Helms won legislation that prohibited the CDC from using federal funds to "promote, encourage, and condone homosexual sexual activities or the intravenous use of illegal drugs."[49]

The effects of this restrictive legislation were certainly more mixed than the authors intended. Not only did ASOs like SFAF get around the decision (as evidenced by their decision to print sexually explicit material with money not from the CDC, as described in the preceding chapter), but parts of the federal government, including PHS and the State Department, seemed undeterred by the decision. In both cases, agency officials continued to talk about the need for condoms, sexual frankness, and the reality of drug use.

The ruling was effective, however, in carving out a leadership role for the president, even though Reagan did little more than he had since signing the original memo at the end of 1985. At subsequent DPC meetings, attention turned from questioning Koop's moral reasoning and toward the ways the president could more effectively deal with AIDS. Presidential advisors were adamant that the president be seen as taking a leadership role on AIDS, even though they did little to change the content of the administration's AIDS policy. This sleight of hand suggested how important a strong executive branch was to conservatism in the 1980s, despite repeated calls for local control that seemed intent on decentralizing political power.

At the April 1, 1987, DPC meeting, members brainstormed how to make the president seem more active in his response to AIDS. They discussed the need to create a presidential commission on AIDS, a national mailing on AIDS, and a policy for widespread testing for HIV. Roper briefed the council about hopes to produce and distribute a PHS mailing on AIDS to "every household in America" and asked about the need for an "AIDS Policy Board." Bauer and Bennett quickly opposed the idea of a mailing unless it came through the DPC first. Burned by Koop, they feared that the content of the brochure would run counter to the president's stated beliefs on marriage and abstinence. Bennett, in particular, did not want to see a pamphlet that made the argument that "fear of AIDS is as bad as the disease itself." Bauer also rejected the need for an AIDS Policy Board, suggesting that it would undercut the DPC; instead, he insisted on a presidential commission on AIDS with a "very short timeframe and a narrow and specific agenda."[50]

Forming the Presidential Commission on the Human Immunodeficiency Virus Epidemic, or the "AIDS Commission," as it was called among White House staffers, not only showed presidential leadership on AIDS but also allowed the White House to mark the limits of what AIDS prevention should look like. T. Kenneth Cribb, a domestic advisor to the president who worked in both Reagan administrations, admitted that "the President has not taken a prominent role in the AIDS debate to this point." He went on to suggest that Reagan "speak out in a visible and forceful way . . . [and] exercise leadership." Cribb also wanted to control the content of that leadership: "We must reject approaches that encourage the type of behavior that leads to AIDS: a. Free needles for drug users; b. Free condoms for so-called 'safe sex.'"[51] Bauer echoed Cribb's assessment: "Authority and direction exercised by the President would instill confidence that the Nation is mobilizing its talent and resources to confront a very serious public health issue."[52] On May 1, 1987, Reagan approved the creation of the AIDS Commission and simultaneously delayed the development of a national mailing.[53] The president asked Bauer to take the lead in forming the commission, using the February principles that emphasized "local control" and "responsible sexual behavior based on fidelity, commitment, and maturity, placing sexuality within the context of marriage."[54]

Instead of highlighting presidential leadership, the commission proved contentious from the very start. It took several months for the commission members to be named, particularly because of the lobbying by AIDS activists and conservative activists alike. Beyond the lobbying, administration officials had to figure out how to choose representatives who would satisfy their constituents. To that end, Bauer strongly opposed including a gay representative on the commission. He explained to Reagan,

> Those pushing us the hardest to name a homosexual are generally not our friends but rather our opponents. They will not be satisfied with one gay, but rather they will sense that if enough pressure is exerted we will cave on other issues. . . . While it is true that homosexuals have been major victims of AIDS, they are also responsible for its spread. Recent studies show the average gay man with AIDS has had over 150 different sexual partners in the previous 12 months. . . . If you feel we must appoint a homosexual, I would recommend a "reformed" homosexual—this is someone not currently living a gay life style.[55]

While Reagan ultimately appointed a gay man to the commission, he initialed the document, suggesting that he had considered Bauer's suggestions.

By the end of July, three months after the president had called for it, the White House announced the thirteen commission members, eight of whom were doctors. The group included Dr. Theresa Crenshaw, a California sex therapist who had been corresponding with Bauer for over a year about the regularity with which condoms failed; Dr. Frank Lilly, a gay geneticist from New York City who worked on retroviruses and cancer;

Dr. Woodrow Myers, the health commissioner of Indiana who oversaw the decision to allow Ryan White to attend public school (and would go on to be the health commissioner of New York City); John Cardinal O'Connor of New York; Admiral James Watkins, a retired naval officer; and Dr. William Walsh, the founding director of Project HOPE, an NGO often funded by USAID, which provided health care to people in the developing world (Walsh was also the uncle of William Bennett). The president charged the group's leader, Dr. Eugene Mayberry, the CEO of the Mayo Clinic in Rochester, Minnesota, with delivering a report within ninety days.[56] Taken together, the choice of commissioners allowed the administration to reinforce its claim that it would address AIDS as a medical rather than a political condition, even though most of the appointees had been chosen because of their conservative credentials.

Despite intense lobbying, none of the AIDS activists described in the previous chapters was considered for membership on the commission. This snub enraged AIDS service providers and led the National Association of People with AIDS to sue the president, albeit unsuccessfully.[57] Because of the decision not to include a person with AIDS on the commission, the group reasoned that the commission would be unable to accurately assess the consequences of the epidemic. Other activist groups, such as ACT UP, protested a commission visit to New York City.[58]

Even though activists tried to change the composition of the commission, internal turmoil ultimately disrupted the group more than anything else. Mayberry and Myers left the commission in October, claiming that they were unable to accomplish their goals within a group shaped so profoundly by political ideology. When Mayberry departed as head of the commission, Admiral Watkins moved into the position. The administration hoped that a social conservative with administrative and military experience would have little problem supporting its AIDS policy.[59]

Watkins, like Koop, disappointed his supporters within the administration. In his first report to the president, delivered ninety days after the commission began, he outlined the need for an extensive governmental response to AIDS, particularly as it related to the connection between drug use and HIV. The interim report called for drug treatment programs as a way to deal with the spread of AIDS and suggested that more than 3,000 new facilities for drug treatment be developed before a discussion of controlling drug trafficking was undertaken.[60] The commission wanted the federal government to provide funding for both case management and programs that would help clients with educational and vocational training as a way to deal with some of the long-term causes of drug abuse.

The final report of the presidential commission, published in June 1988, laid out hundreds of recommendations for dealing with AIDS, including the need for a stronger and better-funded public health system, protection of privacy for HIV-positive people, prevention and treatment of intravenous drug use, and education programs for adults and children. In essence, the report called on the federal government to increase dramatically the resources it devoted to AIDS. In so doing, the report paid particular attention to the connection between AIDS and poverty. One section of the report, devoted to homelessness and AIDS, harshly criticized an underfunded social welfare net, most notably the health care system for the poor. "Although the Medicaid program was designed to be the nation's health insurance program for the poor, Medicaid currently provides health care coverage for only about 40 percent of those with incomes below the poverty line. Management of the HIV epidemic presents additional new problems in prevention and care for a population already receiving inadequate health services."[61]

While the presidential commission laid out an explicit and comprehensive initiative to deal with AIDS and drug use, and the defunding of the welfare state, it did not do the same when it came to discussions of sexual practice. Despite arguing that the "Commission firmly believes that it is possible to develop educational materials and programs that clearly convey an explicit message without promoting high-risk behaviors," the report did not provide many details as to what that might look like.[62] In the chapter on patient care, the commission included a brief discussion of the role of the health care provider in caring for the "homosexual man" who might have been abandoned by his family but had friends around him who should be "included in care decisions."[63] The commission praised "the homosexual community" for "the development and growth of community-based organizations" and even called on the federal government to provide presumably gay community-based organizations more contracts and funding, but not one of its recommendations explicitly mentioned the needs of gay people.

Perhaps we can attribute the privileging of poverty over sexuality to the power of an antidrug message in the Reagan-appointed commission. In contrast to First Lady Nancy Reagan's "Just Say No" campaign, the report's minute details exposed the inadequacy of "saying no." In so doing, it suggested that it was more acceptable to talk about the connection between poverty and drug use than about sexuality. The content of the report replicated patterns that disconnected discussions of sexuality and poverty. When the report described poor people affected by HIV/AIDS, they were often understood to be African American and Latino, and heterosexual. The very few times a discussion of "homosexuality" appeared, race and class disappeared from the discussion, implying that all gay men were white and middle class.

Despite the elision of sexual practice, even the most ardent opponents of the commission seemed pleasantly surprised by its interim and final reports. While they recognized that parts of the report lacked detail, they appreciated that the commission recognized the work of gay community-based organizations and called for a response to AIDS that embraced "compassion, justice and dignity."[64] Jeff Levi, the executive director of the National Gay and Lesbian Task Force, reiterated that "it is *because* of a need to protect the public health that we must *also* protect civil liberties, not the other way around."[65] Here Levi acknowledged that the commission had reversed the relationship between civil rights and public health.

Those same commission documents infuriated White House staff, particularly the sections on drug treatment policy, which threatened to require a major increase in government spending. Robert Sweet told Nancy Risque, the Cabinet secretary, that "the recommendations were obviously drafted by those who have an intimate knowledge of federal programs, especially within PHS. It appears to be a wish list, without regard to costs or benefits to the American people."[66] Contemporaneous reporters claimed that the administration buried the report.[67] As soon as the document was released to the public, administration spokespeople claimed that 40 percent of the 362 commission recommendations were "completed, ongoing, or planned."[68]

In lieu of addressing the other 217 suggestions, the administration produced a "Ten-Point Presidential Action Plan" in August 1988.[69] Testing for the presence of HIV was one of the first points in the plan, a position championed by Bauer, who made the case for routine testing: "In the face of mounting infection and casualties from this deadly disease AIDS, it is time to stop treating this as a politically protected epidemic. . . . Testing is called for because many Americans are entitled to know the information it will provide. . . . We must not permit special interest groups to stand in the way of the health measures that have to be taken."[70] Several scientific advancements made testing a conceivable policy action. First, the ability to test was made possible by the 1984 discovery that AIDS was caused by a virus.[71] It took another year and a half for the ELISA test to be developed to detect the presence of the virus, and two years after that, the Western Blot test, a more accurate, though expensive, test was approved. With the advent of a proven AIDS test, the federal government was the first institution to begin a testing program, starting with the Department of Defense's testing of all armed services personnel in 1985. Despite the range of opposition from both the presidential commission members and AIDS service providers (who feared testing would do little to help people with AIDS and potentially expose them to invasions of privacy), Bauer hailed the possibilities of testing and made it the leading initiative in the ten-point plan.[72]

In addition to calling for testing, Bauer also rejected what he saw as the commission's association with a "gay agenda." Fearing that public services would be turned over to homosexuals, Bauer wrote, "The President needs careful advice on how to avoid mistakes that will allow activists courts to turn our well-meaning efforts into a civil rights crusade based on sexual preferences."[73] Here, Bauer equated "well-meaning" with protecting the public's health and "civil rights crusade" with politicizing a health problem.

Even though the presidential commission's recommendations were not implemented, they provide a powerful alternative to the administration's refusal to fully fund governmental AIDS work.[74] In his attempt to prevent another version of Koop's report by carefully choosing the commission members and maintaining presidential authority, Bauer was unable, in the end, to control the content of the report. Not only did the commission reject the presidential principles concerning fidelity and local control, but it articulated the reasons why a federal response was uniquely necessary. Even though the group included an overwhelming majority of self-identified conservatives, the final report called for a significant increase in state-based resources to deal with AIDS, suggesting that a consensus did not exist among conservatives on the need for small government or on the subject of what counted as effective AIDS prevention. While conservative lobbying, both from within the commission and from outside, was able to keep sexuality out of the report, it failed to stop the call for major governmental spending, a stance that ran counter to economic conservative positions that revered market mechanisms.

At the same time that Bauer tried to contain the commission's report, he faced another threat to the presidential principles when HHS began to develop a new brochure titled *Understanding AIDS*, to be sent to every American household at the end of 1987. On December 22, 1987, Congress passed a continuing resolution authorizing the distribution of the brochure by June 1988 "without necessary clearance of the content by any official."[75] HHS set to work to produce a document that would answer people's questions about AIDS and suggest what they could do to avoid infection with HIV.

The decision scared presidential advisors who feared that the brochure's content would subvert the letter and spirit of the principles and undermine presidential power in the process. One of the biggest concerns of Bill Graham (the science and technology advisor to the president) was that "routine testing" was not included in the message.[76] Theresa Crenshaw, who had been appointed to the AIDS Commission several months earlier, argued that "'America Responds to AIDS' [the larger campaign that encompassed *Understanding AIDS*] contains a number of medically and scientifically inaccurate facts as well as misleading statements." Most disturbing to her were its recommendation that people regularly use condoms and the idea that not everyone needed to be tested.[77] When suggesting talking points for the president, James Warner, Bauer's aide, was particularly aggrieved and called the congressional resolution a "monstrosity" symbolizing all that was wrong with the way Congress tried to promote the "gradual dilution or attenuation of the executive powers."[78]

Beyond trying to change the content, Bauer argued that the brochure violated the president's right to exercise executive power. At Bauer's request, Arthur B. Culvahouse, counsel to the president, reasoned,

> If the provision in question were interpreted so as to require that the Director of the CDC [the subset of HHS in charge of developing the document's content] distribute the AIDS mailing to the public prior to any approval or even review by the Director's superiors, including the DPC and the President, the Director would be effectively severed from his superiors in the executive branch with respect to this one area of his responsibility. This independence is inconsistent with the right of the President to control his subordinates within the executive branch.[79]

Within a month, the Justice Department concurred with Culvahouse and suggested that the congressional resolution violated the separation of powers.[80] Bauer took all of his concerns to Attorney General Edwin Meese, in hopes that the DPC would shut down the CDC's efforts. In attacking the brochure, Bauer pointed out that it "promotes condoms, assumes widespread sexual promiscuity among young people, and is medically inaccurate by making categorical statements about the way AIDS cannot be transmitted. It will very likely be offensive to a majority of Americans because of the explicit manner in which it discusses anal intercourse and other sensitive matters."[81] He also feared that the brochure would mislead people into thinking certain behaviors were safe; in particular he was troubled by the statement, "You won't get AIDS from a kiss," noting that the "CDC's own publications advise about the possibility of infection via intimate kissing." Returning to a common administration theme, Bauer also complained that the mailer discouraged routine testing and therefore ran counter to the president's policy on testing.[82] To temper the message, Bauer suggested that a letter from the president including the sentiment that abstinence was the only way to protect yourself from AIDS and that "medicine and morality truly teach the same lesson about halting AIDS in its tracks" accompany the brochure.[83]

Bauer's efforts to stop the CDC failed. First, the agency's 1988 budget increased 30 percent, or almost $200 million.[84] Then, in June 1988, the CDC announced that it would send out more than 100 million copies of *Understanding AIDS*.[85] The brochure opened with a description of AIDS and HIV and cautioned, "*Who you are has nothing to do with whether you are in danger of being infected with the AIDS virus. What matters is what you do.*"[86] In the section titled, "What is all the talk about condoms?" the booklet cautioned that "condoms were not foolproof" but called on people to use them and provided information on how best to do so. The mailing had images of people with AIDS, gay and straight, as well as people who worked in ASOs.

The response to the brochure was overwhelmingly positive and sparked few, if any, protests.[87] By returning to the ideas first presented by Koop two year earlier, *Understanding AIDS* provided citizens with a way to imagine safer sexual practices. As one of the final national AIDS documents produced during the Reagan administration, the brochure was the last salvo in the battle over what domestic AIDS education would look like. In this case, HHS seems to have been successful in presenting material that Bauer found morally and constitutionally problematic. While Bauer and other self-identified social conservatives tried to redefine public health as a private, rather than a federally funded, responsibility, they were not uniformly successful. As a consequence, the federal government funded AIDS prevention materials that were anathema to many social conservatives, an outcome repeated when Reagan's State Department designed AIDS prevention for the global South.

AIDS Emerges as a Global Pandemic

By the mid-1980s, as members of the Reagan administration fought over what to do about AIDS in the United States, a new set of concerns became apparent as mounting evidence indicated that AIDS was a global problem. A disparate group of governmental and nongovernmental institutions, and a critical mass of researchers studying, detailing, and publishing on AIDS around the world, crafted an epidemiological picture of AIDS that showed consistent spread of the disease in all corners of the globe. In a relatively short period of time, the stunning accumulation of data begged for a global response. By 1987, the U.S. federal government began to design AIDS work that acknowledged the global AIDS pandemic and insisted on frank conversation about sexual practice, but the implementing agency, the State Department, struggled to obtain sufficient resources to carry out the program.

The U.S. federal government was not the first institutional body to address the global implications of AIDS. That job fell to the World Health Organization (WHO), the first international body that accepted the charge of documenting and responding to AIDS. In 1983, the WHO held its first meetings on AIDS in Geneva, but it would take another three years before it established the Special Programme on AIDS (SPA), its coordinating body on the AIDS pandemic.[88] SPA's global AIDS plan had three deceptively simple objectives: "to prevent HIV transmission; to take care of HIV-infected persons; and to unite national and international efforts for global AIDS control."[89] In August 1986, Dr. Jonathan Mann, an expert in global health inequalities who had been working on AIDS in Zaire for the CDC, became the head of SPA.[90] When Mann started work at SPA, the program had only one full-time staff member in addition to Mann and an annual budget of $580,000.[91] Over the next few years, Mann began the process of transforming SPA from a chronically underfunded and understaffed program to one of the most important institutions fighting the spread of HIV/

AIDS worldwide. Within a year of starting, he "established an impressive network of collaboration with researchers, governments and donors. His efforts have started to galvanize the international system into action."[92] In 1988, SPA expanded its work and renamed itself the Global Programme on AIDS (GPA).[93] It became the main clearinghouse for AIDS prevention and treatment projects aimed at alleviating the effects of the global AIDS pandemic; it also served as the first institution to connect the response to AIDS to the need for human rights.[94] According to anthropologist Cristiana Bastos, "Connections with Third World countries and activists organizations were a priority for the GPA. Non-governmental organizations (NGOS) throughout the world praised Mann's leadership and contributed to the GPA's innovative energy."[95] In late 1990, GPA went through a process of restructuring, and Mann left the helm to take a position at Harvard University.

While Mann documented the health effects of the global AIDS pandemic, a growing number of social scientific researchers, most notably anthropologists, joined medical investigators to detail the global epidemiology of AIDS in new ways. Unlike their medical counterparts who had been accumulating epidemiological data on AIDS since as early as 1983, social scientists described how weak economies in the global South were unable to provide the kind of health care its citizens needed; at the same they talked about cultural roadblocks that made AIDS prevention difficult to implement.[96] The social scientific reports provided a basis for the argument that AIDS could be addressed best by a sustained commitment to human rights.

NGOS also became part of the matrix of institutions defining and responding to AIDS as a global concern that required more than medical solutions. The Panos Institute exemplified this effort. Panos, an NGO with autonomous offices in both the North and the South, opened in 1986 committed to giving voice to development efforts led by actors in the global South. Panos placed the eradication of the AIDS epidemic at the heart of its mission. In his brief account of the origins of Panos, Jon Tinker, the first head of the NGO, recalls that the AIDS pandemic made Panos "visible."[97]

In the summer of 1986, Panos employee Renée Sabatier, a researcher from Quebec who would go on to serve as the director of the AIDS and Development Information Unit at Panos, began work on the first book-length account of AIDS in the global South, titled *AIDS and the Third World*. Sabatier made a series of important and prescient arguments about AIDS in the global South, including that every nation on earth had people with AIDS; that education was likely the best hope against AIDS (given the unlikelihood of the development of a vaccine); and finally, that people across the global were taking action to fight AIDS, even though they faced chronic underfunding and denial of the problem.[98] Published first as a sixty-one-page booklet in plastic ring binders, AIDS and the Third World became the most widely read and republished Panos dossier. Mann reportedly explained that in nearly all 100 countries he visited while running GPA, he was shown a well-read copy of the dossier and was told how important it had been to the initiation of national AIDS work.[99] In 1989, Panos released a trade edition of the text, increasing its use among academic researchers, journalists, and policymakers.[100]

Taken together, the work of GPA, academics, and NGOS such as Panos forced a change in how AIDS was understood. It could no longer be seen as a national problem and had become a transnational concern. Press accounts of the international scope of AIDS reflected this shift. At the same time that researchers extended the AIDS map, the news media based in the United States began to publish reports on the state of the global AIDS pandemic, most notably the status of AIDS on the African continent. Newspaper reporters likely got their information from the growing number of NGOS and researchers, but in the process they simplified stories and conflated information. In 1985 and 1986, pieces not only appeared in major daily newspapers such as the *New York Times*, the *Washington Post*, and the *San Francisco Chronicle* but also in weekly magazines, including *Newsweek* and *Time*.[101] Reporters depicted cataclysmic suffering on the African continent and promoted a sense that improvement would be all but impossible. In an article for *Newsweek*, Rod Nordland described AIDS in Africa:

> If apocalypse is the right word, medical research is only beginning to comprehend it. The epidemiology on AIDS in Africa is still in its infancy. There is not enough money for full-blown study. . . . Blood screening is too rare to allow for confident projections of infection rates in anything but the most general terms. . . . Indeed, many AIDS victims die without ever knowing they had the disease; African practice, in some quarters, is not to inform the patient of a positive AIDS diagnosis. After all, nothing can be done to alter the outcome.[102]

In addition to treating "Africa" as a single place instead of a continent with more than fifty countries, the reporter portrayed a sense of political and medical dysfunction when it came to Africans' abilities to deal with the state of AIDS. This disheartening (at best) or neo-imperial (at worst) representation permeated most popular accounts of AIDS on the African continent, a point substantiated by a large body of literature on media representations of AIDS in the global South.[103]

Excluding Immigrants with AIDS

The combination of increasing academic and popular international research and reporting about AIDS plus historical fears of immigrants as vectors for disease created the conditions under which the U.S. government, through PHS, began excluding immigrants with HIV beginning in 1986 by adding AIDS to the list of dangerous and contagious diseases.[104] While it is not entirely clear why HHS prompted the president to take an action that antagonized immigrants with AIDS and ran counter to its AIDS prevention initiatives within the United States, the agency's decision reflected its role in tracking the health of immigrants beginning in the late nineteenth century.[105] As early as 1891, PHS performed health checks on all immigrants seeking residency in the United States.[106] Almost 100 years later, the decision to add AIDS to the list of excludable diseases allowed HHS and PHS to appeal to those in the administration who wanted to control people with AIDS, without necessarily affecting the shape of the domestic agenda. In the end, the decision of whom to test grew out of historical policies that saw immigrants as threats to the nation's public health as well as the idea increasingly common in 1986 that AIDS originated outside the United States, most notably on the African continent.

Over the course of the twentieth century, Congress passed legislation to keep selected groups defined as undesirable or unhealthy out of the United States. In 1882 and again in 1924, the state limited and prevented Asian immigration, basing the exclusion on racist conceptions of the Chinese. Historian Nayan Shah argues that the public health establishment, including PHS, figured Chinese immigrants as "medical menaces."[107] In 1952, over President Harry Truman's veto, the U.S. Senate passed the Immigration and Nationality Act, also known as the McCarran-Walter Act, which prevented the immigration of "sexual deviates" (i.e., homosexuals) and members of the Communist Party. Here the language shifted from the need to be physically healthy to the need to be mentally healthy and stable.

Legislation in 1961 gave PHS flexibility to change the specific grounds for exclusion based on "medical progress," under the assumption that public health officials could best determine what diseases threatened U.S. citizens.[108] By 1987, HHS argued that "the exclusion of those with HIV infection is entirely justified in the national interest on public health grounds, based on both medical and economic considerations."[109] HHS feared the cost of treating noncitizens with HIV as well as the potential health threat HIV-positive immigrants posed to U.S. citizens.

The decision, however, did not receive universal approval from other agencies in the federal government. While the INS concurred with HHS, arguing that "AIDS represents a very serious threat to the public health and should be a basis for denying immigrant visas," much to the surprise of presidential advisors, the U.S. State Department rejected the policy. In so doing, it served as a lone voice of opposition to the administration's exclusionary policy.[110]

In addition to its dismissal of mandatory testing of immigrants, the State Department began to articulate a position that acknowledged the extent of the AIDS pandemic in the global South, most particularly on the African continent, and the role the pandemic would play in creating political instability in the region if it were left untreated. In direct response to a request to review HHS policy, Deputy Secretary of State John C. Whitehead wrote,

> Adoption of the proposed rule would also carry political risks. AIDS is seen in many nations as a cultural threat of Western origin, and the U.S. is widely perceived as the principal exporter of the AIDS virus. Not only would the proposed rule complicate bilateral relations, but it would put the U.S. in the position of contradicting the World Health Organization (WHO), which has stated that there is no justification for travel restrictions at this time. This could undermine the WHO AIDS program, which we are trying to encourage, and also invite reciprocal measures by others nations against the far greater number of American travelers.[111]

Whitehead's comments highlighted two areas of concern, both of which became central tenets of the State Department's AIDS work over the next decade. First, he noted that southern nations believed that AIDS had not necessarily come from Africa; rather, they believed that the U.S. government created the AIDS virus and released it into the world's population.

Developed in response to what many African nations saw as the racist myth of Africa as a chronically sick continent, this narrative of the origins of AIDS was also fueled by Soviet propaganda that accused the U.S. Army of engineering HIV at Ft. Detrick, in Maryland, and dispersing it on the African continent.[112] Rather than protecting the United States, Whitehead suggested that a policy of exclusion would inflame anti-U.S. sentiments in the global South. Not only would the policy run counter to the WHO's rejection of travel restrictions on people with AIDS, but it would also make the United States look like a dishonest broker in the eyes of states in the global South. Second, Whitehead recognized that SPA was the international institution most likely to change the course of the AIDS pandemic. His praise was reflected in increased, albeit limited, funding for the organization from the State Department.[113]

Despite Whitehead's objections, HHS continued to pursue its policy of restricting immigrants with HIV. But because the dispute between State and HHS "pit[ted] public health policy against foreign policy considerations," an executive order would not be sufficient.[114] Instead HHS was forced to begin the process of changing the Immigration and Nationality Act, an action that required congressional approval. In April 1987 the agency sought to amend section 212(a)(6), which listed the "dangerous contagious diseases," so that it included HIV/AIDS.[115]

Support among White House staff was strong enough to override the concerns of the State Department. The WGHP recommended that the DPC and the president take up the proposed rule change and work out any "diplomatic problems" that arose from the legislation.[116] At the April 28, 1987, DPC meeting, advisors discussed the role testing should play in AIDS policy for HIV in general, and testing of immigrants in particular, arguing that this strategy would "protect innocent victims from the disease" and deal with "international implications of AIDS" at the same time.[117] Summing up a sense of unease over the testing policy, Nancy Risque, one of the president's main aides, wrote, "There will be differences of opinion within the Administration about this one [testing immigrants] and *it will raise highly contentious issues about testing and the question of international retaliation*."[118] Later that day, the president announced a decision regarding AIDS testing that included the creation of a nationwide incidence study and mandatory testing for all aliens, immigrants, and federal prisoners.[119]

Within days of the announcement, Reagan gave his first speech exclusively devoted to AIDS, specifically the role of HIV testing in U.S. policy.

Reagan explained that AIDS was not a "casually contagious disease. . . . Experts tell us you don't get it from telephones or swimming pools or drinking fountains."[120] But Reagan concluded his speech with a call for widespread testing of couples applying for marriage licenses, inmates incarcerated in federal prisons, and foreigners seeking legal immigration status in the United States. He claimed that "AIDS is surreptitiously spreading throughout our population, and yet we have no accurate measure of its scope. It is time we knew exactly what we were facing. And that is why I support routine testing."[121] In language eerily reminiscent of the Cold War he was fighting with the Soviet Union and communism, Reagan wanted to stop the "surreptitious" invasion by finding all the people who tested positive for HIV.

With the president making the case for widespread testing, the U.S. Senate began to debate amending the Immigration and Nationality Act to include HIV/AIDS as a dangerous contagious disease. Proposed by North Carolina Republican Jesse Helms, this amendment called for the testing of both potential immigrants to the United States and couples seeking marriage licenses. Over the course of two months, the Senate twice debated the merits of the Helms amendment. The first time the amendment was offered, it failed to garner sufficient support. The second time, sponsors removed the call for testing soon-to-be married heterosexual couples, leaving only immigrants, and the amendment passed by a unanimous vote.[122] The majority-Democratic House of Representatives soon followed suit, and HIV was added to a list of excludable diseases that included five other venereal diseases, as well as infectious leprosy and active tuberculosis.[123] With congressional approval, Attorney General Edwin Meese announced the federal government's policy to test both immigrants and federal prisoners.[124]

The policy change found support from a wide variety of actors. Surgeon General Koop, who opposed testing generally, accepted the need for mandatory tests of all immigrants and federal prisoners.[125] A New York Times editorial appearing on the heels of Reagan's speech rejected forced testing for everyone except these two groups.[126] The general public also seemed convinced by the debate, even though they remained skeptical of the public health benefits. A July 1987 Gallup Poll found that 90 percent of the 1,005 people questioned felt that prospective immigrants should be tested for AIDS, and 66 percent wanted testing of all foreign visitors. Slightly fewer, 52 percent, thought all American citizens should be screened. Strangely, however, only 6 percent believed testing was the best way to prevent AIDS.[127] While testing would not retard the spread of AIDS, it made people feel like they were doing something to protect themselves.

The decision to exclude HIV-positive immigrants sparked protests among AIDS activists who rejected discrimination against immigrants with AIDS and all actions that might lead to mandatory testing for U.S. residents. Days after the Helms amendment passed, the American Civil Liberties Union's Nan Hunter called the policy "too little, too late and tragically beside the point" in a *New York Times* op-ed piece.[128] In the ACLU's annual report, the organization went even further, claiming that the United States was "much more an 'exporter' than an 'importer' of AIDS."[129] In so doing, the ACLU presented an argument that turned the idea that AIDS originated in Africa on its head. The United States could be viewed as an original source for AIDS.

The Third World AIDS Advisory Task Force (TWAATF) criticized the new legislation that sought to control immigration, on the grounds that it was racially discriminatory. At TWAATF's monthly meeting that coincided with the passage of the HIV ban, members discussed the implications of the law for "Third World people," arguing that they would be disproportionately affected. Here, the membership reasoned that people in power viewed immigrants and people of color within the United States similarly. TWAATF feared that if mandatory testing for immigrants were instituted, people of color living within the United States would be the next group to be subjected to the practice. Both groups were represented as dangerous people whose actions needed to be monitored, either in the form of residence exclusion or in limitations to their welfare.[130]

In an unusual alliance, parts of the foreign policy establishment, including the State Department, the Central Intelligence Agency, and the National Security Council, worked to temper the new policy as well. While its original concerns did not keep the legislation from passing, the State Department continued to question the logic and limit the reach of the immigration policy, particularly in the case of immigrants from Soviet-bloc countries. The department called for an exception to the testing policy that would allow an immigrant with HIV from the Soviet Union or one of its satellites to be admitted to the United States. This would require the State Department to work with PHS, and vice versa. "The potential effect of testing refugees in camps in first-asylum countries and the difficulties posed by some admissions programs, such as those for Soviet Jews, Vietnamese, and Cuban political prisoners, are of particular concern. [PHS] will work closely with the Department of State to ensure that the testing program is implemented with respect to refugees in a way that will protect both the affected refugees and U.S. foreign and humanitarian policy interests served by the refugee admissions program."[131] The State Department also managed to add HIV-positive status to the grounds for seeking political asylum.[132] The irony of these two-pronged policy exceptions should not be underestimated. At the same time that the U.S. government excluded immigrants with HIV, foreign policy concerns, particularly those related to weakening Soviet communism by welcoming refugees from Soviet allies, allowed the State Department to argue that the United States should be a safe haven for certain people with HIV who faced discrimination in their home countries.

Mirroring the State Department's actions, the Central Intelligence Agency expressed opposition to the testing policy and, in the process, reiterated the potential catastrophic effects AIDS would have on the African continent. A June 1987 Special National Intelligence Estimate, written by the assistant national intelligence officer for Africa, defined the continental AIDS problem as dangerous to U.S. interests. The intelligence officer tasked with researching and compiling the strategic document consulted a wide range of intelligence organizations, from the Central Intelligence Agency to the National Security Agency, before finalizing the intelligence estimate. The estimate suggested that exporting U.S. AIDS policy to the African continent, particularly the impulse to limit condom distribution and call for immigrant testing, would ultimately hurt strategic interests in the region. Not only did the intelligence estimate recommend easing travel restrictions, but it also explained that "condom use is perhaps the single best hope for lessening the catastrophic spread of the virus today."[133]

> *The United States and other Western countries will probably be asked to increase greatly their assistance to Africa.* A refusal to divert or create new development funds to take on the enormous costs of upgrading health infrastructures will open doors to harsh criticism by beleaguered African countries. . . . A fall in tourist revenues, mandatory testing of African students, and the possibility of visa and immigration restrictions will inflame anti-Western rhetoric and negatively affect bilateral relations.[134]

The national intelligence estimate further explained that AIDS threatened to derail young elites seeking foreign education. The report articulated alternatives to status quo policies of exclusion and called for prevention based on strengthening the internal infrastructure of foreign states. The National Foreign Intelligence Board approved the classified document on June 2, just one day after Reagan's speech calling for testing.

The extent to which the foreign policy establishment disagreed with Reagan and most of his domestic advisors over what to do about immigrants with HIV exposes, again, the fissures AIDS created among modern conservatives. With some in the State Department fearing that an exclusionary AIDS policy hurt the U.S. global standing vis-à-vis the Soviet Union, and other sectors of the government arguing that HIV needed to be contained outside the nation, regardless of its effect on bilateral relations, the Reagan administration was divided about the kind of international AIDS work it would develop and support. The response the State Department developed in the aftermath of both the immigration ban and Reagan's guidelines on fidelity, marriage, and AIDS continued a course of action on AIDS that most presidential advisors vehemently advised against.

The State Department's Response to AIDS in the Global South

Much like it had during the 1950s and 1960s with the promotion of civil rights as a tactic in the Cold War, the State Department recognized that a more capacious AIDS policy that helped other countries deal with AIDS had the potential to promote the standing of the United States. In describing the actions of the State Department in the immediate postwar period, historian Mary Dudziak concludes that "race in America was thought to have a critical impact on U.S. prestige abroad."[135] Twenty-five years later, as the State Department began to create AIDS policy, it built on both the notion that U.S.-based solutions that attended to sexual expression required exportation and its opposition to changes in the Immigration and Nationality Act to insert AIDS work into its diplomatic project. The limits of this approach became apparent over the next several years, as the State Department struggled to receive adequate funding in federal budget allocations, largely because staff seemed unwilling to articulate arguments for resources. The problems associated with promoting individual behavior change in a vacuum where nothing else changed, most notably economic circumstances, also became evident. That said, the State Department's policy ran counter to domestic policy recommendation made by Gary Bauer but, in the process, produced a new form of American exceptionalism that hindered how the U.S. government curbed the spread of the global AIDS pandemic.[136]

Beyond the State Department's opposition to the immigration ruling, by the late 1980s the agency's employees and intelligence officers had collected examples of the evidence detailing the extent of global AIDS and had begun to define AIDS as a national security issue within a Cold War model.[137] Herman Cohen, the director of African affairs for the National Security Council (who had been the ambassador to Senegal and Gambia from 1977 to 1980 and would go on to be named the assistant secretary of state for African affairs from 1989 to 1993 in the George H. W. Bush administration), read two key reports that helped shape State Department thinking: a briefing paper on AIDS in Africa produced by Polaris, an African American–owned, San Francisco–based research firm that worked with SFAF on its program for people of color, and a document titled "AIDS and Poverty in the Developing World," produced by the Overseas Development Council, an NGO based in Washington, D.C.[138] Both reports suggested that the best way to deal with AIDS was to link it to international economic development efforts. The reports argued that because AIDS had the potential to devastate most developing economies, the U.S. government had an obligation to help control the spread of the pandemic, not through exclusion of immigrants and travelers, but instead by bolstering health care infrastructures, particularly at the WHO.

State Department employees did not just collect work from outside venues; more importantly, they began to produce their own assessments of AIDS in the global South. In April 1987, John D. Negroponte, the former ambassador to Honduras and assistant secretary of state for oceans and international environmental and scientific affairs, and Chas Freeman, a foreign service officer who would become the ambassador to Saudi Arabia in 1989, sent a four-page "secret" memorandum titled "AIDS and the Death of Modern African Societies" to the secretary of state.[139] This memo provided Secretary Shultz and Deputy Secretary Whitehead with a view of AIDS on the African continent that appeared similar to contemporary reports of the devastating consequences of AIDS for the countries in sub-Saharan Africa.[140] But unlike many contemporary newspaper accounts, the memo strongly recommended that the U.S. government take a leading role in addressing AIDS, a point that has all but been missed in earlier accounts of federal action.

Using powerful images and phrases to draw attention to their claims, Negroponte and Freeman called attention to how AIDS looked in parts of central Africa. "The enormity of the AIDS pandemic is just now beginning to be realized. . . . Calamity is unfolding in a swath of a half-dozen countries across central Africa, including several important and influential friends and allies, such as Zaire, Zambia, and Tanzania. It is difficult to overstate the impact on these societies of the likely loss of much of their modern sectors, but that is precisely what a number of them are facing."[141] Their position mirrored other reports of how grave the AIDS epidemic was becoming in many African countries, but it also highlighted the fact that national security needed to be part of the decision-making calculus.

The information was far from value-neutral, however. Negroponte and Freeman enumerated grim details of AIDS in Africa and, in the process, betrayed a particular political reaction to AIDS, one that saw the U.S. government as best suited technically to assist African countries suffering through national AIDS epidemics but not obligated to pay for the necessary action. The writers not only relied on some of the worst-case statistics about the state of epidemiology, suggesting that "*up to one-third of all adults in many urban areas* of Central and East Africa *may now be infected with AIDS*," but they also employed worst-case scenarios in terms of the ultimate outcome: "What this means, unless our data are fundamentally wrong, is that *by the mid-1990s two-thirds or more of the modern, educated elite and perhaps half of the overall urban* population in highly infected countries such as Burundi, Rwanda, Tanzania, Uganda, Zaire and Zambia *will probably have died. . . .* In Africa, AIDS *has the potential to devastate entire* societies, erasing the hundred year-old impact of modern European technology and thrusting whole nations back into the early iron age."[142] The final sentence exposed the political consequences of statistical analysis. For Negroponte and Freeman, AIDS posed more of a threat precisely because it had the potential to wipe out the benefits of a century of European imperialism. Negroponte and Freeman seemed immune to postcolonial critiques from African intellectuals who saw these kinds of descriptions as problematic at best and racist at worst.[143]

While we do not know how Negroponte and Freeman collected their data, if we consider the document alongside concurrent reports on AIDS in the global South, we can begin to delineate the larger political implications of one of the first known reports on AIDS from the State Department archive. AIDS *in the Third World*, the seminal dossier created by the Panos

Institute, identified Negroponte's and Freeman's argument as a "doomsday scenario."[144] Even though Panos considered Negroponte and Freeman's scenario plausible, it cautioned against leaving the response to such a tremendous problem to "government action — or inaction."[145] Panos feared that using arguments about the death of Africa would spur defeatism rather than action.

Given the sharp differences in tone and politics between Panos and Negroponte and Freeman, I was wholly unprepared to find agreement between the two on the question of Africa as the geographical originator of AIDS. *Blaming Others*, the second Panos dossier penned by Renée Sabatier, argued that the scientific model that looked for the roots of AIDS on the African continent had racist implications.[146] Somewhat surprisingly, Negroponte and Freeman agreed and refused the question of etiology: "There is now no point in debating where AIDS came from; the relevant question is where it is likely to take us, and *what we can do about it*."[147] Negroponte and Freeman likely spoke with State Department staff working on the African continent before they reached this conclusion. In a declassified cable from Elinor Constable, the U.S. ambassador to Kenya, Constable described the fears of the government of Kenya: "While reacting responsibly at the technical level to the AIDS problem, the [government of Kenya] and Kenyans in general are still hypersensitive and highly defensive in their public reactions to allegations about the prevalence and risk of AIDS in Kenya. From the African perspective foreign characterizations of the AIDS situation on this continent are racist and exaggerated."[148]

Panos and Negroponte and Freeman did not, however, agree on how to characterize various national responses to AIDS. Where Panos emphasized the ways southern nations responded to these racist representation with action, Negroponte and Freeman found fault in a range of national responses to AIDS, particularly those undertaken (or not undertaken) by the Soviet Union and various African nations. Similar to Whitehead a year earlier, the State Department employees accused the Soviets of starting conspiracy theories that "AIDS originated in U.S. germ warfare experiments," but they went beyond that criticism to include a comment on Africans as "defensive" and "unwilling to face up to it." They asked, "How do we deal with African suspicions, fed to a degree by the Soviets, that AIDS is a 'white man's creation' developed by the West in order to keep Africa permanently weak — and the corresponding (albeit still relatively low-level) fear in our own society that African students, visitors and professional people are all

AIDS carriers about to spread their plague in this country?"[149] Unlike the questions that found fault in other nations, the final question suggested that Negroponte and Freeman were equally concerned with the effect U.S. policy would have on how the U.S. public perceived Africans.

In response to what they saw as a series of unacceptable positions that ranged from inaction to propaganda, Freeman and Negroponte asked how the United States would answer the following questions: "Can we stimulate African leaders to quickly take necessary steps to retard a further spread of disease? What is our role in a humanitarian crisis brought on by a disease that is both incurable and invariably fatal? Does it make sense to continue to support economic development efforts and technical and military training programs in countries that may be doomed to social and economic collapse in the near term? If not, how should our assistance be refocussed?" The writers ended this section with a sense of urgency: "This 'heads-up' is intended to signal the magnitude of the problem and some of its implications for US interests."[150]

The document posed many more questions than answers, making it more of a prod than a definitive plan for the State Department. In part, Negroponte and Freeman's resistance to spending money on AIDS made answers hard to come by: "For the time being, we believe it is important to recognize both the magnitude and impact of the problem as well as the limitations on what we can do. It is, we believe, imperative that the U.S. not give the impression that we can — through a massive 'task force' approach to the problem, deal with it by hurling resources into the void."[151] The writers wanted to avoid spending a large percentage of the State Department's budget on AIDS, but at the same time they did not shy away from a description of the implications of inaction.

The cautious approach that the memo implicitly called for found voice in reports from Ambassador Constable in Kenya:

We will need to continue this low-key, almost backdoor approach
in our attempts to assist the [government of Kenya] in its anti-AIDS
efforts.... I also understand that A.I.D. is gearing up for a major, Af-
rica-wide undertaking to combat AIDS. While this program undoubt-
edly will have much to offer Kenya, I must caution that the project will
have to be handled extremely delicately. If we find it necessary to pick
up the pace and take a more active approach in Kenya, we must be

careful not to get too far out in front of what the local traffic will bear or we would end up doing more harm than good.[152]

While it is not clear if Constable favored less AIDS funding, her guarded position served as a justification for a careful (i.e., underfunded) response to AIDS. Constable's argument foreshadowed the ambivalence inherent in the State Department response to AIDS: on one hand, it acknowledged the long-term effects of untreated AIDS; but on the other hand, the department seemed unwilling or unable to devote sufficient resources to funding programs that tried to deal with these problems, and it was also convinced that African states would fail to address AIDS.

Despite, or perhaps because of, the department's hesitance, beginning in late 1987, USAID, the State Department agency charged with distributing foreign aid, established the AIDS Technical Support Program. The program had three parts: funding the WHO's AIDS program, donating close to a quarter of the agency's budget; AIDSTECH, a project intended to support various forms of AIDS work, including policies for keeping the blood supply free from HIV, fortifying government AIDS programs, and designing schemes for condom distribution; and a program called AIDSCOM, designed to help countries in the global South develop communication strategies for AIDS prevention.[153]

From its inception, the support program was underfunded. The combined programs received $68 million, just under half of the total domestic AIDS budget for 1986, to be spent in the five years between 1987 and 1992.[154] In part, this sum reflected the diminutive size of the State Department budget: a bit more than $1 billion per year after 1985 (HHS's was fourteen times that amount), or .03 percent of the total federal budget.[155] But it also seems likely that the ambivalence State Department employees had about the role funding could play in halting the spread of the disease contributed to the anemic allocation to fight the global AIDS pandemic. In 1989, one year into President George H. W. Bush's term, in response to the calls of organizations such as the National Gay and Lesbian Task Force, AIDS became a specific line item in the State Department's budget when USAID allocated $30 million for "research, treatment, and control" of AIDS in addition to the money already being spent on the AIDS Technical Support Program.[156]

Although funding was insufficient to address what was clearly a global problem by 1987, it is still worthwhile to investigate the content of the policies produced with USAID funding, just as I did with domestic AIDS policy. USAID hired a combination of academic researchers and organizations that had experience working in family planning, the model for its nascent AIDS work. Family Health International, a North Carolina–based reproductive health policymaking organization, oversaw AIDSTECH; the Academy for Educational Development, a nonprofit in Washington, D.C., with a history of designing family planning material for the federal government, created and ran AIDSCOM. These two NGOs developed programs with various universities, including Johns Hopkins University and the Annenberg School for Communication at the University of Pennsylvania, each of which lent public health expertise in the field of reproductive and sexual health. These myriad organizations shared a commitment to social scientific research on sexual practices and the need for government intervention to change behavior. Their ideas centered on condom distribution and establishing focus groups with women, commercial sex workers, and men who had sex with men.[157]

AIDSTECH provided technical and administrative support for national AIDS programs established in the global South and tried to "complement" WHO activities.[158] Over the course of five years, AIDSTECH integrated various degrees of sexual content into its AIDS prevention programs. It distributed 48 million condoms, 23 million of them through social marketing programs where patrons were expected to pay a small sum for the condom. In addition to distributing condoms, AIDSTECH trained 5,200 peer educators in hopes of teaching people how and why to use condoms.[159] Working in conjunction with local NGOs, the program used "rapid ethnographic research" to develop profiles of locations where they hoped to implement projects and to determine which people would be best suited to serve as peer educators.[160]

AIDSCOM took a slightly different approach. Designed as a communication program to provide people with new knowledge about AIDS, one of AIDSCOM's slogans was "Education is not enough" (see ill. 3.2). For AIDSCOM, disseminating information about AIDS was insufficient to solve the problems created by the disease; instead, community-based solutions combined with international funding needed to be brought to bear on the AIDS pandemic. In particular, AIDSCOM staff emphasized the need to attend to the ways gender and sexual inequality limited communication and individual behavior change. In a self-assessment of their work on the African

3.2 | AIDSCOM. Courtesy of National Library of Medicine.

continent, AIDSCOM members highlighted seven underlying premises of
their six-year-long project, four of which spoke directly to the centrality of
gender and sexuality in AIDS work:

1   Everyone matters; for example, it is as important to educate and
    counsel a commercial sex worker as it is to educate and counsel
    her customer;
2. High-risk behavior vs. high-risk group . . . A man who identified
    as heterosexual would not listen to messages targeting gay men,
    even if he had regular sexual intercourse with other men;
3. Explicit discussion of sex and sexuality . . . The impact of this
    [sexual] taboo on HIV/AIDS prevention can be profound, since sex
    and sexuality must be discussed openly to prevent the bulk of HIV
    transmission. . . . The range of sexual orientations also must be
    discussed. Increasing numbers of indigenous African lesbian and
    gay organizations have indicated that many of their members are

involved in heterosexual marriages, since it is culturally expected that everyone will marry and have children;

4. Status of women in society . . . Considering that women frequently lack the autonomy to protect themselves from HIV infection, AIDSCOM concluded that when designing prevention strategies for women, it is important to look at women less in terms of their biological differences from men and more in terms of the social relationship between men and women.[161]

This document highlights the extent to which the AIDSCOM program, which coincided with the end of Reagan's second term and the entire term of George H. W. Bush, flew in the face of the guidelines on fidelity and marriage Reagan implemented in 1987. AIDSCOM strategies — "explicit discussion of sex and sexuality" and attending to the "social relationships between men and women" — also bore a stunning similarity to documents written by nascent AIDS activists a decade earlier.

By 1991, five years into the program, USAID reported it had "developed and launched over 650 HIV/AIDS activities in 74 countries."[162] In yearly reports to Congress, USAID regularly detailed its efforts to include women in its programs and to distribute condoms. Between 1987 and 1990, "USAID condom shipments to Africa increased five-fold in response to increased demand . . . from just under 34 million in 1987 to just over 176 million in 1990."[163] In this respect, the State Department funded programs that looked more like the work being done by NGOs and international agencies, such as Panos and WHO, as well as the ASOs described earlier in this book, than the policies promoted by Reagan's domestic policy advisors.

With an underlying goal of securing individual behavior change, particularly in sexual situations, USAID's AIDS work potentially focused on sexuality to the exclusion of other factors such as poverty. Unlike the Presidential Commission on HIV, whose simultaneous report attended to poverty to the exclusion of sexuality, in the global South, USAID emphasized a northern notion of sexual freedom that was, in fact, anathema in parts of the global South. In her work on USAID's AIDS work in Nepal, anthropologist Stacy Pigg argues, "Contemporary Western common sense about sexuality has a history. Internationally, the recent push to address sexual health and to link it to reproductive health programs has generated calls to make the 'open and frank' discussion of sexuality — in essence, a medicalized discussion of sexuality — a public health priority. Such calls, in familiar colonial fashion, risk branding other social histories of sexuality as 'backward' traditions in need of correction."[164] Pigg then wonders, "Might international solidarity risk becoming an imperialism of expertise that overlooks the histories that inform local politics of AIDS?"[165] Timothy Wright, an anthropologist specializing in Bolivia, describes the work he did for USAID in the 1980s. "While project personnel increasingly talked about 'the gay community,' in fact, this was by no means a monolithic or unified group. . . . In short, men-who-have-sex-with-men who were too rich or too poor or too masculine or too effeminate were unlikely to be attracted to the gay center or welcomed as members of the emerging 'gay community.'"[166]

When the State Department performed its own internal evaluation of its AIDS work from 1987 to 1992, it concluded not that the agency had overemphasized individual change or ignored local politics but, rather, that global AIDS work was underfunded and that African states were incapable of creating the conditions necessary for behavior change. In its 1992 report *The Global AIDS Disaster: Implications for the 1990s*, the State Department reiterated some of the key findings in the 1987 Special National Intelligence Estimate, but it emphasized that "the unanswered question is whether greatly expanded programs could reverse the long-term trend." Instead of providing a rationale for increasing funding for AIDS work, the writers deferred and explained, "Most likely, the question will remain unanswered, since anti-AIDS resources will probably grow only moderately during the 1990s."[167]

Nowhere was this truer than on the African continent, where the report estimated that 7 million people were infected with HIV. Instead of calling on the U.S. government to fund the work of the State Department, however, the document's authors grew frustrated with the prospects of dealing with AIDS in Africa. In an increasingly defeatist tone, particularly in discussions of Africans, the report explained, "Africans are not changing their sexual behavior fast enough to affect the course of the epidemic, even though the basics of HIV transmission have now been widely publicized."[168] As we will see in the next chapter, this did not always prove true, given the extensive and consistent work of numerous NGOs across the continent.

Just as the *Global AIDS Disaster* report came out, USAID awarded Family Health International a second contract for $168 million to create a program called AIDS Control and Prevention (AIDSCAP), which lasted from 1991 to 1997.[169] Over the course of six years, AIDSCAP worked in forty-five countries and, according to its own report, reached 19 million people and distributed or sold 254 million condoms.[170] While this represented a significant expansion from the initial funding and the content of the program, including encouraging behavior change with attention to how gender inequality affected the decisions women made, the scale of the AIDSCAP project did not come close to addressing the scope of the global AIDS pandemic, which by 1997 infected 30.6 million people.[171] By the mid-1990s, funding, not models for how to prevent the spread of HIV, became the most pressing concern international AIDS workers faced.

AFTER REAGAN ADMINISTRATION OFFICIALS first questioned what the federal government should do to deal with the problem of AIDS in 1985, the federal government implemented policies and actions that, surprisingly, came from a wide range of ideological positions among self-identified conservatives. On one hand, Bauer and Bennett emphasized teaching that sex should only happen in heterosexual marriage, that testing was necessary for finding people with AIDS, and that maintaining a strong executive branch was the only way to accomplish these goals. These ideological warrants allowed Bauer, once in the position of senior domestic advisor, to argue that federal AIDS policy needed to reject discussions of sexuality and the use of condoms. On the other hand, Surgeon General Koop and the Presidential Commission on HIV insisted on the exact opposite program. In both cases, condoms and well-funded state programs were the only way to effectively deal with AIDS in the United States. The State Department followed the lead of the latter, shying away from the arguments made by Bauer, to distribute more condoms than almost any other federal agency. The State Department's AIDS advocacy appeared similar to the stance the agency took during the John F. Kennedy administration, when the fight against racial inequality in the United States was used to win allies against the Soviet Union.

Considering domestic and international responses that emphasized the need to talk about sex and to distribute condoms in tandem allows us to see that inadequate funding for programs served as more of a liability to success than did ideological disagreements. Put more simply, because federal AIDS work in the United States and the global South was chronically underfunded, federal AIDS workers, whether the surgeon general or the head of USAID, were often able to make arguments that ran counter to standard strands of social conservatism. The lack of funding made it possible to voice a set of ideas that could not find a voice in other governmental arenas. And while they were not adequately funded, it did not diminish the content of the arguments that were fundamentally at odds with other conservative discourses in the 1980s.

In the next chapter we will see what happened when a private organization, the Ford Foundation, rejected the constraints on what could be talked about and, in the process, developed an explicitly feminist response to AIDS in the global South, an action State Department officials were not able to achieve.

4 | AIDS, Reproductive Rights, and
Economic Empowerment

*The Ford Foundation's Response to AIDS
in the Global South, 1987–1995*

IN OCTOBER 1987 the Associação Brasileira Interdisciplinar de AIDS (Brazilian Interdisciplinary AIDS Association, or ABIA), a newly formed Brazilian NGO, approached the Ford Foundation with a request to fund its research project "The Social Impact of AIDS in Brazil."[1] ABIA's diverse membership of academics, doctors, religious leaders, state and municipal health authorities, and gay activists worked together to address what was quickly becoming a national AIDS epidemic. The association had roots in the redemocratization movement that emerged in the shadow of two decades of military dictatorship. Taking its cue from other political organizing efforts begun in the newly democratic Brazil, ABIA approached the nascent Brazilian AIDS epidemic as a social and political problem. In its initial proposal, ABIA asked Ford to finance a national database to track the response of government and Brazilian civil society to AIDS. In addition to serving as a clearinghouse, ABIA planned an education drive that targeted Brazilians at risk for contracting AIDS, most notably "men from a lower income group, unwittingly labeled as 'bisexuals' . . . [and] haemopiliacs."[2]

ABIA's attention to how and why class and sexuality mattered when dealing with AIDS prevention in Brazil became a hallmark of the new organization's mission. ABIA's president, the preeminent Brazilian political scientist Herbert de Souza, wrote, "Taking into account . . . patterns of Brazilian male sexual behavior, notably heterogeneous as to practices and practitioners, and the lax policies of blood banks — we propose as an initial hypothesis, that the virus will spread rapidly among the working-class population, not only because they count on fewer resources, but because their social and sexual practices differ from those of the middle and upper classes, where AIDS preventive strategies are formulated and are more efficacious."[3] For de Souza, attention to sexual behavior required understanding the personal effects of economic inequality. To concretize how sexuality and class intersected in the evolution of sexual practices, ABIA sought to establish a "socioeconomic profile of notified cases of AIDS sufferers" to dispel the notion that wealthy Brazilians were more at risk for contracting AIDS than the poor. The proposal concluded that the best way to accomplish the goals of accurately detailing the Brazilian AIDS epidemic was to institute a "socio-anthropological" investigation of the disease.[4]

ABIA's proposal appealed to Ford Foundation staff working to develop a philanthropic response to AIDS, in part because of ABIA's attention to the health effects of economic inequality and in part because of its desire to harness a social scientific, as opposed to medical, response to AIDS. In his assessment of the grant, Peter Fry, a program officer in the Rio office and an Anglo-Brazilian anthropologist whose ethnographic work focused on homosexuality in Brazil, praised ABIA's decision "to conduct research on [AIDS's] social impact, including such issues as the social characteristics of AIDS patients, the importance of religious affiliation, [and] social class and race on AIDS patients' survival."[5] Ford responded favorably to ABIA's application and awarded the organization its first grant to address AIDS outside the United States. Over the course of the next year, Ford distributed a dozen more grants to NGOs hoping to prevent the spread of AIDS in various national contexts.

As an institution, Ford saw its AIDS work as growing out of its longstanding commitment to dealing with the social and political problems created by global poverty. In its first official proposal to deal with AIDS, "The AIDS Challenge," ratified by the Board of Trustees in December 1987, Ford allocated resources to address the global AIDS pandemic because the disease endangered "a broad cross section of the population in developing nations and compounds their already serious public health, development, and poverty problems." Ford staff members cautioned that "AIDS threatens to push poor nations even deeper into poverty."[6] As we saw in the previous chapter, Ford was not alone in this increasingly global view of AIDS in the mid- to late 1980s. Working in conjunction with state-based institutions such as USAID as well as private organizations, including the Rockefeller Foundation, Ford promulgated the idea that the best way to deal with AIDS in the global South was to connect it to economic development projects.

To address the extensive problems created by AIDS, "The AIDS Challenge" argued, Ford had to "build on its many years of close, mutually trusting relationships with university-based social science and behavioral researchers, with human rights activists, and with government policy makers. Free of constraints that inhibit government funds the Foundation could work flexibly and sensitively with indigenous groups on such delicate topics as patterns of sexual behavior and how they might be modified to prevent AIDS." Ford also planned to tap into "close relationships with local women's organizations" but did not detail what that would look like in the "AIDS Challenge" document.[7]

Given the slight attention paid to women's health in the document, few would have expected that by 1990 Ford's AIDS work would become explicitly feminist in orientation. The main catalyst for this transformation was the arrival of José Barzelatto, a Chilean doctor who had previously worked at the WHO and joined the foundation in 1989 as a senior consultant in the Reproductive Health and Population Program. Three years later, Barzelatto became the head of the program, which oversaw all of the grants awarded to AIDS workers in the global North and South between 1991 and 1996. In the process, Barzelatto made the Ford Foundation's response to AIDS in the global South one of the most extensive feminist responses to AIDS initiated by a U.S.-based institution. The grants the foundation funded under Barzelatto's leadership recognized the transnational nature of AIDS but, more importantly, insisted that feminist solutions that connected gender equality with sexual freedom and originated among women organizers in the global South take center stage in coping with AIDS. In addition to seeing links between gender and sexuality, Barzelatto encouraged Ford program officers in field offices from Lagos to Bangkok to Rio to locate and support activists who articulated connections between women's experiences and economic inequality. In so doing, the Ford Foundation became one of the first U.S. institutions to reiterate the argument that came primarily from the global South, that addressing AIDS required creating the conditions under which women achieved gender *and* economic equality. In combining arguments about economic development, reproductive rights, and sexual health, Ford's AIDS program presaged discussions that would occur over the course of the next decade, particularly the idea that poverty affected an individual's sexual behavior.[8]

This chapter details how and why Ford transformed its "AIDS Challenge" from a program that considered, but did not make central, the needs of women into a strategy for AIDS and reproductive health that explicitly centered on the needs of women, reproductive rights, and economic development. I document this change by analyzing just over half of the 100 grants the foundation gave to organizations working on AIDS in the global South between 1988 and approximately 1993.[9] I chose the grants (53 in total) by determining the four most heavily funded countries and regions — Brazil, Thailand, Haiti, and western Africa, primarily Nigeria and Senegal — and then looking at all the grants Ford made to organizations that provided resources for some form of AIDS prevention. I found that after Barzelatto's arrival in 1989, Ford awarded most of its AIDS prevention money to organizations working to incorporate gender analysis with AIDS and economic development.

This investigation of Ford's AIDS work in the global South serves several purposes, then. First, it suggests that some of the strongest and clearest feminist responses to AIDS in the late 1980s came from the global South. While scholars have pointed out the failure of most U.S. feminists to launch a sustained critique of AIDS, Ford's funding patterns highlight the power of southern feminist voices in shaping the foundation's institutional response.[10] When Ford began to fund AIDS in the global South in 1987–88, just two years after the WHO and at the same time as USAID (both of which were discussed in the previous chapter), it did so with a much more explicitly feminist agenda than either agency. Second, the chapter builds on the revisions scholars have made to the characterization of U.S. feminism in the 1980s and 1990s.[11] The feminist AIDS workers funded by Ford departed from the models promulgated by white, second-wave feminists, where gender discrimination was understood as separate and apart from other forms of discrimination. At the Ford Foundation, concerns for how and why gender mattered in relation to changing economic and racial inequality became central to the struggle against the global AIDS pandemic, a position that originally found voice among the foundation's grantees in the global South. Finally, the analysis here questions the argument that philanthropy around reproductive health often produced a form of (un)intentional imperialism.[12] While I have no intention of making a general claim about the benefits of philanthropy, my investigation of Ford in the late 1980s and early 1990s found Ford staff struggling, more successfully than not, to imbue the foundation's AIDS work with various forms of feminism that integrated gender, race, and class analyses and understandings and placing the ideas and actions of people from the South at the center of the AIDS project.

Taken together, these related claims about feminism and AIDS work force us, again, to reevaluate characterizations of the political landscape of the United States in the 1980s and 1990s. To be sure, conservative ideology, defined by members of the New Right in the case of AIDS as requiring a singular focus on sex within marriage and discussions of abstinence, played a critical role in shaping the U.S. response to AIDS as a global pandemic. But the New Right was not alone in making arguments about what the content of sexual conversations should be. Just as we saw in earlier chapters, responding to AIDS provided private institutions with an opportunity to circumvent governmental restrictions and ideology and offer an alternative to what they saw as the Right's restrictive programs and approaches. The Ford Foundation was key in situating AIDS work in a larger movement to address reproductive and sexual health. As a philanthropic institution with significant assets, Ford influenced the direction AIDS work took in a period when resources, especially federal money, were difficult to obtain. Beyond that, it supported organizations that made some of the earliest critiques in the 1990s of globalization and neoliberalism. While Ford's activist work was by no means as antiestablishment as people protesting at Wall Street, the subject of the final chapter, the projects the foundation helped sustain produced radical changes in myriad local environments. In the process, Ford became a site where progressive critiques of the Reagan administration's response to AIDS emerged, and the foundation's efforts should be situated alongside the work of AIDS activists in ACT UP.

The Ford Foundation before AIDS:
Population Control and Its Feminist Critics

When the Ford Foundation first opened its doors in Detroit, Michigan, in 1936, the organization was mainly concerned with local issues. In 1948, one year after the death of its founder, Henry Ford, the foundation created a committee to plan an expansion to make it the nation's largest private charity. H. Rowan Gaither Jr., a San Francisco lawyer who had served as the chairman of the Rand Corporation and was also involved in defense work, headed the effort. Gaither convened a committee with seven other members, all of whom worked at some point in their careers in a U.S.

university and also had connections to the government, or more particularly to the military-industrial complex.[13] The committee redefined Ford's mission as a philanthropy working to improve "human welfare" through a commitment to "democratic principles."[14] Using this language, the Ford Foundation situated itself at the center of an emerging discourse of postwar American liberalism, committed to spreading democracy as an answer to Soviet expansion and the threat of communism.[15] It also coupled a strong stance against communism with a belief in the power of democracy and the state. This led Ford to fund projects on poverty and education in the United States, while in the developing world the foundation's larger goals morphed into projects that supported postwar development efforts.[16]

As was the case with other philanthropic organizations and governmental agencies involved in postwar development projects, Ford placed a heavy emphasis on the need to control population growth as a "means of promoting economic development."[17] Population controllers, as those interested in limiting population came to be called, argued that the only way to ensure economic growth in the developing world was to limit the number of people using resources. By the mid-1960s, a decade after it became a national foundation, Ford, along with the Rockefeller Foundation, became a major player in population control efforts in both the United States and the developing world.[18] Ford employed methods to medically manage women's fertility, namely, funding projects that developed contraception and provided sterilization for women with the intention of making the world more economically and politically stable. This neo-Malthusian model was very much in vogue in the 1960s, thanks to such popular mainstream works as Paul Ehrlich's *Population Bomb*.[19]

In its earliest instance, Ford's demographic perspective all but ignored the centrality of women's experiences in attempts to regulate childbearing and avoided thinking about the importance of women's health apart from development and population control questions. Focusing on the imperialist tendencies of the demographic/medical model, feminists in the North and South, by the 1970s, forced a major shift in how institutions such as Ford implemented their population control and development efforts. Instead of a model that saw population control as instrumental to development or that claimed women's fertility was best controlled by medical intervention, activists argued that development was the best form of contraceptive, the southern position articulated at the 1974 World Population Conference held in Bucharest.[20] According to feminist scholars Gita Sen,

Adrienne Germain, and Lincoln Chen (the last two of whom worked at the Ford Foundation in the 1970s and were instrumental in changing how Ford approached population control), activists forced a shift in thinking about the relationship between population control and development and, in the process, "strengthened emergent understanding of the relationships among advances in education, the status of women, and human fertility."[21] Feminist critics of population control quickly became central players in the international women's health movement that emerged in the late 1970s.[22]

Southern critics not only insisted on women-centered health efforts as a way to promote family planning; they also articulated an alternative to economic development as implemented by national and international institutions. While women had been key actors in the development project at the United Nations since the 1950s, the UN announcement that 1975–85 would be the Decade for Women served as a catalyst for feminist activism.[23] According to Caribbean feminist scholar and activist Peggy Antrobus, the Decade for Women "facilitated the growth of a global women's movement of the greatest diversity and decentralization, a movement that expanded its agenda from a narrow definition of 'women's issues' to one that embraced a range of concerns for human welfare."[24] Similarly, as historian Estelle Freedman notes, "the impoverishment of women represented a major obstacle to economic justice, and the UN Decade For Women provided a forum for reviewing development policy through the lens of gender."[25] "By the end of the UN Decade for Women," Freedman concludes, "women in the developing world had redefined feminism, rejecting the myth of global sisterhood in favor of a more heterogeneous and flexible framework."[26] They also promoted a new model for putting women's needs at the center of development efforts: the theory of Gender and Development (as opposed to the earlier paradigm, Women in Development) "addressed issues such as the relationships of men and women to natural resources and the impact of male migration on women's work and responsibilities."[27]

The growing vociferousness and relevance of feminists from the global South and North had a dramatic effect on the Ford Foundation. The foundation not only began to pay increasing attention to women's issues, but it did so in a way that acknowledged transnational feminist concerns. Answering the calls for more consistent attention to women's issues at the foundation, made by female staff members, including Susan Berresford, a program officer in Social Development who joined Ford in 1970 after graduating from Radcliffe College and working in antipoverty programs, by

1980 Ford's Board of Trustees, working in conjunction with the new president of the foundation, Franklin Thomas, more than doubled the amount of money that could be spent on global women's issues.[28] Thomas, the first African American to run a major philanthropic institution, deepened the connection between domestic and international efforts and strengthened Ford's feminist stances. Bringing his experience as the president of the Bedford Stuyvesant Restoration Corporation, a community development corporation created by Robert Kennedy in 1966 as an antipoverty program, Thomas came to Ford with a strong desire to connect international and domestic poverty programs, as well as civil rights with human rights.[29] In a 2008 interview, Berresford, who worked with and for Thomas for more than twenty-five years and became the president of Ford when Thomas retired in 1996, recalled that "Thomas saw no sharp distinction between domestic and international. He acknowledged both the commonalities and the differences, but wanted to move the foundation away from the silo model with one side working on the domestic, the other working on the international."[30]

Thomas encouraged the staff to spend the larger allocation on feminist projects that were not an "exportation of American values."[31] Staff members did this by listening to, and supporting, southern women's demands for both economic and gender equality.

> By the late 1970s it had become increasingly clear that the empowerment of women was an issue of indigenous concern in the Third World, and all field offices had begun at least exploratory grant making. The resulting women's programs . . . focused on three related areas: improving women's productive capacity and opportunities for employment and earning income; promoting sex equity in education; and understanding and reducing cultural constraints on women's social and economic participation.[32]

In one of his first acts as president, Thomas ended Ford's decades-long work in population control, reasoning that it was unsuccessful in promoting women's health or creating lasting solutions for poverty. Thomas replaced population control with more holistic programs in child survival and women's health.[33] For example, working in conjunction with several Scandinavian development agencies, Ford funded Development Alternatives with Women for a New Era, a feminist organization based in the global South committed to critiquing development, neoliberalism, and a range of international institutions.[34] This kind of funding placed Ford on a short list of philanthropies that supported the expansion of global feminism in the late 1980s and early 1990s.[35]

The AIDS Challenge

By the mid-1980s, on the heels of Ford's feminist transformations in reproductive health, the foundation slowly began to consider its role in the growing AIDS crisis. The foundation, like most, if not all, major philanthropies in the 1980s, was reluctant to work on AIDS. Because Ford had neither undertaken programs to address single diseases nor considered health one of its main areas of interest, AIDS was not an immediate natural fit.[36] Beyond Ford's lack of a focus on health, Susan Berresford, who by the mid-1980s was vice president of the U.S. and International Affairs Program, remembered that caution seemed warranted because "AIDS was so pervasive that there was a fear that it could take over what the foundation would do. We needed to define a program with clear edges." Even though the foundation had more than a decade's worth of experience as a philanthropy that strived to think about women's health needs as a function of their economic needs, Berresford explained that "the foundation was careful, very careful, not to become the national source for AIDS funding."[37]

While the intellectual case could, and would, be made that Ford's mission as a foundation committed to human welfare required it to act on AIDS, personal events catalyzed the Board of Trustees to usher the Ford Foundation into AIDS work. In the mid-1980s several employees at the New York headquarters died from AIDS. Shep Forman, Ford's director of Human Rights and Governance and the first coordinator of Ford's AIDS funding, recalled that "six men, all of them working in the human rights field, got sick and died. This was horrific at both a personal level and for the foundation."[38] Michael Seltzer, a consultant Forman hired to draft Ford's "AIDS Challenge" document, confirmed Forman's account, reporting that "the deaths of the employees triggered an institutional response that figured AIDS as more than a health issue."[39]

The job of moving the Board of Trustees out of their grief and into a more institutional response to AIDS fell to Forman, an anthropologist specializing in Latin America, and his colleague Richard Horovitz, a historian of Africa. Both men joined Ford in the late 1970s and worked in field offices in their areas of expertise, Forman in Rio de Janeiro, Brazil, and Horovitz in Dakar, Senegal. Forman returned to New York in 1980 and became the program officer in charge of Human Rights and Governance in 1981. Five years later, Susan Berresford charged Forman with the task of designing a foundationwide response to AIDS that connected AIDS work to Ford's commitment to promoting human rights.[40] Forman not only provided the intellectual expertise to connect AIDS work to human rights work; he also addressed "questions of public policy and rights as well as local prevention and care issues."[41]

As Forman developed an AIDS plan in the vein of the foundation's human rights work, Richard Horovitz labored in the Dakar field office to "create a space for doing human rights work in Ford's West African initiatives."[42] In addition to his commitment to human rights, Horovitz was known throughout the foundation as a gay man, in part because he openly lived in Dakar with his lover, the African American poet Melvin Dixon. In 1985, Horovitz left his post in West Africa and returned to the New York City headquarters. By 1987–88, Horovitz's boss, William Carmichael, placed Horovitz in charge of the foundation's AIDS work in developing countries. Horovitz brought his knowledge of West Africa and his experience as a gay man to his new role as Forman's partner in the effort and regularly represented what he saw as the immediate needs of developing countries.[43]

Horovitz wanted the nascent AIDS program to build on the lessons learned in the changes taking place in Ford's population control work as it became more focused on women's and children's health. He emphasized the need to connect with "indigenous" researchers as well as the role social scientific research should play in a disease too often dealt with strictly as a medical condition. Horovitz recognized that Ford did not have the resources to fund large-scale medical investigations (a project, according to the foundation, better left to governmental agencies), but, more importantly, he understood the role social science could play in encouraging changes in sexual behavior.[44] As the nascent AIDS program developed, however, Horovitz did not always integrate investigations of sexuality and of gender.

The lack of immediate connection between AIDS and gender in the Developing Country Program was due, at least in part, to the fact that alongside Ford's budding AIDS program, field office staff members were in the throes of revamping the child survival and reproductive health programs to excise the last vestiges of the population control ideology that privileged the medical regulation of fertility over women's ability to maintain control over their own fertility. The energy expended on that project had the effect of making conversations about AIDS and about women's health more parallel than intersecting. At a February 1988 meeting of the foundation's staff held in Bangkok, Thailand, program officers from several of the East Asian and South Asian offices joined their counterparts from West Africa to discuss a wide range of subjects, including community epidemiology and management, building capacity in women's reproductive health, and a strategy for AIDS.[45] But the AIDS strategy seemed somewhat separate from the reproductive health programs. In describing how to better deal with child survival and reproductive health programs, staff members emphasized a framework that "focused on social problems and the social issues in health improvement rather than on specific diseases. Attention would be given to household behavior, health care systems behavior, and the socio-economic environment as they affect health." The strategy on AIDS emphasized none of these principles and instead called for "research on sexual behavior and the risk of HIV infection."[46]

The lack of concrete connections between reproductive health and AIDS, even in the face of the simultaneity of the conversations, also may have been the result of the fact that several of the foundation's strongest reproductive health and child survival programs existed in countries that had not yet experienced a dramatic increase in the number of AIDS cases. This meant that the program officers at the Bangkok meeting, except for staff from the Lagos field office, were not actively seeking links to AIDS workers. At the same time, the program officers taking the first steps to secure AIDS funding, most notably the representatives from Brazil, witnessed a very different epidemic, one that had a substantial number of cases among gay and bisexual men.[47] In Brazil, the connection between reproductive health and AIDS activism would take several more years to develop, evidenced in the absence of Rio-based program officers from the two-day Bangkok meeting.[48]

After the Bangkok meeting, Ford instituted a global AIDS plan that funded organizations working on individual behavior change as well as those that paid attention to how the "socio-economic environment" affected health. In the ten remaining months of 1988, Ford gave a total of thirteen grants to organizations that dealt with AIDS in five southern countries: Thailand, Haiti, Senegal, Brazil, and Mexico. Of the thirteen grants, I was able to examine nine, using the strategy of looking at the countries receiving the overwhelming majority of Ford funding as well as grants targeting educational, as opposed to care provision, programs.[49]

The Ford Foundation's rationale for supporting these programs in its first round of AIDS grantmaking emphasized global epidemiology and the foundation's local standing in the chosen countries. First, Ford highlighted the epidemiological differences among Brazil, Thailand, Haiti, and Senegal. In the process, the foundation developed a kind of narrative of the AIDS epidemic, telling a story about how AIDS had developed in each country and what projections lay ahead. Both Brazil and Haiti were at the forefront of the global epidemiology: Brazil had the highest number of reported AIDS cases after the United States for much of the 1980s and early 1990s,[50] and Haiti had been associated with AIDS since 1982, when Haitians became the only national group marked as at risk for AIDS.[51] Unlike Brazil and Haiti, neither Thailand nor Senegal yet had reputations as countries with AIDS problems. In Thailand, Ford and other public health agencies recognized that "all signs point to a rapid spread of the virus among high-risk groups."[52] The same was true in Senegal, where Ford was concerned about a lack of AIDS prevention information, as compared with East Africa, the United States, and Europe. Ford staff noted that Senegal had been slow to develop "AIDS control and education programs."[53]

In justifying its decision to sponsor AIDS work in such varied locations, Ford also stressed the need to fund programs that attended to the needs of heterosexuals in particular. Here, the United States became a point of epidemiological exception, serving as the country, along with Brazil to some extent, where the majority of cases occurred among gay men and, therefore, was fundamentally different from national epidemics across the global South.[54] Alternatively, Ford intended to promote social scientific work in Senegal, Thailand, and Haiti on the connection between AIDS and commercial sex work. In this model, program officers often conflated, in studies and programs, representations of women and commercial sex workers such that they became interchangeable subjects. In effect, commercial sex workers, who were always women, regularly appeared as the main vector by which heterosexual men were exposed to AIDS and, therefore, required sustained attention.

Beyond the epidemiology, all of the Ford-funded programs, except those in Haiti, were based in countries where the foundation maintained strong field offices. This meant that the program officers in these locations were well connected to "indigenous" institutions working on issues pertinent to

AIDS. Field officers looked for grantees that articulated a commitment to using social scientific models to build a response to AIDS. With a model in place to coordinate myriad local efforts, Richard Horovitz hoped that the foundation would "move forward rapidly to help indigenous institutions cope with this latest threat to human wellbeing and development."[55]

The Ford Foundation initiated the first phase of its AIDS work in the global South still clinging, to a certain extent, to population control models. While staff members had learned lessons over the course of the 1980s about the problems associated with relying on medical models to control fertility and had seen the benefits derived from giving women agency to control their reproductive lives, they had not fully translated those examples into models for funding local AIDS work. Not only did the Ford Foundation fund groups that had long histories in population control, but it also awarded several grants to organizations that represented women as vectors for disease instead of agents of action.

Ford's initial sponsorship of AIDS work in Thailand, in the summer of 1988, exemplified how betwixt and between the foundation was when it came to the role population control models would play in its plans to deal with AIDS. Beginning in July, Ford awarded three grants, totaling almost $150,000. More than 85 percent of the total expenditure went to two northern NGOs that specialized in population control efforts working in Thailand, with the rest going to a small Thai NGO that focused on women who worked in the sex industry. Ford awarded its first grant ($48,000) to the Program for Appropriate Technology in Health/Thailand (PATH); the second grant ($80,000) went to the Population Council. Both NGOs proposed to work with locally based Thai institutions to design counseling techniques to curb the spread of AIDS.[56] The last and smallest grant ($19,000) in this initial trio went to a Thai NGO, EMPOWER (Education Means Empowerment of Women Engaged in Recreation). With Ford's support, EMPOWER designed a program to provide Thai women in the entertainment industry options for preventing the spread of HIV.[57]

Both the Population Council and PATH had long histories as organizations that distributed contraception to reduce fertility in the developing world.[58] Starting in 1952 with funding from the Rockefeller and Ford foundations, the Population Council worked to limit population growth with the intention of making the world more economically and politically stable. PATH followed a similar course. Originally founded in 1977 as the Program for the Introduction and Adaptation of Contraceptive Technology and based in Seattle, Washington, PATH maintained more than a dozen offices around the world; the organization engaged in population control through attempts to limit women's fertility using medical models.[59]

In its request for Ford funding, the Population Council planned to join forces with the Venereal Disease Division of Thailand's Ministry of Public Health, the National Family Planning Program, and a Thai university to investigate the sexual behavior of certain Thai teenagers and young adults and develop, test, and evaluate AIDS prevention materials. The grant "relied on a corps of 61 volunteer peer counselors" to talk to university students about AIDS in addition to conducting discussions about other STDs and unwanted pregnancy.[60] The project was designed to test the hypothesis that "greater knowledge about AIDS prevention will be associated with greater use of condoms."[61]

The results of the grant to the Population Council were mixed. In its final report to Ford, the Population Council lamented that, in comparison to a control group that received no specific education on AIDS, the AIDS education group "did not further increase their knowledge or decrease their risk behavior."[62] Despite the results, in the final assessment of the grant, Ford staff in Bangkok called the AIDS prevention education "essential" because it targeted "groups of respected status in society" as opposed to "prostitutes and intravenous drug abusers."[63]

Like the Population Council, PATH wanted to use counselors to help promote individual behavior change and curb the spread of AIDS. Unlike the Population Council, PATH proposed working with several Bangkok NGOs targeting "high risk groups — intravenous drug abusers, workers in the entertainment industry, and the gay community."[64] It sought to provide "counseling services for high-risk groups, mounting information and education campaigns for the general public and conducting research on social factors accelerating the spread of the disease among certain segments of the Thai population."[65] This "client-centered interpersonal communication" utilized a psychosocial model of behavior change, reasoning that AIDS counseling would encourage commercial sex workers and intravenous drug users to change their high-risk activity, although the specific modifications were never described in the final reports.[66]

The model of encouraging individual change, as opposed to societal change, made the grantees less able to understand how a range of factors complicated women's actions. Employing population control models, even if implicitly or in name only, the grants to the Population Council and

PATH supported AIDS work that essentially ignored gender and economic inequality as factors to explain how and why AIDS spread as it did. While both organizations had worked with women before, especially in attempts to limit fertility, each viewed women, who appeared in their plans only as commercial sex workers, as vectors for men to become infected with HIV. In one of its reports to Ford, PATH cited an example of a commercial sex worker who said, "'I'm not afraid of AIDS but I am afraid of starving.'" PATH argued that this quote suggested that the subject was "indifferent to AIDS," rather than seeing that the woman's relationship to AIDS was structured by her experience of living in poverty.[67] The writers of that same report never mentioned the needs of female commercial sex workers as having anything to do with their experiences as impoverished women. The Population Council grant seemed more concerned with the health of the young men who often patronized female prostitutes than with the health needs of the commercial sex workers themselves.

EMPOWER took an approach very different from that of either the Population Council or PATH. The three-year-old organization, with four full-time staff members, proposed engaging "women employed in the entertainment industry" in the bars where they worked. According to David Winder, a Southeast Asian program officer, EMPOWER saw the need for change among women *and* men. EMPOWER planned to "encourage the awareness of the AIDS risk, increase the confidence of the workers to the stage where they can insist on the use of condoms in their work and encourage responsible behavior on the part of customers and bar owners."[68] Unlike the Population Council, which focused on the risk posed by commercial sex workers, EMPOWER saw both commercial sex workers and their customers as requiring care and education. EMPOWER's goal of encouraging behavior change in the context of "enhanc[ing] the rights of women who receive little attention from human rights groups" suggested that the organization saw AIDS education as part of larger political change that worked to guarantee the rights of women.[69]

The EMPOWER grant was Ford's first to an organization engaged in feminist AIDS work. Over the course of the next ten years, EMPOWER became a model for Ford's feminist AIDS work and received more AIDS funding than any other Thai NGO in Ford's catalog. I will return to EMPOWER later in the chapter when I discuss the evolution of Ford's grantmaking, but this brief description should illustrate Ford's ongoing struggle to find organizations engaged in AIDS work that broke out of the population control models of the late 1970s.

Ford's initial AIDS funding in Haiti and Senegal looked very different from its contemporaneous grants in Thailand. In Haiti and Senegal, the overwhelming majority of funds went directly to institutions committed to addressing women's experience of AIDS, although the grantees employed very different notions of the role women could play in AIDS prevention efforts. In July 1988, Ford awarded a grant of $105,000 to the Haitian NGO the Centre de Promotion des Femmes Ouvrières (Center for the Promotion of Women Factory Workers, or CPFO) to create a project that educated female factory workers about AIDS. A few months later it supported the work of a French NGO, Implementing Agency for Cooperation and Training (IMPACT), with just under $50,000 to develop an alternative plan to educate Haitian prostitutes to use condoms.[70]

CPFO spoke directly to factory workers employed in the industrial zone of Port-au-Prince, Haiti's capital, in hopes of tapping into a powerful social and political network centered around women's work. According to the CPFO plan, using "a participatory, adult, nonformal education methodology, the program staff will train a group of some forty 'Women Promoters', who will in turn reach approximately 3,000 women workers via 'Roundtables' and condom distribution. Through additional outreach to co-workers, family and partners, and community members, an even larger number of persons will be reached."[71] CPFO's staff wanted to access the feminized labor force in which 70 percent of light assembly industry workers were women. The NGO reasoned that this would allow women to disseminate AIDS information throughout the city. In addition to focusing on women workers, CPFO wanted to empower women with a "strong emphasis on involving the intended beneficiaries in decision making regarding the orientation, selection and implementation of its programs."[72] CPFO trained women factory workers in "such areas as personal and human development, literacy and post literacy, civic and legal issues, women's health and family planning, and professional and microenterprise development," all in an attempt to limit the spread of AIDS.[73] Citing "remarkable progress" a year and half later, Ford supplemented the grant with another $80,000.[74] With the second grant, CPFO hired and trained an additional forty health promoters and collaborated with the Haitian Medical Association "to provide technical assistance and training to other private and governmental

AIDS preventive education initiatives. CPFO staff will also broaden the content of its training materials to include a component on the reproductive system and on family planning."[75]

Funding for CPFO's project almost did not happen because Ford initially wanted to focus on women prostitutes instead of women workers. In an internal memo from Michele Heisler, an assistant program officer, to Richard Horovitz, Heisler wrote, "I had the chance to quickly review the . . . Center for the Promotion of Women Factory Worker's education program for Haitian women factory workers. Although I met with members of the Center on my recent trip to Haiti and was impressed with their work in other areas, it seems more pressing now to work with the target group of prostitutes, as outlined in the IMPACT project."[76] While Heisler provided no further justification for her statement, her rationale was likely based on the idea that female commercial sex workers put the general public (i.e., men) at more risk than female factory workers did. There is no record of her assessment of the CPFO project's impulse to empower female factory workers to protect themselves and, in the process, pass that information on to men. Put more simply, Heisler seemed to support IMPACT, at least initially, because it was more concerned with the ultimate effect the grant would have on heterosexual men, while CPFO focused first and foremost on women and did not seem as interested in attending to men.

IMPACT initially proposed establishing prevention programs for prostitutes in Haitian, Brazilian, and Philippine cities. IMPACT reasoned that heterosexuals in developing countries had "a high number of partners — specially [sic] including female prostitutes."[77] Despite the lack of specificity in the proposal, the foundation funded the Haitian portion of the effort.[78] Using Ford funds, IMPACT talked to 33,000 people and distributed more than 500,000 condoms to men and women in urban Haiti.[79] In its attempt to make prostitutes "systematically" use condoms, IMPACT pictured these women as vectors of disease transmission. While IMPACT mentioned the possibility that prostitutes would be advised "to look for more respectable jobs," in the end, that did not become part of the program.[80]

In Ford's final assessment of its short-lived AIDS work in Haiti, the foundation acknowledged that CPFO, not IMPACT, dealt with "risky sexual practices . . . often a function of economic/social insecurity."[81] The approach differed significantly from IMPACT's as well as the Population Council and PATH efforts in Thailand. CPFO understood that the best way to change risky sexual practices was to change women's underlying economic circumstances. It pushed for microenterprise development, reasoning that increased condom use would not happen solely from education but, rather, required economic incentives that resembled economic development strategies.[82] Finally, CPFO viewed women as active agents, not victims, a position that Ford would go on to emphasize in its subsequent AIDS and reproductive health projects. In deciding to deal with women workers as opposed to female prostitutes, CPFO underscored the fact that all women, not just those who were sex workers, were at risk for HIV. This was the first time these arguments — that sexual practice was a function of economic insecurity and that women's empowerment was a vital piece of effective AIDS work — appeared in Ford's AIDS archive, and they would be repeated often as the foundation sought explicitly feminist responses to AIDS.[83]

While the foundation ceased its funding in Haiti in the early 1990s, the consciousness produced in Port-au-Prince that addressing women's economic needs could be an effective form of AIDS prevention ran parallel to projects Ford funded in other places, most notably in West Africa.[84] In August 1988, the foundation provided scholars at Senegal's Cheikh Anta Diop University with about $75,000 for two projects: a seminar on AIDS for members of the African press and a research project that would work with commercial sex workers in Kaolack, Senegal, a commercial center for West Africa.[85] The press seminar took almost a year to implement, and Ford declined to fund the project's follow-up, in part because women's issues were not sufficiently incorporated into the agenda, but the second grant enjoyed a different fate.[86]

Senegalese researchers planned to "investigate the relationship between sexually transmitted disease and the transmission of AIDS, examine the mode of mother-child transmission, and . . . evaluate the effect of education and condom distribution on the incidence of AIDS and other sexually transmitted diseases."[87] The project's base at Cheikh Anta Diop, a university named after Senegal's preeminent historian and anthropologist, with West African researchers leading the effort, fulfilled the foundation's mission, promoted by Horovitz, to support indigenous institutions. "This might be the institution we have been looking for," William Duggan, a Ford program officer in the Dakar office, commented, to "take the lead in activities in our region using the special appropriation for AIDS."[88] Beyond satisfying Ford's desire to support indigenous researchers, staff members working on the project were impressed because "it was the first time they had seen professors coming out of the university into the community."[89]

Over the life of the Senegalese project, about two years, a gender analysis that combined women's needs with economic empowerment became more and more central.[90] In a site visit nine months into the grant's term, Nicola Jones, a program officer in Ford's Lagos field office, described the successes and failures of the Kaolack project. Staff members worked with registered prostitutes and the police, who referred women to the program, to encourage the use of condoms. The organizers expressed concerns that women were not interested in attending group meetings with clinic staff, but they refused to disempower women in the process of getting them into sessions. "While the reaction of the two male social workers was to mobilise the police to bring them in," Jones wrote, "the female sexologist . . . recognised the importance of the women's own motivation, and the power of peer influence. This is one of the reasons why the team are now talking about setting up an income generating scheme which would provide women with an alternative source of revenue to that from prostitution."[91]

The final grants the Ford Foundation awarded in 1988, the initial phase of AIDS work undertaken as part of the "AIDS Challenge," went to a trio of Brazilian organizations. All three of the chosen organizations — the São Paulo and Rio de Janeiro Support Groups for the Prevention of AIDS (GAPA — São Paulo and GAPA — Rio) and ABIA, which received the first AIDS grant in 1987 — emphasized attending to the needs of sexually active homosexual and bisexual men and hemophiliacs, two groups with a significant percentage of people with AIDS in Brazil.

Two of the grantees, GAPA — São Paulo and ABIA, were equally interested in detailing the class implications of AIDS in Brazil. As a support group, GAPA — São Paulo paid particular attention to the needs of "poorer homosexual men and other low-income groups."[92] ABIA continued to serve as a clearinghouse for information dissemination in the absence of a governmental response. As the only national NGO of the three applicants, ABIA promised to track the government's response to AIDS, conduct research, and distribute "relevant information and educational material."[93] Ford's grant of $267,000 in 1988, its largest AIDS grant to date in any country except the United States, was designed, at least in part, to allow ABIA to counter the belief that most Brazilian AIDS cases were among wealthy gay men.[94]

That the Brazilian AIDS grants did not mention the impact of AIDS on women had more to do with epidemiology than with Ford's commitment to women. By the late 1980s, global epidemiological trends suggested that women were increasingly at risk for becoming infected with HIV, but not all countries fell into that pattern. The sex ratios among people with AIDS varied widely, ranging from eight to one (men to women) in the United States, to four to one in Latin America, to two to one in Southeast Asia, to one and a half to one in the Caribbean, to one to one in sub-Saharan Africa.[95] These statistics partially explained why Ford awarded grants to organizations working with women in Thailand, Haiti, and Senegal, but not in Brazil.

But epidemiology alone did not determine the grants Ford awarded in the first phase of its "AIDS Challenge." Richard Horovitz and Shep Forman led the Ford Foundation in mapping out an initial response to the global AIDS pandemic that successfully defined the disease as both a political and a health crisis. For the most part, this decision required attention to building the capacities of indigenous researchers, but because neither man was connected to feminist activism, their work did not necessarily guarantee that southern feminists received the same consideration.

Moving toward a Combined Reproductive Health
and AIDS Strategy

After Ford's initial grants during 1988, the year following the "AIDS Challenge," subtle yet significant changes began to appear in the grants the foundation made to locally based organizations and international NGOs addressing AIDS in the global South. Over the course of the next few years, Ford understood and responded to AIDS as part and parcel of its reproductive and sexual health policies, and in the process the foundation placed the gendered and economic needs of women and men directly at the center of its AIDS programming. In effect, Ford's AIDS work after 1989 expanded to simultaneously include a systematic analysis of gender and a commitment to addressing the ways economic inequality affected the course of AIDS. The changes were noticeable and in fact had some of their roots in all three of Ford's major funding sites — western Africa, Brazil, and Thailand.

A series of staff moves at Ford between 1989 and 1991 affected the course of the foundation's second phase of AIDS programming. First, Richard Horovitz left the foundation to work at the Panos Institute office in Washington, D.C. Employed by Ford for almost a decade, Horovitz took a job at an NGO with roots in sustainable development. Next, President Franklin Thomas promoted Susan Berresford to vice president in charge of world-wide programming. Berresford brought with her two commitments that directly affected the foundation's AIDS work: establishing connections between U.S. and international funding without making the U.S. example universal, and promoting the central role of feminism in the foundation's grantmaking.[96]

In one of her first acts as vice president, Berresford hired Dr. José Barzelatto as a senior advisor on population in the Urban Poverty Program. A Chilean medical doctor working in the area of medical ethics, Barzelatto had previously worked at the WHO, where he specialized in reproductive and sexual health. Berresford chose Barzelatto because he was "highly respected in international feminist and reproductive health communities and knew research and politics."[97] Upon his arrival, Ford's board charged Barzelatto with "a broad review of the Foundation's population work and its relationship to our AIDS, child survival, fair start, and women's reproductive heath programming."[98]

Barzelatto set to work establishing a program that combined reproductive and sexual health. Barzelatto's mission, as he articulated it, was to connect sex and sexuality more directly to reproductive health. In effect, he wanted to combine an analysis of gender with an analysis of sexuality. "[The] biomedical approach to fertility, combined with cultural myths and taboos, has prevented population programs from adequately addressing sexuality and gender issues," he argued. "Amazingly, even though sexuality is at the core of reproductive life, until AIDS, family planning programs operated quite successfully without even mentioning the word 'sex.'"[99]

Soon after he started at Ford, Barzelatto created an office environment that facilitated his broad vision. He hired Margaret Hempel—a recent graduate of the Woodrow Wilson School at Princeton with a master's degree in international studies and a certificate in demography—as his program assistant. Hempel immediately became a central actor in Barzelatto's plans to reinvigorate Ford's reproductive health program. With her knowledge of demography and her experience in U.S. reproductive health activism in the 1980s, Hempel served as a translator between organizations that had medical models for dealing with AIDS and reproductive health, and those that approached the issues as social and political problems.[100]

As had been the case with Horovitz, who championed the work of indigenous researchers, Barzelatto regularly looked outward, toward the foundation's field offices, to identify promising new programs. Over the course of five years, Barzelatto returned again and again to examples provided by the work of Ford program officers in various field offices. Traveling regularly, holding meetings, and consistently listening to what local people had to say about their work, as well as providing spaces for Ford staff to talk to one another in yearly meetings of the entire reproductive health staff, Barzelatto amassed tremendous amounts of information from NGOs dealing with AIDS and reproductive health in individual countries. He discovered examples of AIDS work that preceded his tenure at Ford and developed strategies to improve upon them. Illustrating how this worked in practice, Hempel remembered that grants often had "three, four, or five program officers working on one grant. We never made an international grant that affected a country without deep consultation with field officers in that country."[101] In the process, people in the field offices and the activists on the ground they funded fundamentally reshaped the institution's AIDS program from the bottom up.

The model of listening to local actors, particularly southern feminists advocating holistic approaches to women's health, exposed Barzelatto to the work of international women's health activists. Political theorist and activist Rosalind Petchesky argues that during the 1980s and 1990s women from the South, with their origins in the struggles against population control, "not only embraced the concept of reproductive rights but also enlarged that concept to include a broad perspective on women's reproductive health needs."[102] As the movement's ideological scope expanded, so, too, did the number of people involved in the activism. According to feminist scholars Claudia Garcia-Moreno and Amparo Claro, between 1988 and 1992 the membership of the Women's Global Network for Reproductive Rights, an organization based in the South, doubled.[103]

Between 1989 and 1995, the infusion of local feminist and women-centered projects had a dramatic effect on Ford's reproductive health program. This transformation, in turn, affected the scope and content of grants to support AIDS work. Ford funded locally based AIDS organizations with female constituencies that also deeply cared about economic empowerment. These organizations argued that economic health provided a necessary prerequisite for physical, reproductive, and sexual health. The new set of local NGOs suggested that individual behavior changes were not sufficient to change the course of a national AIDS epidemic: AIDS was a political crisis that required political solutions, a point also being made by U.S. AIDS activists, which will be discussed in the next chapter.

Several of the local models Barzelatto looked to came out of the Lagos, Nigeria, field office, where program officer Nicola Jones had been working since 1988. Jones — a British expatriate with a long history of feminist organizing in London and a French Ph.D. in social policy and a specialization in demography and development — was one of the first program officers in the field to develop a reproductive health program that included AIDS.[104] She began her work squarely in women's health, trying to fund medical activists treating vesico vaginal fistula, a painful and debilitating condition that affects women after difficult childbirths. Soon thereafter, Jones began to identify nascent AIDS organizations in West Africa "that focus on public education and community involvement" and that required support.[105] To that end, Jones funded a number of projects, including STOPAIDS, a Nigerian AIDS NGO run by a woman named Pearl Nwashili; sponsored a Nigerian research project on sexual behavior and a subsequent training program for health care workers based on the results; provided a supplement to the Senegalese project on commercial sex workers from the first phase of AIDS funding; and awarded several grants to the Society for Women and AIDS in Africa (SWAA), an organization with female members from across the continent. Jones's supervisor at the foundation, Anne Kubisch, recalled that Jones's work in Lagos "became the model that Barzelatto was always able to use. . . . She gave his strategy something concrete, actual grants that combined reproductive health and AIDS."[106]

Jones's first major AIDS grant went to STOPAIDS, an NGO based in Lagos. STOPAIDS sought to foster "public enlightenment" in two motor parks in the city on the southwestern coast of Nigeria.[107] Although not explicitly feminist or women-centered in terms of the population it targeted, STOPAIDS emphasized that the lowest-income groups that inhabited Nigerian motor parks — truck drivers, passengers, "touts, loafers, and various kinds of traders" — required particular attention because of their low levels of literacy and access to media.[108] STOPAIDS proposed establishing "open discussion of sex and sexuality" and "dispel[ing] myths about AIDS high risk behaviors and other health issues."[109] The organization's staff, the majority of whom were women, would do this through "intensive daily chatting" with park regulars, developing illustrated materials for people who could not read, and providing basic health care, including blood pressure checks, to drivers, who would then relax enough to talk with staff members about sexual practices.[110] STOPAIDS saw itself as an organization dedicated to doing something to contain the spread of AIDS among the most mobile, yet impoverished, sectors of the Nigerian population: "For the first time in the history of Nigeria the work domain of this class of our population are made to become vantage points for [a] health education program."[111]

STOPAIDS, like CPFO in Haiti, saw a grassroots response as a way to contain the expanding AIDS epidemic in Nigeria. STOPAIDS workers wanted to incorporate "the ideas and inputs of the park users into the activities . . . [to] make the programme sensitive and adaptable to environmental conditions and customs."[112] STOPAIDS planned to exploit the "extremely efficient informal information networks [that] exist within such parks."[113] With the networks committed to the fight against AIDS, STOPAIDS workers disseminated condoms, basic health care, and information about AIDS to park users.

According to self-reports and Ford site visits, STOPAIDS was incredibly efficient and effective. Within months of receiving the grant, it established two multilingual kiosks in two motor parks, keeping detailed records of each treatment dispensed and referral made. Employing a completely non-uniformed staff in an attempt to make visitors more comfortable, the two kiosks were used by more than 14,500 visitors.[114] People went to the kiosks in search of a wide range of assistance, including help with general health problems, headaches, infections, and mental health.[115] In 1990, Barzelatto toured the STOPAIDS Iddo motor park site to see for himself what the organization had accomplished by targeting an entire class of people as opposed to particular segments, such as commercial sex workers or truckers.[116] Jones remembered that Barzelatto praised the work and exclaimed, "This is what I've been thinking of. You are doing it."[117] Between 1990 and 2003, Ford awarded more than $1.5 million to STOPAIDS in five grant actions.[118] While not explicitly connected to reproductive health, STOPAIDS was one of several grantees that developed a model for preventing the spread of AIDS among impoverished people by using workplaces as intervention sites.

Jones's recognition of explicitly feminist programs began with her visits to the Senegalese project that worked with commercial sex workers, described earlier in the chapter. In what was a common practice, Jones used site visits as an opportunity to talk with AIDS workers about how they might develop their projects with increased Ford support. At Kaolack, Jones pushed researchers beyond income generation for women and toward a more feminist analysis of women's economic and sexual circumstances. After a discussion with William Duggan, Jones's colleague in West Africa, Edwige Bienvenue Ba, the only woman in a leadership role at the project, moved beyond "reconversion and reinsertion of prostitutes" and called for the "reconversion of the entire society to permit women to take control of their reproductive lives." Duggan encouraged Ba to think about future projects "in the context of a wider theme of social transformation."[119] The resulting grant, although falling far short of the revolutionary potential Duggan recommended, funded Ba's follow-up on the Kaolack project. In 1990, Ba headed an anthropological study that "provide[d] information on sexual attitudes and behavior [among Kaolack prostitutes and their children] that would contribute to the elaboration of an enlarged community-based preventive education program."[120] The Kaolack project gave women the space to "take control," according to Jones. Through a system of solidarity, she concluded, "women, however poor, had ways of empowering themselves."[121]

Jones's most lasting and consistent support for feminist AIDS work came in the form of grants to SWAA. Formed in June 1988 by several African women professionals, SWAA planned to work with all African women, not just commercial sex workers.[122] In its initial proposal to Ford, SWAA argued that "African women recognize the importance and urgency of developing AIDS control programs for women, by women in Africa. This opinion was formulated from the peculiar social, cultural and religious settings of most African women and the need to develop programs suitable for them — particularly program strategies for rural women."[123] SWAA proposed a three-day workshop on women and AIDS that combined several Ford initiatives with sessions on "AIDS and Family Planning, Women in the Sex Trades, and Sex education for young women and girls."[124] SWAA hoped this would allow the organization to "pursue collaborations with groups and individuals and with those who recognize the great value in an empowered role for women in shaping strategies against the AIDS virus."[125]

Ford's first assessments of SWAA, made by Richard Horovitz in 1989, heralded the association's feminist worldview. Horovitz praised the organization for "its recognition that AIDS poses a problem for all sexually active women, not just groups, such as prostitutes engaged in high risk-activities."[126] He also applauded the fact that "SWAA's initiatives might thus contribute not only to AIDS control and women's reproductive health but also to women's empowerment."[127]

Jones built on Horovitz's approbation and, over the next five years, helped SWAA expand its efforts on the African continent. In 1990, Ford sponsored SWAA's second conference on women and AIDS in Africa, at which a four-day workshop addressed ways to "reduce the transmission of AIDS and to mitigate the adverse physical, social, and economic impact of the AIDS pandemic on African women."[128] The next year Jones oversaw a grant to support the establishment of a Nigerian chapter of SWAA. The chapter intended to keep the national incidence of AIDS low by working with "poorly educated women in particular" to encourage "sexual empowerment . . . both inside and outside of marriage."[129] Ford saw the Nigerian chapter as part of its long-term objective "to support the development of an intermediary framework for women's reproductive health in Nigeria."[130] SWAA became a signature grantee for the Reproductive Health and Population Program, receiving almost $1 million between 1993 and 2002.[131]

All three West African grantees Jones helped to develop — STOPAIDS, the Kaolack project, and SWAA — became models for addressing the issues associated with women and AIDS. In 1990, SWAA teamed with the Panos Institute to produce the dossier *Triple Jeopardy: Women and AIDS*. The book featured STOPAIDS and Kaolack as constructive examples of what Africans were doing to deal with the AIDS pandemic.[132] Far from silent on the effects AIDS had on women, West African feminists were some of the most vociferous critics of governmental inaction on the African continent.[133]

The links between Jones's work in West Africa and Barzelatto's attempt to craft an institutional mission on AIDS and reproductive health at the foundation resulted in a 1991 document Barzelatto wrote titled *Reproductive Health: A Strategy for the 1990s*. "It seems timely now," the document noted, "for the Foundation to reorient its programming into a holistic concern for reproductive health and rights, as many governments and organizations around the world are beginning to question past approaches and are seeking new ways to achieve more effective and more just population and health programs."[134] The new plan placed a "special emphasis" on AIDS "in view of the magnitude of the consequences expected from this pandemic and because it is mainly a sexually transmitted disease for which there will be no biomedical solution in the future."[135]

Barzelatto's 1991 plan revealed a new commitment to seeing how structural inequalities, as opposed to cultural traditions or individual irresponsibility, hampered women's freedom and made the spread of AIDS more likely. In a series of questions, Barzelatto suggested his desire to see the foundation move well beyond attempts to change individual behavior to embrace an approach that addressed key structural issues such as women's economic circumstances. "Who are the disadvantaged in a given society and how does the way they live affect their reproductive health?" Posing the question this way, Barzelatto refused to see individual action as unrelated to people's relative social and economic advantages. Women with more wealth and social capital often had an easier time negotiating their reproductive life. The next question — "What are the constraints limiting behavior change among persons at risk of AIDS in Thailand?" — acknowledged that education alone was insufficient to change behavior. Instead of programs that criticized subjects for refusing to adopt particular changes in behavior, the question suggested that Barzelatto envisioned a broader, more encompassing socioeconomic model for realizing change. Finally, Barzelatto asked, "How have structural adjustment programs affected household economics and reproductive health?"[136] By wondering about the ways macroeconomic policy (structural adjustment programs) related to health, Barzelatto echoed many of the powerful critiques of neoliberalism coming from southern feminists.[137]

Within two years of adopting this new reproductive health strategy, Barzelatto implemented a new phase of the Ford Foundation's work in the global South. In the first programmatic review for Ford's board of trustees, the authors, likely Barzelatto and Hempel, explained,

> Experience over the last thirty years has shown that much more attention needs to be given to the cultural, social and economic factors that contribute to high fertility, poor maternal health and the spread of sexually transmitted diseases, including HIV/AIDS. Furthermore, focusing only on the social and economic consequences of these problems is not enough. A much more comprehensive approach is needed if we are to see the transition to small, healthy family norms in a manner that is respectful of human rights and that ensures increased equity and quality of life for all people.[138]

In this passage, not only did the writers call attention to the needs of connecting economic inequality and gender inequality when thinking about AIDS; they, more importantly, redefined women's rights as human rights situating the foundation's HIV/AIDS program within a universalist structure and idiom.

The attention to AIDS also broadened Ford's efforts in the area of sexuality studies, apart from issues of sexual health. "We need to know much more about what people do sexually. With reference to HIV, we need to better understand how couples negotiate sex, and why, for example, men and women use or encourage the use of condoms in some relationships and not in others."[139] By paying attention to sexual networks and economic networks in tandem, Ford hoped to understand "how an individual's sexual behavior may be affected by family, peers and the larger social and economic context in which one lives. We need to know more about how sexual networks are influenced by social context, ethnicity and social position."[140]

The foundation's new reproductive and sexual health strategy had an immediate impact in Brazil. By the end of 1991, a group of consultants including Richard Parker, feminist anthropologist Nancy Scheper-Hughes, and Brazilian feminist and reproductive rights activist Sonia Corrêa complied a report on the practical consequences of combining reproductive health work with AIDS work. Citing Barzelatto's reproductive health strategy, the consultants explained that field office staff needed to "build upon both the reality of local circumstances and the background of existing program activities in ways that will fundamentally contribute to the broad goals of the new initiative."[141] While the report ultimately strongly recommended linking the two areas, the writers cautioned against fully conflating AIDS prevention and reproductive health. Each consultant "emphasized the importance of maintaining and developing a range of important activities in the areas of both AIDS and reproductive health that do not necessarily cross or intersect — issues related to health promotion for gay and bisexual men, the incidence of unnecessary or unwanted sterilization among women, and so on."[142]

Despite the caution, changing conditions on the ground over the course of the early 1990s, most notably the evolving epidemiology of AIDS in Brazil that increasingly affected women as well as men who had sex with men, pushed Ford to increase support for Brazilian AIDS workers who attended to the needs of women. When Ford awarded its first grant, in 1989, to the Center for Study and Research in Collective Health (the Center), located in the Institute of Social Medicine at the State University of Rio de Janeiro, it called for a research project on "the relationship between sexuality and AIDS" but at no point mentioned women.[143] Less than three years later, in 1992, the program officers justifying the grant took special care to note that the Center's new grant to document the increasing heterosexual epidemiology of Brazilian AIDS "would contribute to the Foundation's AIDS and Reproductive Health and Population program, which seems to strengthen the nongovernmental and social science responses to AIDS in Brazil and develop new programs on the points of intersection between AIDS and reproductive health."[144] In his description of the project, William Carmichael argued for the "importance of encouraging, whenever possible, ASOS and AIDS researchers to incorporate issues relating to women's reproductive health and reproductive rights into their existing range of activities."[145] Pleased with the Center's accomplishments, especially its interdisciplinary approach to AIDS as well as its consistent collaboration with the WHO's GPA and the Brazilian Ministry of Health, Ford nearly doubled the amount of funding it originally provided to the organization in 1993. In justifying the expansion to support graduate training programs and pilot projects on sexual behavior, Joan Dassin, a program officer in the Rio office, wrote, "Increasingly, researchers are examining the role of human sexuality and gender relations, particularly women's inequality, as key factors in the balance between health and disease and, more broadly, of well-being or its absence. Worldwide, this perspective has been stimulated successively by the women's movement, the gay rights movement and the spread of AIDS."[146]

ABIA, Ford's first southern AIDS grantee, also began to develop a more women-focused program in Brazil. Building on its earlier work on lower-class men, ABIA proposed to create prevention material for "women, adolescents, homosexual men and poor families living in urban peripheral areas."[147] A year later, in December 1992, ABIA's attention to women's reproductive health was even stronger in its request to "incorporate issues specific to women's reproductive health into its ongoing monitoring of key policy issues in the prevention and treatment of HIV/AIDS."[148]

Citing the rapid expansion of reported cases of HIV/AIDS among Brazilian women, Ford saw a unique opportunity to bring together people working on AIDS and those working on reproductive health in a feminist context. Dassin echoed the 1991 consultancy report, explaining that "while AIDS service organizations have been quick to point to the threats to Brazilian women posted by AIDS, they have generally failed to situate this concern within a broader range of women's reproductive health issues. Similarly, while women's organizations have developed an impressive range of activities to promote women's reproductive health, they have been slow to recognize and respond to the potential importance of AIDS."[149] Ford recognized that ABIA's proposal responded to this disconnect by building "collaborative relationships with leading feminist organizations."[150]

The integrated AIDS and reproductive health model developing in West Africa and Brazil made space for Ford to seek out grantees that imagined commercial sex workers as economic agents who required more than education to change their behavior. Nowhere was this truer than in Thailand, where Ford sought out grantees, particularly after Barzelatto took over, that presented prostitution as a decision Thai women made under very difficult economic conditions and that also resisted models that represented female sex workers as vectors for men to become infected with HIV. As described earlier in the chapter, the Ford Foundation's first grant with an explicit feminist perspective on prostitution went to the Thai NGO EMPOWER. The initial award was very small, less than $20,000, but over the course of the next ten years, under Barzelatto's leadership, Ford funding for EMPOWER grew to almost $600,000 in three separate grants. This amount represented the largest cumulative grant Ford gave in Thailand.

From the beginning, EMPOWER combined education with economic alternatives. Every time EMPOWER organized a session on AIDS education, it also provided money to give women access to alternative forms of employment through job training. This strategy recognized that it was not culture alone that influenced women's decisions about sex work but, rather, economic inequality that limited women's ability to support themselves. In 1993, Ford extended funding for the Honey Bee Special (or "condom show") drama group, provided small fellowships for women who wanted to attend school, and created a cooperative restaurant where women could learn business skills.[151] Within five years of its first grant, EMPOWER had opened four education/training centers in various Thai cities, including Bangkok and Chiang Mai, the city reported to have the highest rate of AIDS in the nation.[152]

EMPOWER staff saw their AIDS prevention efforts as part of a larger movement for social change, even though it made their work more difficult. "EMPOWER has learned that it is *hard* for a small organization to get recognition and reputation in the country. It is *harder* for the people at the grass root level to have their voices and expressions heard. It is *hardest* for the work implementing for justice and improvement of human condition to be supported."[153]

Despite the difficulties, Ford praised EMPOWER's AIDS work. In her final evaluation of EMPOWER's first grant, Thai consultant Marjorie Muecke commended the organization's reach. "EMPOWER encompasses a veritable cornucopia of feasible ideas and strategies for extending AIDS-preventive education not only to entertainment workers, but to the public at large. . . . Its strategy to contain HIV infections in society and to reduce social prejudice against women simultaneously is to teach safe sex to the population at large, with a focus on bar owners, customers, and workers."[154] Muecke, an anthropologist specializing in the study of Thai women whom Ford hired as a consultant in 1989, was especially pleased that EMPOWER resisted adopting a punitive stance toward clients and workers.[155] Over the course of the next half decade, EMPOWER maintained this commitment with an "emphasis on empowering women in the commercial sex trade rather than condemning them, [which] has placed the organization in a unique position in the Thai NGO community as a strong advocate for women's rights as well as an organization working on AIDS prevention. EMPOWER's work clearly demonstrates how closely related HIV/AIDS and women's empowerment are to each other."[156]

As the EMPOWER program grew, Ford sought out other Thai organizations that focused on job retraining for female commercial sex workers and moved toward an explicit critique of standard development projects that used moral arguments toconvince women that they should abandon prostitution. In October 1990, Ford funded the Population and Community Development Association (PDA), the largest NGO in Thailand, to study "the economic implications of the AIDS pandemic and identify ways of strengthening prevention education."[157] In addition to documenting the impact of AIDS on the Thai economy, PDA proposed a project that would retrain low-income commercial sex workers and provide them with alternative economic opportunities. In 1992, with Ford's monetary assistance, PDA piloted a training program for eighteen "low income female commercial sex workers" in "hair styling and beauty care." After completing the program, two of the trainees then borrowed funds to open beauty shops that became profitable within several months.[158] A year later, PDA expanded the program to northern Thailand to include a small-scale loan program that would "address the multidimensional factors surrounding young women's entrance into the commercial sex industry [and] sustain the benefits of the project in the villages over the long term."[159]

In subsequent assessments of the grant, Ford acknowledged PDA's ability to shift the conversation about AIDS from one that centered on health to one that also focused on economics. According to its report written with

Ford funds, PDA "succeeded in reframing the World Bank's vision of AIDS from being 'only' a health problem to being a *development problem*."[160] Confirming Ford's report, in a 2003 interview Mechai Viravaidya, the head of PDA, argued, "[PDA] said that HIV is not a medical problem, it's a behavioral problem, a societal problem, a development problem."[161] In this model, coping with AIDS served as a form of sustainable development, and vice versa.

Three of the four countries that received the most Ford funding after 1991, Thailand, Brazil, and Senegal, experienced significant reductions in the number of people affected by AIDS. Between 1991 and 2003 Thailand witnessed a dramatic decrease in the incidence of AIDS, from 143,000 to 19,000 cases. The commitment to prevention education in Senegal and Brazil had similar results.[162] By supporting local AIDS workers and attending to the ways that health required more than the absence of disease, Ford played a role in this success story because program staff championed NGOs that integrated women's rights and economic security into AIDS programs. That, when coupled with major infusions of state sponsorship for AIDS treatment and prevention, suggested that it was possible to contain the effects of AIDS in the global South.

In 1996, Ford's philanthropic work in the field of AIDS and reproductive health shifted in its form but not its content. That year, Susan Berresford became president of the Ford Foundation, the first woman to run a major U.S. philanthropy, and began the process of reorganizing how the foundation organized its intellectual work. Hoping to continue her commitment to feminist principles that led her to hire Barzelatto in 1989, Berresford debated if, and how, the foundation's reproductive health work should be organized.

Together, Berresford and Barzelatto launched an extensive review process of the Reproductive Health and Population program. The subsequent report praised the program under Barzelatto's leadership for "playing a defining role in advancing understanding of reproductive health, and addressing the reproductive health and self-determination needs of disadvantaged people, especially women."[163] The report concluded with a suggestion to "increase inter- and trans-divisional programming, in the areas of education, culture and religion, governance and human rights, and in social development and poverty alleviation."[164] With that information, Berresford decided it was time to "disaggregate RHP as opposed to keep it in one place." She proposed, instead, to "integrate work on reproductive health and AIDS into all of the foundation's work."[165] With the program disbanded, in 1997 Barzelatto retired from the Ford Foundation.

While I have not been able to obtain archival documents about the reorganization of either the Reproductive Health and Population program or the foundation more generally, one way to explain what happened in 1996 is to assume that the program under Barzelatto was so successful that it became a victim of its own success. Although the work was far from complete, the ideas generated by the program, particularly the emphasis on the transformative potential of applying women's empowerment to community health, needed to suffuse Ford's entire grantmaking process, not just the targeted area. The problem with this model, according to former Ford consultant Michael Seltzer, who worked on the original "AIDS Challenge" document in 1987, was that it made "HIV/AIDS everybody's responsibility and nobody's responsibility."[166]

WHEN FORD FIRST BEGAN TO address the problems associated with AIDS in the mid-1980s, it responded with the resources it had available at the time. This meant that the foundation looked to previous population control efforts that had tried simultaneously to control population by supporting contraceptive research and dissemination and to establish models that empowered women to make decision about their own bodies. In the case of population control and its transformation into reproductive health, these two disparate models forced Ford to resist the idea that medical solutions alone were sufficient to make people healthy. When the extent of the global AIDS pandemic began to take shape, Ford did not yet have a mechanism for centering a social science response to AIDS that put attention to gender and economic equality at its center. While staff members, including Shep Forman and Richard Horovitz, knew they wanted to deal with AIDS as a political and social problem and were able to initiate an AIDS program that attended to human rights work, they struggled to find locally based actors proposing AIDS work that attended to the needs of women and men as gendered beings.

Consistent and persistent attention to gender, sexuality, and economic inequality gave new meaning to the social scientific AIDS programs Ford funded. When Ford consciously linked its work on reproductive health to AIDS, at the behest of José Barzelatto, it gave its AIDS program a kind of intellectual weight that it would not have otherwise had. As a medical doctor, Barzelatto could have promoted medical solutions. Instead, he listened to what other disciplines and actors in the global South had to say about AIDS and created, according to anthropologist and former Ford consultant in Brazil Richard Parker, the "glory years of the program, when it was far more progressive than it would be after he left. It was far more feminist than anywhere else. . . . He pushed the envelope."[167]

Ford's response to AIDS between 1989 and 1995 was unique at a moment when unique responses to AIDS were in relatively short supply. In less than five years, Ford realized a commitment to West African, Brazilian, and Thai local organizations, as well as those in dozens of other southern countries, that led a transformation in how the philanthropic institution dealt with AIDS. As I have tried to show throughout the chapter, Ford's vision came as much from activism in the South as it did from ideas in the North. Foundation staff consistently amplified the voices of feminists working on AIDS as an economic and political problem. In the process, the Ford Foundation took part in the beginnings of a conversation among global southerners and northerners about the relationship among poverty, gender inequality, and AIDS, a topic that will be explored in greater detail in the next chapter and the epilogue.

5 | Drugs into Bodies, Bodies into Health Care

The AIDS Coalition to Unleash Power and the Struggle over How Best to Fight AIDS

SEVERAL HUNDRED PROTESTERS stormed the opening session of the Fifth International Conference on AIDS, held in Montreal, Canada, in June 1989. Contingents from the New York chapter of ACT UP and Toronto's AIDS Action Now! took over the podium to read the "Montreal Manifesto" to the audience of several thousand AIDS researchers.[1] The manifesto's ten demands underscored the need for universal rights for all people living with AIDS. The first called for access to treatment for AIDS, a position that by 1989 had gained currency through ACT UP's activism targeting major pharmaceutical companies such as Burroughs Wellcome and the Food and Drug Administration (FDA), the federal agency that oversaw the regulation of all U.S. drugs. Subsequent planks demanded "an international code of rights" for people with HIV, drawing particular attention to the "reproductive rights of women with HIV" and the "unique problems and needs of intravenous drug users . . . and prisoners." The document ended by demanding the establishment of "an international development fund to assist poor and developing countries to meet their health responsibilities, including the provision of condoms, facilities for clean blood supply and adequate supplies of sterile needles," and identification of poverty as a "critical co-factor in HIV disease," a model that required the "conversion of military spending worldwide to medical health and basic social services."[2]

The breadth and audacity of the Montreal Manifesto's demands illustrated the scope of AIDS activism in the late 1980s. Activists, protesting for the first time at an international AIDS conference, made several critical arguments that linked science and politics, all of which functioned as a political critique of the status quo. First, by combining a broad call for rights for people with AIDS with a demand that emphasized the specific circumstances of disenfranchised populations — women and intravenous drug users had particular needs that were not necessarily considered when dealing with gay men — the Montreal protesters recognized that addressing AIDS without understanding the larger political and economic context in which the disease had emerged would not help all people with AIDS equally. Second, the activists acknowledged that all people would benefit from advances in AIDS treatment and prevention only if the tangible products of that progress were affordable. That is, availability of treatment (meaning its existence) did little for people who could not afford that treatment or for people for whom HIV was one of many health problems. In this manifesto, treatment meant more than drugs; it meant dealing with the effects of poverty.

The protest in Montreal was one of literally hundreds where ACT UP used various forms of civil disobedience to effect change after it formed in March 1987. Functioning as a coalition of activists with varying political perspectives, ACT UP consistently and persistently used direct action and civil disobedience — occupying buildings, making confrontational art, and shouting down speakers at public forums — to demand an end to the AIDS crisis. From the beginning, ACT UP's definition of "end" was broad. Means to achieve that end included agitating for more AIDS treatment; insisting on increased public awareness of the effects of AIDS; calling for an end to homophobia, racism, and sexism because of their roles as cofactors in the spread of AIDS; and demanding universal health care. Relying on direct action, ACT UP presented itself as the antithesis of other contemporary AIDS workers — whether they were in the federal government or at ASOs — who seemed unwilling to muster the appropriate level of indignation about the state of the AIDS pandemic.

Over the course of the group's first four years of existence, ACT UP was wildly successful. Members, for example, fought the state and the pharmaceutical industry to transform the development process for drugs, changed the clinical definition of AIDS so that more women were included, oversaw the expansion of independent housing for people with AIDS, and generally made the AIDS crisis visible through the conscious and consistent manipulation of the popular media. Members of ACT UP also vehemently fought with one another over matters ranging from what protests should be about to how to deal with the racism and sexism that manifested at regular meetings and in the group's decisions. This dynamic environment produced energy to effect change. In his recollections of ACT UP's first two or three years, Jim Eigo, an activist who worked on treatment access, remembered that "when people who were thinking on different issues came up with very particular targets that all of the membership . . . could get behind and put their bodies on the line for . . . it worked . . . splendidly."[3]

By 1991 the New York chapter of ACT UP, the first and largest chapter, began to splinter as members could no longer agree on how to prioritize the kinds of issues highlighted in the Montreal Manifesto. Disagreements proliferated and grew louder over what activism for more treatment should look like as well as what the struggle against racism and sexism should entail and where it fit within a social movement organized around AIDS. While these positions were not inherently exclusive, when the question became what the group's priorities should be, the various contingents were unable to continue working together.

The consequences of ACT UP's breakup were put in sharp relief when scientists, with the help of treatment activists who had fundamentally changed the way the government regulated the testing of AIDS drugs, discovered an effective AIDS treatment regimen in 1996. The drugs existed because of the decade-long work of activists who learned the science of AIDS and schooled research scientists in more participatory models of drug development. The new drugs, however, were exorbitantly expensive, in part because at the same time that ACT UP grew in strength, the pharmaceutical industry lobbied the federal government successfully to extend trade protections for drugs in development and keep drug prices high. By the mid-1990s, multilateral trade agreements protected drugs to treat AIDS in a way that was unheard of a decade earlier.[4] These regulatory changes made it all but impossible for activists to accomplish their primary goal to make treatment affordable for the overwhelming majority of people with AIDS.

We know much of this story from the voluminous interdisciplinary literature on ACT UP as a social movement that had been organized to deal with AIDS. Scholars have written critically about ACT UP, emphasizing the internal battles and contradictions within the group and its ultimate disintegration in 1991–92.[5] Filmmakers and video artists — most if not all of whom were once members of ACT UP — have documented and archived the spectacular nature and effectiveness of ACT UP's early protests; their films underscored the central role artistic production played in this model of AIDS activism.[6] Read and viewed together, these scholarly and artistic interpretations present a picture of ACT UP that often places the eventual splintering of the group back in time, thus coloring overall interpretations of the organization's work between 1987 and 1991.

In this final chapter, I bring these diverse accounts together to yield a different conclusion. First, I detail the political effects of ACT UP's activism in the late 1980s and early 1990s in order to return, for a final time, to one of my key arguments: that responses to AIDS served as the basis for political opposition to modern conservatism. Second, by situating the discussion of ACT UP at the conclusion of a book that considers the evolution of AIDS work over the course of the 1980s, I want to demonstrate that ACT UP emerged out of the wide range of AIDS work, both successful and unsuccessful, that preceded it. While ACT UP defined its mission as mounting a radical response to AIDS, it was neither alone nor completely successful in making arguments against the state, a position that was shared by most of the actors introduced in the preceding chapters. While ACT UP tapped into and expanded on the solutions articulated earlier in the decade by gays and lesbians inside and outside AIDS service, at the same time it replicated models used in San Francisco that fell short when addressing the ways racism and sexism functioned in the AIDS epidemic. Through the use of oral histories and ACT UP's extensive written archive, the chapter begins with an account of the moments in ACT UP's history when it was able to integrate direct action and advocacy to effect changes in both the state's AIDS apparatus and the broader public's perception of the disease. The chapter concludes almost ten years later when ACT UP members were forced to acknowledge, however reluctantly, that direct action had not produced the conditions under which all people with AIDS would receive treatment.[7]

Building an AIDS Coalition

From its first meeting held at New York City's Gay and Lesbian Community Center in the Greenwich Village neighborhood in March 1987, ACT UP was a raucous, defiant, and diverse organization. People with varying degrees of political involvement and diverse sexual orientations were drawn to ACT UP. ACT UP became a home for gays and lesbians who had been active in the gay and lesbian liberation movement of the 1970s, as well as people who worked in the Central American solidarity movement and the peace movement. Several of the first women who joined ACT UP brought their experiences in the reproductive rights and women's movements. Unlike the people who had long histories of organizing for political and social change, a significant number of ACT UP members had never taken part in political activism before attending an ACT UP meeting. While ACT UP's membership was overwhelmingly white and male, women and people of color played an important role in the group from its inception.

The variety of members shared a commitment to using direct action to fight AIDS. In the speech often credited with starting ACT UP, Larry Kramer, who by 1987 was frustrated with the proliferation of ASOs and the lack of massive direct action, exclaimed to the more than 200 people in the room that "we must immediately rethink the structure of our community. . . . Every one of us here is capable of doing something. Of doing something strong. We have to go after the FDA — fast. That means coordinated protests, pickets, arrests."[8] While Kramer's speech certainly served as a rallying cry, ACT UP's evolution as a social movement also built on the intellectual infrastructure created by early AIDS workers like Michael Callen and Richard Berkowitz, discussed in the first chapter, who argued that gay communities could act in healthy ways if given the chance, as well as on fellow activists who had long histories of organizing for social change. Within months of the Kramer speech, ACT UP's regular Monday night meeting had several hundred attendees who organized protests across New York City to demand more attention for AIDS.

On March 24, 1987, at its first major protest, ACT UP held a "die-in" in front of Trinity Church on Wall Street, one of the oldest religious institutions in Manhattan. ACT UP announced seven demands at this protest, several of which echoed the kinds of arguments being made by Surgeon General Koop, including the immediate release of drugs at affordable prices by the FDA, a "massive public education" campaign to stop AIDS, and the "establishment of a coordinated, comprehensive, and compassionate national policy on AIDS." The leaflet for the rally concluded, "President Reagan, nobody is in charge. . . . AIDS IS EVERYBODY'S BUSINESS NOW."[9] In this early protest, ACT UP articulated the position that AIDS was a political problem because of the chronic underfunding of AIDS work and profound governmental resistance to sexually explicit AIDS prevention. The protest drew hundreds of people, seventeen of whom were arrested for disorderly conduct when they lay down in the street pretending to be dead.[10]

In conjunction with civil disobedience, ACT UP relied on the political and rhetorical power of art and the media. Artist-activists illustrated each ACT UP protest and infused AIDS education with provocative images and graphic design. Ann Northrop, a longtime ACT UP member who joined the group after working for television networks for two decades, argued that ACT UP's "actions were planned specifically to be dramatic, to get media attention."[11] In ACT UP, politics and art intermingled, giving way to an aesthetic and structural critique of local and national governments as well as pharmaceutical companies.[12]

A desire for sexual liberation also spurred ACT UP's political agenda of ending the AIDS crisis. Most members of ACT UP refused the idea that AIDS spelled the end of gay sex; instead, they embraced a radical sexual politics where sex could be safe and healthy. Using language very similar to that employed by Callen and Berkowitz in *How to Have Sex in an Epidemic*, ACT UP member Richard Deagle recounted that "it was a political act to fuck with rubbers. The whole thing was — there was this whole idea — the epidemic stops with me. The government's not going to take care of us, we have to take care of ourselves."[13] Other ACT UP activists talked about what it was like to find lovers, of both the same sex and the opposite sex, at meetings and protests. Lesbians and gay men became lovers, and many same-sex couples also began and ended their relationships at ACT UP meetings. Filmmaker Jean Carlomusto recalled that fellow filmmaker Gregg Bordowitz slept with all the women Carlomusto was attracted to and that "men were having sex with men, the women were having sex with women, men and women were having sex with each other."[14] For many, these sexual liaisons served as a place to practice safe sex. Peter Staley remembered that "very quickly in ACT UP it became very PC to sleep with somebody who was positive. To, as a way of saying I'm not afraid of this, that safe sex works — it's a political statement. And God bless 'em! Because I was dying to get back into the ball game and all of a sudden I was in high demand and it was just fabulous."[15]

ACT UP's structure as a coalition mirrored its protest style and sexual energy. A wide range of AIDS activists, "united in anger," came together under the name ACT UP. When ACT UP started in 1987, it had six separate committees: Issues, charged with accumulating information about AIDS; Actions, which planned protests; Fundraising; Outreach; Media; and Co-ordinating, the group that served as a kind of steering committee for ACT UP and approved expenditures. By the end of 1988, just over a year later, the number of committees had more than doubled to include various constituencies and issues.[16] Within months of one another in early 1988, four new committees formed that concretized what it meant for ACT UP to work on "issues" and "actions." With a desire to accumulate information, a group of activists committed to pushing for the development of AIDS drugs formed under the name Treatment and Data Committee (T&D). T&D members reasoned that pushing for more treatment and empowering people with AIDS would effect change in treatment options. To increase the possibilities for action, several other committees worked to expand the definition of treatment access to include universal health care and equity in the provision of social services. The Majority Action Committee (MAC) and the Women's Caucus not only focused on the particular needs of people of color (the "majority" of people who had AIDS) and women, but their members also believed that the best way to do this was to connect a struggle for treatment with prevention efforts. Each group focused on the racism and sexism that suffused not only the state's and the medical establishment's responses to AIDS but also ACT UP itself. In addition to MAC and the Women's Caucus, the Housing Committee formed to argue that for treatment activism to be effective for the wide range of people affected by AIDS, it had to include more than a struggle for AIDS drugs; the group also had to agitate for more social services for poor people, most notably housing and health care. In the beginning, these contingents struck a balance between critiquing one another's work and participating in each other's protests.

Drugs into Bodies: The Treatment and Data Committee

T&D claimed, first and foremost, that people with AIDS needed more drugs to treat illnesses associated with AIDS.[17] In 1987 when ACT UP began, only one drug, azidothymidine (AZT), created by research scientists at Burroughs Wellcome, had received federal approval and was in use by doctors treating people with AIDS. T&D members implored the federal government and the pharmaceutical industry to research and produce more treatment options. To underscore their demands, T&D organized protests at key institutions in the medical establishment, including holding die-ins at pharmaceutical headquarters, splattering blood in front of the FDA, and occupying the National Institutes of Health.

T&D followed up on these protests with regular, yet contentious, meetings with scientists and public health officials. T&D reasoned that only when people with AIDS controlled the course of their own treatment would scientists and drug companies change how they produced and subsequently tested drugs. Sociologist Steven Epstein argues that people with AIDS "press[ed] demands about what should be studied in the first place, how the protocols should be worded, and how the results should inform regulatory policy-making."[18] Over the course of the late 1980s and early 1990s, members of T&D became lay AIDS experts who effectively challenged the medical establishment's drug development protocol.

Despite a shared commitment to the idea that people with AIDS should control medical care, one of the first members of what would become T&D was a self-defined "Queens housewife" who seemed to have no direct connection to AIDS.[19] Iris Long, a research chemist who had never been politically active, attended her first ACT UP meeting in the spring of 1987 with the intention of finding a place to talk about developing treatment options for AIDS. Drawn to ACT UP through her work with Dr. Joseph Sonnabend (the physician who treated and worked with Michael Callen and Richard Berkowitz) and his Community Research Initiative, a project that allowed people with AIDS to take part in discussions about what drug trials to begin, Long spoke at the first ACT UP meeting she attended about her desire to investigate the drug approval process.[20] As a political novice, Long relied on her scientific knowledge to shape her evolving political awareness. In time she came to understand that political change was the only way to create more treatment options. In a 2003 interview, Long recounted, "[People in ACT UP] had to put pressure on the FDA and change the FDA — how they did business, because the drug development system was just taking too long. There was too much bureaucracy. Trials couldn't be done, because of the FDA. Drugs couldn't be approved and gotten by the public or whatever because of this long process."[21]

About half a dozen people joined Long in her scientific democracy project. David Kirschenbaum — an architecture student at Pratt Institute who had arrived in New York after leaving Case Western Reserve University in Ohio, where he majored in biomedical engineering — participated by collecting and processing data about various drug trials.[22] With the help of another early committee member, David Barr, who worked at Lambda Legal Defense Fund, T&D filed Freedom of Information Act requests with the FDA and the National Institute of Allergies and Infectious Diseases (NIAID), the two government agencies working directly on drug development and authorization, to ensure the release of information about how drug trials functioned, including the racial and gender breakdown of test subjects.[23] This early action provided T&D with the kind of information that provided justification for its subsequent intervention in how drug trials were run.

Soon thereafter, Jim Eigo, who had been active in anti-Vietnam politics as a high school student in Philadelphia and, after college, was an activist in Central American solidarity work in New York, joined T&D and became Long's "guy Friday."[24] Eigo remembered that ACT UP was "the first intensive political work" he did that "was rooted in the gay community."[25] As an HIV-negative gay man, he was drawn specifically to T&D because he understood that people with AIDS needed to be directly involved in their own treatment. "But, even those of us in the group who were not HIV-positive, follow[ed] that lead and wound up putting our bodies on the line, in some way — whether it was being arrested or in other ways. . . . I have to say, at the time, most of the people who met in that room, had come to a point where grief was not enough. They were angry, and in that anger they were quite prepared to shut down the whole city, if need be."[26]

Over the course of the first few months of T&D's existence, HIV-positive men became central players in the group. Mark Harrington, an openly gay white man who arrived in New York after graduating from Harvard, joined ACT UP in 1988, got arrested at his first protest, and almost immediately began planning major demonstrations to call for more treatment options.[27] Harrington took to treatment activism even though he had never before been politically active, in part because he assumed, but did not know if, he was HIV-positive (Harrington resisted getting tested until the 1990s). Harrington's perceived HIV status drew him to people, including Sonnabend, who were developing a community-based medical response to AIDS. Working alongside a doctor who empowered his patients to think about their own care, Harrington began to imagine how people with AIDS could be involved in the development of AIDS research, a belief that would become central to T&D's work.[28]

Peter Staley, a closeted Wall Street trader, joined ACT UP and T&D after Harrington. Staley, a white man from a wealthy family, came to ACT UP after receiving a positive HIV test result in 1985. He had first gone to a support group at GMHC but found the experience less than satisfying. "I was building up a lot of anger," Staley recalled, "and I really felt that the way this was going to break politically was the expression of that anger in a very activist way."[29] Within a year, Staley had come out to his employer,

J. P. Morgan; left his job because he was too sick to work; and become a regular participant in ACT UP, first as a member of the fundraising committee, then in T&D, where he was dedicated to "access to drugs and . . . a much quicker approval process."[30]

The mix of people teaching and learning the science of drug treatment, coupled with the accumulation of data on what was being tested and on whom, created the basis for action. Two nearly simultaneous actions — one a scientific intervention, the other a protest, both of which came to fruition only a few months after T&D began meeting — sent these individuals and the larger membership of ACT UP on a course that literally changed how prescription drugs got to people with AIDS. In 1988, emboldened by his scientific education from people like Long and Kirschenbaum, Jim Eigo wrote a letter to Anthony Fauci, the head of NIAID, recommending a new way of testing the effectiveness of AIDS drugs. Calling the proposal "parallel trials," Eigo suggested that the federal agency develop a supplement to standard drug trials that tested the efficacy of treatment. Eigo recommended that researchers have access to a "parallel" trial where people who did not qualify for official inclusion in a particular trial, because of other drugs they were taking or because they were too sick, were still able to take the drug. Researchers could then access the parallel results when deciding how and if to continue the drug's development.[31]

As the proposal made its way through NIAID, the entire membership of ACT UP planned a protest that served as a catalyst for new action. Recognizing the power direct action played in producing political change, several T&D members began conversations with people in the Actions Committee of ACT UP to develop a protest that punctuated the work of T&D. In their accounts of the initial conversation, David Barr, a T&D member, and Gregg Bordowitz, an Actions Committee member, recalled that discussion centered around two related ideas: the need for an action that would unify the members of ACT UP New York and one that would serve as a national protest that all the chapters of ACT UP could join.[32] Unlike previous protests about governmental actions that took place at the White House or the Congress, Barr and Bordowitz pushed to hold the protest at the FDA, the agency that oversaw the drug trials run by pharmaceutical researchers. In his account of the lead-up to the FDA action, Bordowitz explained that activists from other parts of the country had to be convinced that the FDA should be the target, but that once that happened, it made "the AIDS activist movement significant, and singular, and directly address[ed] the

THE GOVERNMENT HAS BLOOD ON ITS HANDS

ONE AIDS DEATH EVERY HALF HOUR

5.1 | The Government Has Blood on Its Hands. Gran Fury Collection, Manuscripts and Archives Division, The New York Public Library, Astor, Lenox and Tilden Foundations.

issues that were specific to us. [It] demanded a new kind of thinking, a savvier notion of what the target should be, a savvier way of dealing with the media."[33] They began by building a consensus for the protest among ACT UP New York members, providing them with an "FDA Handbook," written by Jim Eigo and Mark Harrington, that detailed the role of the FDA in AIDS treatment.

The first FDA protest, which came to be known as "Seize Control of the FDA," took place on October 11, 1988. More than 1,500 protesters from across the country descended upon the FDA offices in Rockville, Maryland, just outside Washington, D.C., to demand that the agency speed up the discovery of drugs to treat AIDS and that people with AIDS be able to play a role in that process.[34] The protesters, with contingents from MAC and the Women's Caucus, creatively articulated their demands by covering the building that housed the FDA with posters, including one that read, "The Government Has Blood on Its Hands" (ill. 5.1). Almost 200 people were arrested in the daylong protest.

By all accounts, the protest was hugely successful. Within two weeks of the FDA protest, the agency changed its regulations to allow for a speeded-up drug evaluation process.[35] Seven months later, Fauci acceded to the recommendations made by Eigo about parallel trails. Fauci renamed the idea "parallel track" and implemented it. Eigo recalled that Fauci adopted the proposal because "we were able to find a great need, narrow our focus, articulate it, through the people who were working intensively in the area of drugs and then . . . back it up through the people in ACT UP, who just came en masse . . . and put their bodies on the line."[36]

The parallel track victory exposed a related problem, however; the drug trials were not including the range of people with AIDS. Building on data collected from the Freedom of Information requests about drug trials, David Kirschenbaum documented the consistent exclusion of people of color and women from drug protocols because some scientists feared that their presence in the trials would skew the data.[37] Eigo used this information to focus his attention on the state of AIDS clinical trials and communities of color. In April 1989, Eigo indicated that only 9 percent of the participants in New York City's AIDS Program trials were black, while they accounted for 33 percent of the city's AIDS cases.[38] Eigo knew that drug trials provided a place where drugs would get into bodies, but he worried that too few people of color with AIDS were included, either because they were considered too sick for inclusion in the study or because they lacked access to doctors designing the trials.[39] Eigo hoped to work with MAC, which pushed for solutions that connected treatment, equal access, and prevention to diversify protocols and provide drugs for all people with AIDS.

Not all the members of T&D followed Eigo and Kirshenbaum in their efforts to look at the limits of drug trials. After the FDA protest, several members redoubled their efforts to work exclusively on speeding up drug development, and in the process they became more and more scientifically oriented. Mark Harrington created a system of "drug buddies," where T&D members were charged with "call[ing] the investigator, if there was one, and try[ing] to find the literature about it, and maybe writ[ing] a little report about it, and bring[ing] it to the group, to see what could happen next."[40] T&D would then report this information to the general ACT UP membership. But the reports did not always serve the purpose of providing people with AIDS with knowledge about available drugs. Andrew Vélez, an ACT UP member who facilitated Monday night meetings, remembered how he felt when listening to T&D accounts:

> T&D people were not good at representing themselves and giving the information to the floor. So, there was this sort of white boy, exclusive club about it. They really did themselves an injustice to a certain extent, and that is not to say there wasn't arrogance, there was. But, often — like, when I would be facilitating a meeting, I would say to them, "Speak slowly and clearly." Just a simple thing like that. It was so difficult to get people to do that when they were talking to the floor.

And then, you would get these very bright guys in Treatment and Data who would use phrases and terminology that most of the floor didn't know what any of it meant — technical terms — and it would confuse and then ultimately anger, and just cause all kinds of bad stuff.[41]

Even though T&D members were unable to accomplish it, the committee members had begun their work with the idea that science had to be democratized and made more participatory. Eigo argued that several treatment activists, himself included, ultimately wanted to push for universal health care.[42] This participatory and expansive model existed in direct opposition to the idea that scientific studies were the exclusive purview of scientists. T&D members assumed a space next to doctors and scientists and built on the idea, first heralded by people like Michael Callen and Richard Berkowitz, that people with AIDS had something to say. The T&D model had significant political implications in terms of how it redefined the meaning of how the government protected the health of its citizens.

At the same time that T&D agitated for change at the FDA, NIAID, and pharmaceutical companies, other ACT UP members developed alternative arguments for thinking about ending AIDS that did not rely so exclusively on the language of science, even when in service to a larger political project. Claiming that treatment development, even when supported with direct action, would be insufficient to end the AIDS crisis for all people affected by it, three committees came to symbolize this alternative approach: MAC, the Women's Caucus, and the Housing Committee. While they had different foci, the ACT UP members who joined these contingents supported the provision of universal health care and basic social services, particularly housing and drug treatment, to all people with AIDS as a way to ensure health. This broader definition of treatment as a way to end AIDS allowed advocates to claim that the only way to get drugs into bodies was to deal with structural inequalities that made it difficult for certain people to access health care more generally.

"Getting the Bodies . . . Access to Health Care":
The Majority Action Committee

MAC began, according to one of its first members, Jose Fidelino, a Filipino gay man who grew up in Kansas, as a place where people of color "wouldn't feel alone" in what was otherwise a very white group.[43] It quickly became a committee dedicated to protesting the racism members experienced in the medical and social service establishments as well as within ACT UP itself. The founding members of MAC took their name "Majority Action" to highlight the fact that people of color were the majority of people with AIDS worldwide, even though they were regularly referred to as "minorities." Emboldened by a national AIDS protest action in the spring of 1988 and concerned that most white AIDS activists discounted the specific needs of people of color, several gay men of color and a few straight white women came together in MAC to educate "all minority communities" about the growing AIDS crisis and provide its members with a place to discuss the unique problems faced by communities of color. MAC also worked directly with other AIDS-related organizations to foster change for, and in, communities of color.[44]

From its inception, MAC connected AIDS in communities of color to long-standing manifestations of inequality in the United States. In its 1988 statement of purpose, MAC called for "national action against the holocaust, which is caused not only by illness but by homophobia, racism, sexism, indifference and profiteering at the expense of the dying."[45] Racism encouraged the spread of AIDS, not because HIV knew that a given body was black, the other white, but, rather, because the social, economic, and political realities of life in 1980s America made certain groups more susceptible to infection. For MAC, solutions needed to address the relationship among AIDS, racism, and economic discrimination.[46]

The position that more than a virus caused the rapid spread of AIDS in communities of color became quite clear in protests initiated at the CDC's Second National Conference on AIDS in Minority Communities, held in Washington, D.C., in August 1988. More than 2,000 people registered for the three-day conference, attending workshops and discussions each day. The CDC leadership intended the conference to show the agency's concern for the increasing AIDS problem in minority communities. But MAC members in attendance questioned the efficacy of the event. After they returned from Washington, members of the committee wrote a lengthy response to the event targeted to the larger membership of ACT UP. MAC's concerns centered on the connection between treatment and prevention, and the reallocation, not increase, proposed to pay for services for people of color. The critique began by explaining that for the spread of AIDS to be controlled in minority communities, prevention and treatment issues needed to be on equal footing. "By [the federal government's] focus only on prevention, the many persons of color already infected with HIV are rendered invisible, or seen only as vectors of transmission to the uninfected — then left for dead. . . . In separating 'prevention' issues from treatment issues, an effective approach to prevention of HIV transmission in communities of color simply cannot be formulated."[47]

These were some of the clearest attacks on the false dichotomy between funding for treatment and funding for prevention. MAC vehemently rejected the idea that the available funding could be reshuffled. Ultimately, in MAC's analysis, change would occur only if there was a massive increase in the resources allocated for communities of color. "Future conferences must be designed so that all of us can, in the highest sense, come together to work in developing the most effective responses to the AIDS crisis for all of our communities."[48]

Back in New York, MAC worked toward these goals in several ways. First, members committed themselves to sustaining community outreach, actions, they acknowledged, that did not put direct action into practice in the same way as protests.[49] They went to churches in Harlem to talk about the work of ACT UP, according to member Kendall Thomas, a black gay man who taught at Columbia Law School, to commemorate "a day of solidarity and remembrance in churches in New York City — predominantly black and Latino churches in New York City — for a day of solidarity and remembrance of people who were living with and/or people who had died from HIV/AIDS."[50] In addition to church outreach, MAC organized alongside organizations such as the Brooklyn AIDS Task Force to hold "community speakouts" to talk with people who did not attend Monday night meetings.[51] In addition to talking to non–ACT UP members, MAC also made sure that people of color in ACT UP attended protests and AIDS conferences.[52]

Beyond its critique of a singular focus on treatment activism, MAC expanded its demands to include the provision of basic health care for all people with AIDS. Fidelino remembered that the goals of MAC members were very different from those of people in T&D:

Everyone was talking about empowerment, and how good it felt. But [MAC] took the position that asking the government to take care of you is not empowerment. And that's what a lot of people in ACT UP, that was their goal. They . . . wanted the government to take care of them, as the government takes care of any suburban white person. Which is, I suppose, equality, of a sort. But it's not empowerment. And it was just odd, where a lot of people were focusing on getting the drugs into bodies. And we were focused on getting the bodies just primary access to health care.[53]

MAC was the first sector of ACT UP to question the need to rely solely on direct action as the way to end the AIDS crisis. In ways that were reminiscent of AIDS workers in San Francisco's TWAATF, MAC members tried to blur the line between service and activism by reasoning that in some locations, providing information was a form of profound direct action.

"Women Say No to Cosmo": The Women's Caucus

Concurrent with the work that MAC did, women in ACT UP also considered the benefits of forming their own caucus. The idea began at "dyke dinners," where many of the lesbians in ACT UP gathered to talk about their activism. Lesbians took a leading role in the Women's Caucus from the very beginning. "The lesbians within ACT UP were very strong and vocal about not wanting to be made invisible once again," remembered videomaker Jean Carlomusto.[54] At least initially, almost all the women in the caucus were white, but that did not prevent them from acknowledging that the overwhelming majority of women with AIDS were women of color.

The new caucus gave women space to think about activist projects they could undertake in addition to the protests they regularly attended as ACT UP members. Building on their experiences in women's health, most particularly reproductive rights struggles in the 1970s and 1980s, where they learned firsthand that health issues had profound social and political implications, caucus members embraced the need to find political solutions to the particular medical problems women with AIDS faced. Marion Banzhaf, who joined ACT UP after more than a decade of work in radical politics and women's and lesbian health, remembered that the Women's Caucus wanted "to share information about the women's movement, and how other people had actually forced the FDA to do certain things before [ACT UP] had."[55] Maxine Wolfe, an academic at the City University of New York whose long history of political activism led her to be one of the most active women in ACT UP, refused to separate medicine from politics. Wolfe argued that only activism that targeted institutional power would benefit most women with AIDS.[56]

The women's first target for direct action, even before the official formation of the caucus, was *Cosmopolitan* magazine. In January 1988, the magazine published an article titled "Reassuring News about AIDS: A Doctor Tells Why You May Not be at Risk," written by psychiatrist Robert Gould. As the title indicated, the article reported that AIDS posed no threat to heterosexual women. Not surprisingly, a discussion of Gould's piece ensued at the next dyke dinner, where the attendees decided to plan a protest, much in the vein of the kinds of protests feminists had organized in the 1970s.[57] Citing the popular media as a site of contention and power, the caucus took over the offices of *Cosmopolitan* and forced the magazine to retract the article.[58]

While the *Cosmopolitan* protest marked the first Women's Caucus action, it was only partially representative of the work the caucus undertook. Over the next several years, the caucus increasingly addressed the intersection of racism and sexism in the AIDS epidemic. In part, this evolution occurred because more women of color joined ACT UP, but it also happened because the original members, white lesbians all, chose to respond to the racial reality of the evolving epidemic as it affected women. One of the new members of ACT UP, Katrina Haslip, was an HIV-positive, African American, Muslim woman who had served prison time in the Bedford Hills Women's Correctional Facility. Haslip arrived at her first ACT UP meeting having created the AIDS Counseling and Education program in 1988 in Bedford Hills. The program counseled incarcerated HIV-positive women on how to survive prison, practice safer sex, and cope with AIDS after release.

The influx of HIV-positive women into ACT UP, most of whom were also women of color, pushed the Women's Caucus to design actions and advocacy projects that dealt with the intersection of race and gender. Two projects symbolized this effort: the campaign to expand the CDC's definition of AIDS to include women, and the publishing of *Women, AIDS, and Activism*. Both projects had explicit political and scientific implications and underscored that the Women's Caucus adopted a strategy to integrate scientifically based activism with direct action to accomplish change.

The Women's Caucus decision to target the CDC grew out of the fact that AIDS affected women differently than it did men, a situation that the caucus members documented and publicized. While both men and women could be infected with HIV in similar ways — through unprotected vaginal or anal intercourse or intravenous drug use — the more advanced stages of AIDS did not manifest themselves the same way in women as in men. For men, full-blown AIDS often caused KS, while women experienced bacterial pneumonia, pelvic inflammatory disease, and cervical cancer. This meant that even as the number of women with HIV increased during the 1980s, very few were actually diagnosed with AIDS and instead were categorized as having the less advanced ARC. In recounting her work on the CDC campaign, Maxine Wolfe pointed out that "many women had been dying of bacterial pneumonia, which was ridiculous, like it was an epidemic of bacterial pneumonia. But, it wasn't. It was HIV, really."[59]

The economic and political implications of this medical ignorance became clear when caucus members began to work with women outside ACT UP who advocated for women with AIDS to receive Social Security benefits. Functioning as an advocate for her client at a federal poverty center in the Hell's Kitchen neighborhood of New York City, Terry McGovern, a lesbian lawyer, found that her female clients, many of whom had been referred to her by the Women's Prison Association, were regularly diagnosed with either HIV or ARC, but not AIDS, because their doctors used the CDC's definition of the disease. In the process, these women effectively were denied the Social Security benefits that men with AIDS had fought hard to secure, and won, in the late 1980s. In 1989, McGovern approached ACT UP to organize an action that would call attention to the problem.[60]

Within less than a year, ACT UP, working with McGovern, had organized several protests, enlisted the support of ACT UP women's caucuses from around the country, and filed a lawsuit against the Social Security Administration for relying on the CDC's overly limited definition of AIDS.[61] At a protest held on October 2, 1990, to coincide with McGovern filing the lawsuit, 200 activists participated in the action targeting the HHS office that ultimately oversaw the distribution of Social Security benefits.[62] Women with AIDS, who were actually being denied benefits, not only participated in the protests but also became the experts their fellow protesters listened to. In describing the events that took place in Washington, Jean Carlomusto explained:

Whenever a woman was going to speak about her case we sounded these horns and everybody sat down and shut up. And it was really

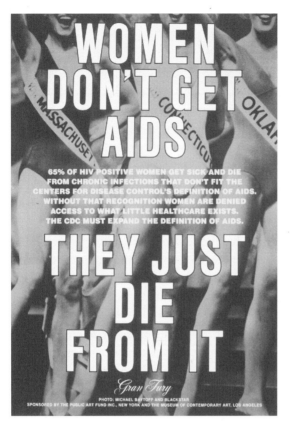

5.2 | Women Don't Get
AIDS. Gran Fury Collection,
Manuscripts and Archives
Division, The New York
Public Library, Astor, Lenox
and Tilden Foundations.

notable, because before that we were all chanting, we were march-
ing and chanting. "How many more have to die before you say they
qualify," was one of the chants I remember. But when that horn went
off, everybody shut up. And I remember specifically when Iris De
La Cruz [one of the women of color who joined ACT UP] took the
megaphone and spoke about not being able to get health care. She said
her physician didn't take food stamps. Clearly women — their needs
weren't being met.[63]

McGovern concurred with Carlomusto, reporting that the protest and lawsuit forced people to "see positive women as leaders."[64]

As was often the case with ACT UP protests, artists/activists provided
stunning illustrations to accompany the chants. For the CDC battle, Gran
Fury, the artists' collective that worked with ACT UP, designed a poster
that read, "Women Don't Get AIDS, They Just Die From It" (ill. 5.2). The

problem with the poster, however, was that its designers did not utilize a representation of women with AIDS or of the women engaged in ACT UP protests. Instead, underneath the text, an image of white beauty contestants appeared. This raised questions about the political implications of graphics produced to be visually arresting. Despite the contradictory representation, ACT UP protesters carried the poster at the Washington rally, and Gran Fury installed 100 copies, half in Spanish and half in English, at bus stops across New York City.[65]

After a battle with the government over the wording of the definition of AIDS, as well as an internal battle among caucus members about what a victory would look like, the CDC announced that it planned to change the definition of AIDS to include cervical cancer, tuberculosis, and a T-cell (the cells that help ward off infection) count below 200. The new definition provided for the inclusion not only of women but also of poor people and intravenous drug users, who were more likely also to have tuberculosis. Under the new model, the number of women with AIDS in the United States increased almost 50 percent.[66]

The CDC definition project, with its use of direct action and scientific knowledge accumulation, suggested that the Women's Caucus sometimes employed techniques similar to those of T&D in terms of dealing with government regulators, but the Women's Caucus did so in an environment where their political critique of science as a historically sexist enterprise remained central. It also provides evidence that gender difference did more than create schisms within ACT UP; it also produced projects that brought the membership together. Wolfe remembered the extent to which a significant number of ACT UP members joined in the CDC project. "There were gay men, there were women of color, straight women of color, lesbians of color. . . . It was every possible kind of person came together to work on that thing. . . . That's what was amazing about it."[67] McGovern confirmed Wolfe's account while acknowledging that some in T&D did not support the project: "There's a lot of men from ACT UP typing the papers at night, and there was a huge volunteer effort from within ACT UP, and not kind of the most known people."[68]

At the same time that it enacted its direct action strategy to change the CDC definition of AIDS and secure equitable Social Security benefits for women with AIDS, the Women's Caucus also published a book that became one of the most widely cited texts on the extent of U.S. feminist AIDS activism. In 1990, South End Press released *Women, AIDS, and Activism*, a book that documented the medical and political effects AIDS had on women and detailed U.S.-based feminist responses to AIDS. The culmination of a year's work, the project grew out of a series of teach-ins on women and AIDS held in 1989. It represented a sustained effort not only to talk about how the AIDS epidemic affected all women, across race, class, and sexual orientation, but also to prove that without a broader definition of AIDS — for both treatment and prevention — whole groups would be left without help. The preface spelled out the authors' intentions: "We realized that different questions needed to be asked, in order to establish future research priorities, to identify women's treatment issues, to make demands for change in the health care system, and to overcome the barriers to fighting HIV infection."[69]

The book's editors made interpretations of racism central to the text and the AIDS crisis. In her introductory essay to the section "Race, Women, and AIDS," Marion Banzhaf wrote, "The extent to which white people oppose racism will to a large extent determine how effective they will be in advocating for *all* people with AIDS."[70] The book employed a broad definition of race, including essays on African American women, Caribbean American women, Latinas, and Asian American women, and it also printed first-person reflections of some of the women with AIDS in ACT UP, including Iris De La Cruz, who reflected on her experience as a sex worker and a recovering drug addict. After articulating the issues faced by women with AIDS, the book collective argued for broad actions that would make women's health central to future AIDS activism.

The argument made by the book's writers echoed work by MAC as well as work by feminists of color who had written about the limits of white liberal feminism regarding issues of reproductive rights.[71] Just as choosing to have an abortion was a necessary but insufficient choice for poor women of all colors to make in dealing with their reproductive experiences, women in ACT UP argued that treatment and prevention designed for men, under the guise of being created for everyone, would not satisfy the needs of women. The book's claims also ran parallel to the budding feminist responses in the global South that saw economic equality as critical for securing gender equality, described in the preceding chapter. While there is no evidence that feminists in the United States and in the global South knew of one another's work, the simultaneity of their AIDS work and their parallel organizational/institutional approaches are worth noting. Feminists in various parts of the world were developing similar arguments that attended to politics and economics, instead of biology, as a way to make women healthier in the age of AIDS.

Demand Housing: The People with AIDS Housing Committee

Leading up to the FDA protest in October 1988, the first national ACT UP protest described earlier in the chapter, a group of HIV-positive and HIV-negative members of ACT UP New York decided to focus on the issue of homelessness and AIDS. Concerned about the unavailability of housing for people with AIDS — in 1987 only one institution, Bailey House, provided housing for people with AIDS, and it had fewer than twenty beds — the People with AIDS Housing Committee of ACT UP, known as the Housing Committee, formed to force the New York City government to provide sufficient housing for people with AIDS.

Two of the committee's first members, Eric Sawyer and Gedelia Braverman, both HIV-positive white gay men, discovered their interest in housing before joining ACT UP. Sawyer made a living renovating townhouses in Harlem. Sawyer's lover, Scott, began to get sick in 1984 and ultimately died of AIDS in 1986. At that point, Sawyer recalled, he became more conscious of the growing numbers of people with AIDS who were also homeless. Sawyer attended the first ACT UP meeting at the Gay and Lesbian Community Center, at the urging of Larry Kramer, but went with the intention of finding connections to work on housing for people with AIDS.[72]

Braverman came to ACT UP on a slightly different path. After taking time to mourn the loss of his lover in 1985, Braverman found himself at the 1987 Gay Pride Parade in New York City when ACT UP's float went by — a "quarantine camp," surrounded with barbed wire and marchers with masks and rubber gloves — and he said to himself, "That's where I need to be."[73] Braverman attended his first meeting and found himself drawn to the Housing Committee for two reasons: his lover had worked on housing issues, and Braverman had been hospitalized for complications from HIV and remembered seeing "abandoned young men, who really would have been homeless, if they hadn't come to the hospital."[74]

The Housing Committee's first action was a protest against Donald Trump, the real estate magnate who developed luxury housing in some of New York City's most expensive neighborhoods. In targeting Trump, the activists wanted to expose the tax breaks Trump received from the city as a luxury housing developer, and they demanded that the same kind of support be given to "independent housing" for people with AIDS. As was often the case with ACT UP, the particulars of the protests drew attention to the hypocrisy of ignoring AIDS. On the Friday after Thanksgiving in 1988, the busiest shopping day of the year, the Housing Committee occupied the lobby of the Trump Tower and shut down the intersection at the corner of Fifty-sixth Street and Fifth Avenue in New York's midtown. While no record exists of how many ACT UP members participated, Braverman remembered that many people showed up and helped make the event a success.[75]

In the aftermath of the Trump protest, ACT UP members interested in housing issues continued to develop their agenda. They took part in regular protests, all designed to receive as much media attention as possible. But they also moved beyond direct action. Charles King, a lawyer working at the Coalition for the Homeless; Keith Cylar, King's lover, who worked at the Minority AIDS Task Force; and Lei Chou, a gay art student, joined the Housing Committee, and, working with committee member Rich Jackman, a trained architect, the group began to explore the possibilities of actually creating housing for people with AIDS. The Housing Committee made direct connections with ACT UP members in MAC and the Women's Caucus. Sawyer defined it as the "social justice squad of ACT UP."[76]

So long as the work of the committee remained grounded in direct action, it received support from the larger membership. Lei Chou remembered, "The whole organization started addressing more hands-on delivery issues, rather than focusing just on treatment issues. And, I think Housing Caucus was one of the main pushes, in terms of really targeting agencies, and targeting specific policies, or lack thereof."[77] But targeting specific governmental institutions was one thing; trying to become a housing agency was another one entirely. The decision to pursue the production of housing as a social justice agenda did not receive full-throated support from the group's general membership. Sawyer reported that "ACT UP didn't want to do AIDS housing. . . . They didn't want paid staff. . . . We would come to the floor and tell people about our search for buildings or whatever, and there was a huge outcry of 'You can't have paid staff, you can't get governmental contracts. That's going to limit what we say. It's going to compromise our voice.'"[78]

The battle lines were quickly drawn between T&D and the Housing Committee. Gregg Gonsalves, an active member of T&D, argued, "You had these PWA's [people with AIDS] who were like, 'I don't want to die,

I want to get access to treatment.' Yes, housing and all these other things were important, but they were very mono-focused on, I've got to figure out how to stay alive. And, in a certain sense, maybe a lot of them were middle-class white guys who didn't have to deal with housing, prison issues or all these other issues. And in that sense, there's some sort of class anxieties, and other things that played out."[79] This hostility to housing manifested itself, in one example, when members of T&D asked that the first fifteen minutes of ACT UP meetings be spent sharing information about the latest clinical trials. Sawyer and King replied that in addition to discussions of drug protocols, "life-saving information about housing and access to social services and Medicaid cards [be discussed] as well, because if poor people didn't have a place to live, or didn't have a Medicaid card, and didn't have health insurance, they couldn't afford the drugs."[80]

In 1990, just two years after forming as an ACT UP committee, the Housing Committee split from the main group to become Housing Works, an agency that provided housing for people with AIDS. As an NGO, Housing Works could purchase buildings, receive city contracts, and provide services for people with AIDS. Although the Housing Works contingent was the first faction to leave ACT UP to form an agency where activist intentions and strategies could suffuse service delivery, the departure did not produce an internal disruption over losing a significant committee from ACT UP.

ACT UP's Coalition Begins to Fracture

At the same time that the Housing Committee broke off to form Housing Works, ACT UP experienced physical growth and political success. By January 1991, between 600 and 800 people regularly attended weekly ACT UP meetings.[81] The meetings became so large, ACT UP had to leave its home at the Gay and Lesbian Community Center in Greenwich Village for larger quarters at Cooper Union, where it utilized an auditorium that had been home to labor unions and radical politics dating from the middle of the nineteenth century. Nineteen ninety-one was also the year when treatment activists in T&D and feminist activists in the Women's Caucus began to make headway with the scientific establishment. For T&D, the inroads were defined by two events: the beginning of basic, yet extensive, scientific investigations into the ways HIV functioned in the body, and the creation of the Community Constituency Group (CCG), a community advisory board of people with AIDS that served as a check on the AIDS Clinical Trial Group, the governmental model for regulating drug trials instituted by the National Institutes of Health in 1987.[82] The Women's Caucus's progress was slower but significant. In January 1991, the CDC held the first National Women and HIV Conference in Washington, D.C., an event that the caucus had fought to establish for two years.[83]

Within a month, however, the successes of both contingents were put in jeopardy when ACT UP learned the particulars of a new drug trial identified as AIDS Clinical Trial Group 076. The trial protocol proposed testing the efficacy of AZT in limiting the spread of HIV from pregnant women to their unborn fetuses. As he had with hundreds of protocols over the course of three years, David Kirschenbaum, the data collector in T&D, studied the proposal and reported back to the larger membership what he saw as potential problems. The study, which was to be run, at least in part, in Newark, New Jersey, the city with one of the highest number of women with AIDS in the country, did not inform the women in the study that having a cesarean section significantly decreased the risk of passing HIV on to their newborns. It also only provided the drug to half the women, while the other half would receive a placebo. By detailing the study's problems to the membership, Kirschenbaum hoped to "give women information, so they could make their own choice."[84]

As was sometimes the case, not all the people in the general membership of ACT UP received the information well. A contingent from the Women's Caucus, including Maxine Wolfe, Tracy Morgan, and Heidi Dorow, denounced the trial. Wolfe rejected the trial's focus on babies and not women, reasoning that "the transmission from women to kids was minuscule." But since the trial was organized around "saving babies," Wolfe argued it justified hurting women.[85] Unlike Kirschenbaum, who wanted to modify the trial to inform women more thoroughly of their options, the Women's Caucus members believed the trial needed to be rejected outright because researchers failed to fully inform the female test subjects that AZT might cause birth defects. Carrie Wofford, a reporter covering the story for the gay magazine *Outweek*, supported the caucus's position, comparing the trial to the "Tuskegee syphilis trials" and claiming that 076 was "unnecessary and unethical."[86]

The women rejecting the trial found themselves in opposition not only to members of T&D but also to a racially and gender diverse group of activists who saw potential in the 076 trial. Women's Caucus member Marion Banzhaf and MAC member Andrew Vélez supported the trial, albeit in a modified form, as an opportunity to gain women of color access to drugs.[87] Banzhaf and Vélez represented their positions as empowering the women who consensually took part in the trial because they actively wanted to be part of a protocol that could prevent perinatal transmission. In addition to Banzhaf and Vélez, Nima Eshghi, a member of ACT UP Seattle, who participated in an activism conference for people of color held in New York as the 076 protocol came to light, reported,

> Women of color AIDS activists — some from within ACT UP and some from other AIDS activist organizations — came together and developed an analysis of the 076 "situation," and of ACT UP strategies in general. What we decided collectively was that the voices of women of color have, for the most part, been marginalized within ACT UP. . . . While some might define only acts of civil disobedience as truly radical action — we believe providing access to information and an opportunity to dialogue is equally radical and sometimes more appropriate for certain situations.[88]

The debate came to a head when a group of ACT UP protesters, including Wolfe and Morgan as well as several male members of ACT UP, orchestrated a disruption at the CCG meeting on the 076 protocol held in Washington.[89] CCG arranged the session so that representatives from the affected communities could question the researchers and learn more about the trial. As an attendee at the session, David Barr, an original member of T&D who worked on the Freedom of Information requests on trial inclusion, reported that the protest quickly escalated, with members of ACT UP shouting down the researchers, one of whom was a black female doctor from New York City. Many of the CCG members, a substantial number of whom were people of color, felt silenced.[90] "The conversation then switched from the design of the trial to that ACT UP's action wound up being racist," Marion Banzhaf recalled, "because here was this group of largely people of color; and they didn't let them hear the information and make up their minds for themselves."[91] For Lei Chou, who had been active on housing problems, the events surrounding the 076 trial brought preexisting and submerged gender and racial tensions in the organization to the fore.

I think the whole trial (076) touched on so many hot button issues — feminism, racial inequalities. Everything was just kind of tied up in a knot, with that trial. There was just so many difference — people were screaming and yelling and crying, fighting over it. It was so emotional, and I think, for ACT UP, particularly, being a primarily white organization that race was a very touchy issue — it's always been kind of touchy — when we were out there, screaming for attention about AIDS, all you see are white faces which given the impression that we're speaking for everybody, but at the same time, the fact of the matter is, we don't have that kind of participation from people of color communities.[92]

With ACT UP members locked in a battle over the ethics of the trial, the tactics necessary to change the way the scientific establishment functioned, and how to determine how to empower all people with AIDS, but particularly women and men of color, it was difficult to imagine how the group would return to the functioning coalition that earlier had produced successful actions and advocacy. In an attempt to "get rid of that tension" created in the aftermath of the 076 imbroglio, Maxine Wolfe proposed a six-month moratorium on all ACT UP negotiations with the federal government, an idea that originated with fellow Women's Caucus member Tracy Morgan. While Wolfe suggested that she did not actually support the proposal, she brought it to the floor nonetheless to try to clear the air and give the ACT UP membership a chance to participate, belatedly, in an action that had involved only a handful of members.[93] The floor, including Wolfe, voted down the proposal.

Two months after the failed vote on the moratorium, Peter Staley, a leader of T&D, began to articulate the idea that treatment activists, whom he equated with HIV-positive people, needed to leave ACT UP to form their own organization. In a speech titled "ACT UP: Past, Present and Future" that Staley delivered at a treatment conference held in San Francisco, he argued,

> We deserve praise . . . for our throwing it in people's faces the fact
> that sexism and racism are murdering women and people of color
> as surely as any virus. . . . But a rift has occurred between those of us
> who joined as a matter of survival and those who joined seeking a
> power base from which their social activism could be advanced. The
> common denominator that was missing was the crisis mentality — the

view that time was our ultimate enemy. Defeating racism, sexism, and homophobia will take decades at best, and become a never-ending fight at worst. Successfully countering the anti-abortionists of America's imperialist tendencies will take more time than people with AIDS have.[94]

No record of responses to Staley's speech by either MAC or the Women's Caucus exists, but we do know how ACT UP against the New World Order, a group that formed in response to the Gulf War being waged in the Middle East, rebutted Staley. Members of the newly formed caucus, at least one of whom, George Carter, was also a member of T&D, disagreed with Staley's comments on "crisis mentality." They argued that he had created a false dichotomy between people in T&D and ACT UP who wanted to address the social problems of racism, sexism, and homophobia.

> Peter can't even conceive that some of us on this "side" of the disagreement are in fact ourselves people with HIV and AIDS. . . . Given our daily commitment and personal ties to AIDS work and PWAs, it is grossly unfair to charge that any of us have less of a "crisis mentality" about fighting AIDS than others in ACT UP. . . . We've always advocated a primary focus on specific AIDS survival issues — but survival for all PWAs, not just, for instance, white gay men with health insurance, as crucial as their/our battles are.[95]

Echoing the work of Housing Committee members Eric Sawyer and Gedelia Braverman, ACT UP against the New World Order voiced the idea that people needed to analyze the "root problem" to achieve "both short-term victories for PWAs and long-term changes that will benefit the millions of PWAs who will be diagnosed in future years." In so doing, ACT UP against the New World Order returned to the arguments ACT UP New York supported at the Montreal conference two years earlier.[96]

The rift between people who wanted to focus exclusively on treatment activism and those who saw a need to also fight for "survival issues" or "social justice," however, was simply too great. By the end of 1991, treatment activists in T&D agreed that it was time to break from ACT UP. In January 1992, several of the original T&D members, including Peter Staley and Mark Harrington, but not Jim Eigo, Iris Long, or David Kirschenbaum, left to form a new and independent community-based group for treatment activism, called Treatment Action Group.[97] Staley led the exit so that he could take part in "something that was administratively a little more traditional and structured so that it could handle its growth and that it could grow, and something that also continued to do both inside and outside work, that was willing to do a lot of traditional lobbying, as it were."[98]

Unlike the departure of Housing Committee members a year and half earlier, the T&D exodus hampered the larger ACT UP membership's ability to continue its efforts. Several key members left at this point, including Jean Carlomusto, who was active in both the Women's Caucus and video production. Describing the fighting as "endless," Carlomusto concluded, "People became impatient. . . . So they started attacking people on either end. The movement just began to eat itself up from the inside, and that was painful to watch."[99] Moises Agosto, an HIV-positive Latino man who had worked on multiple committees, including T&D and the Latino Caucus, became disenchanted with both T&D and ACT UP. "The majority of people I looked up to [in T&D] . . . were not really that much into doing work related to access to care and treatment for disenfranchised communities."[100] In 1992, Agosto took his skills as a treatment activist with him to work with the National Latino Lesbian and Gay Organization, noting that he "couldn't be radical just for the sake of being radical."[101]

The effect on ACT UP's agenda was dramatic, especially for the people who stayed in ACT UP. Ann Northrop, who continued to attend ACT UP meetings after the treatment activists split off, argued that the coalition's splintering "diluted the ability or willingness to demand universal health care."[102] Jim Eigo confirmed Northrop's account. As one of the original members of T&D, by the mid-1990s Eigo claimed, "The biggest disappointment of my life was . . . we could [not] hold ACT UP together, to do it just a bit longer or somewhat longer. A lot of us who were working in drug approval, wanted to push the fight to universal health care and to reforming things like Social Security, Medicare and Medicaid."[103]

Treatment Activism after the ACT UP Split

Treatment activism continued after ACT UP, as an organization, began to wane after 1992, but it did so in a space without the critique of science and power that had defined ACT UP's work during the 1980s. Treatment activists continued to demand that drug companies develop drugs and that the federal government test treatments and get them to market, but they did so without the rhetoric of opposition to the scientific establishment. In this shift, treatment activists went from direct action to boardroom negotiations and encouraged drug companies to produce new drugs with the stamp of community approval.

The splintering of ACT UP directly benefited the pharmaceutical industry that had once been the target of the group's massive direct action tactics. Policy analysts Peter Arno and Karyn Feiden argue that by the early 1990s there was "a curious overlapping of interests" between the pharmaceutical industry and treatment activists.[104] Peter Staley identified this shared interest as directly related to profit, in the form of drugs for people with AIDS and money for drug manufacturers. "[Pharmaceutical companies] were all supportive of what the AIDS activists were doing, obviously. In fact, AZT was approved quicker than any drug in history. And all the subsequent AIDS drugs were approved very fast as well, largely because of pressure of AIDS activism. So they stood to benefit greatly."[105]

Interventions by Treatment Action Group made it possible for drug companies to accede to activists' demands and, in the process, appear as though they were building community support while they were, at the same time, maximizing their profits. In 1993, one public relations executive working for big pharmaceutical companies went so far as to explain,

> The battle cry has changed. A few years ago, AIDS activists were at war and pharmaceutical companies were the enemies. Activists marched, picketed and protested to be heard. . . . Today, demonstrations still occur, but more sporadically. Now, the boardroom has taken precedence as the forum for working out differences. Clearly, activists and pharmaceutical companies have come full circle. Companies are more open; activists are more business-like in their approach. As a result, cooperative, productive relationships have taken root and, in some instances, flourished.[106]

One of the agreed-upon demands made through the "cooperative, productive relationships" was a policy of "conditional approval," which allowed drugs that showed promise in certain kinds of tests to be approved on the basis of future studies. If the treatment failed to be safe and effective when drug companies performed follow-up studies after the drug was in widespread use, then the FDA could revoke the license. In so doing, AIDS activists provided pharmaceutical companies with new mechanisms for increasing profits. Sociologist Steven Epstein argues that conditional approval "was designed with the explicit goal of enlisting the pharmaceutical companies by giving them a chance to do what they liked best: earn profits." He concludes that it "was quickly endorsed by the deregulation lobby and by the Quayle Competitiveness Council, the vice-president's commission dedicated to the elimination of regulatory barriers for US industries."[107]

At the same time that treatment activists fought the medical wing of the government to change the mechanism through which drugs got to the market, the U.S. pharmaceutical industry lobbied the arm of the government overseeing trade regulations to guarantee its position as the sole provider of those same drugs. In 1986, a year before the formation of ACT UP, the Reagan administration entered into new negotiations for the General Agreement on Tariffs and Trade (GATT), the international document that had regulated multilateral trade since 1947.[108] According to economic policy analyst Charan Devereaux, the U.S. government pursued, for the first time, a clause intended to secure intellectual property protection for a range of U.S. companies. The government made this decision after consultation with the chairman of Pfizer Pharmaceuticals, Edmund Pratt, and the chairman of IBM, John Opel.[109] To help in the regulation effort, Reagan's U.S. trade representative, Clayton Yeutter, appointed Harvey Bale, a former research chemist, as the first assistant U.S. trade representative for international investment and intellectual property.[110] Bale "became the point man for getting [intellectual property] into the [GATT] talks."[111]

Over the next five years, a time period completely coincidental with the ACT UP story this chapter has narrated, the U.S. government secured, albeit in fits and starts, the rights that the pharmaceutical industry sought in the form of the Trade-Related Intellectual Property Rights Agreement. The agreement required all the countries participating in the GATT negotiations, fifty of whom did not recognize patent protection for medicine in 1986, to acknowledge "patents, trademarks, and copyrights" for a range of products from computer programs to films to medicine.[112]

While the intellectual property negotiations began during the Reagan administration and continued through George H. W. Bush's term, the William J. Clinton administration provided even more support for the pharmaceutical industry than had either the Reagan or Bush administrations. Elected in 1992 and defining himself as a New Democrat, Clinton embraced the need for free trade and economic competitiveness as central to the reclamation of liberalism after twelve years of conservative rule. Clinton argued that increasing global trade would expand the global economy in the aftermath of the Cold War. Coming to power just a few years after the dissolution of the Soviet Union, Clinton became what policy analyst Sheila Slaughter calls an "articulate and ardent" champion of a "'competitiveness' agenda." This strategy allowed Clinton to replace the rhetoric of the Cold War with "the rhetoric of 'global competitiveness' [in] an effort to create a new narrative of heroic proportion."[113]

To accomplish his goal of industry competitiveness, Clinton supported expanding the reach of trade agreements, including completing the GATT negotiations and championing the creation of the North American Free Trade Agreement to open global markets for U.S. industries. In this vein, Clinton and his U.S. trade representative, Mickey Kantor, became central players in the intellectual property discussions begun ten years earlier under Reagan. Building on changes implemented in 1986, when the United States inserted demands for intellectual property protection into the GATT negotiations, U.S. pharmaceutical companies lobbied Clinton and Kantor to further strengthen the Trade-Related Intellectual Property Rights Agreement. Pharmaceutical companies, represented by Harvey Bale, who left his post in Reagan's trade office in 1992 to become the senior vice president of the Pharmaceutical Manufacturers of America, regularly argued for increasing intellectual property protection for drug formulas that were being wrongfully produced in India, a country Bale called a "global instigator."[114] Bale's boss, Gerald Mossinghoff, the president of the Pharmaceutical Manufacturers of America, put the point in sharp relief when he wrote to Kantor that the U.S. trade representative needed to protect pharmaceutical companies from patent-infringing countries (Brazil, Turkey, Argentina, and India), also known as "patent pirates."[115]

The contradictory consequences of a powerful pharmaceutical industry, supported by both treatment activists and the federal government's expanded trade protection, were put in sharp relief in 1996 at the Eleventh International AIDS Conference, held in Vancouver, British Columbia. During the proceedings, drug researchers and activists announced the discovery of protease inhibitors, an effective treatment for AIDS. This medical advancement was due in no small measure to the work of AIDS activists, who had demanded new methods for testing drugs in combination with each other.[116] AIDS activists and researchers believed that these new treatment protocols would lessen suffering and allow people with AIDS to live longer and better lives. With the cost of the drug regimen set at about $20,000 per year, per person, the pharmaceutical manufacturers were more likely than most people with AIDS worldwide to reap the benefits.

Eric Sawyer, the HIV-positive ACT UP member who founded ACT UP's Housing Committee, attended the opening ceremony in Vancouver and felt he needed to do a "reality check": "I mean, everyone is running around — the cure is here, the cure is here. The cure is not here. This isn't the end of AIDS, just the beginning. And, for ninety-nine percent of the people with AIDS, nothing's changed."[117] He went on: "Maybe you've got access to treatment, but what about the three million people that are going to die this year in the developing world, because they don't?"[118] With this question, Sawyer returned to the demands of the 1989 Montreal Manifesto, in spirit, if not in letter. If people with AIDS could not afford treatment, he wondered, the fact that treatments existed would have little effect on their health and well-being.

While Sawyer insisted on articulating the argument that the discovery of treatment options would only have a salubrious effect on the majority of the people with AIDS worldwide if they were able to receive the drugs, the underlying assumptions had a history in ACT UP. Kendall Thomas, a member of ACT UP for several years, who at the same time worked as a law professor at Columbia University, argued that treatment activists in ACT UP failed to embrace a vision that would produce the conditions for widespread access:

> There were any number of . . . gay white men — who had been raised, before they knew they were gay, to this notion that they were where they were because of merit — that the world belonged to them. . . .
> So, people who had been able to live their lives in the closet as gay men were being outed by the fact that their bodies were giving out on them. And that sense of not being willing to acknowledge their invest-ment in the structures of social and economic and gender and racial power — even though that very same structure was killing them — was one of the most painful things in the world for me to watch, because these were smart people. But, this willful refusal to recognize that their investment in this world was also killing them, because it was occluding a vision of the only kind of politics that would be adequate to the crisis we were facing. That willful refusal, to this day, is, for me, one of the most powerful examples of the strength of white supremacy as an ideology and as an institution — the way it can make white people, effectively, commit suicide, in its name, and not even see it as such.[119]

Thomas's stinging critique of T&D as an example of "white supremacy" suggested the foolishness of seeing treatment development and treatment access as separate issues that could be dealt with sequentially. For Thomas, drug development as a singular solution for AIDS, a program that increasingly found voice among people fighting for treatment, reified the conditions that produced the problems with access in the first place. By refusing to see race as anything more than the number of people of color on a particular trial, they left privilege completely unexplored.

A NEW WAVE of global AIDS activism began following the Vancouver conference and the announcement of protease inhibitors. In this iteration of activism, participants focused on bridging the gap between the global haves and have-nots. While it had a base in the United States, the vital center of this new incarnation of AIDS activism shifted squarely to the global South. As the epilogue that follows will suggest, southern AIDS activists, particularly those in South Africa, not only developed their own models of activism based on years of antiapartheid struggle, but they also succeeded where U.S. activists had failed: in the integration of service and activism, and drug availability and affordability.

While ACT UP built on long-standing arguments voiced by AIDS workers in the early 1980s, over the course of five short years, the organization fundamentally changed the course of AIDS work in the United States. Whether in terms of developing new ways of testing drugs and getting them to market, creating a more accurate measure for counting the number of people who had AIDS, providing housing for people with AIDS, or insisting that attention to the effect of racism and sexism not be seen as detrimental to the fight against AIDS, ACT UP saw its mission, even when its members regularly and fundamentally disagreed with one another, as providing an alternative to the political status quo that wanted to test people for HIV and refused to provide anyone with sexually explicit prevention material.

Epilogue | We Struggle against It Together

| *The South African* AIDS *Alliance, 1996–2003*

FOUR YEARS AFTER THE ANNOUNCEMENT in Vancouver about protease inhibitors, at the Thirteenth International AIDS Conference in Durban, South Africa, 5,000 people participated in the Global March for HIV/AIDS Treatment, hoping to secure antiretroviral drugs (ARVs, of which protease inhibitors were a particular class) for all people with AIDS in the global South.[1] The marchers' position on drug treatment for HIV/AIDS existed in direct opposition to the claims of the president of South Africa, Thabo Mbeki, who rejected ARVs as dangerous and questioned the link between HIV and AIDS. But the protesters, most of whom came from two organizations, Treatment Action Campaign (TAC), an AIDS activist organization less than two years old, and the Congress of South African Trade Unions (COSATU), the largest trade union federation in the country, also knew that Mbeki could not be their only target. They carried posters that pictured a bloody hand coupled with the phrase "One AIDS Death Every 10 Minutes: Affordable Drugs Now!" (ill. E.1). To attain their goal of treatment access, protesters demanded research be redirected from the global North to "poor countries and communities." Not only would this end "profiteering" by the pharmaceutical companies and make distribution of drugs more possible, but it would also "sustain development" and help women and children cope with HIV/AIDS.[2] By combining forces, TAC and COSATU articulated a shared project between people with AIDS and people committed to a global class struggle. This "AIDS alliance"[3] solidified an argument that refused the dichotomy between the availability of treatment and the economic equality required to access that treatment, and it also mobilized people to create alternative AIDS services in the face of an inactive state.

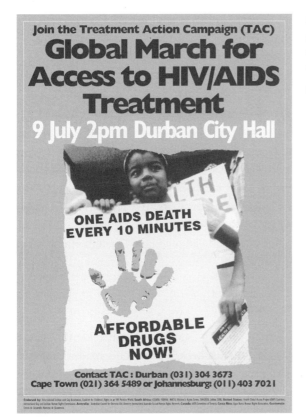

The need to connect AIDS and economic development grew out of the deep connection between AIDS and poverty. By 2000, just under a quarter of the South African population was infected with HIV.[4] This was double the number of people infected in 1997. The rates of poverty were equally dramatic. By 2001, approximately 57 percent of the South African population lived below the poverty line. This percentage had not changed since 1996, the first time the national statistics were collected in a democratic South Africa.[5] At the Durban conference, South African politicians, trade unionists, and AIDS activists faced the twin problems of HIV infection and poverty in ways that called attention to the links between the historical struggles against state-sponsored racial and economic inequality.

The case of how South African AIDS activism emerged, and the course that activism took after the discovery of effective treatment for AIDS, puts U.S. AIDS work in sharp relief, particularly in terms of how change takes place on a local and global level. Instead of seeing the South African case as a direct descendant of U.S. activism, a tempting choice given the link between the style of protest used by TAC and COSATU as well as the similarities between the images carried by protesters (compare ill. 5.1 with ill. E.1), the historical connection more aptly should be made to the southern AIDS workers funded by the Ford Foundation in the late 1980s and early 1990s.[6] In both cases, AIDS workers defined solutions to AIDS as broader than education, direct action, and advocacy. Instead, they centered on eliminating economic inequality as the only way to ensure health. This strategy of putting health within a political-economic framework is why a book about the history of U.S. AIDS work in the late twentieth century must end not in New York but in Durban. To a certain extent, South African AIDS activism, which grew out of a long tradition of protest, succeeded where American activism failed, in a challenge to capitalist medicine through attention to poverty and disease simultaneously.

HIV/AIDS in Democratic South Africa

Although South Africa's first democratically elected president, Nelson Mandela, made some inroads into dealing with AIDS, his government did not enact a comprehensive program for the disease.[7] In fact, its initial actions on AIDS were more contradictory than comprehensive. After the 1994 election, all political will and activity was directed at creating a new government. This consumed the attention that might have been paid to AIDS.[8] Beyond a lack of political energy, historians have criticized President Mandela for saying the right things about AIDS but not being able to implement them. During the first two years of Mandela's presidency, a series of rather public mistakes came to symbolize the new government's response to HIV/AIDS.[9]

Despite his missteps, Mandela oversaw two legislative actions that set the stage for a decade-long struggle by activists to secure affordable ARV treatment for the millions of South Africans with HIV/AIDS: the drafting and ratification of the South African constitution, and the successful amending of the South Africa Medicines and Related Substances Act (Medicines Act) to allow for inexpensive drug imports. The South African constitution, ratified in 1996, enshrined two key rights related to AIDS in its bill of rights: an antidiscrimination clause based on sexual orientation and the right to health care services, including reproductive health care and sufficient food and water.[10] With one of the most extensive and positive rights-granting constitutions in the world, South Africa became one of only a few countries where health care was a constitutional right and equal protection existed for gays and lesbians. Although political scientists and legal scholars debate how far these constitutional guarantees went, the constitutional language became central to AIDS activists' rhetorical strategy after 1996.[11]

Beyond a constitutional requirement to provide health care, or perhaps in an effort to ensure the provision of that health care, Mandela also amended the Medicines Act to make medicine more accessible for all South Africans. In its original form, this act, which was instituted by the apartheid regime in 1965 as a mechanism for regulating the national pharmaceutical industry, did nothing to ensure access to medicines for the majority of South Africans. With a new section 15(c) signed into law in December 1997, two years after the establishment of the World Trade Organization and its intellectual property protections, the Medicines Act allowed parallel importations of drugs so that South Africa could import generic drugs from other southern countries that produced them.[12] Having seen success in Brazil, where the government had instituted a national initiative to produce enough generic drugs to distribute to all HIV-positive Brazilians earlier in the year, South Africa imagined the new amendment would allow it to implement strategies that tapped into generic drugs being produced in Brazil, Thailand, and India.[13]

The newly amended Medicines Act infuriated the pharmaceutical manufacturers, who argued that South Africa's action violated the Trade-Related Intellectual Property Rights Agreement adopted at the final GATT round in 1994 and enforced by the World Trade Organization. The International Federation of Pharmaceutical Manufacturers Associations, the parent organization of the Pharmaceutical Manufacturers of America, whose lobbying in the late 1980s and early 1990s ensured the inclusion of intellectual property rights, publicly chastised South Africa for passing the Medicines Act. The president of the parent organization, Sir Richard Sykes, who also served as the chairman of Glaxo Wellcome, the company formed in a 1995 merger between Glaxo and Burroughs Wellcome (the manufacturer of AZT), argued that if countries were allowed to produce patented drugs and sell them at lower prices, "companies will logically be forced to consider stopping offering concessionary prices, which would certainly have a negative impact on access to medicines in low-income countries."[14] Sykes reasoned that generics threatened to undermine pharmaceutical philanthropy, whereby pharmaceutical companies cut prices or even donated drugs in an effort to create support for their particular brands instead of generics. Members of the international pharmaceutical association clearly wanted South Africans to turn to them instead of generic production facilities in the global South. The threat became concrete in February 1998 when a group of thirty-nine pharmaceutical manufacturers sued the South African government for violating the Trade-Related Intellectual Property Rights Agreement.[15]

An AIDS Alliance Emerges

The combination of a frustrated state apparatus, a quickly expanding epidemic, a hostile industry, and the legacy of antiapartheid struggle produced the conditions ripe for an explosion of AIDS activism. On December 10, 1998, International Human Rights Day, the anniversary of the signing of the UN Declaration of Human Rights, TAC answered the call. Initiated as a subsidiary of the National Association of People with AIDS, one of the first AIDS organizations in South Africa, started in 1994, TAC went beyond its parent organization with calls for massive protest. It joined forces with the AIDS Law Project, housed at the University of Witwatersrand, and COSATU, the federation that had been key in the struggle to overthrow apartheid in the late 1980s.[16] In its first action, TAC and the new alliance orchestrated a mass mobilization of people with HIV/AIDS to gain access to treatment. TAC called for the end to "unnecessary suffering and AIDS-related deaths of thousands of people in Africa, Asia and South America. These human rights violations are the result of poverty and the unaffordability of HIV/AIDS treatment." TAC informed participants that

> the message people living with HIV/AIDS have been getting from government and even health-care workers is that, there is no treatment available for HIV/AIDS, it is an incurable disease and we are all going to die. This message which underlies government policy on treatment is not the whole truth. There are many viable treatment options available for most of the illnesses which affect people living with HIV/AIDS (including treatments which attack the virus directly). The problem with these treatments is affordability. We call on the government and the pharmaceutical industry to work together as a matter of urgency

with NGOs and people living with HIV/AIDS to develop a plan to provide affordable treatment.[17]

In its initial actions, TAC built on the promise and failure of both the government and industry to effect change on behalf of people with HIV/AIDS.

The new tripartite alliance formed among TAC, the AIDS Law Project, and COSATU developed a language to talk about how AIDS affected South Africa and South Africans that built on the demands made by antiapartheid activists who refused to separate racial discrimination from class exploitation.[18] The alliance not only relied on a stark description of the present state of the epidemic that disproportionately infected poor black women, but it also deployed a historical consciousness of how ordinary South Africans had brought about political change through nonracialism and a commitment to workers. The alliance's general philosophy alternately deployed moral, economic, and scientific arguments as justification for comprehensive treatment and prevention funded by both the South African government and the international pharmaceutical industry. Between 1999 and 2003, this coalition, while not always successful, changed the terms of the debate about how to get AIDS treatment to the people who needed it most.

In an attempt to secure the moral high ground for TAC's positions, Zackie Achmat, one of the group's founders and a colored, HIV-positive gay man, took a page from conscientious objectors in the antiapartheid movement and refused to take ARVs until they were available in the public sector.[19] In justifying his decision, Achmat exemplified what TAC meant when it said that dealing with poverty and political disenfranchisement was as important as winning access to treatment.

> For me personally, I . . . in terms of the majority of people with HIV, they don't have a face, they don't have a political understanding, they are desperate, they are poor, they are alone. And to advocate for their medicines is a very difficult task. . . . But me personally, with HIV, as someone who could access medicines through friends and through medical aiders-on, for me I can't look them in the eye when I take medicines and I know they are going to die because they can't get medicine. And I cannot lead them, if that is the case. So my position is based on an understanding that I want, I want the right to life

for myself, but I want the right to life and I want to live in a political community in which that right is extended to every person. If such a political community does not exist and the only reason that you die, or you are allowed to die, is because you are poor, when you are sick, then I do not want to be part, on a conscience basis and on a moral basis, I could not be part of such a community.[20]

Achmat's actions received a tremendous amount of international publicity. His position highlighted the extent of the problem in South Africa and the power of a moral argument about treatment access, which had been central to TAC's activism before and after Achmat's conscientious objection.

As powerful as Achmat's moral stance was, COSATU insisted that the heart of the problem was the capitalist system that produced economic inequalities. At the 1998 COSATU Congress, the head of the National Education, Health, and Allied Workers Union, Vusi Nhlapo, declared, "As a union whose major concern is to keep our nation healthy and educated, we declare HIV/AIDS enemy two of the working class all over the world, as capitalism is our enemy one."[21] This powerful rhetoric not only connected workers who provided care to workers who needed care but, more importantly, explicitly linked disease and politics.

To address the twin enemies of the working class, COSATU designed a popular education campaign that took the message of AIDS prevention to the shop floor. Workers from all the unions in the federations took a pledge to act on HIV/AIDS in 1999 by declaring that every union meeting should include a discussion of HIV/AIDS.[22] The federation also employed the services of a full-time AIDS educator, who trained shop stewards and union organizers about the epidemic.[23] COSATU's public education effort for workers and poor people modeled, at least in part, its popular education strategies of the 1980s.[24]

As it grew and expanded the reach of its message, the AIDS alliance faced opposition, however, from the newly elected president, Thabo Mbeki, whose distrust of drugs used to treat HIV/AIDS became one of the most widely known "facts" about AIDS in South Africa. Within months of the 1999 election that promoted the deputy vice president to president, Mbeki gave his first speech that mentioned HIV/AIDS. The speech was not on AIDS, but it ended with a passage that fundamentally reshaped the boundaries of the debate about how best to treat South Africans with HIV/AIDS.

Concerned to respond appropriately to this threat, many in our country have called on the Government to make the drug AZT available in our public health system. . . . There are legal cases pending in this country, the United Kingdom and the United States against AZT on the basis that this drug is harmful to health. There also exists a large volume of scientific literature alleging that, among other things, the toxicity of this drug is such that it is in fact a danger to health. These are matters of great concern to the Government as it would be irresponsible for us not to head [*sic*] the dire warnings which medical researchers have been making. I have therefore asked the Minister of Health, as a matter of urgency, to go into all these matters so that, to the extent that is possible, we ourselves, including our country's medical authorities, are certain of where the truth lies.[25]

While Mbeki's words scared and angered most people who had been working on AIDS in South Africa and beyond, they also mobilized a strong opposition. Nowhere was this truer than at the 2000 Durban conference. In the lead-up to the conference, and in response to Mbeki's statements about ARVs, 5,000 scientists signed the "Durban Declaration" that presented the case for HIV as the cause of AIDS and the need for effective treatment in the form of ARVs. Once at the conference, hundreds of attendees refused to listen to Mbeki's speech at the opening session, where he called for attention to the health implications of poverty. As Mbeki began his speech and it became clear that he did not plan to talk about HIV or ARVs, the attendees stormed out of the stadium and literally took the conference's theme of "Breaking the Silence" into their own hands.[26]

But it was the words of people who stayed at the opening session that best exemplified "breaking the silence." Joyce Pekane, the second vice president of COSATU, delivered an oration that linked AIDS work and trade unions and criticized Mbeki from within the South African political establishment. Presenting just a few hours after Mbeki, Pekane argued, "There is no doubt that AIDS kills. There is no doubt that poverty kills. These twins of misery, when they work together, are responsible for the absolute devastation we see across Africa. Our campaign must be designed to defeat both, through providing drugs and treatment and distributing more equitably the resources of our country to immediately reduce poverty. The inequality in our country undermines our potential. It is the over-abundance of the one that is responsible for the abject poverty of the other."[27] Pekane exemplified COSATU's AIDS work by claiming that poverty and HIV/AIDS had to be dealt with as two sides of the same coin.

After Durban: The Making of Legal Strategy

With the moral arguments about the imperative of AIDS treatment combined with the economic analysis that saw the need to address the inequalities produced by capitalism, the AIDS alliance of TAC, the AIDS Law Project, and COSATU launched a legal strategy to force the hand of both the pharmaceutical industry and the South African government to provide ARV treatments for HIV/AIDS to all South African regardless of their ability to pay. The first leg of the legal strategy united the AIDS alliance with the South African government in fending off the efforts of the pharmaceutical industry to prevent the state from importing inexpensive drugs. In April 2001, the South African Constitutional Court allowed TAC to join the government's case as a friend of the court. The court reasoned that TAC had a particular interest in the case as an organization whose primary membership was people with AIDS. Within a month of the court's initial decision to grant TAC access to the case, the pharmaceutical manufacturers dropped their suit and announced an undisclosed settlement with the South African government. TAC underscored the moral and economic implications of the decision. "This is a victory by ordinary people against unethical actions by multinational corporations. It has been shown that with a united global effort, concerned citizens can make a difference. Although this court case has dealt with South African legal issues, it is an example that people in all poor countries can defend their essential interests."[28] COSATU celebrated alongside TAC and ran an exuberant image of dozens of AIDS and labor activists popping a bottle of champagne to celebrate their victory on the cover of its monthly magazine.

While the government prevailed in court, it neither imported any AIDS drugs into South Africa nor established delivery systems for existing drugs.[29] The legal victory had little effect on Thabo Mbeki and Minister of Health Manto Tshabalala-Msimang, who still maintained that ARVs were harmful and that HIV did not cause AIDS.[30] At a meeting with the minister of health after the legal victory against the pharmaceutical industry, TAC realized that the government had no intention of using the settlement to import drugs, a decision that infuriated and disappointed the activists.[31] At that point, TAC felt that it had little choice but to sue the government.

TAC's case rested on providing service to pregnant women with HIV. The decision to focus initially on women and children lent credibility to TAC's moral suasion. Building on several years of medical and scientific research that showed that pregnant women given a short course of AZT were much less likely to pass HIV to their unborn babies (based, in large part, on the 076 trial that contributed to the splitting of ACT UP), TAC demanded that "the standard of care in many developed countries" be applied to South African women.[32] TAC saw the development of a system to treat mother-to-child transmission as a way to initiate a plan to treat all South Africans with HIV/AIDS.

In December 2001, TAC won its case against the government. The South African court declared that the government must "plan an effective comprehensive national programme to prevent or reduce the mother-to-child transmission of HIV." This comprehensive program needed to include the provision of counseling and testing as well as formula for nursing mothers.[33] Under this ruling, TAC established regional clinics to provide drug treatment for pregnant women, with the intention of creating a model for a national system. When the pilot projects fell short, TAC hammered the government for failing to meet implementation goals. So, too, did COSATU, whose president, Willie Madisha, pointed to the government's obligation "to look after the most vulnerable of its people." People living with HIV, he insisted, "[have] become the litmus test of our revolution."[34]

The multifaceted strategy of the AIDS alliance pointed to the most promising model for AIDS politics. The AIDS alliance was finally successful, at the end of 2003, when the government announced its plan to implement a comprehensive HIV/AIDS treatment plan.[35] Zackie Achmat responded to the decision by going back on ARV treatment that he had refused for five years.[36] The AIDS alliance continued to struggle greatly to enforce the plan's implementation, but the government's dramatic reversal on ARVs was an unparalleled victory.

As with the struggle against apartheid, TAC and COSATU understood the need for broad coalitions to create change. As Achmat observed after the government announced its ARV reversal, "South Africa needs examples of non-racial, cross-class, inter-generational and gender cooperation on the basis of equality. . . . In the TAC, we struggle against it together. Our non-racialism . . . utilize[s] the privilege, education, skills and resources of our middle-class members, black and white, to develop a strong pro-poor and working-class leadership in the TAC. . . . Genuine non-racialism asserts the equality, dignity and freedom of all people and it is essential to ensure social justice for all."[37] South African AIDS workers harnessed the language of the antiapartheid movement to address one of the most pressing crises since the racist regime.

Infectious Ideas has shown how AIDS workers transformed the political landscape, whether in the United States, Thailand, or South Africa. Over the course of the 1980s, a disparate group of actors — community activists, service and health care providers, government officials, and philanthropists — came together, however uneasily, to address the AIDS crisis. In doing so, they put the debate about what constituted health on the table. More specifically, AIDS workers made the case that health care had to be understood in a broader political context. While they were not entirely successful in creating a new kind of health care system, they changed the terms of the debate about the state's obligation to the health of its citizens.

Notes

Abbreviations

In addition to the abbreviations used in the text, the following appear in the notes.

ACT UP/NY   AIDS Coalition to Unleash Power/New York

AO Records   AIDS Office of the San Francisco Department of Public Health
Records

FFA   Ford Foundation Archives, New York, N.Y.

GLBTHS   Gay, Lesbian, Bisexual, Transgender Historical Society, San Francisco,
Calif.

IGIC   International Gay Information Center Records, New York Public
Library, New York, N.Y.

NLM   National Library of Medicine, Bethesda, Md.

NUA   Northeastern University Archives, Boston, Mass.

NYPL   New York Public Library, New York, N.Y.

PUL   Princeton University Library, Princeton, N.J.

RRPL   Ronald Reagan Presidential Library, Simi Valley, Calif.

SFPL   San Francisco Public Library, San Francisco, Calif.

UCSF   University of California at San Francisco Archives, San Francisco,
Calif.

Prologue

1 My work has been informed by a substantial body of interdisciplinary literature
on the social construction of AIDS. First and foremost, Paula Treichler's assessment of AIDS as an "epidemic of signification" is probably cited by most, if not
all, humanist and social scientific analyses of AIDS. Beyond helping to enumerate
the signification of AIDS, I have tried, throughout this book, to answer Treichler's
call to detail how AIDS has been "democratically determined." See Treichler, *How
to Have Theory*, 39. Cindy Patton's body of work has been equally informative,
particularly her analyses of why gender matters in the AIDS epidemic, as well as

the attention she has paid to the mechanism through which AIDS became understood as a global problem. See Patton, *Sex and Germs*, "Resistance and the Erotic," *Inventing AIDS*, *Last Served*, *Fatal Advice*, "'On Me,'" and "Migratory Vices," and Patton and Kelly, *Making It*.

2   For a sampling of the literature on AIDS and gay sexuality over the course of two decades, see Altman, *AIDS in the Mind of America*; Andriote, *Victory Deferred*; Bayer, *Private Acts*; Bronski, *Pleasure Principle*; Moore, *Beyond Shame*; Preston, *Personal Dispatches*; Rotello, *Sexual Ecology*; and Watney, "Missionary Positions" and *Practices of Freedom*.

3   For analyses that insist on addressing the intersections of race, sexuality, and gender in the U.S. epidemic, see Cohen, "Contested Membership" and *Boundaries of Blackness*; Díaz, *Latino Gay Men and HIV*; Hammonds, "Race, Sex, AIDS," "Missing Persons," and "Seeing AIDS"; and Rodríguez, *Queer Latinidad*, 37–83.

4   For a general text on the evolution of AIDS work globally, see Altman, *Power and Community*. For more specific work on the Brazilian response, see Biehl, "Activist State," and Parker, *Beneath the Equator*.

5   For one of the finest synthetic accounts of this historiographical model, see Gosse, "Introduction I." For a sampling of standard historical narratives of the rise of conservatism, see Berman, *America's Right Turn*; Ehrman, *The Eighties*; Ferguson and Rogers, *Right Turn*; Hodgson, *World Turned Right Side Up*; Kazin, "Grass-Roots Right"; McGirr, "Piety and Property"; and Fraser and Gerstle, *Rise and Fall of the New Deal Order*. On the link between conservatism and neoliberalism, see Harvey, *Brief History of Neoliberalism*.

6   See Formisano, *Boston against Busing*; Gerstle, "Race and the Myth of the Liberal Consensus"; Nicolaides, *My Blue Heaven*; Rieder, *Canarsie*; and Sugrue, "Crabgrass-Roots Politics" and *Urban Crisis*.

7   On the origins of postwar conservatism among college age people, see Andrews, *Other Side of the Sixties*, and Klatch, *Generation Divided*. For an assessment of conservative activism in postwar Orange County, see McGirr, *Suburban Warriors*.

8   Klatch, *Women of the New Right*; Petchesky, "Antiabortion, Antifeminism" and *Abortion and Woman's Choice*; Rymph, *Republican Women*.

9   None of the books cited in n. 5 on the "Right turn" discuss AIDS. Alternatively, a handful of feminist scholars have briefly discussed AIDS in the larger political context. See, for example, Berlant, *Queen of America*, 17–18, and Diamond, *Roads to Dominion*, 290.

10   See Gitlin, *Twilight of Common Dreams*, and Michaels, *Trouble with Diversity*.

11   Michaels, *Trouble with Diversity*, 6.

12   Duggan, *Twilight of Equality?*, x (emphasis in original). For other accounts on how a Left-liberal coalition devolved into neoliberalism, see, for example, Berlant, *Queen of America*; Brown and Halley, *Left Legalism/Left Critique*; and Prashad, *Everybody Was Kung Fu Fighting*. Gosse critiques this argument as well, claiming

that the Right has a more accurate picture of the Left — it prospered and survived well into the 1980s and 1990s — than the Left's self-assessment; see Gosse, "Introduction I," 24–25.

13 Duggan, *Twilight of Equality?*, xii.

14 I make the distinction between political and medical history not because I disagree with the medical historiography on AIDS but, rather, because it seems necessary to change some of the questions asked at the archive and of the sources. Medical historians were among the first historians to write about AIDS. See, for example, Berridge and Strong, *AIDS and Contemporary History*; Fee and Fox, *AIDS: The Burdens* and *AIDS: Chronic Disease*; and Rosenberg, *Explaining Epidemics*.

15 Cindy Patton was the first to caution against drawing too sharp a distinction between early AIDS activism and early AIDS service work. In *Inventing AIDS*, Patton argues that seeing ACT UP as the first example of radical activism ignores earlier radical roots. "It is important to reassess the historical significance of the early years and understand both why, and at what cost, the AIDS service industry emerged, *and* who benefits from a reading of the development of these now powerful groups which severs them from their activist roots" (Patton, *Inventing AIDS*, 20). More recently David Román has argued against what he calls the myth that no AIDS activism existed before ACT UP; see Román, *Acts of Intervention*, xxix. Writing in the context of New York City history, Susan Chambré argues that ACT UP accomplishment were due, at least in part, to the work of many different AIDS organizations; see Chambré, *Fighting for Our Lives*, 5–6.

16 A notable exception is the work of anthropologist Paul Farmer, whose work on the transnational nature of AIDS links, for example, the conditions in Haiti with those in New York. See Farmer, *AIDS and Accusation* and *Infections and Inequalities*.

17 I chose SFAF not only because it was one of the largest ASOs in the country in the early 1980s, but also because it was one of the few ASOs whose archive had been collected and processed.

18 The description of gay men came from Larry Bye, the head of Communication's Technology, one of the marketing firms SFAF hired to help it design prevention efforts. See Larry L. Bye, "Designing Effective Programs to Change AIDS Risk Behaviors: The Experience of San Francisco, California," Nov. 9, 1987, SFAF Records, carton 23, not yet processed, UCSF, 4.

19 For an assessment of the tendency to see race and sexuality as generally parallel, see Somerville, "Queer *Loving*."

20 Historians of Reagan's presidency have, for the most part, ignored AIDS. See Boyer, *Reagan as President*; Cannon, *President Reagan*; Johnson, *Sleepwalking through History*; Rogin, *Ronald Reagan, the Movie*; Troy, *Morning in America*; and Wilentz, *Age of Reagan*.

21 One of the most notable exceptions to this would be the essays collected in Gosse and Moser, *World the Sixties Made*.

Chapter One

1 Paula Treichler and David Román agree that Patton was one of very few feminists writing about AIDS, although Román cites Patton's first feminist work as the 1985 *Sex and Germs*. See Román, *Acts of Intervention*, xix–xx, and Treichler, *How to Have Theory*, 86. By looking at Patton's writing in *GCN*, along with that of her fellow writers, men and women, I have found consistent attention to feminism in discussions of AIDS beginning in 1982.

2 Bob Andrews and Cindy Patton, "Talking about AIDS," *Gay Community News*, June 18, 1983, 6–7.

3 Patton, "Illness as Weapon," 5. Patton consistently continued to make this argument. In 1985, she wrote, "AIDS cannot be viewed outside the quest for sexual liberation" (*Sex and Germs*, 4).

4 For a useful summary of how and why lesbians were excluded from epidemiological study, see Treichler, *How to Have Theory*, 65–66. For accounts of women as caregivers, see Altman, *AIDS in the Mind of America*, 94–96. For more general accounts of lesbians' relationship to AIDS as HIV-positive people and caregivers, see Richardson, *Women and AIDS*, chap. 4, and Stoller, *Lessons from the Damned*, chap 1.

5 Streitmatter, *Unspeakable*, 243–75. Streitmatter levels his most serious attacks on press coverage at the California-based periodicals: the *Bay Area Reporter*, the *San Francisco Sentinel*, and the *Advocate*. He praises the coverage by the *Native* and *GCN* but only emphasizes the legal writing from *GCN*.

6 Kramer, *Reports from the Holocaust*, 44. The article was reprinted all over the country. For interpretations of Kramer's impact, see Mass, *We Must Love One Another*.

7 Kramer, *Reports from the Holocaust*, 46. In *The Normal Heart*, the play Kramer wrote in 1985 about AIDS, he made a similar argument about the changes gay men needed to make.

8 Shilts, *And the Band Played On*, 210.

9 Ibid., 315.

10 Ibid., 316.

11 For the argument that *GCN* was the only gay paper to also embrace feminism, see Streitmatter, *Unspeakable*, 213. Amy Hoffman's memoir about her time at *GCN* confirms this claim as well; see Hoffman, *Army of Ex-Lovers*.

12 Sociologist Elizabeth Armstrong argues that science made AIDS activism more possible: "Once it was established that the source of the disease was viral, the character of the gay identity movement enabled it to respond to the epidemic in a more effective manner than other constituencies affected by the disease" (Armstrong, *Forging Gay Identities*, 155–56).

13 For the first women's health book, see Boston Women's Health Book Collective,

Our Bodies, Ourselves. See also Davis, *Making of "Our Bodies, Ourselves"*; Morgen, *Into Our Own Hands*; Nelson, *Women of Color and the Reproductive Rights Movement*; Silliman, Fried, Ross, and Gutiérrez, *Undivided Rights*; and White, *Black Women's Health Book*. On scientific vs. community knowledge of AIDS, see Epstein, *Impure Science*.

14 John D'Emilio was the first historian to look for the roots of gay liberation in the homophile movement; see D'Emilio, *Sexual Politics, Sexual Communities*. More recently, historians have added to, but not substantially revised, D'Emilio's argument. See, for example, Beemyn, *Creating a Place*; Boyd, *Wide Open Town*; Gallo, *Different Daughters*; Kennedy and Davis, *Boots of Leather*; and Stein, *City of Sisterly and Brotherly Love*.

15 Armstrong, *Forging Gay Identities*; Chasin, *Selling Out*; Vaid, *Virtual Equality*.

16 Diane Feinberg, "AIDS/Health," *Gay Community News*, Nov. 26, 1983.

17 It is important to note that lesbians did not experience STDs in the same way as men. In part this meant that many lesbians held on to the idea that they were not vulnerable to disease just because they were having sex with other women. They assumed that disease was a factor for heterosexual women, but not necessarily for themselves.

18 Berkowitz, *Stayin' Alive*, 53.

19 Ibid., 76.

20 Robert K. Bolan, "Guidelines and Recommendations for Healthful Gay Sexual Activity," pt. 1, *Bay Area Reporter*, July 7, 1981, 20.

21 Ibid., pt. 2, July 16, 1981, 32.

22 There is very little written on gay men's health before 1980. Eric Rofes has a brief description of clinics in the 1970s but explains that many gay men had to find either closeted health care providers or face real homophobia when seeking medical attention for STDs; see Rofes, *Reviving the Tribe*, 114–16. See also Andriote, *Victory Deferred*, 35–39.

23 Patton, "Lesbian and Gay Health Care," 7.

24 "Advocates for Better Health Care — NGHEF," *Advocate*, July 21, 1983, 13–14.

25 Ron Vachon, "Care for Your Rectum," *Gay Community News*, Apr. 25, 1981, 10.

26 Ibid., 12.

27 Ron Vachon, "To Your Health," *Gay Community News*, Aug. 1, 1981, 13.

28 Patton, "Lesbian and Gay Health Care," 8.

29 See Catherine Batza's "Before AIDS: Gay and Lesbian Health in the 1970s," a dissertation in progress at the University of Illinois-Chicago.

30 "Agreements for Meridian Fraternity Membership," 1980, Mass Collection, box 8, folder "Meridian," NYPL, 1.

31 Ibid., 2; John Calendo, "Quiet Good Taste," Oct. 1982, Mass Collection, box 8, folder "Meridian," NYPL, 18. It was not entirely clear where a man would put the pin were he naked in the bathhouse.

32 John Calendo, "Quiet Good Taste," Oct. 1982, Mass Collection, box 8, folder "Meridian," NYPL, 18.

33 Richard Edwards, "Form letter from Meridian," 1980, Mass Collection, box 8, folder "Meridian," NYPL, 1.

34 Mr. Rick, "In Gays We Trust," 4.

35 For quote, see Mass, "Epidemic Continues," 14.

36 Mr. Rick, "In Gays We Trust," 4.

37 For quote, see Mass, "Epidemic Continues," 14.

38 For the first mention of the term "discreet fraternity," see ibid., 13.

39 Lawrence K. Altman, "Rare Cancer Seen in 41 Homosexuals," *New York Times*, July 3, 1981, A20. Altman's analysis was based on the first articles to appear in the CDC's *Morbidity and Mortality Weekly Reports*. See "Kaposi's Sarcoma and Pneumocystis Pneumonia among Homosexual Men" and "Pneumocystis Pneumonia."

40 Lawrence Mass, "Cancer in the Gay Community," *New York Native*, July 27–Aug. 9, 1981, 1.

41 Ibid., 21.

42 The appeal was reprinted in Kramer, *Reports from the Holocaust*, 8.

43 Kramer quotes Chesley in response. See ibid., 9.

44 Quoted in Fain, "Is Our 'Lifestyle' Hazardous?," 21.

45 J. B. Molaghan, "The New 'Gay Disease': Concern Not Panic," *Gay Community News*, Jan. 2, 1982, 3.

46 Mass, "Epidemic Continues," 1.

47 Ibid., 12.

48 Ibid., 13–14.

49 Ibid., 15.

50 Greco, "Report on NYC GRID Briefing," 13; Lawrence Mass, "AID and What to Do about It," *Gay Community News*, Sept. 25, 1982, 3.

51 "Acquired Immune Deficiency," *Bay Area Reporter*, Aug. 5, 1982, 5.

52 Chris Heim, "'Gay Diseases' Theories Examined," *Gay Life*, Aug. 13, 1982, 8.

53 "All About AIDS," *Gay Community News*, Feb. 26, 1983, 11.

54 Greco, "Report on NYC GRID Briefing," 13.

55 Joseph Sonnabend, "Promiscuity Is Bad for Your Health," *New York Native*, Sept. 13–26, 1982, 49.

56 Sonnabend, "Acquired Immunodeficiency Syndrome," 2370.

57 McShane, "Letter," 341.

58 Tom M. Smith, M. D, "Tricking with AIDS," *Bay Area Reporter*, Apr. 14, 1983, 14.

59 Ron Vachon, "Risks and Responsibilities of Recreational Sex," *New York Native*, Apr. 26, 1982, 11.

60 Ibid., 30.

61 American Association of Physicians for Human Rights, "Gay Doctors Recommend Steps for Blood Donation, 'Healthful' Sex," *Advocate*, Apr. 28, 1983, 10–11.

62 The Sisters of Perpetual Indulgence remains a vibrant San Francisco institution. In 2009, it will celebrate its thirtieth anniversary, and over that time its membership has expanded to include "the entire gender spectrum: we have men, women and trans members. We also cover most of the sexual orientation spectrum with gay, bi, and even the odd straight member" (Sister Edith Myflesh, Current Abbess and Mistress of the Web, personal e-mail communication with author, Oct. 6, 2008).

63 The original brochure was reprinted in Lawrence Mass, "Creative Sex, Creative Medicine," *New York Native*, July 19–Aug. 1, 1982, 11. For an updated version of *Play Fair!* created in 1999, see ⟨http://www.thesisters.org/playfair.html⟩. Andriote describes Bobbi Campbell and the Sisters of Perpetual Indulgence; see Andriote, *Victory Deferred*, 55–56, 169–72. Shilts dismisses the Sisters as an embarrassing example of gay liberation; see Shilts, *And the Band Played On*, 467. For an assessment of the performative significance of the Sisters, see Glenn, "Queering the (Sacred) Body Politic."

64 Gordon Murray, "The AIDS Mystery: Crisis and Challenge," *Gay Community News*, Oct. 9, 1982, 7.

65 Ibid., 11.

66 Michael Bronski, "AIDing Our Guilt and Fear," *Gay Community News*, Oct. 9, 1982, 8.

67 Ibid.

68 Ibid., 10.

69 Ibid.

70 Lawrence Mass, "Reason and Metaphor," *Gay Community News*, Oct. 23, 1982, 4.

71 Ibid.

72 Michael Lynch and Bill Lewis, "Illness and Guilt," *Gay Community News*, Nov. 13, 1982, 5. For a biography of Lynch, see Silversides, *AIDS Activist*.

73 Michael Lynch, "Living with Kaposi's," *The Body Politic* (1982), 36–37.

74 Hoffman, *Army of Ex-Lovers*, xiii.

75 Streitmatter, *Unspeakable*, 213.

76 Callen and Berkowitz, "We Know Who We Are," 23.

77 Ibid.

78 In his memoir, Richard Berkowitz describes his connection to Callen through Sonnabend as well as the importance of Sonnabend's arguments about promiscuity for his work with Callen. See Berkowitz, *Stayin' Alive*.

79 Callen and Berkowitz, "We Know Who We Are," 25.

80 In a related example, historian Heather Murray has suggested that some lesbian feminists rejected consumerism in the 1970s, only to create their own consumer culture; see Murray, "Free for All Lesbians."

81 Richard Berkowitz, "When the Epidemic Hits Home," *New York Native*, Dec. 20, 1982, 22.

82 Callen and Berkowitz, "We Know Who We Are," 25.

83 Berkowitz interview.

84 Callen and Berkowitz, "We Know Who We Are," 29.

85 Randy Shilts wrote a few paragraphs about Callen and Berkowitz suggesting that their critics denounced them as "sexual Carrie Nations" (*And the Band Played On*, 210).

86 Jurrist, "In Defense of Promiscuity," 27.

87 Tom Reeves, "On Backlash, Closets, and Sexual Liberation," *Gay Community News*, Mar. 12, 1983, 5.

88 McKusick, Horstman, and Coates, "AIDS." For pilot study, see Leon McKusick, "Report on Community Responses to AIDS Survey," 1983, Alfred Papers, box 8, GLBTHS. These men fit into four classification categories: the "Bathhouse Group," made up of men who left popular bathhouses between 10:00 P.M. and 2:00 A.M.; the "Bar Group," consisting of men who left a gay bar between 6:00 P.M. and 2:00 A.M.; the "No Bar–No Bath Group," men recruited through ads in gay papers; and the "Committed Relationship Group," couples who had participated in a pilot study. Of the 1,550 men, the researchers were able to analyze 655. This study became one of the driving forces behind Dr. Mervyn Silverman's decision to shut down the bathhouses in San Francisco.

89 McKusick, Horstman, and Coates, "AIDS," 495.

90 Jurrist, "In Defense of Promiscuity," 29.

91 Callen and Berkowitz, *How to Have Sex*, 15.

92 Ibid., 27.

93 Ibid., 30–31.

94 Ibid., 39 (emphasis in original).

95 Ibid.

96 The text of Callen's speech appears in Berkowitz, *Stayin' Alive*, 171.

97 Richard Berkowitz, "A Catalyst for Change," *Gay Community News*, Oct. 29, 1983, 5.

98 For an article that confirms this argument but claims that it was never realized, see Silin, "Dangerous Knowledge."

99 Callen and Berkowitz, *How to Have Sex*, 40.

100 Alfred's copy of *How to Have Sex in an Epidemic* can be found in "Not Now Going to Bars or Baths for Sex," 1983, Alfred Papers, box 8, GLBTHS.

101 Richard Royal, "AIDS and Promiscuity," *Gay Community News*, Aug. 13, 1983, 6.

102 Ibid.

103 The Red Queen, "Them and Us," *Bay Area Reporter*, Apr. 7, 1983, 6.

104 D'Emilio and Freedman, *Intimate Matters*, 322. Elizabeth Armstrong argues that

in 1969 and 1970 gay liberation was composed of three analytically distinct currents. Gay power sought the overthrow of capitalism and the creation of a liberated society in which sexual identity categories would no longer be necessary. Gay power activists, who saw themselves as gay revolutionaries, fought for sexual liberation for all, not just rights for gay-identified people. . . . A second strain, which I refer to as gay pride, sought to achieve gay visibility and build a positive gay identity. The third current, inherited from the homophile movement, believed that the situation of gays could be improved through single issue interest group politics seeking gay rights. (*Forging Gay Identities*, 85)

105 Marie Goodwin, "AIDS and the New Morality," *Gay Community News*, Aug. 13, 1983, 6.

106 Amy Hoffman, "Gay Liberation: The Spirit of Stonewall," *Gay Community News*, July 2, 1983, 5.

107 Sue Hyde, "AIDS Quarantines, the Government, and Us," *Gay Community News*, Mar. 24, 1984, 3.

108 Debi Law, "AIDS Lobby and Education Project Proposed," *Gay Community News*, July 9, 1983, 3.

109 Kevin Gordon, "Religion, Moralizing, and AIDS," *Gay Community News*, Dec. 17, 1983, 6.

110 Hal Slate, "AIDS and All: 'It's Still Hot,'" *Bay Area Reporter*, May 5, 1983, 14 (emphasis in original).

111 Not much has been written on gay male manhood, even though there is work on the role homophobia plays in the construction of masculinity. One of the few works to do so is Levine, *Gay Macho*. For a sampling of the documents that refer to masculinity from the gay liberationist activists of the 1970s, see The Red Butterfly, "Comments on Carl Wittman's 'A Gay Manifesto'"; Third World Gay Revolution, "Oppressed Shall Not Become the Oppressor"; and Wittman, "Gay Manifesto." For more general historical accounts of masculinity and brotherhood, see Clawson, *Constructing Brotherhood*; Gilmore, *Manhood in the Making*; Kimmel, *Manhood in America*; and Rotundo, *American Manhood*.

112 PWA Coalition, "Safe Sex Guidelines," 1983, IGIC, Ephemera, folder "PWA Coalition."

113 Nathan Fain, "Coping with a Crisis: AIDS and the Issues It Raises," *Advocate*, Feb. 17, 1983, 17.

114 Patton, "Illness as Weapon," 5.

115 Levine, *Gay Macho*, 5.

116 Quoted in Fain, "Is Our 'Lifestyle' Hazardous?," 21.

117 Patton, "Illness as Weapon," 5.

118 Ibid.

Chapter Two

1 Les Pappas, "Promoting Condoms for Gay Men," 1987, SFAF Records, carton 21, folder "Promoting Condoms for Gay Men Speech by Les Pappas at Atlanta Conference, 1987," UCSF, 9.

2 For two of the earliest uses of the term "safe sex" at SFAF, see Ed Power, "Memo to file," Dec. 28, 1983, SFAF Records, carton 8, folder "Press Releases, 1983–4," UCSF, 1, and Ed Power, "Memo Re: Bathhouse Education Campaign," Aug. 18, 1983, SFAF Records, carton 1, folder 1, UCSF.

3 I am indebted to Paula Treichler's preliminary work on the history of the condom, "Rethinking the Condom" (paper and presentation delivered at the Rutgers Institute for Research on Women, April 9, 2001). For an extensive history of responses to STDs, see Brandt, *No Magic Bullet*.

4 "Condom Results Crucial in AIDS Fight," Dec. 17, 1985, SFAF Records, carton 8, folder "Press Releases, 1985–6," UCSF, 1.

5 Duggan, *Twilight of Equality?*, xii; Prashad, *Everybody Was Kung Fu Fighting*, 63.

6 Boyd, *Wide Open Town*, 2.

7 Broussard, *Black San Francisco*; Massey and Fong, "Segregation and Neighborhood Quality," 19–20.

8 For an analysis of late-twentieth-century racial demography in San Francisco, see DeLeon, "San Francisco."

9 Boyd argues that bars were political spaces that coexisted with homophile activism; see *Wide Open Town*, 14.

10 Sarria's oral history is published in ibid., 20–24.

11 Stryker, *Transgender History*, 63–65. See also Stryker's film, *Screaming Queens: The Riot at Compton's Cafeteria* (Frameline Distribution, 2005).

12 Stryker, *Transgender History*, 68–78.

13 For the first definitive account of homophile activism in San Francisco, see D'Emilio, *Sexual Politics, Sexual Communities*. Boyd revises some of D'Emilio's arguments by paying particular attention to bar culture. For an account of the Daughters of Bilitis that suggests their feminist inklings, see Gallo, *Different Daughters*. For an account of homophile activism in Philadelphia that argues the importance of both men and women, see Stein, *City of Sisterly and Brotherly Love*.

14 Armstrong, *Forging Gay Identities*, 1.

15 Stryker and Van Buskirk, *Gay by the Bay*, 64–67.

16 Armstrong, *Forging Gay Identities*, 149.

17 Ramirez, "'That's *My* Place!,'" 225.

18 Ibid., 228.

19 Armstrong, *Forging Gay Identities*, 135.

20 Cochrane, *When AIDS Began*, xxiv. For a more hagiographic analysis of early epidemiologists, see Oppenheimer, "In the Eye of the Storm," 291–92.

21 Cochrane, *When AIDS Began*, 55–83.

22 I was not able to research the early work of GMHC because the organization's records had not yet been processed at the New York Public Library. San Francisco historical institutions, on the other hand, have done a much better job archiving its early history of AIDS work. For an account of GMHC that suggests the critical role of gay men in the organization, see Kayal, *Bearing Witness*.

23 "Kaposi's Sarcoma Foundation Opens," *Bay Area Reporter*, July 1, 1982, 4.

24 In its 1983 funding applications, SFAF noted that 96 percent of AIDS cases in San Francisco were homosexual. See AIDS/KS Foundation, "Proposal: Acquired Immune Deficiency Syndrome Project," Sept. 19, 1983, SFAF Records, carton 13, folder "Proposal to State . . . ," UCSF, 7. For information on the early structure of SFAF, see the University of California at Berkeley's Regional Oral History Office's "Oral Histories on the AIDS Epidemic in San Francisco" series. In recent years several scholars have turned their attention to the evolution of ASOs in particular, and AIDS work in general, to argue that groups such as SFAF and GMHC became increasingly professionalized over the course of the 1980s. This professionalization not only had a deleterious effect on the services the agencies were able to provide but also erased the political radicalness from the organizations. See Patton, *Inventing AIDS*.

25 AIDS/KS Foundation, "Proposal: Acquired Immune Deficiency Syndrome Project," Sept. 19, 1983, SFAF Records, carton 13, folder "Proposal to State . . . ," 3–4.

26 Ibid., 2–3.

27 *Can We Talk?*, 1983, AIDS History Project Ephemera Collection, box 5, UCSF.

28 AIDS/KS Foundation, "Proposal: Acquired Immune Deficiency Syndrome Project," Sept. 19, 1983, SFAF Records, carton 13, folder "Proposal to State . . . ," UCSF, 9; Rick Crane, "Letter to Jim Felten," Mar. 6, 1984, SFAF Records, carton 13, folder "State Contract . . . ," UCSF, 4.

29 Ed Power, "Memo Re: Bathhouse Education Campaign," Aug. 18, 1983, SFAF Records, carton 1, folder 1, UCSF; Ed Power, "Memo to file," Dec. 28, 1983, SFAF Records, carton 8, folder "Press Releases, 1983–4," UCSF, 1.

30 For a useful analysis of the bathhouse controversy, see Bayer, *Private Acts*.

31 Pappas interview.

32 Rick Crane, "Letter to Jim Felten," Mar. 6, 1984, SFAF Records, carton 13, folder "State Contract . . . ," UCSF, 1.

33 Billy S. Jones, "Memo to AIDS/KS Foundation, et al.," July 21, 1983, SFAF Records, carton 1, folder 1, UCSF, 1.

34 For contemporaneous examples, see Beam, *In the Life*, and Hemphill, *Brother to Brother*. For an account of the development of black gay responses to AIDS, see Cohen, *Boundaries of Blackness*.

35 Ed Power, "Bathhouses/AIDS Education," Feb. 20, 1984, SFAF Records, carton 8, folder "Press Releases, 1983–4," UCSF, 1.

36 "You Can Have Fun (and be safe, too)," 1984, SFAF Records, carton 19, folder "You Can Have Fun . . . ," UCSF, 1.

37 For an analysis of the use of interracial couples in early AIDS prevention, see Stoller, *Lessons from the Damned*, 53–57. She argues that interracial gay couples were acceptable because no procreation was possible.

38 Cohen, *Consumers' Republic*, 309.

39 Manoff, *Social Marketing*, 6. For another contemporaneous source on health marketing, see Festervand, "Focus Group."

40 Harvey, *Every Child*, 4.

41 Stoller, *Lessons from the Damned*, 45.

42 Puckett regularly communicated with the San Francisco Department of Public Health's AIDS Activity Office. In 1986 he reported on a series of six new ads SFAF wanted to run in the *Bay Area Reporter* after showing them to a focus group of gay men. See Sam Puckett, "Letter to Jeff Amory," Oct. 29, 1986, AIDS History Project Ephemera Collection, box 5, UCSF.

43 Pappas interview. Pappas left SFAF in the early 1990s to form his own social marketing firm, called Better World Advertising. Now, SFAF and other progressive groups contract Better World to create advertisements and educational campaigns for them.

44 Research and Decisions Corporation, "Designing an Effective AIDS Prevention Campaign Strategy for San Francisco," 1984, SFAF Records, carton 13, folder "Research and Decisions Corp," UCSF, 1.

45 Ibid., 7–9. Stoller argues that R and D was run by white gay men; while she does not name the people, I assume she means Larry Bye, the vice president of research at R and D.

46 Ibid., 2.

47 "SFAF Receives Research Grant," May 7, 1984, SFAF Records, carton 8, folder "Press Releases, 1983–4," UCSF, 1.

48 Research and Decisions Corporation, "Designing an Effective AIDS Prevention Campaign Strategy for San Francisco," 1984, SFAF Records, carton 13, folder "Research and Decisions Corp," UCSF, 1.

49 Ibid., 14.

50 Les Pappas, "Model for AIDS Prevention Campaign in Gay Community Business," 1985, SFAF Records, carton 27, folder "Model for AIDS Prevention Campaign . . . ," UCSF, 1–2.

51 Ibid., 11.

52 Ibid., 12.

53 For a discussion of the Tavern Guild, see Boyd, *Wide Open Town*, 223–26.

54 Les Pappas, "Model for AIDS Prevention Campaign in Gay Community Business," 1985, SFAF Records, carton 27, folder "Model for AIDS Prevention Campaign . . . ," UCSF, 12.

55 Bernie Wagner, "Memo to Tom Mossmiller," Aug. 28, 1985, SFAF Records, carton 22, not yet processed, UCSF, 1.

56 Les Pappas, "Model for AIDS Prevention Campaign in Gay Community Business," 1985, SFAF Records, carton 27, folder "Model for AIDS Prevention Campaign . . . ," UCSF, 13.

57 "Local Businesses Support Action to Make Condoms Readily Available," Apr. 29, 1985, SFAF Records, carton 8, folder "Press Releases, 1985–6," UCSF, 1.

58 Les Pappas, "Model for AIDS Prevention Campaign in Gay Community Business," 1985, SFAF Records, carton 27, folder "Model for AIDS Prevention Campaign . . . ," UCSF, 13–14.

59 "Local Businesses Support Action to Make Condoms Readily Available," Apr. 29, 1985, SFAF Records, carton 8, folder "Press Releases, 1985–6," UCSF, 1.

60 SFAF, "A Comprehensive AIDS Education/Prevention Plan for FY 1984–85," June 18, 1984, SFAF Records, carton 16, folder "Comprehensive AIDS Education," UCSF, 9.

61 Ernesto Hinojos, "Handwritten Memo," 1985, SFAF Records, carton 22, not yet processed, UCSF.

62 Armstrong, *Forging Gay Identities*, 134. For examples of gay men of color describing what it was like to be excluded because of racism, see Ramirez, "'That's *My* Place!,'" and Wat, *Making of a Gay Asian Community*.

63 TWAATF, "Letter to Executive Director, AIDS Clinic," Sept. 18, 1985, Ward 84/86 Records, box 2, folder "Letter to P. Volberding," UCSF, 3; TWAATF, "Organizational Chart," Aug. 12, 1986, TWAATF Records, box 1, folder "History, Organization, and Policy Statements (1987–1991)," UCSF.

64 "Minutes for TWAATF Meeting," Aug. 27, 1985, SFAF Records, carton 22, not yet processed, UCSF, 1.

65 Hank Tavera, "The Third World AIDS Advisory Taskforce," Nov. 1990, TWAATF Records, box 1, folder "History, Organization, and Policy Statements (1987–1991)," UCSF, 1.

66 Hank Tavera, "Letter to Don Francis," Apr. 15, 1990, TWAATF Records, box 1, folder "Meeting Minutes (9/86–10/90)," UCSF, 1.

67 Hank Tavera, "Letter to Douglas P. Holloway," Apr. 15, 1990, TWAATF Records, box 1, folder "Meeting Minutes (9/86–10/90)," UCSF, 2.

68 Amanda Houston-Hamilton, "A Constant Increase: AIDS In Ethnic Communities," Oct. 1986, SFAF Records, carton 8, folder "People of Color Caucus, 1986–1989," UCSF, 2.

69 Ibid.

70 The Multicultural AIDS Resource Center used the article to justify the hiring of a training coordinator for Third World Outreach. See "Third World Educational Outreach," 1986, Multicultural AIDS Resource Center Records, carton 1, folder "Third World AIDS Researchers," UCSF, 1. SFAF's POCC used the document to

argue for affirmative action at the agency. See Hank Tavera, "Arguments Supporting the Inclusion of People of Color . . .," Jan. 30, 1987, SFAF Records, carton 8, folder "People of Color Caucus, 1986–1989," UCSF.

71 TWAATF, "Information for People of Color," Dec. 1985, Bromfield St. Educational Foundation, box 7, folder 19, NUA; TWAATF, "Organizational Chart," Aug. 12, 1986, TWAATF Records, box 1, folder "History, Organization, and Policy Statements (1987–1991)," UCSF.

72 TWAATF, "Information for People of Color," Dec. 1985, Bromfield St. Educational Foundation, box 7, folder 19, NUA.

73 Lyn Paleo, "Letter to TWAATF Members," Dec. 14, 1988, SFAF Records, carton 22, not yet processed, UCSF.

74 TWAATF, "Western Regional Conference on AIDS and Ethnic Minorities, April 25–27, 1986," Apr. 25, 1986, TWAATF Records, box 1, folder "Western Regional Conference on AIDS and Ethnic Minorities, 1986; planning (1985–86)," UCSF.

75 "Board Minutes," May 16, 1985, SFAF Records, carton 1, folder 3, UCSF, 3.

76 Tavera interview.

77 Mitch Bart, "Letter to Michael Bala," July 1, 1986, SFAF Records, carton 17, folder "Client and Staff Ethnicity," UCSF, 2–4.

78 In addition to general outreach to communities of color, SFAF built connections specifically with the Latino community through attempts to develop bilingual educational materials. See Ernesto Hinojos, "Letter to Ramon Sevilla," Sept. 27, 1985; Ernesto Hinojos, "Memo Re: Collection of Data on Ethnic Minority Outreach," Sept. 12, 1985; and Ernesto Hinojos, "PSA," Oct. 15, 1985, all in SFAF Records, carton 22, not yet processed, UCSF.

79 Unfortunately, no copy of the poster is in the archives, but given their description of it as "cartoonish," I assume it was the Cruse image discussed in Chapter 1. See ill. 1.3.

80 "Third World Gay and Bisexual Men," Oct. and Dec. 1985, SFAF Records, carton 19, folder "Report on Focus Groups: Third World Gay and Bisexual Men," UCSF, 5.

81 Ibid.

82 Ibid., 3.

83 Ibid.

84 Ibid., 6.

85 Larry L. Bye, "Memo to SFAF," Aug. 1, 1986, SFAF Records, carton 19, folder "Summary of Major Findings from Focus Groups . . .," UCSF, 1.

86 Ibid., 2.

87 Ibid., 5.

88 By expressing concerns about sexual respectability, these community leaders used strategies similar to those employed by the black Baptist women. See the chapter "The Politics of Respectability" in Higginbotham, *Righteous Discontent*, 185–230.

For more general literature on black respectability, see Carbado, *Black Men on Race, Gender, and Sexuality*, and Collins, *Black Sexual Politics*.

89 Larry L. Bye, "Memo to SFAF," Aug. 1, 1986, SFAF Records, carton 19, folder "Summary of Major Findings from Focus Groups . . .," UCSF, 3. For an analysis of resistance to needle exchange, see Cohen, *Boundaries of Blackness*.

90 For quote, see Larry L. Bye, "Memo to SFAF," Aug. 1, 1986, SFAF Records, carton 19, folder "Summary of Major Findings from Focus Groups . . .," UCSF, 4. SFAF was not the only AIDS organization in San Francisco to use social marketing. The Stop AIDS Project used R and D to develop small support groups where men talked about how to practice safe sex. "The Stop AIDS project will be the equivalent of a community meeting of 1,000 San Francisco gay and bisexual men, conducted in small confidential groups of 10–12 men per group so that each individual will have an opportunity to fully participate in the discussion. . . . All gay and bisexual men are invited to participate in this important dialogue" ("The Stop AIDS Project: A Community Experiment in Communication," 1985, SFAF Records, carton 8, folder "Early Fundraising Papers," UCSF, 1). This model for community education was also quite a dangerous endeavor. The Traditional Values Coalition, a California right-wing organization, tried to defund the group in 2001–2.

91 People of Color Caucus, "Minutes of May 4, 1988 POCC meeting," May 4, 1988, SFAF Records, carton 8, folder "People of Color Caucus, 1986–1989," UCSF, 1.

92 Gay Men's Caucus, "Memo re: attached articles," Jan. 12, 1988, AO Records, box 2, folder "Minority Issues, 1987– ," SFPL.

93 Miguel Ramirez, "Memo re: Response to SF Chronicle and Gay Men's Caucus," Jan. 13, 1988, AO Records, box 2, folder "Minority Issues, 1987– ," SFPL.

94 People of Color Caucus, "Statement of Purpose," Dec. 2–3, 1986, SFAF Records, carton 8, folder "People of Color Caucus, 1986–1989," UCSF, 3.

95 Hank Tavera, "Memo to the POCC," Sept. 19, 1988, SFAF Records, carton 8, folder "People of Color Caucus, 1986–1989," UCSF, 1.

96 People of Color Caucus, "Minutes of September 28, 1988 POCC meeting," Sept. 28, 1988, SFAF Records, carton 8, folder "People of Color Caucus, 1986–1989," UCSF, 1.

97 Ibid., 2.

98 Ibid.

99 Jackson Peyton, "Memo To Kevin Cox Re: Long Range Planning," 1988, SFAF Records, carton 8, folder "Gay Men's Caucus," UCSF, 1.

100 Ibid.

101 Chuck Frutchey, "Letter to George Lemp," May 24, 1989, SFAF Records, carton 15, folder "1989 Gay/Bisexual Survey," UCSF, 3.

102 Ibid., 6.

103 Ernesto Hinojos, "Letter to Dr. Rutherford," Oct. 23, 1989, AO Records, box 17, folder "SFAF: Six Other Proposals," SFPL, 1.

104 SFAF, "Get Carried Away . . . with Condoms," 1989, AO Records, carton 17, folder "SFAF: Six Other Proposals," SFPL, 1. Because the publisher expressed concerns about this image, it has been removed.

105 Ibid.

106 Ernesto Hinojos, "Letter to Dr. Rutherford," Oct. 23, 1989, AO Records, box 17, folder "SFAF: Six Other Proposals," SFPL, 2.

107 Philip Hilts, "Study Says Many Gay Black Men Don't Guard Against AIDS," *New York Times*, June 15, 1990.

108 "Centers for Disease Control Guidance," Jan. 30, 1986, SFAF Records, carton 18, folder "Federal Materials Review 1988," UCSF, 1.

109 Domestic Policy Council, "Decision Memorandum on AIDS in America," Apr. 30, 1987, Ball Files, box OA 15332, folder "WLB — 1987 Health — AIDS [1 of 2]," RRPL, 2.

110 Jeff Amory, "Letter to Leo Sandars," Apr. 17, 1986, SFAF Records, carton 18, folder "Federal Materials Review 1988," UCSF, 1.

111 CDC Educational Materials Review Panel, "Minutes for 1/31/90," Jan. 31, 1990, AO Records, box 17, folder "SFAF: Six Other Proposals," SFPL, 1.

112 Victoria Sanabria, "Summary of Findings: Input of Latin Gay and Bisexual Health Education Providers," Dec. 26, 1989, SFAF Records, carton 19, folder "Summary of Findings: Input of Latin Gay and Bisexual Health Education Providers, 1989," UCSF, 1.

113 Ibid., 2.

114 Ibid.

115 Released in 1988, "Get it On/Dress for the Occasion," was the first poster in a series produced by SFAF intended to increase gay men's condom use. Because the publisher expressed concerns about this image, it has been removed. See "Focus Group Research on AIDS Educational Material Among Three Groups: General Population, Gay and Bisexual Men, & Sexually Active Heterosexual Women," Nov. 23, 1987, SFAF Records, carton 19, folder "Evaluation of AIDS Educational Media Materials for English and Spanish Speaking Populations, 1987," UCSF, 1.

116 Victoria Sanabria, "Summary of Findings: Input of Latin Gay and Bisexual Health Education Providers," Dec. 26, 1989, SFAF Records, carton 19, folder "Summary of Findings: Input of Latin Gay and Bisexual Health Education Providers, 1989," UCSF, 3.

117 "Field Testing," Mar. 8, 1990, AO Records, carton 17, folder "SFAF: Poster Targeting Gay Latino Men," SFPL, 1. Because the publisher expressed concerns about this image, it has been removed.

118 "Summary of Major Findings," Mar. 8, 1990, AO Records, carton 17, folder "SFAF: Poster Targeting Gay Latino Men," SFPL, 1.

119 "AIDS Office Material Evaluation Sheet," Mar. 8, 1990, AO Records, carton 17, folder "SFAF: Poster Targeting Gay Latino Men," SFPL, 1.

120 Juan Cruz, "Memo Re: The Poster . . . ," May 21, 1990, AO Records, carton 17, folder "SFAF: Poster Targeting Gay Latino Men," SFPL, 1.

121 Sandra Hernandez, M.D., "Letter to Les Pappas," June 11, 1990, AO Records, carton 17, folder "SFAF: Poster Targeting Gay Latino Men," SFPL, 2.

122 Les Pappas, "Letter to Sandra Hernandez," June 18, 1990, AO Records, carton 17, folder "SFAF: Poster Targeting Gay Latino Men," SFPL, 1.

123 Sociologist Joshua Gamson questions whether "sociopolitical strategies" based on identity "eventually undermine themselves" (Gamson, "Must Identity Movements Self-Destruct?," 391). This chapter has attempted to provide a historically based assessment of this question to suggest that it may not always be so.

124 SFAF, "Bilingual/Multicultural Services Program," Feb. 1992, SFAF Records, carton 16, folder "BMSP," UCSF, attachment B, 2.

125 Larry L. Bye, "Designing Effective Programs to Change AIDS Risk Behaviors: The Experience of San Francisco, California," Nov. 9, 1987, SFAF Records, carton 23, not yet processed, UCSF, 4.

126 United States AIDS Program, "United States Cases Reported to CDC," *AIDS Weekly Surveillance Report*, Dec. 28, 1987, 5. The number of people who had died in the United States by the end of 1987 was likely much higher, however. The 27,909 represented the number of known deaths as a subset of the almost 50,000 reported cases of AIDS.

Chapter Three

1 For first draft, see Working Group on Health Policy, "Memorandum for the Domestic Policy Council (DRAFT)," Oct. 29, 1985, Bell Files, box OA 17965, folder "DPC Health Working Group AIDS (1)," RRPL, 5. For cover letter notifying Patrick Buchanan and Linda Chavez about the changes, see Carl Anderson, "Memorandum for Patrick J. Buchanan," Nov. 1985, Bell Files, box OA 17965, folder "DPC Health Working Group AIDS (1)," RRPL. For the final version of the document that went to the DPC with the call for a special report, see Working Group on Health Policy, "Memo for the DPC Re: What should the federal government do to deal with the problem of AIDS?," Dec. 16, 1985, Sweet Files, box OA 16630, folder "Working Group on Health Policy AIDS [5 of 13]," RRPL, 5.

2 This was the twenty-fifth meeting of the DPC and the first on AIDS that Reagan attended. Of those twenty-five meetings, Reagan attended five.

3 Domestic Policy Council, "Memorandum for the President," Dec. 1985, Bledsoe Files, box OA 17012, folder "320-AIDS Policy (2)," RRPL.

4 William Roper, "Memo for the Working Group on Health Policy," Apr. 2, 1986, Sweet Files, box OA 16785, folder "[US Public Health Service AIDS Information Packet] [2 of 2]," RRPL, 1. Roper used the term "AIDS" in the document even

though HIV had been discovered, a slippage that was quite common within the administration.

5 Shilts, *And the Band Played On*, 55, 213–12, 224–25, 273, 290–91, 293–98, 328–29, 397–99, 452–53, 473–74, 525–27, 534–35, 572–73, 585–89.

6 While many gay theorists have criticized Shilts's position on the gay community's complicity in the spread of the AIDS epidemic, they have not criticized his argument about the failure of the federal government to act. See Bersani, "Is the Rectum a Grave?"; Bordowitz, *AIDS Crisis Is Ridiculous*; and Crimp, "How to Have Promiscuity" and "Randy Shilts' Miserable Failure." For a sociological account that relies heavily on Shilts, see Perrow and Guillen, *AIDS Disaster*.

7 AP, "Government, Gay Activists, Scientists Share Blame on AIDS, Author Declares," *San Diego Union-Tribune*, Oct. 8, 1987, B17; James Beckett, "AIDS Crisis Requires Worldwide Cooperation," *St. Petersburg Times*, Nov. 16, 1987, 13A; Margaret Engel, "AIDS and Prejudice: One Reporter's Account of the Nation's Response," *Washington Post*, Dec. 1, 1987, Z10; H. Jack Geiger, "Plenty of Blame to Go Around," *New York Times*, Nov. 8, 1987, Book Review section, 9; Daniel Greenberg, "And the Band Played On: Book Review," *Nation*, Nov. 7, 1987, 526; Joan O'Conner Hamilton, "How Politics as Usual Made AIDS a Megakiller," *Business Week*, Nov. 9, 1987, 18; William A. Henry, II, "The Appalling Saga of Patient Zero," *Time*, Oct. 19, 1987, 40; Henry Klingeman, "And the Band Played On Book Review," *National Review*, Dec. 4, 1987, 50; Christopher Lehmann-Haupt, "Books of the Times," *New York Times*, Oct. 26, 1987, C20; Jim Miller, "The Making of an Epidemic," *Newsweek*, Oct. 19, 1987, 91; Bob Sipchen, "The AIDS Chronicles," *Los Angeles Times*, Oct. 9, 1987, pt. 5, p. 1; Nicholas Wade, "The Editorial Notebook," *New York Times*, Nov. 10, 1987, A34.

8 For examples of the many books on Reagan that barely cover AIDS, see Cannon, *President Reagan*; Johnson, *Sleepwalking through History*; Troy, *Morning in America*; and Wilentz, *Age of Reagan*.

9 Diamond, *Roads to Dominion*, 274. See also Klatch, *Women of the New Right* and *A Generation Divided*, and Rymph, *Republican Women*.

10 For a discussion of how social and economic conservatisms affected AIDS in African American communities, see Cohen, *Boundaries of Blackness*. Cindy Patton's large body of work on AIDS also addresses how modern conservatism shaped AIDS. See, in particular, Patton, *Sex and Germs*, chap. 7, and Patton, "'On Me.'" For a complementary argument on conservative backlash, see Bronski, *Pleasure Principle*. Principal activists, such as ACT UP (discussed in more detail in the final chapter) saw Reagan as a criminal who failed to act on AIDS. For a useful discussion of how visual images and performance played a role in that argument, see Crimp, *AIDS*; Crimp and Rolston, *AIDS Demographics*; Kushner, *Angels in America*; Román, *Acts of Intervention*; and Schulman, *My American History* and *Stage Struck*.

11 William B. Turner makes a somewhat similar argument about disagreement among Reagan appointees but concludes the Reagan administration actually did little to make AIDS a priority. See Turner, "Mirror Images."

12 Kaplan, *Anarchy of Empire*, 1.

13 Judi Buckalew, "Memo for Faith Ryan Whittlesey Re: AIDS meeting at HHS, June 21, 1983," Aug. 1, 1983, Whittlesey Files, box OA 11288, folder "AIDS," RRPL, 1.

14 Virginia Apuzzo, "Letter to Judi Buckalew," June 30, 1983, Buckalew Files, box OA 10223, folder "1983-AIDS Background (3 of 5)," RRPL, 1. I have found no other record in the archive of further contact between members of the political arm of the Reagan administration and gay and lesbian activists.

15 Judi Buckalew, "Memo for Faith Ryan Whittlesey Re: AIDS meeting on Tuesday, August 2, 1983 with the Conservative Caucus," Aug. 3, 1983, Whittlesey Files, box OA 11288, folder "AIDS," RRPL, 1.

16 The Department of Health and Human Services houses PHS, the agency charged with investigating infectious and communicable disease in the United States. For a useful historical account of PHS's evolving work, see Parascandola, "Public Health Service."

17 "AIDS Briefing for Domestic Policy Council Executive Staff and Members," Aug. 27, 1985, Bledsoe Files, box OA 17012, folder "320-AIDS Policy (3)," RRPL, 1. Beginning in 1982–83, reports circulated about the "4-Hs" at risk for AIDS: Homosexuals, Hemophiliacs, Heroin Users, and Haitians. It is worth noting that the briefers described three of the four original "Hs" in their talk. Haitians were left out, because by 1985 the FDA had removed them from the groups that were prevented from giving blood. For a discussion of the 4-Hs, see Treichler, *How to Have Theory*, 20. For the FDA decision, see AP, "Haitians Removed from AIDS Risk List," *New York Times*, Apr. 10, 1985, A13.

18 "AIDS Briefing for Domestic Policy Council Executive Staff and Members," Aug. 27, 1985, Bledsoe Files, box OA 17012, folder "320-AIDS Policy (3)," RRPL, 3. In May 1984 two groups of scientists — one in the United States, the other in France — completed studies that connected a then-unnamed and unique retrovirus with AIDS. The French scientists, headed by Luc Montagnier of the Pasteur Institute, named the virus Lymphadenopathy Associated Virus (LAV), while the American scientists, headed by Robert Gallo of the National Cancer Institute at the National Institutes of Health, named it Human T-Lymphotropic Virus-III (HTLV-III). After a series of heated discussions, the virus was renamed Human Immunodeficiency Virus (HIV) in 1986. For a good synopsis of the events that transpired between the French and American scientists, as well as the simultaneous political dealings that created the agreement, see Grmek, *History of AIDS*.

19 Dick Hafer, *Homosexuality: Legitimate, Alternate Deathstyle* (1986), Bell Files, box OA 17965, folder "AIDS (8)," RRPL. See also Plymouth Rock Foundation, "FAC-

Sheet," July 15, 1983, and H. L. Richardson, "Richardson Report," July 15, 1983, Buckalew Files, box OA 10223, folder "1983-AIDS Background (2 of 5)," RRPL.

20 Dick Hafer, *Homosexuality: Legitimate, Alternate Deathstyle* (1986), Bell Files, box OA 17965, folder "AIDS (8)," RRPL, 59–77. For other examples of material on AIDS from right-wing activists collected by White House staff, see Plymouth Rock Foundation, "FAC-Sheet," July 15, 1983, and H. L. Richardson, "Richardson Report," July 15, 1983, Buckalew Files, box OA 10223, folder "1983-AIDS Background (2 of 5)," RRPL.

21 William Dannemeyer, "Letter to The President," Nov. 22, 1985, Bell Files, box OA 17965, folder "AIDS (10)," RRPL, 2–4.

22 Ibid., 4.

23 Newt Gingrich, "Letter to Dr. James Mason," Oct. 10, 1985, Bell Files, box OA 17965, folder "AIDS (10)," RRPL, 2.

24 There is now little doubt that the Reagan administration forced deep reductions in spending for social welfare and antipoverty programs. The literature on this subject is too vast to recount here. See, for example, Edsall, *New Politics of Inequality*; Sidel, *Women and Children Last*; and Wilson, *Truly Disadvantaged*.

25 Public Health Service, "Briefing Material for Domestic Policy Council Working Group on Health Policy," Oct. 17, 1985, Sweet Files, box OA 16630, folder "Working Group on Health Policy AIDS [10 of 13]," RRPL, 1.

26 Federal budgets are very confusing and hard to use. The actual amount of money spent in a given fiscal year is verified and published two years later. For the 1986 HHS budget expenditures, see U.S. Executive Office of the President, *Appendix Budget — Fiscal Year 1988*, I-K9–I-K10. I am indebted to Katie Batza for her hard work on demystifying the federal budget process and archive.

27 U.S. Executive Office of the President, *Budget — Fiscal Year 1985*, 8-82–8-96; U.S. Executive Office of the President, *Budget — Fiscal Year 1986*, 8-88–8-105; U.S. Executive Office of the President, *Budget — Fiscal Year 1987*, 6d-108–6d-131; U.S. Executive Office of the President, *Budget — Fiscal Year 1988*, 4-86–4-102; U.S. Executive Office of the President, *Budget — Fiscal Year 1989*, 6f-72–6f-87. For an analysis of how little the federal government actually spent on AIDS, see Perrow and Guillen, *AIDS Disaster*.

28 Gary Bauer, "The Family: Preserving America's Future" (1986) ⟨http://www.eric .ed.gov/ERICWebPortal/custom/portlets/recordDetails/detailmini.jsp?_ nfpb=true&_&ERICExtSearch_SearchValue_0=ED316515&ERICExtSearch_ SearchType_0=no&accno=ED316515⟩ (accessed Mar. 15, 2008).

29 Gary Bauer, "Memo to William L. Roper," Jan. 16, 1987, Sweet Files, box OA 16630, folder "Working Group on Health Policy AIDS [5 of 13]," RRPL, 1.

30 In addition to Koop's rejection of his conservative image, people who worked for him came to see him as the antithesis of social conservatism. Willard Cates, who began working for the CDC's Abortion Surveillance Unit in 1973 feared the

loss of his job in 1981 when Koop became surgeon general. Much to his surprise, Cates noted that Koop "turned out to be arguably the best surgeon general we've had in my lifetime in terms of a very independently minded, health-oriented, grandfather figure, and it sort of changed my mind about who should be surgeon general" (Cates interview, 65).

31 C. Everett Koop, "[Notes on the] Surgeon General's Report on AIDS" (1986) ⟨http://profiles.nlm.nih.gov/QQ/Views/Exhibit/documents/aids.html⟩ (accessed May 20, 2007).

32 C. Everett Koop, "Statement by C. Everett Koop, M.D.," Oct. 22, 1986, Sweet Files, box OA 16785, folder "[US Public Health Service AIDS Information Packet] [2 of 2]," RRPL, 3.

33 Ibid.

34 C. Everett Koop, "Surgeon General's Report on Acquired Immune Deficiency Syndrome" (1986) ⟨http://profiles.nlm.nih.gov/QQ/Views/Exhibit/documents/aids.html⟩ (accessed May 20, 2007), 4.

35 Koop, *Koop*, 216.

36 Gil Gerald, "Letter to C. Everett Koop, M.D.," Oct. 24, 1986, Koop Papers, box 114, file 1, NLM, 1. Editorials in the *New York Times* and the *Washington Post* praised Koop's actions, while the editorial at the *Washington Times*, a much more conservative newspaper, suggested that Koop needed "to heal himself." See editorial, "A Doctor's Good Advice," *Washington Post*, Oct. 24, 1986, A26; editorial, "Dr. Koop's Decent AIDS Dissent," *New York Times*, Oct. 25, 1986, A26; and editorial, "Flying the Koop," *Washington Times*, Oct. 27, 1986, A26.

37 Koop, *Koop*, 212.

38 C. Everett Koop, "Speech to the Joint Session on AIDS of the California Legislature," Mar. 6, 1987, Bauer Files, box OA 19222, folder "AIDS VII (5 of 5)," RRPL, 9.

39 Koop, *Koop*, 134.

40 William Bennett, "Note to Gary," 1987, Bauer Files, box OA 19222, folder "AIDS VII (5 of 5)," RRPL, 1 (emphasis in original).

41 Robert Sweet, "Memo for Gary Bauer Re: PHS Plans to Distribute Information on AIDS . . . ," Mar. 13, 1987, Sweet Files, box OA 16630, folder "Working Group on Health Policy AIDS [9 of 13]," RRPL, 1.

42 "Minutes DPC," Jan. 21, 1987, Bledsoe Files, box OA 17012, folder "320-AIDS Policy (1)," RRPL, 2.

43 John Klenk, "Note to Gary L. Bauer," Aug. 10, 1987, Sweet Files, box OA 16784, folder "AIDS/Klenk [1 of 2]," RRPL, 1.

44 These brochures would soon resurface when Senator Jesse Helms held them up on the Senate floor and said, "The comic books do not encourage and change any of the perverted sexual behavior [*sic*]. In fact, the comic book promotes sodomy and the homosexual lifestyle as an acceptable alternative in American society." Helms

went on to call for a ban on sexually explicit material in AIDS education, which passed 94 to 2. See Helms, "Departments," S14202.

45 Gary Bauer, "Memo to Howard H. Baker, Jr.," Mar. 24, 1987, WHORM Subject File, ID# 480629, FG 022-10, RRPL; Gary Bauer et al., "Memorandum for Howard Baker (DRAFT)," May 28, 1987, Risque Files, box OA 18383, folder "AIDS Binder (6)," RRPL.

46 John Klenk, "Memorandum to Winnie Austermann," Dec. 1986, Bell Files, box OA 17965, folder "AIDS (5)," RRPL, 1. The memo then found its way to the White House and subsequently to conservative activist Phyllis Schlafly, who proposed replacing the final principle with

Sex education cannot be taught by the public schools in any way that condons [sic] sex outside of marriage, or appears to imply that such is healthy or socially acceptable behavior, if contraceptives and/or condoms are used, because this offends the first amendment rights of those who believe that all sex outside of marriage is morally wrong. . . . Public school children must also be protected against the use of sexually explicit language in the classroom which the child may find offensive or embarrassing, and be protected against the use of psycho-logically disturbing films such as the birth of a baby. (Phyllis Schlafly, Dec. 19, 1986, Sweet Files, box OA 16784, folder "AIDS Testing [1 of 4]," RRPL, 1.

47 Gary Bauer, "Memo to William L. Roper," Jan. 16, 1987, Sweet Files, box OA 16630, folder "Working Group on Health Policy AIDS [5 of 13]," RRPL, 1. Other White House aides followed Bauer's lead, writing memos on principles for AIDS preven-tion and control. See, in particular, Bob Sweet's advice not to "make condoms a panacea" and "urge that sex be heterosexual and monogamous (within marriage)" (Robert Sweet, "Memo to Chuck Hobbs re: AIDS," Jan. 7, 1987, Hobbs Files, OA 18529, box 1, folder "AIDS [1]," RRPL, 2).

48 Domestic Policy Council, "Memorandum for the President," Feb. 10, 1987, Bledsoe Files, box OA 17012, folder "320-AIDS Policy (1)," RRPL, 2.

49 Helms, "Departments," S14204 in daily edition.

50 "Minutes DPC," Apr. 1, 1987, MacDonald Files, box OA 16756, folder "HIV (1)," RRPL, 3. Gary Bauer's main aide in the West Wing, James Warner, originally sug-gested the idea that "the mission of the commission should be restricted to fact findings" as opposed to policymaking. See James Warner, "Memorandum for Rhett Dawson," Apr. 22, 1987, Warner Files, box OA 18329, folder "AIDS: Com-ment on SJ Res. 190," RRPL, 1.

51 T. Kenneth Cribb Jr., "Memorandum for Howard Baker, Jr. (DRAFT)," Mar. 23, 1987, Risque Files, box OA 18383, folder "AIDS Commission (8)," RRPL, 4.

52 William Ball et al., "Memorandum for Howard H. Baker, Jr., Chief of Staff to the President," Mar. 6, 1987, Risque Files, box OA 18383, folder "AIDS Binder (1)," RRPL, 2.

53 Domestic Policy Council, "Memorandum for the President," May 1, 1987, Risque Files, box OA 18383, folder "AIDS Binder (3)," RRPL; "Minutes DPC," May 4, 1987, Risque Files, box OA 18383, folder "AIDS Binder (5)," RRPL.

54 Domestic Policy Council, "Memorandum for the President," May 1, 1987, Risque Files, box OA 18383, folder "AIDS Binder (3)," RRPL.

55 Gary Bauer, "Memorandum for the President," June 30, 1987, Bauer Files, box OA 19222, folder "AIDS [1 of 3]," RRPL, 1.

56 Office of the Press Secretary, "Statement by the Assistant to the President for Press Relations," July 23, 1987, Baker Files, box 1, folder "AIDS," RRPL. For Crenshaw correspondence, see Theresa Crenshaw, "AIDS," Nov. 1986, Bell Files, box OA 17965, folder "AIDS (7)," RRPL.

57 C. Christopher Cox, "Memo Re: *Decision in National Association of People with AIDS v. Reagan*," Dec. 17, 1987, Cox Files, box OA 16350, folder "AIDS Commission (1)," RRPL.

58 "Presidential Commission Action, New York 2/18/88," Feb. 18, 1988, ACT UP/NY Records, box 13, folder 8, NYPL.

59 On the departure of Mayberry and Myers, see Philip Boffey, "Leaders of AIDS Panel Quit Amid Feuds and Criticism," *New York Times*, Oct. 8, 1987, A18, and Sandra Boodman, "Top Officers of AIDS Panel Step Down Over Infighting," *Washington Post*, Oct. 8, 1987, A1. On Watkins, see Sally Squires, "Setting the Course on AIDS," *Washington Post*, June 7, 1988, Z14.

60 James D. Watkins, "Chairman's Recommendations," Feb. 29, 1988, Risque Files, box OA 18383, folder "AIDS Commission (3)," RRPL, 7.

61 *Report of the Presidential Commission*, 94. The CDC did not keep data on socioeconomic status and AIDS in the 1980s. Cases were divided by race, gender, and region. See "HIV and AIDS — United States, 1981–2000" (2001) ⟨http://www.cdc.gov/mmwr/preview/mmwrhtml/mm5021a2.htm#tab1⟩ (accessed Mar. 22, 2008).

62 James D. Watkins, "Chairman's Draft Recommendations for the Final Report," June 2, 1988, Mack-Bryan Files, box OA 19246, folder "PMB AIDS Commission Litigation (2 of 4)," RRPL, 127.

63 *Report of the Presidential Commission*, 14.

64 James D. Watkins, "Chairman's Draft Recommendations for the Final Report," June 2, 1988, Mack-Bryan Files, box OA 19246, folder "PMB AIDS Commission Litigation (2 of 4)," RRPL, 143.

65 Jeffrey Levi, "Letter to Ian Donald MacDonald, M.D.," July 13, 1988, MacDonald Files, box OA 16757, folder "Responses to Recommendations 14 July 88 (7)," RRPL, 1 (emphasis in original).

66 Robert Sweet, "Memo to Nancy J. Risque," July 5, 1988, Bauer Files, box OA 19222, folder "AIDS VI (1 of 3)," RRPL, 2.

67 Sandra Boodman, "Reagan Turns Aside AIDS Panel Report," *Washington Post*,

Aug. 3, 1988, A1; Marlene Cimons, "Reagan May Overrule AIDS Panel," *San Francisco Chronicle*, Aug. 1, 1988, A1.

68 Ian MacDonald, "Memorandum for the President," July 27, 1988, Risque Files, box OA 18383, folder "AIDS [10 Point Action Plan]," RRPL, 1.

69 Ronald Reagan, "Memorandum for the Secretary of Health and Human Services," Aug. 5, 1988, Risque Files, box OA 18383, folder "AIDS [10 Point Action Plan]," RRPL.

70 Gary Bauer, "AIDS: The Case for Routine Testing," ca. 1987, Warner Files, box OA 18329, folder "AIDS: Testing: Gary," RRPL, 1–3.

71 For a useful discussion of the history of the how HIV became known as "the virus that causes AIDS," see Epstein, *Impure Science*, 79–104.

72 Ronald Bayer argues that the debate over testing "forced a confrontation" over what measures would most effectively change people's behavior. See Bayer, *Private Acts*, chaps. 4 and 5. See also Patton, *Sex and Germs*, 37–38, and *Inventing AIDS*, 36–40. Testing was a main agenda item at several DPC meetings. See Ralph Bledsoe, "Memo for the DPC Re: Meeting on April 8, 1987," Apr. 7, 1987, WHORM Subject File FG010-03, folder 317302, RRPL.

73 Gary Bauer, "Memo for Donald Ian MacDonald," July 26, 1988, Bauer Files, box OA 19222, folder "AIDS I (4 of 4)," RRPL, 2.

74 Contemporaneous assessments of the presidential commission were positive. See Banks, "Review: AIDS and Government"; Edwards and Beil, "Pessimistic Outlook in AIDS Reports"; Murphy, "No Time for an AIDS Backlash"; Perrow and Guillen, *AIDS Disaster*, 179; and Stoddard and Rieman, "AIDS and the Rights of the Individual."

75 I have been unable to locate the original congressional resolution, but the White House memos on the subject are quite clearly opposed to the congressional effort. See Arthur B. Culvahouse Jr., "Memo to Gary L. Bauer," Feb. 22, 1988, Bauer Files, box OA 19222, folder "AIDS II (3 of 3)," RRPL, 1.

76 William Graham, "Handwritten Letter to Nancy Risque," Sept. 30, 1987, Risque Files, box OA 18383, folder "AIDS Binder (7)," RRPL.

77 Theresa Crenshaw, "America Responds to AIDS: Evaluation by Dr. Theresa L. Crenshaw," 1987, Risque Files, box OA 18383, folder "AIDS Binder (7)," RRPL, 1–2. The information moved up the political chain when Rhett Dawson, an assistant to the president for operations, conveyed Crenshaw's concerns about the campaign to Nancy Risque. See Rhett Dawson, "Handwritten Letter to Nancy Risque," Oct. 3, 1987, Risque Files, box OA 18383, folder "AIDS Binder (7)," RRPL.

78 James Warner, "Memo for Gary L. Bauer," Feb. 22, 1988, Bauer Files, box OA 19222, folder "AIDS VI (1 of 3)," RRPL, 1.

79 Arthur B. Culvahouse Jr., "Memo to Gary L. Bauer," Feb. 22, 1988, Bauer Files, box OA 19222, folder "AIDS II (3 of 3)," RRPL, 3.

80 Charles J. Cooper, "Memo for the Honorable A. B. Culvahouse, Council to the President," Mar. 11, 1988, Sweet Files, box OA 16785, folder "AIDS Mailer," RRPL.

81 Gary Bauer, "Memo for Edwin Meese III," Mar. 25, 1988, Bauer Files, box OA 19222, folder "AIDS II (1 of 3)," RRPL, 1.

82 Gary Bauer, "Memo for Howard H. Baker," Mar. 29, 1988, Bauer Files, box OA 19222, folder "AIDS II (3 of 3)," RRPL, 1–2.

83 "RRNATAIDS," Mar. 24, 1988, Bauer Files, box OA 19222, folder "AIDS II (1 of 3)," RRPL, 3–4. Many people, both close advisors and opponents of the president, had been calling on Reagan to speak directly to the American public in the form of a television appearance or letter. Bauer drafted a letter, but I have not been able to determine if it was mailed with the brochure. I assume it was not, because no record of it has been kept in either the Reagan archive or Koop's archive.

84 U.S. Executive Office of the President, *Appendix Budget — Fiscal Year 1990*, I-K11–I-K13.

85 Otis Bowen, "Memo to Gary Bauer," May 3, 1988, Bauer Files, box OA 19222, folder "AIDS IV (3 of 3)," RRPL.

86 *Understanding AIDS*, 2 (emphasis in original).

87 Sandra Boodman, "HHS AIDS Brochure: Frank, Explicit and Ready to Be Mailed," *Washington Post*, May 5, 1988, A21; Bruce Lambert, "Flood of Phone Calls on AIDS Tied to Mailing," *New York Times*, July 3, 1988, A12; Don Phillips, "Conservatives Warn of AIDS Brochure," *Washington Post*, May 28, 1988.

88 Panos Institute, *AIDS and the Third World*, 1st ed., 47.

89 Mann, "World Health Organization's Global Strategy," 733. See also Behrman, *Invisible People*, 44, and World Health Organization, "Global AIDS Fact File," June 1988, PHS Surgeon General's Office AIDS Records, box 6, file 43, NLM.

90 For a useful description of Mann's work in Zaire, see Cameron, "Deafening Silence."

91 Panos Institute, *AIDS and the Third World*, 1st ed., 48.

92 Ibid., 2nd ed., 49.

93 U.S. Agency for International Development, *HIV Infection and AIDS* (1991), 7.

94 I have found no substantial historical account of the GPA, so I pieced together as much as possible from disparate sources. For a brief discussion of the formation of the SPA/GPA, see Bastos, *Global Responses to AIDS*, chap. 3. Bastos argues that the WHO's program was at its height between 1989 and 1990. For a brief discussion of AIDS and human rights, see Gruskin, Mann, and Tarantola, "Past, Present, and Future."

95 Bastos, *Global Responses to AIDS*, 65.

96 For a useful bibliography on medical research on AIDS in the global South in the early 1980s, see Sabatier, "AIDS in the Developing World." For some of the first published social scientific research on AIDS in Africa, see Schoepf, "Women,

AIDS, and Economic Crisis." Beyond that, for a small sampling of early social scientific investigations of AIDS in the global South, see Abramson and Herdt, "Assessment of Sexual Practices"; Bolton, Lewis, and Orozco, "AIDS Literature for Anthropologists"; Farmer, *AIDS and Accusation*; Mann, "World Health Organization's Global Strategy"; Mann, Tarantola, and Netter, *AIDS in the World*; Schoepf, "Ethical, Methodological, and Political Issues"; and Sepulveda, Fineberg, and Mann, *AIDS Prevention through Education*.

97 Tinker, "Earthscan-Panos," 54.

98 Panos Institute, *AIDS and the Third World*, 1st ed. For more of Sabatier's work, see Sabatier, "AIDS in the Developing World." Beyond *AIDS and the Third World*, Panos published several important dossiers on AIDS over the course of the late 1980s and early 1990s. See Panos Institute, *Triple Jeopardy*, and Sabatier, *Blaming Others*.

99 Tinker, "Earthscan-Panos," 55.

100 Panos Institute, *AIDS and the Third World*, trade ed.

101 Much of the earliest journalistic work on AIDS outside the United States focused on Haiti because public health officials believed Haitians were a particular risk group. See Lawrence K. Altman, "AIDS Now Seen as a Worldwide Health Problem," *New York Times*, Nov. 29, 1983, C1; Lawrence K. Altman, "Concern Over AIDS Grows Internationally," *New York Times*, May 24, 1983, C1; Lawrence K. Altman, "The Confusing Haitian Connection to AIDS," *New York Times*, Aug. 16, 1983, C2; Lawrence K. Altman, "Debate Grows on U.S. Listing of Haitians in AIDS Category," *New York Times*, July 31, 1983, A1; Christine Russell, "Body's Immune System Disease Seen Occurring Also in Equatorial Africa," *Washington Post*, Apr. 2, 1983, A7; Christine Russell, "Disease of Immune System Becoming a U.S. Epidemic," *Washington Post*, Mar. 17, 1983, A1; Jean Seligmann, "The AIDS Epidemic: The Search for A Cure," *Newsweek*, Apr. 18, 1983, 74–79; Karlis Streips, "AIDS-Haitian Connection: Questions and Controversy," *Gay Life*, Nov. 3, 1983, 1; Ronald Sullivan, "City Takes Haitians Off List of High-Risk AIDS Groups," *New York Times*, July 29, 1983, B3; UPI, "Researchers Reporting U.S. Haitian AIDS Tie," *New York Times*, Oct. 20, 1983, A22; and Claudia Wallis, "The Deadly Spread of AIDS," *Time*, Sept. 6, 1982, 55. Haitians were not removed from the list of risk groups until 1985. See AP, "Haitians Removed from AIDS Risk List," *New York Times*, Apr. 10, 1985, A13. By 1985, the focus had shifted from Haiti to Central Africa, where reporters wrote about an "AIDS Belt" fueled by heterosexual behavior. See Lawrence K. Altman, "AIDS in Africa: A Pattern of Mystery," *New York Times*, Nov. 8, 1985, A1; Lawrence K. Altman, "Heterosexuals and AIDS: New Data Examined," *New York Times*, Jan. 22, 1985, C1; Lawrence K. Altman, "New Support from Africa as W.H.O. Plans Effort on AIDS," *New York Times*, Dec. 22, 1985, A29; Lawrence K. Altman, "Key World Health Official Warns of Epidemic of Prejudice on AIDS," *New York Times*, June 3, 1987, A1; Daniel Q. Haney, "Study Says Prostitutes, Cus-

tomers May Be Key to AIDS in Africa," *AP*, Feb. 12, 1986; Boyce Rensberger, "AIDS Potential Seen Worsening; Risk From Virus Climbs," *Washington Post*, Jan. 10, 1986, A1; and Jan Ziegler, "AIDS: Panic and Progress in 1985," *UPI*, Dec. 18, 1985. Although his book came out in 1987, Randy Shilts's *And the Band Played On* also made a powerful case for fearing travelers between the African continent and the United States. His subsequently disproven account of "Patient Zero," a French-Canadian flight attendant accused of being the first person with AIDS in the United States, made for captivating reporting. See, for example, AP, "Canadian Said to Have Had Key Role in Spread of AIDS," *New York Times*, Oct. 7 1987, B7; AP, "Montreal Man Described as Typhoid Mary of AIDS," *San Diego Union-Tribune*, Oct. 8 1987, B17; Cheryl Clark, "Band's a Gripping History of Death March of AIDS," *San Diego Union-Tribune*, Oct. 18, 1987, Books section, 3; H. Jack Geiger, "Plenty of Blame to Go Around," *New York Times*, Nov. 8 1987, Book Review section, 9; Christopher Lehmann-Haupt, "Books of the Times," *New York Times*, Oct. 26, 1987, C20; and Nicholas Wade, "The Editorial Notebook," *New York Times*, Nov. 10, 1987, A34.

102 Rod Nordland, Ray Wilkinson, and Ruth Marshall, "Africa in the Plague Years," *Newsweek*, Nov. 24, 1986, 44.

103 Patton, "From Nation to Family"; Treichler, "Third World"; Watney, "Missionary Positions."

104 In 1987 most AIDS workers regularly referred to "people infected with HIV," but the government's initial efforts were to place the term "AIDS," not "HIV," on the list. By the time the legislation passed, it named HIV and AIDS as excludable diseases.

105 Most accounts of the HIV ban suggest that explicit and implicit racism played a role in why immigrants with HIV got excluded. None of these accounts have explored how and why the State Department opposed the legislative change. See Fairchild and Tynan, "Policies of Containment"; Golumbic, "Closing the Open Door"; Konvicka, "Give Us Your Tired, Your Poor, Your Huddled Masses"; Kraut, *Silent Travelers*; LeMay, *Anatomy of a Public Policy*; Markel and Stern, "Foreignness of Germs"; Reimers, *Unwelcome Strangers*, 84–86; and Shoop, "Health Based Exclusion."

106 Parascandola, "Public Health Service." For a longer historical account of the medical gaze of immigration authorities, see Fairchild, *Science at the Borders*.

107 Shah, *Contagious Divides*, 2.

108 The McCarran-Walter Act was not fully rescinded until October 1990. See editorial, "Two Reasons to Rejoice on Immigration," *New York Times*, Oct. 29, 1990.

109 The quote was included in the Final Rule published in U.S. Department of Health and Human Services, "42 CFR Part 34," 32543. See also Somerville, "Queer Loving."

110 Wendy L. Gramm, "Memo for Joseph R. Wright, Jr.," Mar. 25, 1986, Sweet Files,

box OA 16785, folder "[US Public Health Service AIDS Information Packet] [2 of 2]," RRPL, 1.

111 Whitehead signed the letter as acting secretary of state, because George P. Shultz, the secretary of state, was not in Washington and left Whitehead in charge of the department. For the quote, see John C. Whitehead, "Letter to James C. Miller, III, Director, Office of Management and Budget," Mar. 21, 1986, Sweet Files, box OA 16785, folder "[US Public Health Service AIDS Information Packet] [2 of 2]," RRPL, 2.

112 For notes on the disinformation campaign, see "Eighth US-USSR Joint Committee Meeting, Health and Science," 1987, Bledsoe Files, box OA 17012, folder "320-AIDS Policy (2)," RRPL.

113 In 1987, USAID provided $5 million of funding to the WHO, about a third of its AIDS budget. By 1988, the ratio of WHO funding and other AIDS work was 1:1, with each receiving $15 million. See U.S. Congress, House, Select Committee on Hunger, *AIDS and the Developing World*, 72, 80.

114 Wendy L. Gramm, "Memo for Joseph R. Wright, Jr.," Mar. 25, 1986, Sweet Files, box OA 16785, folder "[US Public Health Service AIDS Information Packet] [2 of 2]," RRPL, 2.

115 Robert Sweet, "Memo for Gary Bauer Re: AIDS Testing for Immigrants," Apr. 28, 1987, Sweet Files, box OA 16784, folder "AIDS Testing [3 of 4]," RRPL. See also U.S. Congress, House, Committee on the Judiciary, *Grounds for Exclusion of Aliens*, and Bernard Weinraub, "Health Officials Seek AIDS Test for Immigrants," *New York Times*, May 16, 1987, A1.

116 The first memo in the archives suggests that staff tried to get immigration on the DPC's agenda in 1986. See Joe Wright, "Memo for Al Kingon," Mar. 27, 1986, Sweet Files, box OA 16785, folder "[US Public Health Service AIDS Information Packet] [2 of 2]," RRPL. For the minutes of the WGHP discussion, see William Roper, "Memo for the Working Group on Health Policy," Apr. 2, 1986, Sweet Files, box OA 16785, folder "[US Public Health Service AIDS Information Packet] [2 of 2]," RRPL, 2.

117 Domestic Policy Council, "Decision Memorandum on AIDS in America," Apr. 30, 1987, Ball Files, box OA 15332, folder "WLB — 1987 Health — AIDS [1 of 2]," RRPL, 2.

118 Nancy Risque, "Memorandum for Senator Baker, et al.," May 8, 1987, Risque Files, box OA 18383, folder "AIDS Binder (4)," RRPL, 1 (emphasis in original).

119 Edwin Meese III, "Memo for the DPC," June 12, 1987, Ball Files, box OA 15332, folder "WLB — 1987 Health — AIDS [1 of 2]," RRPL, 1.

120 Ronald Reagan, "Remarks to the American Foundation For AIDS Research Awards Dinner," May 31, 1987, Sweet Files, box OA 16629, folder "HPWG: AIDS #2 [2 of 6]," RRPL, 2.

121 Ibid., 4. For press account, see Boffey, "Reagan Urges," A1.

122 "Supplemental Appropriations, 1987," *Congressional Record*, June 2, 1987, S7410–S7415 (daily ed.). One of the four senators who did not vote was Robert Dole, a Republican from Kansas. He believed that false positives meant that marriage applicants should not be tested because the risk of incorrect results was likely and quite painful. He did not, however, apply this argument to immigrants. For a full discussion of the making of this legislation, see Brier, "Immigrant Infection."

123 U.S. Congress, House, Committee on the Judiciary, *Grounds for Exclusion of Aliens*, 84.

124 Department of Justice, "For Immediate Release," June 7, 1987, Sweet Files, box OA 16629, folder "HPWG: AIDS #2 [4 of 6]," RRPL; Robert Pear, "AIDS Test Ordered For U.S. Prisoners and Immigration," *New York Times*, June 9, 1987, A1.

125 For Koop quote, see Boffey, "Reagan Urges," B5.

126 Editorial, "Forced AIDS Tests. Then What?," *New York Times*, June 7, 1987, D28.

127 Congressional Research Service, *American Public Opinion on AIDS*, 20.

128 Nan Hunter, "Reagan's 'Weak, Coercive' AIDS Plan," *New York Times*, June 12, 1987, A31. See also Judy Rabinovitz and Nan Hunter, "A Maginot Line Against AIDS," *New York Newsday*, May 22, 1989.

129 ACLU, "Annual Report," 1987–88, American Civil Liberties Union Records, box 390, folder 3, PUL.

130 This sentiment was echoed by the National Minority AIDS Council. "But as citizens of color who are considered by many lawmakers as among that population directly responsible for overburdening the health and welfare systems, we must consider their action as one in a series that will play itself out against all of us fighting against both the spread of HIV and the discrimination against those infected with HIV. We must not miss this opportunity to stop what is intended by many to become the basis for a federal government ruling on mandatory testing and discrimination in all of the communities impacted by HIV" (National Minority AIDS Council, "HIV: A National Public Health Threat," ca. 1990, AO Records, carton 6, folder "Immigration Law and HIV," SFPL, 1). By 1990, protests had replaced editorials as the main means of criticizing the immigration legislation. For a full description of the protests that ensued at the last International AIDS Conference held in the United States in 1990, see Brier, "Immigrant Infection."

131 U.S. Department of Health and Human Services, "42 CFR Part 34," 32542.

132 Jonathan Moore, "Memorandum for Gary L. Bauer," Aug. 1, 1987, Bauer Files, box OA 19222, folder "AIDS and Refugees," RRPL.

133 "Sub-Saharan Africa: Implications of the AIDS Pandemic," June 1987, Cohen Files, OA92241, box 2, folder "AIDS in Africa [1 of 2]," RRPL, 10.

134 Ibid., 6 (emphasis in original).

135 Dudziak, *Cold War Civil Rights*, 250. For other work on Cold War civil rights, see Borstelmann, *Cold War and the Color Line*, and Romano, "No Diplomatic Immunity."

136 The literature on American exceptionalism is simply too great to repeat here, but I am indebted to the work of Jasbir Puar and Amit Rai, who have advanced the claim that the United States promotes a particular form of American exceptionalism based on gender and sexuality. See Puar and Rai, "Monster, Terrorist, Fag" and "Remaking of a Model Minority."

137 Most accounts of how and when AIDS became a national security issue point to the Clinton administration. See Johnson, "AIDS as a US National Security Threat."

138 Noel Day, "A Briefing Paper in AIDS in Africa," Dec. 1986, Cohen Files, OA92241, box 2, folder "AIDS in Africa [2 of 2]," RRPL; Overseas Development Council, "AIDS and Poverty in the Developing World," 1987, Cohen Files, OA92241, box 2, folder "AIDS in Africa [1 of 2]," RRPL. The notes of Cohen's deputy director, Alison Rosenberg, on the top corner of the Overseas Development Council document suggest that by 1987 AIDS material warranted collection; she wrote, "Do we have an AIDS file? If not, I'll file this in my safe."

139 Chas W. Freeman and John D. Negroponte, "Information Memorandum Re: AIDS and the Death of Modern African Societies," Apr. 10, 1987, Cohen Files, OA92241, box 2, folder "AIDS in Africa [2 of 2]," RRPL. It should be noted that Negroponte took the position as assistant secretary after returning from Honduras, where many have argued he played an active role in trying to overthrow the democratically elected government of Nicaragua. See ⟨http://www.gwu.edu/~nsarchiv/NSAEBB/NSAEBB151/index.htm⟩.

140 After describing how he became the deputy secretary of state, Whitehead writes in his 2005 memoir that "George Shultz had great respect for the professional Foreign Service officers in the Department, too. . . . [He relied] heavily on the in-house staff of experts, and I followed his lead, always drawing on the State Department's specialists to work on whatever problem was at hand." See Whitehead, *Life in Leadership*, 144. See also Whitehead, *African Development*, where Whitehead mentioned AIDS in the context of African development policy.

141 Chas W. Freeman and John D. Negroponte, "Information Memorandum Re: AIDS and the Death of Modern African Societies," Apr. 10, 1987, Cohen Files, OA92241, box 2, folder "AIDS in Africa [2 of 2]," RRPL, 1.

142 Ibid., 2 (emphasis in original).

143 Chirimuuta and Chirimuuta, *AIDS, Africa, and Racism*.

144 Panos Institute, *AIDS and the Third World*, 2nd ed., 21.

145 Ibid., 22.

146 Sabatier, *Blaming Others*.

147 Chas W. Freeman and John D. Negroponte, "Information Memorandum Re: AIDS and the Death of Modern African Societies," Apr. 10, 1987, Cohen Files, OA92241, box 2, folder "AIDS in Africa [2 of 2]," RRPL, 2 (emphasis in original).

148 Elinor Green Constable, "Cable Re: The AIDS Issue in Kenya," June 1987, Cohen Files, OA92241, box 2, folder "AIDS in Africa [1 of 2]," RRPL, 2.

149 Chas W. Freeman and John D. Negroponte, "Information Memorandum Re: AIDS and the Death of Modern African Societies," Apr. 10, 1987, Cohen Files, OA92241, box 2, folder "AIDS in Africa [2 of 2]," RRPL, 2.

150 Ibid., 1.

151 Ibid., 3.

152 Elinor Green Constable, "Cable Re: The AIDS Issue in Kenya," June 1987, Cohen Files, OA92241, box 2, folder "AIDS in Africa [1 of 2]," RRPL, 2.

153 In 1990, USAID provided 27 percent of the $77 million, or just over $20 million. Sweden gave more than $16 million. See U.S. Agency for International Development, *HIV Infection and AIDS* (1991), 2. On AIDSCOM and AIDSTECH, see U.S. Congress, House, Select Committee on Hunger, *AIDS and the Developing World*, 74.

154 Norine C. Jewell et al., "First Interim Evaluation: Public Health Communication (AIDSCOM) and Technical Support (AIDSTECH)," Dec. 21, 1989, USAID Document #PD-ABI-192, 6, in author's possession.

155 U.S. Office of Management and Budget, *Historic Tables*. See also Whitehead's critical speeches on the State Department's budget: *Foreign Affairs Budget*, *African Development*, and *U.S. Trade Policy*.

156 Beyond the demand that $20 million be added to international efforts, the National Gay and Lesbian Task Force also demanded $680 million more for the domestic AIDS budget. See NGLTF, "An Analysis of President Reagan's FY 1989 AIDS Budget," ca. 1988, Bromfield St. Educational Foundation, box 7, folder 17, NUA. For the budget increase, see U.S. Office of Management and Budget, *Budget of the United States Government*.

157 U.S. Agency for International Development, *HIV Infection and AIDS* (1990), 32.

158 Joyce Frame, "Letter to Robert Hughes," Sept. 16, 1987, USAID Document #PDABF455, 9, in author's possession.

159 AIDSTECH, "AIDSTECH Final Report, Volume 1," 1993, USAID Document #PD-ABJ-655, 4–6, in author's possession.

160 AIDSTECH, *Tools*, 29. See also Family Health International, *Making Prevention Work*.

161 AIDSCOM, "AIDSCOM Lessons Learned: AIDS Prevention in Africa," ca. 1994, USAID Document #PN-ABQ-409, 1–2, in author's possession.

162 U.S. Agency for International Development, *HIV Infection and AIDS* (1991), 1.

163 Ibid., 2. In 1987 and 1988, USAID spent $3 million on condoms for the projects in the global South. See U.S. Congress, House, Select Committee on Hunger, *AIDS and the Developing World*, 80.

164 Pigg, "Expecting the Epidemic," 113.

165　Ibid., 115. See also Adams and Pigg, *Sex in Development*.

166　Wright, "Gay Organizations, NGOs, and the Globalization of Sexual Identity," 100–102. For a short overview of gay issues and development, see Lind and Share, "Queering Development."

167　U.S. Department of State, *Global AIDS Disaster*, 9.

168　Ibid., 5.

169　AIDSTECH, "AIDSTECH Final Report, Volume 1," 1993, USAID Document #PD-ABJ-655, 4–6.

170　Family Health International, *Making Prevention Work*, 5.

171　UNAIDS, "Report on Global HIV/AIDS Epidemic" (1997), ⟨http://www.unaids .org/en/KnowledgeCentre/HIVData/default.asp⟩ (accessed July 16, 2008).

Chapter Four

1　A handful of scholars have written about ABIA in English. See Bastos, *Global Responses to AIDS*, chap. 4, and Parker, *Beneath the Equator*.

2　Herbert de Souza, "The Social Impact of AIDS in Brazil," Oct. 9, 1987, 1, and Peter Fry, "Memo to William Carmichael through Michele Heisler," Oct. 19, 1987, PA885-0207, FFA.

3　Herbert de Souza, "The Social Impact of AIDS in Brazil," Oct. 9, 1987, PA885-0207, FFA, 1.

4　Ibid., 2.

5　Peter Fry, "Memo to William Carmichael through Michele Heisler," Oct. 19, 1987, PA885-0207, FFA, 2. See also Peter Fry, "Memo to William Carmichael through Michele Heisler," July 8, 1988, PA885-0207, FFA. For an example of Fry's work in English, see Peter Fry, "Male Homosexuality and Spirit Possession in Brazil." For an assessment of his work within the field of Brazilian sexuality studies, see Parker, *Beneath the Equator*. Over the course of the next twenty-five years, Ford gave ABIA just over $1.75 million. Because I am only able to view Ford Foundation grants that have been closed for ten years, I was only able to analyze the first three grants, totaling just over $500,000.

6　Ford Foundation, "The AIDS Challenge: A Ford Foundation Response," Dec. 1987, FFA, 34, 37. Rockefeller was the only American foundation to give an international grant before Ford. See Seltzer, "Meeting the Challenge," 31. For the research conducted under the grant, see Schoepf, "Women, AIDS, and Economic Crisis."

7　Ford Foundation, "The AIDS Challenge: A Ford Foundation Response," Dec. 1987, FFA, 40–41.

8　See, for example, Farmer, *Infections and Inequalities*.

9　By 2012 or so, it will be possible to look at grants from the late 1990s and early 2000s, a critical period in the history of AIDS, particularly because of the advent of protease inhibitors in 1996 (an event discussed in the final chapter and epilogue). Beyond Ford's archive, I have tried to gain access to the archives at the Rockefeller Foundation and the MacArthur Foundation, both of which worked alongside Ford in the 1980s. The archival policy at Rockefeller requires that twenty years elapse before researchers can look at grant files. At the time of writing this book, I was not yet able to look at any grants. MacArthur's archive is completely closed to outside researchers.

10 Paula Treichler argues that "few feminists challenged the biomedical account of AIDS" (*How to Have Theory*, 42). Beyond the quote, see chaps. 2 and 8 for an important analysis of women, feminism, and AIDS activism. In the conclusion to her essay "Missing Persons," Hammonds writes, "African American feminists need to intervene in the public and scientific debates about AIDS, making plain the impact that medical and public health policy will have on African American women" (22). See also Hammonds, "Seeing AIDS"; Patton and Kelly, *Making It*; ACT UP/ NY Women and AIDS Book Group, *Women, AIDS, and Activism*; Gorna, *Vamps, Virgins, and Victims*; and King, *Theory in Its Feminist Travels*.

11 Gutiérrez, *Fertile Matters*; Moraga and Anzaldua, *This Bridge Called My Back*; Springer, *Living for the Revolution*; Mohanty, Russo, and Torres, *Third World Women*; Silliman, Fried, Ross, and Gutiérrez, *Undivided Rights*; Nelson, *Women of Color and the Reproductive Rights Movement*.

12 Looking at population control efforts, Hartmann argues for a kind of imperial similarity between USAID and Ford. See Hartmann, *Reproductive Rights and Wrongs*, 58–59. Donaldson, Warwick, and Harkavy disagree, although the male authors seem rather unconcerned with the role women might play as actors in fertility control. See Donaldson, *Nature against Us*, 65–67; Harkavy, *Curbing Population Growth*, 29–39, 129–200; and Warwick, *Bitter Pills*, 51–56. More general arguments about the limits of northern philanthropy can be found in Adams and Pigg, *Sex in Development*, and Justice, *Policies, Plans, and People*.

13 The connection between private foundations and the research university goes back to the nineteenth century. See O'Connor, *Poverty Knowledge*.

14 Gaither, *Report of the Study for the Ford Foundation*, 9–14.

15 For a useful historiographic review of postwar foreign policy, see McMahon, "Republic as Empire."

16 For historical accounts of development, see Escobar, *Encountering Development*, and Hess, "Waging the Cold War." For an analysis of Ford's history as a major philanthropic institution, see Magat, *Ford Foundation at Work*. Most of the historical analysis of Ford's work has focused on the foundation's efforts and programs within the United States. See O'Connor, "Ford Foundation and Philanthropic Activism" and *Poverty Knowledge*, and Raynor, "Ford Foundation's War on Poverty." The limited material on Ford and international development has often made a harsh critique of the foundation as culturally imperialist. See Seybold, "Ford Foundation and the Triumph of Behavioralism," and Weissman, *Trojan Horse*.

17 Warwick, *Bitter Pills*, 52.

18 For a historical account of Ford's and Rockefeller's population control work, see Critchlow, "Implementing Family Planning Policy," and Harkavy, *Curbing Population Growth*. For an internal Ford report on its population policies, see Caldwell and Caldwell, *Limiting Population Growth*.

19 The most recognized version of the argument originated in Ehrlich, *Population Bomb*. For a useful analysis of the population control establishment in the 1960s and 1970s, see Dixon-Mueller, *Population Policy and Women's Rights*, chap. 3, and Warwick, *Bitter Pills*.

20 Corrêa, *Population and Reproductive Rights*, 1. The position also found voice among a few mainstream population controllers. In his speech at the Bucharest conference, John D. Rockefeller III, one of the original leaders of the population control movement and the grandson of the Rockefeller Foundation's founder, John D. Rockefeller Sr., argued that the "provision of contraception information and services alone simply is not enough and will not be enough until women have alternatives to prolonged child-bearing and child-rearing." See Rockefeller, "Population Growth," 515–16.

21 Sen, Germain, and Chen, "Reconsidering Population Policies," 4. Adrienne Germain was also interviewed by Rebecca Sharpless in conjunction with the Sophia Smith Collection's Population and Reproductive Health Oral History Project. See Germain interview.

22 In their discussion of the emergent international women's health movement, Claudia Garcia-Moreno and Amparo Claro write, "A central tenet of the international women's health movement is that women's health and rights, not macroeconomic objectives, are of paramount concern" (Garcia-Moreno and Claro, "Challenges from the Women's Health Movement," 47). See also Petchesky and Corrêa, "Reproductive and Sexual Rights." For more general information on feminist critiques of population control, see Caldwell and Caldwell, *Limiting Population Growth*; Connelly, *Fatal Misconceptions*; Gordon, *Woman's Body, Woman's Right*; Hartmann, *Reproductive Rights and Wrongs*; Packard, "Visions of Health and Development"; Shapiro, *Population Control Politics*; and Sharpless, "Population Science, Private Foundations, and Development Aid."

23 Basu, *Challenge of Local Feminisms*; Jain, *Women, Development, and the UN*; Moser, "Gender Planning in the Third World"; Porter and Judd, *Feminists Doing Development*; Simmons, *Perspectives on Development*.

24 Antrobus, *Global Women's Movement*, 37.

25 Freedman, *No Turning Back*, 113.

26 Ibid., 117. Women's work had long historical roots. In 1970, Danish social scientist Ester Boserup wrote the first investigation of how gender affected development, in reality and practice. Her book, *Woman's Role in Economic Development*, was the first text in the field that would soon come to be known as Women in Develop-

ment (WID); see Boserup, *Woman's Role in Economic Development*. Freedman notes that some "scholars have noted that WID represented 'liberal feminism writ global,' for it rested upon liberal values of individualism, self-interest, and private property" (Freedman, *No Turning Back*, 114).

27 Freedman, *No Turning Back*, 115. For a good summary of the transition from Women in Development to Gender and Development, see Bhavnani, Foran, and Kurian, "Introduction to Women, Culture, and Development."

28 Berresford interview; Ford Foundation, *Women in the World*, 2.

29 For a brief but useful history of the Bedford Stuyvesant Restoration Corporation and community development corporations more generally, see Johnson, "Community Development Corporations."

30 Berresford interview.

31 For quote, see *Created Equal*, 23. In my interview with Berresford, she confirmed the point, using identical language.

32 *Created Equal*, 23.

33 Harkavy, *Curbing Population Growth*, 188–89.

34 For discussions of the work of Development Alternatives with Women for a New Era, see Corrêa, *Population and Reproductive Rights*, and Sen and Grown, *Development, Crises, and Alternative Visions*.

35 For analyses of global feminism in this period, see Mohanty, Russo, and Torres, *Third World Women*; Petchesky, *Global Prescriptions*; and Porter and Judd, *Feminists Doing Development*.

36 Ford was far from alone in its initial reluctance. In fact, in some of its first AIDS grants, Ford awarded money to an organization called Funders Concerned About AIDS in hopes of encouraging other philanthropies to incorporate AIDS into their missions. See Shepard Forman, "Recommendation for Delegated-Authority Grant," Aug. 12, 1988, PA885-1018, FFA, 2. The final evaluation of Funders Concerned About AIDS put an even sharper point on the argument, "For funders, the established structure of program areas, funding restrictions regarding single-disease initiatives, and the inexperience of new grassroots organizations in seeking funds all conspired to make grantmaking difficult" (Marjorie Muecke, "Memo to Files [885-1018]," Oct. 3, 1994, PA885-1018, FFA, 1). For an assessment of how various foundations initially responded to AIDS, see Seltzer, "Meeting the Challenge." Seltzer wrote this report as a consultant at Ford. He went on to work as a consultant for several years and serve as the first executive director of Funders Concerned About AIDS.

37 Berresford interview.

38 Forman interview.

39 Seltzer interview. Susan Berresford agreed that the death of people Ford "treasured" was a major catalyst for the foundation's actions; see Berresford interview.

40 Forman interview.

41 *Child Survival/Reproductive Health Programs*, attachment c.

42 Kubisch interview. Richard Horovitz left Ford in 1989 to serve as the executive director of the Panos Institute. He died of AIDS in 1991 at age forty-four. His partner, Melvin Dixon, died a year later. For his obituary, see "Richard Horovitz, 44, Foundation Executive," *New York Times*, July 20, 1991. Michael Seltzer described Horovitz's commitment to seeing AIDS funding for the global South. In part, his work with Funders Concerned About AIDS and his legacy encouraged the organization to pay equal attention to the United States and international programming. See FCAA, "International AIDS Grantmaking: A Donor's Report," Dec. 1991; "International AIDS Grantmaking," Mar. 1992; and "International AIDS Grantmaking: A Guide for Corporations, Foundations and Other Donors," Mar. 1993, PA885-1018, FFA.

43 Horovitz died of AIDS in 1991. While I have found no evidence that he was openly HIV-positive in 1987 or that his sero-status affected the kind of work he did in New York, the connection between his HIV status and his desire to develop responses to AIDS deserves noting.

44 *Child Survival/Reproductive Health Programs*, attachment c, 2.

45 Ibid., iii.

46 Ibid., iv.

47 Richard Parker, "The Social Dimensions of AIDS in Brazil: Report on a Consultancy for the Ford Foundation," Feb. 1989, PA890-0445, FFA, 5.

48 Scheper-Hughes, Adams, Corrêa, and Parker, "Reproductive Health and AIDS in Brazil."

49 I would have liked to look at one more grant, one given to the Panos Institute for "an indigenous language project," but it would not be available until the end of 2008.

50 For the first reference to the number of reported cases, see Peter Fry, "Memo to William Carmichael through Michele Heisler," Oct. 19, 1987, PA885-0207, FFA, 2. The statistic naming Brazil as the nation with the second highest number of reported cases of AIDS after the United States regularly appeared in the first few paragraphs of Ford grants to programs in Brazil. It is not entirely clear that it was accurate, however. The Panos Institute's statistics suggested that Brazil was third in reported cases, after the United States and France. Brazil did have the highest number of reported cases in the global South. See Panos Institute, *AIDS and the Third World*, 2nd ed., 54.

51 For the earliest and, in many ways, finest investigations of AIDS and Haiti, see Farmer, *AIDS and Accusation*, and Treichler, "Third World."

52 William Carmichael, "Recommendation for Grant/FAP Action," July 7, 1988, PA880-0783, FFA, 3.

53 William Duggan, "Memo to William Carmichael," Aug. 16, 1988, PA885-1186, FFA, 3.

54 In a 1989 report on AIDS in Brazil written for Ford, anthropologist Richard Parker

noted, "Even in Brazil itself, the shape of the epidemic has been interpreted as roughly parallel to the AIDS epidemic in the United States. . . . Virtually no attention has been directed to the social dimensions of AIDS in Brazil — a context that clearly differs in a number of important respects when compared to many of the other societies where the spread of AIDS has been most severe" (Richard Parker, "The Social Dimensions of AIDS in Brazil: Report on a Consultancy for the Ford Foundation," Feb. 1989, PA890-0445, FFA, 2).

55 *Child Survival/Reproductive Health Programs*, attachment c.

56 William Carmichael, "Recommendation for Grant/FAP Action," July 7, 1988, PA880-0783, FFA, 4.

57 See David Winder, "Memo to the Files," June 2, 1988, PA885-0991, FFA.

58 See Donaldson, *Nature against Us*. For a historical account of Ford's population control work, see Critchlow, "Implementing Family Planning Policy," and Harkavy, *Curbing Population Growth*.

59 For a brief history of the Population Council, see Critchlow, *Intended Consequences*, 4. For PATH, see Harkavy, *Curbing Population Growth*, 116–17.

60 William Carmichael, "Recommendation for Grant/FAP Action," July 7, 1988, PA880-0783, FFA, 5–6.

61 Marjorie Muecke, "Memo to David Winder," Jan. 9, 1990, PA880-0782, FFA, 1.

62 The Population Council, "Final Report: AIDS Prevention Among Adolescents and Young Adults: An Experimental Study in Thailand," Jan. 1992, PA880-0782, FFA, 8.

63 Marjorie Muecke, "Memo to David Winder," Dec. 29, 1991, PA880-0782, FFA, 2.

64 William Carmichael, "Recommendation for Grant/FAP Action," July 7, 1988, PA880-0783, FFA, 2.

65 Ibid., 4.

66 Marjorie Muecke, "Memo to David Winder," Sept. 7, 1990, PA880-0783, FFA, 2.

67 PATH/Thailand, "Interim Project Report for September 1988–December 1989," Apr. 1990, PA880-0783, FFA, 6.

68 David Winder, "Memo to the Files," June 2, 1988, PA885-0991, FFA, 2.

69 Ibid., 3.

70 William Carmichael, "Recommendation for Grant/FAP Action," July 21, 1988, PA880-0890, FFA; Thomas Trebat, "Recommendation for Grant/FAP Action — Supplement," Jan. 25, 1990, PA880-0890, FFA.

71 Center for the Promotion of Women Factory Workers, "AIDS Prevention Program for Factory Women Workers," Mar. 1988, PA880-0890, FFA, 1.

72 William Carmichael, "Recommendation for Grant/FAP Action," July 21, 1988, PA880-0890, FFA, 6.

73 Ibid., 5.

74 Thomas Trebat, "Recommendation for Grant/FAP Action — Supplement," Jan. 25, 1990, PA880-0890, FFA.

75 Nancy Feller, "Letter to Brenda Leggett," Feb. 20, 1990, PA880-0890, FFA, 1.

76 Michele Heisler, "Memo to Richard Horovitz," Apr. 7, 1988, PA880-0890, FFA, 1.

77 IMPACT, "AIDS: A Prevention Campaign in the Third World Focused on a Specific Target Group," Apr. 1988, PA880-0890, FFA, 1.

78 Michele Heisler and Richard Horovitz, "Memo to William D. Carmichael," Jan. 17, 1989, PA895-0260, FFA, 2.

79 Michele Heisler and Rebecca Nichols, "Memo to Thomas Trebat," Nov. 27, 1991, PA895-0260, FFA, 1.

80 IMPACT, "AIDS: Extension of Prevention Campaigns Focused on Specific Target Groups in Haiti," Nov. 1988, PA895-0260, FFA, 9.

81 Shareen Hertel, "Recommendation for Grant/FAP Action," Apr. 16, 1992, PA880-0890, FFA, 1.

82 Center for the Promotion of Women Factory Workers, "AIDS Prevention Program for Factory Women Workers," Mar. 1988, PA880-0890, FFA, 5.

83 The CPFO project also predates one of the more famous examples of microenterprise development as a form of AIDS prevention for commercial sex workers, the Sonagachi Project in Calcutta, India, which began in 1991. See Jana, Basu, Rotherdam-Borus, and Newman, "Sonagachi Project."

84 Ford saw its philanthropy in Haiti as "experimental" but hoped to "elicit support from other funders . . . including the U.S. Agency for International Development, [which] had already expressed interest in supporting an expanded program if the pilot phase proves successful" (Michele Heisler, "Recommendation for DAG," Aug. 13, 1990, PA905-1442, FFA, 3–4). Political instability in the country also affected Ford's decision to end funding. Shareen Hertel, a New York–based Ford staff member, described "the backdrop of political tension and general social instability which intensified in Haiti during the months preceding the military coup of September 1991." She concluded that these pressures "directly affected not only the target population involved but CPFO itself," presumably precluding further Ford funding. See Shareen Hertel, "Recommendation for Grant/FAP Action," Apr. 16, 1992, PA880-0890, FFA, 2.

85 See William Duggan, "Memo to William Carmichael," Aug. 16, 1988, PA885-1138, and "Memo to William Carmichael," Aug. 16, 1988, PA885-1186, FFA.

86 Nicola Jones, "Memo to Grant File via William Duggan," Feb. 20, 1990, PA885-1138, FFA.

87 William Duggan, "Memo to William Carmichael," Aug. 16, 1988, PA885-1186, FFA, 5.

88 William Duggan, "Memo to Nicola Jones," July 15, 1988, PA885-1186, FFA, 2.

89 Nicola Jones, "Memo to File #885-1186," Apr. 25, 1989, PA885-1186, FFA, 2.

90 Some scholars have started to problematize the use of the term "empowerment." For an argument about how "empowerment" was co-opted by mainstream development institutions, see Parpart, Rai, and Staudt, *Rethinking Empowerment*. This

does not seem to be the case with the Ford Foundation, whose use of "empowerment" recognized feminist critiques of development from the 1970s and 1980s.

91 Nicola Jones, "Memo to File #885-1186," Apr. 25, 1989, PA885-1186, FFA, 1–2.

92 William Carmichael, "Recommendation for Grant/FAP Action," Sept. 1, 1988, PA880-1065, FFA, 8.

93 Ibid., 5.

94 Richard Parker, "The Social Dimensions of AIDS in Brazil: Report on a Consultancy for the Ford Foundation," Feb. 1989, PA890-0445, FFA, 4.

95 Mann, Tarantola, and Netter, *AIDS in the World*, 20–21.

96 Berresford interview.

97 Ibid.

98 Ford Foundation, "Preliminary Spending Level, Budget . . . for FY 1990 and 1991," June 1989, FFA, 87.

99 Barzelatto, *Introduction to The Colectivo*, 1. Barzelatto's 2006 obituaries confirmed this. One former colleague wrote that Barzelatto thought "that healthy human reproduction was a question of human rights, and that it was improper to hide that reproduction was inextricably related to sex" (Faúndes, "In Memoriam: José Barzelatto," 181). In another obituary, Stephen Isaacs, of the Center for Health and Social Policy, explained, "'His efforts to put ethics, religion, and women's health at the centre of the Ford Foundation's work in the lead up to the International Conference on Population and Development in 1994 had a major impact. . . . As a result, he can be credited with the Cairo Declaration's emphasis on the importance of reproductive health, its widespread acceptance after that, and the improvement in women's lives that followed'" (Pincock, "José Barzelatto"). See also Faúndes and Hardy, "From Birth Control to Reproductive Health." For some of Barzelatto's work, see Barzelatto, "Ethics and Human Values in Family Planning."

100 Hempel interview.

101 Ibid.

102 Petchesky, *Global Prescriptions*, 4. For an account of how Development Alternatives with Women for a New Era addressed health concerns in the late 1980s and 1990s, see Corrêa, *Population and Reproductive Rights*.

103 Garcia-Moreno and Claro, "Challenges from the Women's Health Movement," 48.

104 Jones interview.

105 John Gerhart, "Memo to Franklin A. Thomas," Dec. 14, 1989, PA900-0264, FFA, 4.

106 Kubisch interview.

107 Nicola Jones, "Memo to STOPAIDS Log File," Nov. 9, 1988, PA895-0785, FFA.

108 STOPAIDS, "Project Proposal on AIDS Campaign at Motor Parks in Lagos," Nov. 1988, PA895-0785, FFA, 2.

109 Ibid., 3.

110 Bernard Nwabuko, "Narrative of Final Report," Oct. 1990, PA895-0783, FFA, 4.

111 Ibid., Appendix 1.

112 Bernard Nwabuko, "Letter to The High Commissioner of Canada in Nigeria," Apr. 10, 1990, PA895-0783, FFA, 2.

113 William Duggan, "Memo to William D. Carmichael," Mar. 30, 1989, PA895-0783, FFA, 4. While the grant was officially authored by Duggan, it appears that Jones drafted it and took the lead on evaluating its progress.

114 Bernard Nwabuko, "Narrative of Final Report," Oct. 1990, PA895-0783, FFA, 3.

115 Nicola Jones, "Memo to STOPAIDS Grant File," Jan. 18, 1990, PA895-0785, FFA, 1.

116 Bernard Nwabuko, "Narrative of Final Report," Oct. 1990, PA895-0783, FFA, Appendix 1, 3. I was unable to find Barzelatto's notes on his visit.

117 Jones interview.

118 I am unable to look at this grant, PA #900-1222. It will be available in 2013.

119 William Duggan, "Memo to Nikki Jones," Mar. 23, 1990, PA885-1186, FFA, 1.

120 John Gerhart, "Recommendation for Grant Action," Aug. 9, 1990, PA885-1186, FFA, 7. Similar models would become much more common in the 1990s. See, in particular, work on the Sonagachi Project in Calcutta, India: Jana, Basu, Rotherdam-Borus, and Newman, "Sonagachi Project."

121 Jones interview.

122 Richard Horovitz, "Memo to William Charmichael (DAG)," Jan. 17, 1989, PA895-0230, FFA, 3.

123 Fathia Mahmoud, "Project Proposal for the Society for Women and AIDS in Africa," Dec. 1988, PA895-0230, FFA, 1.

124 Ibid., 4.

125 Ibid., 5.

126 Richard Horovitz, "Memo to William Charmichael (DAG)," Jan. 17, 1989, PA895-0230, FFA, 3.

127 Ibid.

128 William Duggan, "Recommendation for Delegated-Authority Grant," Apr. 9, 1990, PA905-0736, FFA, 4.

129 SWAA-Nigeria, "Programme Proposal, 1991–1992," Mar. 1991, PA915-0846, FFA, 2–3.

130 William Duggan, "Recommendation for Delegated-Authority Grant," May 21, 1991, PA915-0846, FFA, 6. Over the next two years, Ford not only provided more funding for SWAA but also worked to help the organization grow as an institution. See, for example, Barry Gaberman, "Recommendation for Grant," June 3, 1993, PA930-0820, FFA. This grant awarded SWAA $100,000 for organizational planning.

131 I am unable to look at this grant, PA #930-1223. It will be available in 2012.

132 Panos Institute, *Triple Jeopardy*, 84, 90.

133 For an account of Nigerian feminism in the 1980s and 1990s, see Amadiume, *Daughters of the Goddess*.

134 Ford Foundation, *Reproductive Health*, 23.

135 Ford Foundation, "Preliminary Spending Level . . . for FY 1992 and 1993," June 1991, FFA, 88–89.

136 Ford Foundation, *Reproductive Health*, 28–29.

137 For feminist critiques of neoliberal development policies, see Bhavnani, Foran, and Kurian, "Introduction to Women, Culture, and Development"; Burgeron, "Political Economy"; Chua, Bhavnani, and Foran, "Women, Culture, Development"; Jackson and Pearson, *Feminist Visions of Development*; Jain, *Women, Development, and the* UN; Marchand and Parpart, *Feminism/Postmodernism/Development*; Parpart, Rai, and Staudt, *Rethinking Empowerment*; and Porter and Judd, *Feminists Doing Development*.

138 Ford Foundation, *Reproductive Health and Population Program*, 2.

139 Ibid., 62–63.

140 Ibid., 66.

141 Scheper-Hughes, Adams, Corrêa, and Parker, "Reproductive Health and AIDS in Brazil," 2.

142 Ibid., 58.

143 William Carmichael, "Recommendation for Grant/FAP Action," Mar. 30, 1989, PA890-0445, FFA, 5. This was the last Brazilian grant where Horovitz and Forman were the liaisons. After 1989, either Barzelatto or someone from his office was the liaison.

144 Thomas Trebat, "Recommendation for Grant/FAP Action," Jan. 9, 1992, PA890-0445, FFA, 2.

145 Ibid., 4.

146 Joan Dassin and Jose Barzelatto, "Recommendation for Grant/FAP Action," June 3, 1993, PA890-0445?, FFA, 3.

147 Thomas Trebat, "Recommendation for Grant/FAP Action — Supplement," Jan. 17, 1991, PA880-1068, FFA, 5.

148 Joan Dassin, "Recommendation for Grant/FAP Action," Dec. 3, 1992, PA930-0217, FFA, 2.

149 Ibid., 3.

150 Ibid., 4.

151 Peter Geithner, "Recommendation for Grant," Sept. 9, 1993, PA910-0107, FFA, 6–7.

152 EMPOWER, "Final Report 1991–92–93: AIDS Education for Workers in Entertainment Industry," Mar. 1996, PA910-0107, FFA, 2. For statistics on Chiang Mai, see Muecke's published research, "Mother Sold Food, Daughter Sells Her Body."

153 EMPOWER, "Education for Workers in Entertainment Industry," Sept. 1990, PA910-0107, FFA, 8 (emphasis in original).

154 Marjorie Muecke, "Memo to David Winder," Sept. 7, 1990, PA885-0991, FFA, 1.

155 Muecke interview. Other Thai grantees working with commercial sex workers resisted punitive methods as well. In June 1989 Ford provided a grant to Prince Songkla University to study regional variations in prostitution. While the study and the grant were small, Muecke reported that the work had important implications for how women should be targeted as recipients of AIDS prevention and education. "Unlike the epidemiological and political approach that focuses upon female prostitutes as nodes of HIV transmission in society, this grantee views female prostitutes as being at serious risk for contracting HIV from their male clients, and therefore in need of health education intervention to increase their ability to protect themselves from HIV. This perspective is consistent with the Foundation's concern with women's rights" (Marjorie Muecke, "Memo to David Winder," Dec. 28, 1991, PA895-1097, FFA, 1).

156 Rebecca Firestone, "Memo to Gary Suwannarat," Oct. 7, 1997, PA910-0112, FFA, 4. Ford gave its final grant to EMPOWER in 1997, PA #970-1418, but it will not be accessible until 2010.

157 Peter Geithner, "Recommendation for Grant," Oct. 18, 1990, PA910-0112, FFA, 8.

158 Mechai Viravaidya, "Progress Report," Mar. 18, 1993, PA910-0112, FFA, 2.

159 John P. Baker, "PDA Progress Report," May 18, 1994, PA910-0112, FFA, 3.

160 Marjorie Muecke, "Memo to David Winder," Jan. 3, 1992, PA910-0112, FFA, 3 (emphasis in original).

161 Viravaidya interview, 7.

162 Global HIV Prevention Working Group, *Bringing HIV Prevention to Scale*, 18.

163 Rebecca Cook et al., "The Ford Foundation's Reproductive Health and Population Program: A Five Year Review," Dec. 1996, FFA, 63.

164 Ibid., 67.

165 Berresford interview.

166 Seltzer interview.

167 Parker interview.

Chapter Five

1 Throughout the chapter, I use the acronym ACT UP to refer to the New York chapter of ACT UP. ACT UP began in New York and spread across the country to other cities between 1987 and 1990. Historical accounts of the various ACT UP chapters have yet to be written, except for the San Francisco and Chicago chapters. On San Francisco, see Gamson, "Silence, Death" and "Must Identity Movements Self-Destruct?" On Chicago, see Gould, *Moving Politics*.

2 AIDS Action Now! and ACT UP/NY, "Montreal Manifesto" (1989), ⟨http://www.gaylib.com/text/misc12.htm⟩ (accessed Jan. 11, 2007); AIDS Activism Center, "Demonstration to Protest Conference's Exclusion of Lesbian and Prostitutes'

Rights Issue," June 6, 1989, ACT UP/NY Records, box 117, folder 6, NYPL, 1. For an account of how this protest fits into the history of Canadian AIDS activism, see Silversides, *AIDS Activist*. For a reflection on Montreal by a member of ACT UP/NY, see Ron Goldberg, "Conference Call: When PWAs First Sat at the High Table," *POZ*, July 1998.

3 Eigo interview, 21.

4 On the Orphan Drug Act, see Arno, Bonuck, and Davis, "Rare Diseases, Drug Development, and AIDS." On pharmaceutical lobbying in the mid-1980s, see Devereaux, Lawrence, and Watkins, *Case Studies in US Trade Negotiation*.

5 In one of the first dissertations on ACT UP, Gilbert Elbaz laid out the demography of the group, explaining that its overwhelmingly white, gay, male, and young membership was not always able to accomplish the broad goals it set out to address; see Elbaz, "Sociology of AIDS Activism." Subsequent accounts by scholars, including Peter Cohen and Nancy Stoller, emphasized ACT UP as a paradoxical movement that called for social change but struggled with internal problems of sexism, racism, and classism. See Cohen, "'All They Needed'" and *Love and Anger*, and Stoller, *Lessons from the Damned*. Former members of ACT UP, many of whom are also academicians, have described their experiences of the contradictions inherent in ACT UP but also tried to emphasize the work of women, especially lesbians, and people of color in the group. See, for example, Crimp, *Melancholia and Moralism*; Cvetkovich, *Archive of Feelings*; Wolfe, "ACT UP"; and Wolfe and Sommella, "This Is about People Dying." Many of the scholars cited above have also described the conditions that produced the splintering of ACT UP in the early 1990s. For work specifically on the subject, however, see Edwards, "AIDS, Race, and the Rise and Decline," and Smith and Siplon, *Drugs into Bodies*. For contemporaneous accounts of the breakdown of ACT UP New York and ACT UP San Francisco, which experienced a similar split, see Tim Kingston, "Acting Up Is Hard to Do," *San Francisco Bay Times*, Oct. 1, 1990, and Donna Minkowitz, "ACT UP at a Crossroads," *Village Voice*, June 5, 1990.

6 See, for example, Gregg Bordowitz and Jean Carlomusto, *Seize Control of the* FDA (1988); James Wentzy, *Fight Back, Fight AIDS: 15 Years of* ACT UP (2002); and Jean Carlomusto and Maria Maggenti, *Doctors, Liars and Women: AIDS Activists Say No to Cosmo* (1988). In addition to these films, the New York Public Library's AIDS Activist Videotape Collection, 1983–2000, is a comprehensive collection of moving images produced by a dozen AIDS activists, most of whom were active in or affiliated with ACT UP.

7 I am indebted to the ACT UP Oral History Project. Sarah Schulman, Jim Hubbard, and Jim Wentzy have interviewed almost 100 surviving members of ACT UP New York, transcribed each interview, and posted them online as a digital archive.

8 Kramer, *Reports from the Holocaust*, 136. In many ways the discussion over the

origins of ACT UP mirrors the one about the origins of the gay and lesbian liberation movement. In the latter case, the Stonewall Riots have come to signify the beginning of the movement, when in fact lots of activism and organizing occurred before the riots, making the birth of the movement possible. A similar lore exists for ACT UP. Larry Kramer, one of the first members of the group, writes that his speech at the Lesbian and Gay Community Center in Greenwich Village was the catalyst for ACT UP. Many activists and scholars have since written about the radical gay and lesbian activism of the 1980s and its role in the formation of the group. See, for example, Wolfe and Sommella, "This Is about People Dying."

9   ACT UP, "Massive AIDS Demonstration" (1987), ⟨http://www.actupny.org/documents/1stFlyer.html⟩ (accessed May 13, 2007).

10   Amy Bauer, a member of ACT UP who provided civil disobedience training for hundreds of other members, recalled that at the first ACT UP protest, organizers gave the police a list of the people who were prepared to be arrested. See Bauer interview, 25.

11   Northrop interview, 23.

12   For an assessment of the visual art produced by ACT UP members, see Meyer, *Outlaw Representation*, 225–75.

13   Deagle interview, 47.

14   Carlomusto interview, 21–23. At the time, many of the lesbians felt uncomfortable talking about the relationship they had with men. For accounts that detail the painful secrecy many lesbians felt they needed to maintain, see Cvetkovich, *Archive of Feelings*, 189–97.

15   Staley interview, 27.

16   Crimp, *Melancholia and Moralism*, 189.

17   T&D was certainly not the only group working to insert people with AIDS into the treatment agenda. In San Francisco, Martin Delaney formed Project Inform in 1985. For a discussion of Delaney and Project Inform, see Epstein, "Activism, Drug Regulation."

18   Ibid., 692.

19   Eigo interview, 19.

20   For a description of Community Research Initiative, see Chambré, *Fighting for Our Lives*, 143–45, and Epstein, *Impure Science*, 217–19.

21   Long interview, 18.

22   Kirschenbaum interview, 9–17.

23   Barr interview, 21–22.

24   Eigo interview, 20.

25   Ibid., 10.

26   Ibid., 16–17.

27   Harrington interview, 11.

28   Ibid., 12.

29 Staley interview, 11–12.

30 Ibid., 31.

31 Eigo interview, 28–31. See also Epstein, *Impure Science* and "Activism, Drug Regulation."

32 Barr interview, 33; Bordowitz interview, 23–24.

33 Bordowitz interview, 24. See also Gregg Bordowitz and Jean Carlomusto's video, *Seize Control of the* FDA (1988), New York Public Library, AIDS Activist Videotape Collection, 1983–2000.

34 The account of the FDA protest relies on several descriptions of the action. See Bordowitz, *AIDS Crisis Is Ridiculous*, 237–38; Crimp and Rolston, *AIDS Demographics*, 76–830; and Epstein, *Impure Science*, 224–26.

35 Michael Specter, "FDA Amends Rules to Speed AIDS Drugs," *Washington Post*, Oct. 20, 1988, A1.

36 Eigo interview, 26.

37 Kirschenbaum interview, 20–22.

38 Jim Eigo, "Treatment and Data Update: AIDS Clinical Trials and Communities of Color," ca. 1989, ACT UP/NY Records, box 31, folder 2, NYPL, 1.

39 Ibid., 2.

40 Harrington interview, 16.

41 Vélez interview, 34–35.

42 Eigo interview, 32.

43 Fidelino interview, 11.

44 Elbaz, "Sociology of AIDS Activism," 65.

45 MAC, "The Majority Action Committee," ca. 1988, ACT UP/NY Records, box 35, folder 14, NYPL, 1. Almost identical language appeared in a 1988 MAC call to action. See MAC, "A Call to Action," ca. 1988, ACT UP/NY Records, box 35, folder 14, NYPL, 1.

46 MAC, "Manifesto," ca. 1989, ACT UP/NY Records, box 31, folder 2, NYPL, 1.

47 MAC, "Response to the 1988 CDC Conference," Aug. 17, 1988, ACT UP/NY Records, box 35, folder 14, NYPL, 1.

48 Ibid., 2.

49 See Medley interview, 15–16. For a general account of the development of MAC, see Elbaz, "Sociology of AIDS Activism," 246.

50 Thomas interview, 13.

51 "Meeting Minutes, February 27, 1989," ACT UP/NY Records, box 4, folder 1, NYPL, 2–3.

52 Medley interview, 16.

53 Fidelino interview, 12.

54 Carlomusto interview, 22.

55 Banzhaf interview, 50.

56 Wolfe interview, 97.

57 Freedman, *No Turning Back*, 214–15.

58 See Treichler, *How to Have Theory*, 235–77.

59 Wolfe interview, 82.

60 McGovern interview, 15.

61 Josh Barbanel, "U.S. Sued Over AIDS Benefits," *New York Times*, Oct. 2, 1990, B3.

62 Chris Nealon, "Actions Focus on Women with AIDS/HIV," *Gay Community News*, Oct. 13, 1990, 1.

63 Carlomusto interview, 29–30.

64 McGovern interview, 21.

65 "Gran Fury, Guerrilla Girls, Barbara Kruger," *New York Times*, Mar. 8, 1991, C30.

66 CDC, "Estimated Number and Proportion of AIDS Cases among Female Adults" (2006), ⟨http://www.cdc.gov/hiv/topics/surveillance/resources/slides/women/index.htm⟩ (accessed July 3, 2008).

67 Wolfe interview, 94.

68 McGovern interview, 22.

69 ACT UP/NY Women and AIDS Book Group, *Women, AIDS, and Activism*, 3.

70 Ibid., 81.

71 Nelson, *Women of Color and the Reproductive Rights Movement*; Petchesky, *Abortion and Woman's Choice*; Silliman, Fried, Ross, and Gutiérrez, *Undivided Rights*.

72 Sawyer interview, 13–14.

73 Braverman interview, 9. For a description and image of the ACT UP float, see Crimp and Rolston, *AIDS Demographics*, 34.

74 Braverman interview, 13.

75 Ibid., 14–15.

76 Sawyer interview, 19.

77 Chou interview, 10.

78 Sawyer interview, 3.

79 Gonsalves interview, 41.

80 Sawyer interview, 18.

81 "Minutes for January 21 meeting," Jan. 21, 1991, ACT UP/NY Records, box 5, folder 4, NYPL, 3.

82 Epstein writes about the formation of the AIDS Clinical Trial Group in *Impure Science*, 211. For comments on scientific investigation and the CCG, see Harrington interview, 38, 43, and Arno and Feiden, *Against the Odds*, 196.

83 Marea Murray, "'It Is Time to Come': An Activist's Perspective on the First National Women and HIV Conference," *Gay Community News*, Jan. 13, 1991, 1.

84 Kirschenbaum interview, 36–37.

85 Wolfe interview, 110.

86 Carrie Wofford, "Sitting at the Table," *Outweek*, Apr. 3, 1991, 22.

87 For quote about T&D, see Kirschenbaum interview, 36. See also Banzhaf inter-

view, 56–68, and Andrew Vélez, "An Open Letter to ACT UP," Apr. 1, 1991, ACT UP/NY Records, box 8, folder 11, NYPL, 1–2.

88 Nima Eshghi, "II National People of Color AIDS Activist Conference," 1991, ACT UP/NY Records, box 31, folder 2, NYPL, 1–2.

89 While no record of the ACT UP contingent exists, Barr, who was at the session, remembered that men joined the women's caucus members. See Barr interview, 89.

90 Ibid.

91 Banzhaf interview, 61.

92 Chou interview, 27.

93 Wolfe interview, 97.

94 Peter Staley, "ACT UP: Past, Present and Future," May 20, 1991, ACT UP/NY Records, box 5, folder 7, NYPL, 1–3.

95 ACT UP against the New World Order, "Reply to Peter Staley's Speech," June 17, 1991, ACT UP/NY Records, box 29, folder 1, NYPL, 1–2.

96 Ibid., 4.

97 Harrington interview, 59.

98 Staley interview, 56.

99 Carlomusto interview, 44.

100 Agosto interview, 28.

101 Ibid., 30.

102 Northrop interview, 38.

103 Eigo interview, 32.

104 Arno and Feiden, *Against the Odds*, 33.

105 Staley interview, 34.

106 Moravick, "AIDS Activists and Pharmaceuticals."

107 Epstein, "Activism, Drug Regulation," 702.

108 Free trade has been a key component of the postwar economic project. At the 1944 Bretton Woods Conference, the United States and Great Brittan met to develop a system for postwar economic policy. Together, the two nations created GATT, the International Monetary Fund, and the World Bank. These organizations created in the aftermath of World War II made trade and economic development central to the liberal Cold War project that tried to manage the expansion of communism with the expansion of free-market economic policy. See, for example, Aaronson, *Trade and the American Dream*; Lovett, Eckes, and Brinkman, *U.S. Trade Policy*; and Smith, *Endgame*.

109 Devereaux, Lawrence, and Watkins, *Case Studies in US Trade Negotiation*, 52.

110 Ibid., 53.

111 Ibid., 56.

112 Ibid., 38, 77.

113 Slaughter and Rhoades, "Emergence of a Competitive Research and Development Policy Coalition," 304.

114 "US PMA Warning Over GATT," *Pharma Marketletter*, Dec. 13, 1993, 1.

115 "USA 'Must Keep Pressing Patent Pirates,'" *Pharma Marketletter*, Mar. 7, 1994, 1. For a list of countries, see "US PMA Says GATT is 'Seriously Flawed,'" *Pharma Marketletter*, Jan. 31, 1994, 1.

116 Epstein, "Activism, Drug Regulation."

117 Sawyer interview, 40.

118 For quote, see ibid., 41. For an account of the disjuncture between the argument about the end of AIDS and the reality of AIDS in 1996, see Román, "Not-About-AIDS."

119 Thomas interview, 15.

Epilogue

1 TAC, "TAC News, 17 July 2000" (2000), ⟨http://www.tac.org.za/newsletter/2000/ns000717.txt⟩ (accessed Dec. 28, 2006).

2 TAC and Health GAP, "Global March for HIV/AIDS Treatment" (2000), ⟨http://tac.org.za/news_2000.html⟩ (accessed Dec. 28, 2006).

3 I employ the term "AIDS alliance" not because it is a term that TAC or COSATU used but, rather, because it calls to mind the original Tripartite Alliance between COSATU, the South African Communist Party, and the African National Congress, formed in the 1980s in the fight against apartheid.

4 Gouws and Karim, "HIV Infection in South Africa," 56.

5 Craig Schwabe, "Fact Sheet: Poverty in South Africa" (2004), ⟨http://www.sarpn.org.za/documents/d0000990/index.php⟩ (accessed July 29, 2008). For an extensive analysis of the health effects of the links between HIV/AIDS and poverty in South Africa, see DeCoteau, "Bio-Politics of HIV/AIDS."

6 I am indebted to Gregg Bordowitz's account of his experiences at the Durban conference. He writes, "This is just like 1989 was for us" but concludes that his initial position was "enormously arrogant and not correct" (Bordowitz, *AIDS Crisis Is Ridiculous*, 274). For examples of texts that center the U.S. story, see Behrman, *Invisible People*; Sawyer, "ACT UP Founder"; Schoofs, "South Africa Acts Up"; and Smith and Siplon, *Drugs into Bodies*.

7 According to Mark Heywood, who would become the director of the AIDS Law Project, "In the early 1990s, it seemed that the Liberation Movement was committed to a holistic AIDS prevention strategy." The soon-to-be government's 1992 AIDS Plan, unlike contemporaneous models in the United States, "proposed a holistic and multi-sectoral response, including education and prevention, counseling, health care, welfare, and research. The inclusion of a section on law reform and human rights demonstrated an understanding of the relationship between

human rights and public health." See Heywood and Cornell, "Human Rights and AIDS in South Africa," 66.

8   Ibid. 67; Schneider, "On the Fault-Line," 146–47.

9   Anthropologist Virginia van der Vliet argues that the mid-1990s were the best of times and the worst of times for AIDS in South Africa; see van der Vliet, "South Africa Divided," 54. Mandela spearheaded the creation of *Serafina II*, a musical about AIDS designed in the South African activist tradition of using performance to effect political transformation. The cost of the play was exorbitant, and in the end, it had little effect on its viewers. In addition to *Serafina*, Mandela's term also witnessed what has come to be known as the Virodene controversy. In this case, South African researchers claimed to cure AIDS with a drug that had no scientific support. For further discussion of these failures, see Fassin, *When Bodies Remember*; Kauffman and Lindauer, *AIDS and South Africa*; and Schoofs, "South Africa Acts Up."

10 "South African Constitution — Bill of Rights" (1996), ⟨http://www.info.gov.za/documents/constitution/1996/96cons2.htm#27⟩ (accessed Mar. 13, 2007).

11 For an analysis of the practical implications of the South African Bill of Rights, see Ellmann, "Constitutional Confluence."

12 "Section 15C: Amendments to the South African Medicines and Related Substances Control Act No. 101 of 1965" (1997), ⟨http://lists.essential.org/pipermail/pharm-policy/2001-January/000607.html⟩ (accessed Mar. 16, 2007). For a longer description of the legal implications of the Medicines Act, see Snyder, "South Africa's Medicines and Related Substances Control Amendment Act."

13 While it is from three years later, a TAC pamphlet on Brazil's policy suggests that it served as a model for South Africa. See TAC, *Brazil Fact Sheet* (ca. 2000) (Mar. 18, 2007). For an analysis of Brazil's actions, see Biehl, "Activist State."

14 "South Africa Will Disregard Int. Agreements: Zuma," *Pharma Marketletter*, Nov. 20, 1998.

15 Pharmaceutical Manufacturers' Association of South Africa, "Case number 4183/98" (1998), ⟨http://www.cptech.org/ip/health/sa/pharmasuit.html⟩ (accessed Mar. 18, 2007).

16 In its earliest actions, COSATU presented itself as a key player in the struggle against apartheid and subscribed to the position that effective social movements required active union participation. For an overview of social movement unionism, see Von Holt, *Transition from Below*, 8–11, and Wood, "South African Trade Unions in a Time of Adjustment," 134. By the late 1980s, after a decade of violent strikes and protest, unions "emerged as an influential, politically engaged, and strong working-class movement" (Marx, *Lessons of Struggle*, 220). Marx also provides a detailed account of the differing political and ideological positions, most notably the debate between people who supported Black Consciousness and those who supported varying forms of trade unionism, within the antiapartheid strug-

gle. Friedman argues that by 1982, unions had come of age as political actors; see Friedman, *Building Tomorrow Today*. For accounts of the move beyond the shop floor to the political arena or "social movement unionism," see Lambert, "Trade Unions"; Lambert and Webster, "Re-emergence of Political Unionism"; and Murray, *South Africa*. COSATU was certainly not the first federation of unions in South Africa. Unions played a role in the liberation movement as early as the 1950s. The historical and sociological literature on trade unions in South Africa is vast. For a historiographic assessment of South African labor history, see Lewis, "South African Labor History." See also Baskin, *Striking Back*; Fine and Davis, *Beyond Apartheid*; Friedman, *Building Tomorrow Today*; Lambert, "Trade Unions"; Lambert and Webster, "Re-emergence of Political Unionism"; and Marx, *Lessons of Struggle*. In 1990, COSATU formed the Tripartite Alliance with the African National Congress and the South African Communist Party. Together they detailed a shared ideological mission of nonracialism and workers' political potential in the fight to topple a violently racist system that required strict labor control. See Baskin, *Striking Back*, 425, and Webster and Buhlungu, "Between Marginalisation and Revitalisation?," 232–33.

17   TAC, "Day of Action" (1998), ⟨http://tac.org.za/treat.html⟩ (accessed Dec. 28, 2006).

18   Most of the literature on TAC ignores its relationship with COSATU. See Krista Johnson, "AIDS and the Politics of Rights in South Africa"; Schneider, "On the Fault-Line"; and Schoofs, "South Africa Acts Up." The exceptions are Dwyer, "Commentary"; Friedman and Mottiar, "Rewarding Engagement?"; Lethbridge, "Combining Worker and User Interests"; and Robins, "'Long Live Zackie, Long Live.'" All these authors make passing references to COSATU.

19   For an autobiographical account, see Achmat, "My Childhood as an Adult Molester." For journalistic accounts, see Samantha Power, "The AIDS Rebel," *New Yorker*, May 19, 2003, and Schoofs, "South Africa Acts Up." Several films have been made about TAC; one of the best at analyzing Achmat is Brian Tilley's *It's My Life* (2001).

20   Author transcription from Brian Tilley, *It's My Life* (2001).

21   "HIV/AIDS Declared Enemy of the People," *Shopsteward*, June 1998.

22   "Pledge of Representatives of Workers," *Shopsteward*, Sept./Oct. 1999.

23   COSATU, "COSATU Campaign Against HIV/AIDS: A Guide for Shopstewards" (1999–2000), ⟨http://www.cosatu.org.za/docs/2000/hivbook.htm⟩ (accessed Dec. 23, 2007). See also Kim Jurgensen, "Tackling HIV/AIDS," *Shopsteward*, Jan./Feb. 1999.

24   Jeremy Baskin argues that COSATU's workerist and populist positions allowed the rank and file to combine an analysis of race and class in the struggle against apartheid; see Baskin, *Striking Back*, 95. With a tradition of worker control and power of the shop steward built into the trade unions allied under COSATU, many

individual unions not only mobilized workers for protests against apartheid but also educated members on how to be political agents. See Buhlungu, "Building of the Democratic Tradition," 134. COSATU's commitment to education using popular culture meant that workers wrote plays about political struggle that were performed by their comrades. By the end of the 1980s, this strategy of worker education was essential to the federation's political organizing. See Baskin, *Striking Back*, 246. See also the third part of Brown et al., *History from South Africa*.

25 Thabo Mbeki, "Address to the National Council of Provinces" (1999), ⟨http://www .anc.org.za/ancdocs/history/mbeki/1999/tm1028.html⟩ (accessed Jan. 15, 2008).

26 See "Declaration for AIDS Sufferers" and "Durban Declaration." For news coverage, see Jon Jeter and David Brown, "Hundreds Walk Out On Mbeki: S. African's Speech On AIDS Protested," *Washington Post*, July 10, 2000.

27 Joyce Pekane, "Durban Address," *Shopsteward*, Oct. 2000. COSATU's president, Willie Madisha, explicitly supported the position that HIV causes AIDS. "We believe that indeed HIV causes AIDS and that is not disputable. . . . All this talk and debate about the cause of AIDS prevents people from trying to deal with the problem." See Jaspreet Kindra and Glenda Daniels, "COSATU Slams Govt AIDS Policy," *Mail and Guardian*, Sept. 8, 2000.

28 TAC, "Urgent Press Release 19 April 2001" (2001), ⟨http://www.tac.org.za/newsletter /2001/ns010419.txt⟩ (accessed Dec. 29, 2006).

29 Zackie Achmat and Mark Heywood, "Letter to Manto Tchabalala-Msimang" (2001), ⟨http://www.tac.org.za/newsletter/2001/ns010508.txt⟩ (accessed Jan. 19, 2008).

30 Mbeki's denial is a very complicated issue. While it has had an incredibly powerful impact on the course of AIDS work in South Africa, I would like to resist seeing it as *the* central narrative. For the most complete delineation of the lines of debate, see Fassin, *When Bodies Remember*.

31 TAC, "TAC Statement 12 June 2001" (2001), ⟨http://www.tac.org.za/newsletter /2001/ns010612.txt⟩ (accessed Dec. 29, 2006).

32 TAC, *Brazil Fact Sheet* (ca. 2000), 1.

33 High Court of South Africa, "Judgement TAC and Others v. Minister of Health and Others" (2001), ⟨http://tac.org.za/news_2001.html⟩ (accessed Dec. 29, 2006).

34 Willie Madisha, "Defeating HIV: Now is the Time!" (2002), ⟨http://sadtu.org .za/portal/index.php?option=com_content&task=view&id=36&Itemid=123⟩ (accessed July 5, 2008).

35 "Cabinet Statement on Treatment Plan for HIV and AIDS" (2003), ⟨http://www. tac.org.za/newsletter/2003/ns20_11_2003.htm#CabinetStatement⟩ (accessed Jan. 5, 2008).

36 Di Caelers, "The Real Battle to Provide Medicine Is On," *Cape Argus*, Dec. 1, 2003.

37 Zackie Achmat, "Living Non-Racialism," *Mail and Guardian*, May 2, 2003.

Bibliography

Archival Materials

George Bush Presidential Library, College Station, Tex.

Ford Foundation Archives, New York, N.Y.

Gay, Lesbian, Bisexual, Transgender Historical Society, San Francisco, Calif.
  Randy Alfred Papers

National Archive of Lesbian, Gay, Bisexual, Transgender History, New York, N.Y.
  Michael Callen Collection

National Library of Medicine, Bethesda, Md.
  C. Everett Koop Papers
  National Commission on AIDS
  PHS Surgeon General's Office AIDS Records

New York Public Library, New York, N.Y.
  AIDS Coalition to Unleash Power/NY Records
  International Gay Information Center Records
  Lawrence Mass Collection

Northeastern University Archives, Boston, Mass.
  Bromfield St. Educational Foundation

Princeton University Library, Princeton, N.J.
  American Civil Liberties Union Records

Ronald Reagan Presidential Library, Simi Valley, Calif.
  Howard L. Baker Files
  William L. Ball Files
  Gary L. Bauer Files
  Mariam Bell Files
  Ralph C. Bledsoe Files
  Judi Buckalew Files
  Herman J. Cohen Files

C. Christopher Cox Files
Charles D. Hobbs Files
Donald Ian MacDonald Files
Patricia Mack-Bryan Files
Nancy J. Risque Files
Robert W. Sweet Files
James H. Warner Files
Faith Ryan Whittlesey Files
WHORM Subject Files

San Francisco Public Library, San Francisco, Calif.

AIDS Office of the San Francisco Department of Public Health Records

University of California at San Francisco Archives, San Francisco, Calif.

AIDS History Project Ephemera Collection
Multicultural AIDS Resource Center Records
San Francisco AIDS Foundation Records
Third World AIDS Advisory Task Force Records

Interviews

Agosto, Moises. Interview with Sarah Schulman. Transcript of audio recording, December 15, 2002. ACT UP Oral History Project, ⟨http://www.actuporalhistory .org⟩.

Banzhaf, Marion. Interview with Sarah Schulman. Transcript of audio recording, April 18, 2007. ACT UP Oral History Project, ⟨http://www.actuporalhistory.org⟩.

Barr, David. Interview with Sarah Schulman. Transcript of audio recording, May 15, 2007. ACT UP Oral History Project, ⟨http://www.actuporalhistory.org⟩.

Bauer, Amy. Interview with Sarah Schulman. Transcript of audio recording, March 7, 2004. ACT UP Oral History Project, ⟨http://www.actuporalhistory.org⟩.

Berkowitz, Richard. Interview with author. July 15, 2005, New York, N.Y. In author's possession.

Berresford, Susan. Phone interview with author. March 25, 2008.

Bordowitz, Gregg. Interview with Sarah Schulman. Transcript of audio recording, December 17, 2002. ACT UP Oral History Project, ⟨http://www.actuporalhistory .org⟩.

Braverman, Gedalia. Interview with Sarah Schulman. Transcript of audio recording, April 20, 2003. ACT UP Oral History Project, ⟨http://www.actuporalhistory.org⟩.

Carlomusto, Jean. Interview with Sarah Schulman. Transcript of audio recording, December 19, 2002. ACT UP Oral History Project, ⟨http://www.actuporalhistory .org⟩.

Cates, Willard. Interview with Rebecca Sharpless. Audio recording, May 25–26,

2004. Population and Reproductive Health Oral History Project, Sophia Smith Collection, Smith College, Northampton, Mass., tape 1.

Chou, Lei. Interview with Sarah Schulman. Transcript of audio recording, May 5, 2003. ACT UP Oral History Project, ⟨http://www.actuporalhistory.org⟩.

Deagle, Richard. Interview with Sarah Schulman. Transcript of audio recording, September 13, 2003. ACT UP Oral History Project, ⟨http://www.actuporalhistory .org⟩.

Eigo, Jim. Interview with Sarah Schulman. Transcript of audio recording, March 5, 2004. ACT UP Oral History Project, ⟨http://www.actuporalhistory.org⟩.

Fidelino, Jose. Interview with Sarah Schulman. Transcript of audio recording, October 13, 2004. ACT UP Oral History Project, ⟨http://www.actuporalhistory.org⟩.

Forman, Shepard. Phone interview with author. April 2, 2008.

Germain, Adrienne. Interview with Rebecca Sharpless. Transcript of audio recording, June 19–20, Sept. 25, 2003. Population and Reproductive Health Oral History Project, Sophia Smith Collection, Smith College, Northampton, Mass.

Gonsalves, Gregg. Interview with Sarah Schulman. Transcript of audio recording, January 19, 2004. ACT UP Oral History Project, ⟨http://www.actuporalhistory.org⟩.

Harrington, Mark. Interview with Sarah Schulman. Transcript of audio recording, March 8, 2003. ACT UP Oral History Project, ⟨http://www.actuporalhistory.org⟩.

Hempel, Margaret. Phone interview with author. April 2, 2008.

Jones, Nicola. Phone interview with author. July 2, 2008.

Kirschenbaum, David. Interview with Sarah Schulman. Transcript of audio recording, October 19, 2003. ACT UP Oral History Project, ⟨http://www .actuporalhistory.org⟩.

Kubisch, Anne. Phone interview with author. April 14, 2008.

Long, Iris. Interview with Sarah Schulman. Transcript of audio recording, May 16, 2003. ACT UP Oral History Project, ⟨http://www.actuporalhistory.org⟩.

McGovern, Terry. Interview with Sarah Schulman. Transcript of audio recording, May 25, 2007. ACT UP Oral History Project, ⟨http://www.actuporalhistory.org⟩.

Medley, Ron. Interview with Sarah Schulman. Transcript of audio recording, December 28, 2003. ACT UP Oral History Project, ⟨http://www.actuporalhistory .org⟩.

Muecke, Marjorie. Phone interview with author. April 29, 2008.

Northrop, Ann. Interview with Sarah Schulman. Transcript of audio recording, May 28, 2004. ACT UP Oral History Project, ⟨http://www.actuporalhistory.org⟩.

Pappas, Les. Phone interview with author. June 5, 2001.

Parker, Richard. Phone interview with author. March 11, 2008.

Sawyer, Eric. Interview with Sarah Schulman. Transcript of audio recording, March 10, 2004. ACT UP Oral History Project, ⟨http://www.actuporalhistory.org⟩.

Seltzer, Michael. Phone interview with author. March 3, 2008.

Staley, Peter. Interview with Sarah Schulman. Transcript of audio recording,

December 9, 2006. ACT UP Oral History Project, ⟨http://www.actuporalhistory .org⟩.

Tavera, Hank. Interview with Horacio Roque Ramirez. May 19, 1995. LGBT/Queer Latina and Latino San Francisco Oral History Project. In author's possession.

Thomas, Kendall. Interview with Sarah Schulman. Transcript of audio recording, May 3, 2003. ACT UP Oral History Project, ⟨http://www.actuporalhistory.org⟩.

Vélez, Andrew. Interview with Sarah Schulman. Transcript of audio recording, February 26, 2004. ACT UP Oral History Project, ⟨http://www.actuporalhistory.org⟩.

Viravaidya, Mechai. Interview with Deborah McFarlane. Transcript of audio recording, October 6, 2003. Population and Reproductive Health Oral History Project, Sophia Smith Collection, Smith College, Northampton, Mass.

Wolfe, Maxine. Interview with Jim Hubbard. Transcript of audio recording, February 19, 2004. ACT UP Oral History Project, ⟨http://www.actuporalhistory.org⟩.

Newspapers and Periodicals

Bay Area Reporter
Gay Community News
Gay Life
Los Angeles Times
Mail and Guardian (South Africa)
New York Daily News
New York Native
New York Newsday
New York Times
San Francisco Chronicle
Village Voice
Washington Post

Published Sources, Reports, and Dissertations

Aaronson, Susan A. *Trade and the American Dream: A Social History of Postwar Trade Policy.* Lexington: University Press of Kentucky, 1996.

Abramson, Paul R., and Gilbert Herdt. "The Assessment of Sexual Practices Relevant to the Transmission of AIDS: A Global Perspective." *Journal of Sex Research* 27, no. 2 (1990): 215–32.

Achmat, Zackie. "My Childhood as an Adult Molester: A Salt River Moffie." In *Defiant Desire: Gay and Lesbian Lives in South Africa*, edited by Mark Gevisser and Edwin Cameron, 325–41. New York: Routledge, 1995.

ACT UP/NY Women and AIDS Book Group. *Women, AIDS, and Activism.* Boston: South End, 1990.

Adams, Vincanne, and Stacy Leigh Pigg, eds. *Sex in Development: Science, Sexuality, and Morality in Global Perspective*. Durham: Duke University Press, 2005.

AIDSTECH. *Tools for Project Evaluation: A Guide for Evaluating AIDS Prevention Interventions*. Durham: Family Health International, 1992.

Altman, Dennis. *AIDS in the Mind of America: The Social, Political, and Psychological Impact of a New Epidemic*. Garden City: Anchor, 1987.

———. *Power and Community: Organizational and Cultural Responses to AIDS*. London: Taylor and Francis, 1994.

Amadiume, Ifi. *Daughters of the Goddess, Daughters of Imperialism: African Women Struggle for Culture, Power, and Democracy*. London: Zed Books, 2000.

Andrews, John A. *The Other Side of the Sixties: Young Americans for Freedom and the Rise of Conservative Politics*. New Brunswick: Rutgers University Press, 1997.

Andriote, John-Manuel. *Victory Deferred: How AIDS Changed Gay Life in America*. Chicago: University of Chicago Press, 1999.

Antrobus, Peggy. *The Global Women's Movement: Origins, Issues, and Strategies*. London: Zed Books, 2004.

Armstrong, Elizabeth. *Forging Gay Identities: Organizing Sexuality in San Francisco, 1950–1994*. Chicago: University of Chicago Press, 2002.

Arno, Peter S., and Karyn L. Feiden. *Against the Odds: The Story of AIDS Drug Development, Politics, and Profits*. New York: Harper Collins, 1992.

Arno, Peter S., Karen Bonuck, and Michael Davis. "Rare Diseases, Drug Development, and AIDS: The Impact of the Orphan Drug Act." *Milbank Quarterly* 73, no. 2 (1995): 231–52.

Banks, Taunya Lovell. "Review: AIDS and Government. A Plan of Action?" *Michigan Law Review* 87, no. 6 (1989): 1321–37.

Barzelatto, José. "Ethics and Human Values in Family Planning." *International Journal of Gynecology and Obstetrics* 28 (1989): 327–30.

———. *Introduction to The Colectivo: A Feminist Sexuality and Health Collective in Brazil*. Edited by Margarita Diaz and Debbie Rogow. *Quality/Calidad/Qualité*, no. 6 (1995): 1–21.

Baskin, Jeremy. *Striking Back: A History of COSATU*. London: Verso, 1991.

Bastos, Cristiana. *Global Responses to AIDS: Science in Emergency*. Bloomington: Indiana University Press, 1999.

Basu, Amrita, ed. *The Challenge of Local Feminisms: Women's Movements in Global Perspective*. Boulder: Westview Press, 1995.

Bayer, Ronald. *Private Acts, Social Consequences: AIDS and the Politics of Public Health*. New Brunswick: Rutgers University Press, 1991.

Beam, Joseph, ed. *In the Life: A Black Gay Anthology*. Boston: Alyson, 1986.

Beemyn, Brett, ed. *Creating a Place for Ourselves: Lesbian, Gay, and Bisexual Community Histories*. New York: Routledge, 1997.

Behrman, Greg. *The Invisible People: How the U.S. Has Slept through the Global AIDS*

Pandemic, the Greatest Humanitarian Catastrophe of Our Time. New York: Free Press, 2004.

Beinhart, William. *Twentieth-Century South Africa.* Oxford: Oxford University Press, 1994.

Berkowitz, Richard. *Stayin' Alive: The Invention of Safe Sex, a Personal History.* Cambridge, Mass.: Westview Press, 2003.

Berlant, Lauren. *The Queen of America Goes to Washington City: Essays on Sex and Citizenship.* Durham: Duke University Press, 1997.

Berman, William. *America's Right Turn: From Nixon to Bush.* Baltimore: Johns Hopkins University Press, 1994.

Berridge, Virginia, and Philip Strong, eds. *AIDS and Contemporary History.* Cambridge: Cambridge University Press, 1993.

Bersani, Leo. "Is the Rectum a Grave?" In *AIDS: Cultural Analysis, Cultural Activism,* edited by Douglas Crimp, 197–222. Cambridge, Mass.: MIT Press, 1988.

Bhavnani, Kum-Kum, John Foran, and Priya A. Kurian. "An Introduction to Women, Culture, and Development." In *Feminist Futures: Re-imagining Women, Culture, and Development,* edited by Kum-Kum Bhavnani, John Foran, and Priya A. Kurian, 1–21. London: Zed Books, 2003.

Biehl, João. "The Activist State: Global Pharmaceuticals, AIDS, and Citizenship in Brazil." *Social Text* 80, no. 3 (2004): 105–32.

Bishop, Ryan. *Night Market: Sexual Cultures in the Thai Economic Miracle.* Edited by Lillian Robinson. New York: Routledge, 1998.

Black, Allida M., ed. *Modern American Queer History.* Philadelphia: Temple University Press, 2001.

Boffey, Philip. "Reagan Urges Wide AIDS Testing But Does Not Call for Compulsion." *New York Times,* June 1, 1987, A1.

Bogecho, Dina, and Melissa Upreti. "The Global Gag Rule: An Antithesis to the Rights-Based Approach to Health." *Health and Human Rights* 9, no. 1 (2006): 17–32.

Bolton, Ralph, Michelle Lewis, and Gail Orozco. "AIDS Literature for Anthropologists: A Working Bibliography." *Journal of Sex Research* 28, no. 2 (1991): 307–46.

Bordowitz, Gregg. *The AIDS Crisis Is Ridiculous and Other Writings, 1986–2003.* Cambridge, Mass.: MIT Press, 2004.

Borstelmann, Thomas. *The Cold War and the Color Line: American Race Relations in the Global Arena.* Cambridge, Mass.: Harvard University Press, 2001.

Boserup, Esther. *Woman's Role in Economic Development.* London: Earthscan Publications, 1989.

Boston Women's Health Book Collective. *Our Bodies, Ourselves.* New York: Simon and Schuster, 1973.

Boyd, Nan Alamilla. *Wide Open Town: A History of Queer San Francisco to 1965*. Berkeley: University of California Press, 2003.

Boyer, Paul, ed. *Reagan as President: Contemporary Views of the Man, His Politics, and His Policies*. Chicago: Ivan R. Dee, 1990.

Brandt, Allan. *No Magic Bullet: A Social History of Venereal Disease in the United States since 1880*. New York: Oxford, 1987.

Brier, Jennifer. "The Immigrant Infection: Images of Race, Nation, and Contagion in Public Debates on AIDS and Immigration." In *Modern American Queer History*, edited by Allida M. Black, 253–70. Philadelphia: Temple University Press, 2001.

Bronski, Michael. *The Pleasure Principle: Sex, Backlash, and the Struggle for Gay Freedom*. New York: St. Martin's Press, 1998.

Broussard, Albert S. *Black San Francisco: The Struggle for Racal Equality in the West, 1900–1954*. Lawrence: University Press of Kansas, 1993.

Brown, Joshua, Patrick Manning, Karen Shapiro, Jon Weiner, Belinda Bozzoli, and Peter Delius, eds. *History from South Africa: Alternative Visions and Practices*. Philadelphia: Temple University Press, 1991.

Brown, Wendy, and Janet Halley, eds. *Left Legalism/Left Critique*. Durham: Duke University Press, 2002.

Buhlungu, Sakhela. "The Building of the Democratic Tradition in South Africa's Trade Unions after 1974." *Democratization* 11, no. 3 (2004): 133–58.

Burgeron, Suzanne. "Political Economy Discourses of Globalization and Feminist Politics." *Signs* 26, no. 4 (2001): 983–1006.

Caldwell, John, and Pat Caldwell. *Limiting Population Growth and the Ford Foundation Contribution*. London: France Pinter, 1986.

Callen, Michael, and Richard Berkowitz. *How to Have Sex in an Epidemic: One Approach*. New York: Tower Press, 1983.

———. "We Know Who We Are: Two Gay Men Declare War on Promiscuity." *New York Native*, November 8, 1982.

Cameron, Edwin. "The Deafening Silence of AIDS." *Health and Human Rights* 5, no. 1 (2000): 7–24.

Cannon, Lou. *President Reagan: The Role of a Lifetime*. New York: Simon and Schuster, 1991.

Carbado, Devon, ed. *Black Men on Race, Gender, and Sexuality*. New York: New York University Press, 1999.

Chambré, Susan. *Fighting for Our Lives: New York's AIDS Community and the Politics of Disease*. New Brunswick: Rutgers University Press, 2006.

Chasin, Alexandra. *Selling Out: The Gay and Lesbian Movement Goes to Market*. New York: St. Martin's Press, 2000.

Chen, Lincoln C., Jaime Sepulveda Amor, and Sheldon J. Segal. *AIDS and Women's Reproductive Health*. New York: Plenum Press, 1991.

Child Survival/Reproductive Health Programs: Ford Foundation Staff Meeting. Vol. 1,
   Proceedings. New York: Ford Foundation, 1988.

Chirimuuta, Richard, and Rosilind Chirimuuta. *AIDS, Africa, and Racism.* London:
   Free Association Books, 1989.

Chua, Peter, Kum-Kum Bhavnani, and John Foran. "Women, Culture, Development:
   A New Paradigm for Development Studies?" *Ethnic and Racial Studies* 23, no. 5
   (2000): 820–41.

Clawson, Mary Ann. *Constructing Brotherhood: Class, Gender, and Fraternalism.*
   Princeton: Princeton University Press, 1989.

Cochrane, Michelle. *When AIDS Began: San Francisco and the Making of an
   Epidemic.* New York: Routledge, 2004.

Cohen, Cathy. *The Boundaries of Blackness: AIDS and the Breakdown of Black Politics.*
   Chicago: University of Chicago Press, 1999.

———. "Contested Membership: Black Gay Identities and the Politics of AIDS." In
   Queer Theory/Sociology, edited by Steven Seidman. Cambridge: Blackwell, 1996.

Cohen, Lizbeth. *A Consumers' Republic: The Politics of Mass Consumption in Postwar
   America.* New York: Knopf, 2003.

Cohen, Peter. "'All They Needed': AIDS, Consumption, and the Politics of Class."
   Journal of the History of Sexuality 8, no. 1 (1997): 86–115.

———. *Love and Anger: Essays on AIDS, Activism, and Politics.* New York: Hayworth
   Press, 1998.

Collins, Patricia Hill. *Black Sexual Politics: African Americans, Gender, and the New
   Racism.* New York: Routledge, 2004.

Congressional Research Service. *American Public Opinion on AIDS.* Washington,
   D.C.: U.S. Government Printing Office, 1989.

Connelly, Matthew. *Fatal Misconceptions: The Struggle to Control World Population.*
   Cambridge, Mass.: Belknap Press, 2008.

Cook, Nerida. "'Dutiful Daughters,' Estranged Sisters: Women in Thailand." In
   Gender and Power in Affluent Asia, edited by Krishna Sen and Maila Stivens,
   250–90. New York: Routledge, 1998.

Cooper, Frederick, and Randall Packard. Introduction to *International Development
   and the Social Sciences*, edited by Frederick Cooper and Randall Packard, 1–41.
   Berkeley: University of California Press, 1997.

Corrêa, Sonia. *Population and Reproductive Rights: Feminist Perspectives from the
   South.* London: Zed Books, 1994.

Crane, Barbara B., and Jennifer Dusenberry. "Power and Politics in International
   Funding for Reproductive Health: The US Global Gag Rule." *Reproductive Health
   Matters* 12, no. 24 (2004): 128–37.

Created Equal: A Report on Ford Foundation Women's Program. New York: Ford
   Foundation, 1986.

Crimp, Douglas. "How to Have Promiscuity in an Epidemic." In *AIDS: Cultural*

Analysis/Cultural Activism, edited by Douglas Crimp, 237–71. Cambridge, Mass.: MIT Press, 1988.

———. *Melancholia and Moralism: Essays on AIDS and Queer Politics*. Cambridge, Mass.: MIT Press, 2002.

———. "Randy Shilts' Miserable Failure." In *A Queer World: The Center for Lesbian and Gay Studies Reader*, edited by Martin Duberman, 641–48. New York: New York University Press, 1997.

———, ed. *AIDS: Cultural Analysis, Cultural Activism*. Cambridge, Mass.: MIT Press, 1988.

Crimp, Douglas, and Adam Rolston. *AIDS Demographics*. Seattle: Bay Press, 1990.

Critchlow, Donald T. "Implementing Family Planning Policy: Philanthropic Foundations and the Modern Welfare State." In *With Us Always: A History of Private Charity and Public Welfare*, edited by Donald T. Critchlow and Charles H. Parker, 211–40. Lanham, Md.: Rowman and Littlefield, 1998.

———. *Intended Consequences: Birth Control, Abortion, and the Federal Government in Modern America*. New York: Oxford, 1999.

Cvetkovich, Ann. *An Archive of Feelings: Trauma, Sexuality, and Lesbian Public Culture*. Durham: Duke University Press, 2003.

Davis, Kathy. *The Making of "Our Bodies, Ourselves": How Feminism Travels across Borders*. Durham: Duke University Press, 2007.

"Declaration for AIDS Sufferers." *Nature* 406, no. 6791 (2000): 1.

DeCoteau, Claire Laurier. "The Bio-Politics of HIV/AIDS in Post Apartheid South Africa." Ph.D. diss., University of Michigan, 2008.

DeLeon, Richard. "San Francisco: The Politics of Race, Land Use, and Ideology." In *Racial Politics in American Cities*, edited by Rufus Browning and Dale Rogers Marshall, 167–98. New York: Longman, 2003.

D'Emilio, John. "After Stonewall." In *Making Trouble*, 234–73. New York: Routledge, 1992.

———. *Sexual Politics, Sexual Communities: The Making of a Homosexual Minority in the United States, 1940–1970*. 2nd ed. Chicago: University of Chicago Press, 1998.

D'Emilio, John, and Estelle Freedman. *Intimate Matters: A History of Sexuality in America*. 2nd ed. Chicago: University of Chicago Press, 1997.

Devereaux, Charan, Robert Z. Lawrence, and Michael D. Watkins. *Case Studies in US Trade Negotiation: Making the Rules*. Vol. 1. Washington, D.C.: Institute for International Economics, 2006.

Diamond, Sara. *Roads to Dominion: Right-Wing Movements and Political Power in the United States*. New York: Guilford, 1995.

Díaz, Rafael M. *Latino Gay Men and HIV: Culture, Sexuality, and Risk Behavior*. New York: Routledge, 1998.

Dixon-Mueller, Ruth. *Population Policy and Women's Rights: Transforming Reproductive Choice*. Westport: Praeger, 1993.

Donaldson, Peter J. *Nature against Us: The United States and the World Population Crisis, 1965–1980*. Chapel Hill: University of North Carolina Press, 1990.

Dudziak, Mary. *Cold War Civil Rights: Race and the Image of American Democracy*. Princeton: Princeton University Press, 2000.

Duggan, Lisa. *The Twilight of Equality? Neoliberalism, Cultural Politics, and the Attack on Democracy*. Boston: Beacon, 2003.

Duggan, Lisa, and Nan Hunter. *Sex Wars: Sexual Dissent and Political Culture*. New York: Routledge, 1995.

"The Durban Declaration." *Nature* 406, no. 6791 (2000): 15.

Dwyer, Peter. "Commentary: Dying to Fight." *Transformation* 53 (2003): 76–80.

Eades, Lindsay Michie. *The End of Apartheid in South Africa*. Westport: Greenwood Press, 1999.

Edsall, Thomas Byrne. *New Politics of Inequality*. New York: Norton, 1984.

Edwards, D. D., and L. Beil. "Pessimistic Outlook in AIDS Reports." *Science News* 133, no. 24 (1988): 372.

Edwards, Jeffrey. "AIDS, Race, and the Rise and Decline of a Militant Oppositional Lesbian and Gay Politics in the US." *New Political Science* 22, no. 4 (2000): 485–506.

Ehrlich, Paul R. *The Population Bomb*. New York: Ballantine, 1968.

Ehrman, John. *The Eighties: America in the Age of Reagan*. New Haven: Yale University Press, 2005.

Elbaz, Gilbert. "Beyond Anger: The Activist Construction of the AIDS Crisis." *Social Justice* 22, no. 4 (1995): 43–86.

———. "The Sociology of AIDS Activism, the Case of ACT UP/New York, 1987–1992." Ph.D. diss., CUNY, 1992.

Ellmann, Stephen. "A Constitutional Confluence: American 'State Action' Law and the Application of South Africa's Socio-economic Rights Guarantee to Private Actors." In *The Post-Apartheid Constitutions: Perspectives on South Africa's Basic Law*, edited by Penelope Andrews and Stephen Ellmann, 440–80. Johannesburg: Witwaterstrand University Press, 2001.

Eng, David. *Racial Castration: Managing Masculinity in Asian America*. Durham: Duke University Press, 2001.

Epstein, Steven. "Activism, Drug Regulation, and the Politics of Therapeutic Evaluation in the AIDS Era: A Case Study of ddC and the 'Surrogate Markers' Debate." *Social Studies of Science* 27, no. 5 (1997): 691–726.

———. *Impure Science: AIDS, Activism, and the Politics of Knowledge*. Berkeley: University of California Press, 1996.

Escobar, Arturo. *Encountering Development: The Making and Unmaking of the Third World*. Princeton: Princeton University Press, 1994.

Escoffier, Jeffrey. "Fabulous Politics: Gay, Lesbian, and Queer Movements, 1969–1999." In *The World the Sixties Made: Politics and Culture in Recent America*, edited by Van Gosse and Richard Moser, 199–218. Philadelphia: Temple University Press, 2003.

Fain, Nathan. "Is Our 'Lifestyle' Hazardous to Our Health?" Pt. 2. *Advocate*, April 1, 1982.

Fairchild, Amy. *Science at the Borders: Immigrant Medical Inspection and the Shaping of the Modern Industrial Labor Force*. Baltimore: Johns Hopkins University Press, 2003.

Fairchild, Amy, and Eileen Tynan. "Policies of Containment: Immigration in an Era of AIDS." *American Journal of Public Health*, no. 84 (1994): 2011–22.

Family Health International. *Making Prevention Work: Global Lessons Learned from the AIDS Control and Prevention (AIDSCAP) Project, 1991–1997*. Durham: Family Health International, 1997.

Farmer, Paul. *AIDS and Accusation: Haiti and the Geography of Blame*. Berkeley: University of California Press, 1992.

———. *Infections and Inequalities: The Modern Plagues*. Berkeley: University of California Press, 1999.

Fassin, Didier. *When Bodies Remember: Experience and Politics of AIDS in South Africa*. Berkeley: University of California Press, 2007.

Faúndes, A., and E. Hardy. "From Birth Control to Reproductive Health." *International Journal of Gynecology and Obstetrics* 49 (1995): 55–62.

Faúndes, Aníbal. "In Memoriam: José Barzelatto." *Reproductive Health Matters* 14, no. 28 (2006): 181–83.

Fee, Elizabeth, and Daniel Fox, eds. *AIDS: The Burdens of History*. Berkeley: University of California Press, 1988.

———, eds. *AIDS: The Making of a Chronic Disease*. Berkeley: University of California Press, 1992.

Ferguson, Thomas, and Joel Rogers. *Right Turn: The Decline of the Democrats and the Future of American Politics*. New York: Hill and Wang, 1986.

Festervand, Troy. "An Introduction and Application of Focus Group Research to the Health Care Industry." *Health Marketing Quarterly* 2, no. 2–3 (1984–5): 199–209.

Fine, Robert, and Dennis Davis. *Beyond Apartheid: Labour and Liberation in South Africa*. London: Pluto Press, 1990.

Finnemore, Martha. "Redefining Development at the World Bank." In *International Development and the Social Sciences*, edited by Frederick Cooper and Randall Packard, 203–27. Berkeley: University of California Press, 1997.

Fitzgerald, Frances. *Way Out There in the Blue: Reagan, Star Wars, and the End of the Cold War*. New York: Simon and Schuster, 2000.

Ford Foundation. *Reproductive Health: A Strategy for the 1990s*. New York: Ford Foundation, 1991.

———. *Reproductive Health and Population Program: A Progress Report, 1990–1992*. New York: Ford Foundation, 1992.

———. *Women in the World: A Ford Foundation Position Paper*. New York: Ford Foundation, 1980.

Formisano, Ronald. *Boston against Busing: Race, Class, and Ethnicity in the 1960s and 1970s*. Chapel Hill: University of North Carolina Press, 1991.

Fraser, Steve, and Gary Gerstle, eds. *The Rise and Fall of the New Deal Order, 1930–1980*. Princeton: Princeton University Press, 1989.

Freedman, Estelle. *No Turning Back: The History of Feminism and the Future of Women*. New York: Ballantine, 2002.

Friedman, Steven. *Building Tomorrow Today: African Workers in Trade Unions, 1970–1984*. Johannesburg: Ravan Press, 1987.

Friedman, Steven, and Shauna Mottiar. "A Rewarding Engagement? The Treatment Action Campaign and the Politics of HIV/AIDS." *Politics and Society* 33, no. 4 (2005): 511–65.

Fry, Peter. "Male Homosexuality and Spirit Possession in Brazil." *Journal of Homosexuality* 11, no. 3/4 (1985): 137–53.

Gaither, H. Rowan, Jr. *Report of the Study for the Ford Foundation on Policy and Program*. Detroit: Ford Foundation, 1949.

Gallo, Marcia M. *Different Daughters: A History of the Daughters of Bilitis and the Rise of the Lesbian Rights Movement*. New York: Carroll and Graf, 2006.

Gamson, Joshua. "Must Identity Movements Self-Destruct? A Queer Dilemma." *Social Problems* 42, no. 3 (1995): 390–407.

———. "Silence, Death, and the Invisible Enemy: AIDS Activism and Social Movement 'Newness.'" *Social Problems* 36, no. 4 (1989): 351–67.

Garcia-Moreno, Claudia, and Amparo Claro. "Challenges from the Women's Health Movement: Women's Rights versus Population Control." In *Population Policies Reconsidered: Health, Empowerment, and Rights*, edited by Gita Sen, Adrienne Germain, and Lincoln C. Chen, 47–61. Cambridge, Mass.: Harvard University Press, 1994.

Gerstle, Gary. "Race and the Myth of the Liberal Consensus." *Journal of American History* 82, no. 2 (1995): 579–86.

Gilmore, David. *Manhood in the Making: Cultural Concepts of Masculinity*. New Haven: Yale University Press, 1990.

Gitlin, Todd. *The Twilight of Common Dreams: Why America Is Wracked by Culture Wars*. New York: Metropolitan Books, 1995.

Glenn, Cathy B. "Queering the (Sacred) Body Politic: Considering the Performative Cultural Politics of the Sisters of Perpetual Indulgence." *Theory and Event* 7, no. 1 (2003). Online journal.

Global HIV Prevention Working Group. *Bringing HIV Prevention to Scale: An Urgent Global Priority*. Seattle: Bill and Melinda Gates Foundation, 2007.

Golumbic, Court E. "Closing the Open Door: The Impact of the Human Immunodeficiency Virus Exclusion on the Legalization Program of the

Immigration Reform and Control Act of 1986." *Yale Journal of International Law* 15 (1990): 162–89.

Gordon, Linda. *Woman's Body, Woman's Right: Birth Control in America*. New York: Penguin, 1990.

Gorna, Robin. *Vamps, Virgins, and Victims: How Can Women Fight AIDS?* New York: Cassell, 1996.

Gosse, Van. "Introduction I: Postmodern America." In *The World the Sixties Made: Politics and Culture in Recent America*, edited by Van Gosse and Richard Moser, 1–36. Philadelphia: Temple University Press, 2003.

Gosse, Van, and Richard Moser, eds. *The World the Sixties Made: Politics and Culture in Recent America*. Philadelphia: Temple University Press, 2003.

Gould, Deborah. "Life in Wartime: Emotions and the Development of ACT UP." *Mobilization* 7, no. 2 (2002): 177–200.

———. *Moving Politics: Emotion and Shifting Political Horizons in the Fight against AIDS*. Chicago: University of Chicago Press, forthcoming.

———. "Sex, Death, and the Politics of Anger: Emotions and Reason in ACT UP's Fight against AIDS." Ph.D. diss., University of Chicago, 2000.

Gouws, Eleanor, and Quarraisha Abdool Karim. "HIV Infection in South Africa: The Evolving Epidemic." In *HIV/AIDS in South Africa*, edited by S. S. Abdool Karim and Q. Abdool Karim, 48–66. New York: Cambridge University Press, 2005.

Greco, Stephen. "Report on NYC GRID Briefing." *Advocate*, July 8, 1982, 13.

Grmek, Mirko D. *History of AIDS: Emergence and Origin of a Modern Pandemic*. Translated by Russell C. Maulitz and Jacalyn Duffin. Princeton: Princeton University Press, 1990.

Gruskin, Sophia, Jonathan Mann, and Daniel Tarantola. "Past, Present, and Future: AIDS and Human Rights." *Health and Human Rights* 2, no. 4 (1998): 1–3.

Gupta, Monica Das, Lincoln C. Chen, and T. N. Krishnan. *Women's Health in India*. Bombay: Oxford University Press, 1995.

Gutiérrez, Elena. *Fertile Matters: The Politics of Mexican-Origin Women's Reproduction*. Austin: University of Texas Press, 2008.

Halchi, Abigail. "AIDS, Anger, and Activism: ACT UP as a Social Movement Organization." In *Waves of Protest: Social Movements since the Sixties*, edited by Jo Freeman and Victoria Johnson, 135–52. Lanham, Md.: Rowman and Littlefield, 1999.

Hammonds, Evelynn. "Missing Persons: African American Women, AIDS, and the History of Disease." *Radical America* 24, no. 2 (1990): 7–23.

———. "Race, Sex, AIDS: The Construction of 'Other.'" *Radical America* 20, no. 6 (1987): 328–40.

———. "Seeing AIDS: Race, Gender, and Representation." In *The Gender Politics of HIV/AIDS in Women: Perspectives on the Pandemic in the United States*, edited by Nancy Goldstein, 113–26. New York: New York University Press, 1997.

Harkavy, Oscar. *Curbing Population Growth: An Insider's Perspective on the Population Movement*. New York: Plenum Press, 1995.

Hartmann, Betsy. *Reproductive Rights and Wrongs: The Global Politics of Population Control*. 2nd ed. Boston: South End, 1995.

Harvey, David. *A Brief History of Neoliberalism*. Oxford: Oxford University Press, 2005.

Harvey, Philip. *Let Every Child Be Wanted: How Social Marketing Is Revolutionizing Contraceptive Use around the World*. Westport: Auburn House, 1999.

Helms, Senator Jesse. "Departments of Labor, Health and Human Services, and Education, and Related Agencies Appropriations, Fiscal Year 1988." *Congressional Record*, October 14, 1987, S14200–14213.

Hemphill, Essex, ed. *Brother to Brother: New Writings by Black Gay Men*. Boston: Alyson, 1991.

Hess, Gary R. "Waging the Cold War in the Third World: The Foundations and the Challenges of Development." In *Charity, Philanthropy, and Civility in American History*, edited by Lawrence Friedman and Mark McGarvie, 319–39. Cambridge: Cambridge University Press, 2003.

Heywood, Mark. "Current Developments: Preventing Mother-to-Child HIV Transmission in South Africa." *South African Journal of Human Rights* 19 (2003): 278–315.

Heywood, Mark, and Morna Cornell. "Human Rights and AIDS in South Africa: From Right Margin to Left Margin." *Health and Human Rights* 2, no. 4 (1998): 60–82.

Higginbotham, Evelyn Brooks. *Righteous Discontent: The Women's Movement in the Black Baptist Church, 1880–1920*. Cambridge, Mass.: Harvard University Press, 1993.

Hilderbrand, Lucas. "Retroactivism." *GLQ* 12, no. 2 (2006): 303–17.

Hodgson, Godfrey. *The World Turned Right Side Up: A History of the Conservative Ascendancy in America*. Boston: Houghton Mifflin, 1996.

Hoffman, Amy. *An Army of Ex-Lovers: My Life at the Gay Community News*. Amherst: University of Massachusetts Press, 2007.

Jackson, Cecile, and Ruth Pearson, eds. *Feminist Visions of Development: Gender, Analysis, and Policy*. London: Routledge, 1998.

Jain, Devaki. *Women, Development, and the UN: A Sixty-Year Quest for Equality and Justice*. Bloomington: Indiana University Press, 2005.

Jana, Smarajit, Ishika Basu, Mary Jane Rotherdam-Borus, and Peter A. Newman. "The Sonagachi Project: A Sustainable Community Intervention Program." *AIDS Education and Prevention* 16, no. 5 (2004): 405–14.

Johnson, E. Patrick, and Mae Henderson, eds. *Black Queer Studies: A Critical Anthology*. Durham: Duke University Press, 2005.

Johnson, Haynes. *Sleepwalking through History: America in the Reagan Years*. New York: Norton, 1991.

Johnson, Karin E. "AIDS as a US National Security Threat: Media Effects and Geographical Imaginations." *Feminist Media Studies* 2, no. 1 (2002): 81–95.

Johnson, Kimberley. "Community Development Corporations, Participation, and Accountability: The Harlem Urban Development Corporation and the Bedford-Stuyvesant Restoration Corporation." *Annals of the American Academy of Political and Social Science* 594 (2004): 109–24.

Johnson, Krista. "AIDS and the Politics of Rights in South Africa: A Contested Terrain." *Human Rights Review* (2006): 115.

Jurrist, Charles. "In Defense of Promiscuity: Hard Questions about Real Life." *New York Native*, December 6, 1982.

Justice, Judith. *Policies, Plans, and People: Culture and Health Development in Nepal.* Berkeley: University of California Press, 1986.

Kaplan, Amy. *The Anarchy of Empire and the Making of U.S. Culture.* Cambridge, Mass.: Harvard University Press, 2002.

"Kaposi's Sarcoma and Pneumocystis Pneumonia among Homosexual Men — New York City and California." *Morbidity and Mortality Weekly Reports* 30, no. 25 (1981): 305–8.

Kauffman, Kyle D., and David L. Lindauer, eds. *AIDS and South Africa: The Social Expression of a Pandemic.* New York: Palgrave, 2004.

Kayal, Philip. *Bearing Witness: Gay Men's Health Crisis and the Politics of AIDS.* Boulder: Westview Press, 1993.

Kazin, Michael. "The Grass-Roots Right: New Histories of U.S. Conservatism in the Twentieth Century." *American Historical Review* 97, no. 1 (1992): 136–55.

Kennedy, Elizabeth Lopovsky, and Madeline D. Davis. *Boots of Leather, Slippers of Gold: The History of a Lesbian Community.* New York: Penguin, 1993.

Kimmel, Michael. *Manhood in America: A Cultural History.* New York: Free Press, 1996.

King, Katie. *Theory in Its Feminist Travels: Conversations in U.S. Women's Movements.* Bloomington: Indiana University Press, 1994.

Klatch, Rebecca. *A Generation Divided: The New Left, the New Right, and the 1960s.* Berkeley: University of California Press, 1999.

———. *Women of the New Right.* Philadelphia: Temple University Press, 1987.

Konvicka, Jason W. "Give Us Your Tired, Your Poor, Your Huddled Masses . . . Except When They Have HIV: An Analysis of Current United States Immigration Policy Regarding HIV-Positive Aliens in Light of Guantanamo Bay." *University of Richmond Law Review* 27 (1993): 531–48.

Koop, C. Everett. *Koop: The Memoirs of America's Family Doctor.* New York: Random House, 1991.

Kramer, Larry. *The Normal Heart.* New York: Samuel French, 1985.

———. *Reports from the Holocaust: The Story of an AIDS Activist.* New York: St. Martin's Press, 1994.

Kraut, Alan. *Silent Travelers: Germs, Genes, and the "Immigrant Menace."* New York: Basic Books, 1994.

Krystall, Abigail, Jotham Anthony Mwaniki, and J. W. Owour. "Kenya." *Studies in Family Planning* 6, no. 8 (1974): 286–91.

Kushner, Tony. *Angels in America*. Pt. 1, *Millennium Approaches*. New York: Theatre Communications Group, 1993.

Lambert, Rob. "Trade Unions, Nationalism, and the Socialist Project in South Africa." *South African Review* 4 (1987): 232–52.

Lambert, Rob, and Eddie Webster. "The Re-emergence of Political Unionism in Contemporary South Africa?" In *Popular Struggles in South Africa*, edited by William Cobbett and Robin Cohen, 20–41. Trenton: African World Press, 1988.

LeMay, Michael C. *Anatomy of a Public Policy: The Reform of Contemporary American Immigration Law*. Westport: Praeger, 1994.

Lethbridge, Jane. "Combining Worker and User Interests in the Health Sector: Trade Unions and NGOs." *Development in Practice* 14, no. 1 and 2 (2004): 234–47.

Levine, Martin P. *Gay Macho: The Life and Death of the Homosexual Clone*. New York: New York University Press, 1998.

Levine, Philippa. *Prostitution, Race, and Politics: Policing Venereal Disease in the British Empire*. New York: Routledge, 2003.

Lewis, John. "South African Labor History: A Historiographical Assessment." In *History from South Africa: Alternative Visions and Practices*, edited by Joshua Brown, Patrick Manning, Karen Shapiro, Jon Weiner, Belinda Bozzoli, and Peter Delius, 165–82. Philadelphia: Temple University Press, 1991.

Lind, Amy, and Jessica Share. "Queering Development: Institutionalized Heterosexuality in Development Theory, Practice, and Politics in Latin America." In *Feminist Futures: Re-imagining Women, Culture, and Development*, edited by Kum-Kum Bhavnani, John Foran, and Priya A. Kurian, 55–73. London: Zed Books, 2003.

Lovett, William A., Alfred E. Eckes Jr., and Richard Brinkman. *U.S. Trade Policy: History, Theory, and the WTO*. 2nd ed. Armonk, N.Y.: M. E. Sharpe, 2004.

Magat, Richard. *The Ford Foundation at Work: Philanthropic Choices, Methods, and Styles*. New York: Plenum Press, 1979.

Mann, Jonathan. "The World Health Organization's Global Strategy for the Prevention and Control of AIDS." *Western Journal of Medicine* 147 (1987): 732–34.

Mann, Jonathan, Daniel Tarantola, and Thomas Netter, eds. *AIDS in the World*. Cambridge, Mass.: Harvard University Press, 1992.

Manoff, Richard K. *Social Marketing: New Imperative for Public Health*. New York: Praeger, 1985.

Marais, Hein. *South Africa: Limits to Change. The Political Economy of Transition*. New York: St. Martin's Press, 1998.

Marchand, Marianne H., and Jane L. Parpart, eds. *Feminism/Postmodernism/ Development*. London: Routledge, 1995.

Markel, Howard, and Alexandra Minna Stern. "The Foreignness of Germs: The

Persistent Association of Immigrants and Disease in American Society." *Milbank Quarterly* 80, no. 4 (2002): 757–88.

Marks, Shula, and Stanley Trapido, eds. *The Politics of Race, Class, and Nationalism in Twentieth-Century South Africa*. London: Longman, 1987.

Marx, Anthony W. *Lessons of Struggle: South African Internal Opposition, 1960–1990*. New York: Oxford University Press, 1992.

Mass, Lawrence. "The Epidemic Continues: Facing a New Case Every Day, Researchers Are Still Bewildered." *New York Native*, March 29, 1982.

———, ed. *We Must Love One Another or Die: The Life and Legacy of Larry Kramer*. New York: St. Martin's Press, 1997.

Massey, Douglas S., and Eric Fong. "Segregation and Neighborhood Quality: Blacks, Hispanics, and Asians in the San Francisco Metropolitan Area." *Social Forces* 69, no. 1 (1990): 15–35.

McGirr, Lisa. "Piety and Property: Conservatism and Right-Wing Movements in the Twentieth Century." In *Perspectives on Modern America*, edited by Harvard Sitkoff, 33–54. New York: Oxford, 2001.

———. *Suburban Warriors: The Origins of the New American Right*. Princeton: Princeton University Press, 2001.

McKusick, Leon, W. Horstman, and T. J. Coates. "AIDS and Sexual Behavior Reported by Gay Men in San Francisco." *American Journal of Public Health*, 75, no. 5 (1985): 493–96.

McMahon, Robert J. "The Republic as Empire: American Foreign Policy in the 'American Century.'" In *Perspectives on Modern America*, edited by Harvard Sitkoff, 80–100. New York: Oxford, 2001.

McShane, Dennis, M.D. "Letter to the Editor." *JAMA* 251, no. 3 (1984): 341.

Meyer, Richard. *Outlaw Representation: Censorship and Homosexuality in Twentieth-Century American Art*. Boston: Beacon, 2002.

Meyerowitz, Joanne, ed. *Not June Cleaver: Women and Gender in Postwar America, 1945–1960*. Philadelphia: Temple University Press, 1994.

Michaels, Walter Benn. *The Trouble with Diversity: How We Learned to Love Identity and Ignore Inequality*. New York: Henry Holt, 2006.

Mohanty, Chandra, Ann Russo, and Lourdes Torres, eds. *Third World Women and the Politics of Feminism*. Bloomington: Indiana University Press, 1991.

Moore, Patrick. *Beyond Shame: Reclaiming the Abandoned History of Radical Gay Sexuality*. Boston: Beacon, 2004.

Moraga, Cherrie, and Gloria Anzaldua, eds. *This Bridge Called My Back: Writings by Radical Women of Color*. New York: Kitchen Table, Women of Color Press, 1983.

Moravick, Ann. "AIDS Activists and Pharmaceuticals: The Struggle for Common Ground." *Public Relations Quarterly* 38, no. 1 (1993): 31–32.

Morgen, Sandra. *Into Our Own Hands: The Women's Health Movement in the United States, 1969–1990*. New Brunswick: Rutgers University Press, 2002.

Moser, Caroline O. N. "Gender Planning in the Third World: Meeting Practical and Strategic Gender Needs." *World Development* 17, no. 11 (1989): 1799–25.

Mr. Rick. "In Gays We Trust." *New York Native*, November 2, 1981.

Muecke, Marjorie. "Mother Sold Food, Daughter Sells Her Body: The Cultural Continuity of Prostitution." *Social Science and Medicine* 35, no. 7 (1992): 891–901.

Murphy, Timothy. "No Time for an AIDS Backlash." *Hastings Center Report* 21, no. 2 (1991): 7–11.

Murray, Heather. "Free for All Lesbians: Lesbian Cultural Production and Consumption in the United States during the 1970s." *Journal of the History of Sexuality* 16, no. 2 (2007): 251–75.

Murray, Martin J. *South Africa: Time of Agony, Time of Destiny. The Upsurge of Popular Protest*. London: Verso, 1987.

Narlikar, Amrita. *The World Trade Organization: A Very Short Introduction*. Oxford: Oxford University Press, 2005.

Nelson, Jennifer. *Women of Color and the Reproductive Rights Movement*. New York: New York University Press, 2003.

"New Directions in Multiethnic, Racial, and Global Queer Studies." *GLQ* 10, no. 1 (2003): 123–37.

Nicolaides, Becky. *My Blue Heaven: Life and Politics in the Working-Class Suburbs of Los Angeles, 1920–1965*. Chicago: University of Chicago Press, 2002.

O'Connor, Alice. "The Ford Foundation and Philanthropic Activism in the 1960s." In *Philanthropic Foundations: New Scholarship, New Possibilities*, edited by Ellen Condliffe Lagemann, 169–94. Bloomington: Indiana University Press, 1999.

———. *Poverty Knowledge: Social Science, Social Policy, and the Poor in Twentieth-Century U.S. History*. Princeton: Princeton University Press, 2001.

Oppenheimer, Gerald. "In the Eye of the Storm: The Epidemiological Construction of AIDS." In *AIDS: The Burdens of History*, edited by Elizabeth Fee and Daniel Fox, 267–300. Berkeley: University of California Press, 1988.

Packard, Randall. "Visions of Health and Development and Their Impact on Public Health Interventions in the Developing World." In *International Development and the Social Sciences*, edited by Frederick Cooper and Randall Packard, 93–115. Berkeley: University of California Press, 1997.

Panos Institute. *AIDS and the Third World*. 1st ed. London: Panos Institute in association with the Norwegian Red Cross, 1986.

———. *AIDS and the Third World*. 2nd ed. London: Panos Institute in association with the Norwegian Red Cross, 1987.

———. *AIDS and the Third World*. Trade ed. London: Panos Institute in association with the Norwegian Red Cross, 1989.

———. *Triple Jeopardy: Women and AIDS*. London: Panos Institute, 1990.

Parascandola, John L. "Public Health Service." In *A Historical Guide to the U.S. Government*, edited by George T. Kurian. New York: Oxford University Press, 1998.

Parker, Richard. *Beneath the Equator: Cultures of Desire, Male Homosexuality, and Emerging Gay Communities in Brazil*. New York: Routledge, 1999.

Parpart, Jane L., Shirin M. Rai, and Kathleen Staudt, eds. *Rethinking Empowerment: Gender and Development in a Global/Local World*. London: Routledge, 2002.

Patton, Cindy. *Fatal Advice: How Safe-Sex Education Went Wrong*. Durham: Duke University Press, 1996.

———. "From Nation to Family: Containing African AIDS." In *The Lesbian and Gay Studies Reader*, edited by Henry Abelove et al., 127–40. New York: Routledge, 1993.

———. "Illness as Weapon." *Gay Community News*, June 30, 1984.

———. *Inventing AIDS*. New York: Routledge, 1990.

———. *Last Served: Gendering the HIV Pandemic*. London: Taylor and Francis, 1994.

———. "Lesbian and Gay Health Care: Moving into the '80s." *Gay Community News*, May 22, 1982.

———. "Migratory Vices." In *Queer Diasporas*, edited by Cindy Patton and Benigno Sanchez-Eppler. Durham: Duke University Press, 2000.

———. "'On Me, Not in Me': Locating Affect in Nationalism after AIDS." *Theory, Culture, and Society* 15, no. 3–4 (1998): 355–73.

———. "Resistance and the Erotic: Reclaiming History, Setting Strategy as We Face AIDS." *Radical America* 20, no. 6 (1987): 68–74.

———. *Sex and Germs: The Politics of AIDS*. Boston: South End, 1985.

Patton, Cindy, and Janis Kelly. *Making It: A Woman's Guide to Sex in the Age of AIDS*. Ithaca: Firebrand, 1987.

Perrow, Charles, and Mauro F. Guillen. *The AIDS Disaster: The Failure of Organizations in New York and the Nation*. New Haven: Yale University Press, 1990.

Petchesky, Rosalind. *Abortion and Woman's Choice: The State, Sexuality, and Reproductive Freedom*. Boston: Northeastern University Press, 1990.

———. "Antiabortion, Antifeminism, and the Rise of the New Right." *Feminist Studies* 7, no. 2 (1981): 206–41.

———. *Global Prescriptions: Gendering Health and Human Rights*. London: Zed Books, 2003.

Petchesky, Rosalind, and Sonia Corrêa. "Reproductive and Sexual Rights: A Feminist Perspective." In *Population Policies Reconsidered: Health, Empowerment, and Rights*, edited by Gita Sen, Adrienne Germain, and Lincoln C. Chen, 107–23. Cambridge, Mass.: Harvard University Press, 1994.

Pigg, Stacy Leigh. "Expecting the Epidemic: A Social History of Representation of Sexual Risk in Nepal." *Feminist Media Studies* 2, no. 1 (2002): 97–125.

Pincock, Stephen. "José Barzelatto." *Lancet* 367 (2006): 1650.

"Pneumocystis Pneumonia — Los Angeles." *Morbidity and Mortality Weekly Reports* 30, no. 21 (1981): 250–52.

Porter, Doug J. "A Plague on the Borders: HIV, Development, and Traveling Identities in the Golden Triangle." In *Sites of Desire/Economies of Pleasure: Sexualities in Asia and the Pacific*, edited by Margaret Jolly and Lenore Manderson. Chicago: University of Chicago Press, 1997.

Porter, Marilyn, and Ellen Judd, eds. *Feminists Doing Development: A Practical Critique*. London: Zed Books, 1999.

Prashad, Vijay. *Everybody Was Kung Fu Fighting: Afro-Asian Connections and the Myth of Cultural Purity*. Boston: Beacon, 2001.

Preston, John, ed. *Personal Dispatches: Writers Confront AIDS*. New York: St. Martin's Press, 1989.

Puar, Jasbir K., and Amit S. Rai. "Monster, Terrorist, Fag: The War on Terrorism and the Production of Docile Patriots." *Social Text* 20, no. 3 (2002): 117–48.

———. "The Remaking of a Model Minority: Perverse Projectiles under the Specter of (Counter)terrorism." *Social Text* 22, no. 3 (2004): 75–104.

Raynor, Gregory K. "The Ford Foundation's War on Poverty: Private Philanthropy and Race Relations in New York City, 1948–1968." In *Philanthropic Foundations: New Scholarship, New Possibilities*, edited by Ellen Condliffe Lagemann, 195–228. Bloomington: Indiana University Press, 1999.

The Red Butterfly. "Comments on Carl Wittman's 'A Gay Manifesto.'" In *We Are Everywhere: A Historical Sourcebook of Gay and Lesbian Politics*, edited by Mark Blasius and Shane Phelan, 389–90. New York: Routledge, 1997.

Reimers, David. *Unwelcome Strangers: American Identity and the Turn against Immigration*. New York: Columbia University Press, 1998.

Report of the Presidential Commission on the Human Immunodeficiency Virus Epidemic. Washington, D.C., 1988.

Richardson, Diane. *Women and AIDS*. New York: Routledge, 1989.

Rieder, Jonathan. *Canarsie: The Jews and Italians of Brooklyn against Liberalism*. Cambridge, Mass.: Harvard University Press, 1985.

Robins, Steven. "'Long Live Zackie, Long Live': AIDS Activism, Science, and Citizenship after Apartheid." *Journal of Southern African Studies* 30, no. 3 (2004): 651–72.

Rockefeller, John D. "Population Growth: The Role of the Developed World." *Population and Development Review* 4, no. 3 (1978): 509–16.

Rodríguez, Juana Maria. *Queer Latinidad: Identity Practices, Discursive Spaces*. New York: New York University Press, 2003.

Rofes, Eric. *Reviving the Tribe: Regenerating Gay Men's Sexuality and Culture in the Ongoing Epidemic*. Binghamton: Harrington Park Press, 1996.

Rogin, Michael Paul. *Ronald Reagan, the Movie*. Berkeley: University of California Press, 1987.

Román, David. *Acts of Intervention: Performance, Gay Culture, and AIDS*. Bloomington: Indiana University Press, 1998.

———. "Not-About-AIDS." *GLQ* 6, no. 1 (2000): 1–28.

Romano, Renee. "No Diplomatic Immunity: African Diplomats, the State Department, and Civil Rights, 1961–1964." *Journal of American History* 87, no. 2 (2000): 546–79.

Roque Ramirez, Horacio N. "'That's *My* Place!': Negotiating Racial, Sexual, and Gender Politics in San Francisco's Gay Latino Alliance, 1975–1983." *Journal of the History of Sexuality* 12, no. 2 (2003): 224–58.

Rosenberg, Charles E. *Explaining Epidemics and Other Studies in the History of Medicine*. Cambridge: Cambridge University Press, 1992.

Rotello, Gabriel. *Sexual Ecology: AIDS and the Destiny of Gay Men*. New York: Dutton, 1997.

Rotundo, Anthony. *American Manhood: Transformations in Masculinity from the Revolution to the Modern Era*. New York: Basic Books, 1993.

Rymph, Catherine E. *Republican Women: Feminism and Conservatism from Suffrage through the Rise of the New Right*. Chapel Hill: University of North Carolina Press, 2006.

Sabatier, Renée. "AIDS in the Developing World." *International Family Planning Perspectives* 13, no. 3 (1987): 96–103.

———. *Blaming Others: Prejudice, Race, and Worldwide AIDS*. London: Panos Institute, 1988.

Sawyer, Eric. "An ACT UP Founder 'Acts Up' for Africa's Access to AIDS." In *From ACT UP to WTO: Urban Protest and Community Building in the Era of Globalization*, edited by Benjamin Shepard and Ronald Hayduk. London: Verso, 2002.

Scheper-Hughes, Nancy, Michael Adams, Sonia Corrêa, and Richard Parker. "Reproductive Health and AIDS in Brazil: A Consultants' Report Prepared for the Ford Foundation." 1991. In author's possession.

Schneider, Helen. "On the Fault-Line: The Politics of AIDS Policy in Contemporary South Africa." *African Studies* 61, no. 1 (2002): 145–67.

Schoepf, Brooke. "Ethical, Methodological, and Political Issues of AIDS Research in Central Africa." *Social Science and Medicine* 33, no. 7 (1991): 749–63.

———. "Women, AIDS, and Economic Crisis in Central Africa." *Canadian Journal of African Studies* 22, no. 3 (1988): 625–44.

Schoofs, Mark. "South Africa Acts Up." *Village Voice*, December 22–28, 1999.

Schulman, Sarah. *My American History: Lesbian and Gay Life during the Reagan/Bush Years*. New York: Routledge, 1994.

———. *Stage Struck: Theater, AIDS, and the Marketing of Gay America*. Durham: Duke University Press, 1998.

Seltzer, Michael. *Meeting the Challenge: Foundation Responses to Acquired Immune Deficiency Syndrome*. New York: Ford Foundation, 1987.

Sen, Gita, and Caren Grown. *Development, Crises, and Alternative Visions: Third World Women's Perspectives*. New York: Monthly Review Press, 1987.

Sen, Gita, Adrienne Germain, and Lincoln C. Chen. "Reconsidering Population Policies: Ethics, Development, and Strategies for Change." In *Population Policies Reconsidered: Health, Empowerment, and Rights*, edited by Gita Sen, Adrienne Germain, and Lincoln C. Chen, 3–14. Cambridge, Mass.: Harvard University Press, 1994.

Sepulveda, Jaime, Harvey Fineberg, and Jonathan Mann, eds. *AIDS Prevention through Education: A World View*. New York: Oxford University Press, 1992.

Seybold, Peter J. "The Ford Foundation and the Triumph of Behavioralism in American Political Science." In *Philanthropy and Cultural Imperialism: The Foundations at Home and Abroad*, edited by Robert F. Arnove, 269–304. Bloomington: Indiana University Press, 1982.

Shah, Nayan. *Contagious Divides: Epidemics and Race in San Francisco's Chinatown*. Berkeley: University of California Press, 2001.

Shapiro, Thomas. *Population Control Politics: Women, Sterilization, and Reproductive Choice*. Philadelphia: Temple University Press, 1985.

Sharpless, John. "Population Science, Private Foundations, and Development Aid." In *International Development and the Social Sciences*, edited by Frederick Cooper and Randall Packard, 176–200. Berkeley: University of California Press, 1997.

Shepard, Benjamin, and Ronald Hayduk, eds. *From ACT UP to WTO: Urban Protest and Community Building in the Era of Globalization*. London: Verso, 2002.

Sherman, Peggy B., and Ellwood F. Oakley. "Pandemics and Panaceas: The World Trade Organization's Efforts to Balance Pharmaceutical Patents and Access to AIDS Drugs." *American Business Law Journal* 41, no. 2/3 (2004): 353–411.

Shilts, Randy. *And the Band Played On: Politics, People, and the AIDS Epidemic*. New York: Penguin, 1987.

Shoop, Lyn G. "Health Based Exclusion Grounds in the United States Immigration Policy: Homosexuals, HIV Infection, and the Medical Examination of Aliens." *Journal of Contemporary Health Law and Policy* 9 (1993): 521–44.

Sidel, Ruth. *Women and Children Last: The Plight of Poor Women in Affluent America*. New York: Viking, 1986.

Silin, Jonathan G. "Dangerous Knowledge." *Christopher Street* 10, no. 5 (1987): 34–40.

Silliman, Jael, Merlene Gerber Fried, Loretta Ross, and Elena R. Gutiérrez. *Undivided Rights: Women of Color Organize for Reproductive Justice*. Cambridge, Mass.: South End, 2004.

Silversides, Ann. *AIDS Activist: Michael Lynch and the Politics of Community*. Toronto: Between the Lines, 2003.

Simmons, Ozzie G. *Perspectives on Development and Population Growth in the Third World*. New York: Plenum Press, 1988.

Slaughter, Sheila, and Gary Rhoades. "The Emergence of a Competitive Research and Development Policy Coalition and Commercialization of Academic Science and Technology." *Science, Technology, and Human Values* 21, no. 3 (1996): 303–39.

Smith, Neil. *The Endgame of Globalization.* New York: Routledge, 2005.

Smith, Raymond A., and Patricia D. Siplon, *Drugs into Bodies: Global AIDS Treatment Activism.* Westport: Praeger, 2006.

Snyder, David Benjamin. "South Africa's Medicines and Related Substances Control Amendment Act: A Spoonfull of Sugar or a Bitter Pill to Swallow?" *Dickinson Journal of International Law* 18, no. 1 (1999): 175–98.

Somerville, Siobhan. "Queer *Loving.*" *GLQ* 11, no. 3 (2005): 335–70.

Sonnabend, Joseph, M.D., et al. "Acquired Immunodeficiency Syndrome, Opportunistic Infections, and Malignancies in Male Homosexuals." *JAMA* 249, no. 17 (1983): 2370–74.

Springer, Kimberly. *Living for the Revolution: Black Feminist Organizations.* Durham: Duke University Press, 2005.

Stein, Marc. *City of Sisterly and Brotherly Love: Lesbian and Gay Philadelphia, 1945–1972.* Chicago: University of Chicago Press, 2000.

Stiglitz, Joseph E. *Globalization and Its Discontents.* New York: Norton, 2002.

Stimpson, Catharine R., and Nina Kressner Cobb. *Women's Studies in the United States: A Report to the Ford Foundation.* New York: Ford Foundation, 1986.

Stoddard, Thomas, and Walter Rieman. "AIDS and the Rights of the Individual: Toward a More Sophisticated Understanding of Discrimination." *Milbank Quarterly* 68, supplement 1 (pt. 1) (1990): 143–74.

Stoller, Nancy E. *Lessons from the Damned: Queers, Whores, and Junkies Respond to AIDS.* New York: Routledge, 1998.

Streitmatter, Roger. *Unspeakable: The Rise of the Gay and Lesbian Press in America.* Boston: Faber and Faber, 1995.

Stryker, Susan. *Transgender History.* Berkeley: Seal Press, 2008.

Stryker, Susan, and Jim Van Buskirk. *Gay by the Bay: A History of Queer Culture in the San Francisco Bay Area.* San Francisco: Chronicle Books, 1996.

Sugrue, Thomas J. "Crabgrass-Roots Politics: Race, Rights, and the Reaction against Liberalism in the Urban North, 1940–1964." *Journal of American History* 82, no. 2 (1995): 551–78.

———. *The Origins of the Urban Crisis: Race and Inequality in Postwar Detroit.* Princeton: Princeton University Press, 2002.

Third World Gay Revolution. "The Oppressed Shall Not Become the Oppressor." In *We Are Everywhere: A Historical Sourcebook of Gay and Lesbian Politics*, edited by Mark Blasius and Shane Phelan, 400–401. New York: Routledge, 1997.

Tinker, Jon. "Earthscan-Panos: Favourite Son, Via Cuckoo-in-the-Nest, to Friendly Rival." In *Evidence for Hope: The Search for Sustainable Development*, edited by Nigel Cross, 40–59. London: Earthscan Publications, 2003.

Treichler, Paula. "AIDS and HIV Infection in the Third World: A First World Chronicle." In *AIDS: The Making of a Chronic Disease*, edited by Elizabeth Fee and Daniel Fox, 377–412. Berkeley: University of California Press, 1992.

———. *How to Have Theory in an Epidemic: Cultural Chronicles of AIDS*. Durham: Duke University Press, 1999.

Troy, Gil. *Morning in America: How Ronald Reagan Invented the 1980s*. Princeton: Princeton University Press, 2005.

Turner, William B. "Mirror Images: Lesbian/Gay Civil Rights in the Carter Administration and Reagan Administrations." In *Creating Change: Public Policy, Civil Rights, and Sexuality*, edited by John D'Emilio, Urvashi Vaid, and William B. Turner, 3–28. New York: St. Martin's Press, 2000.

U.S. Agency for International Development. *HIV Infection and AIDS: A Report to Congress on the USAID Program for Prevention and Control*. Washington, D.C.: U.S. Government Printing Office, 1990.

———. *HIV Infection and AIDS: A Report to Congress on the USAID Program for Prevention and Control*, Washington, D.C.: U.S. Government Printing Office, 1991.

U.S. Congress. House. Committee on the Judiciary. *Grounds for Exclusion of Aliens under the Immigration and Nationality Act*. 100th Cong., 2nd sess., 1988. Washington, D.C.: U.S. Government Printing Office, 1988.

U.S. Congress. House. Select Committee on Hunger. *AIDS and the Developing World: The Impact of Development*. 100th Cong., 1st sess., 1988. Washington, D.C.: U.S. Government Printing Office, 1988.

U.S. Congress. House. Subcommittee on Government Operations. *Federal Response to AIDS*. 98th Cong., 1st sess., 1983. Washington, D.C.: U.S. Government Printing Office, 1983.

U.S. Department of Health and Human Services. "42 CFR Part 34: Medical Examination of Aliens (AIDS)." *Federal Register*, August 28, 1987.

U.S. Department of State. *The Global AIDS Disaster: Implications for the 1990s*. Washington, D.C.: Department of State, 1992.

U.S. Executive Office of the President. *Appendix Budget of the United States Government — Fiscal Year 1988*. Washington, D.C.: U.S. Government Printing Office, 1988.

———. *Appendix Budget of the United States Government — Fiscal Year 1990*. Washington, D.C.: U.S. Government Printing Office, 1990.

———. *Budget of the United States Government — Fiscal Year 1985*. Washington, D.C.: U.S. Government Printing Office, 1985.

———. *Budget of the United States Government — Fiscal Year 1986*. Washington, D.C.: U.S. Government Printing Office, 1986.

———. *Budget of the United States Government — Fiscal Year 1987*. Washington, D.C.: U.S. Government Printing Office, 1987.

———. *Budget of the United States Government — Fiscal Year 1988*. Washington, D.C.: U.S. Government Printing Office, 1988.

———. *Budget of the United States Government — Fiscal Year 1989*. Washington, D.C.: U.S. Government Printing Office, 1989.

U.S. Office of Management and Budget. *Historic Tables, Budget of the United States Government*. Washington, D.C.: Executive Office of the President, Office of Management and Budget, 1984–88.

———. *Budget of the United States Government*. Washington, D.C.: Executive Office of the President, Office of Management and Budget, 1991.

Understanding AIDS. Rockville, Md.: U.S. Department of Health and Human Services, 1988.

Vaid, Urvashi. *Virtual Equality: The Mainstreaming of Gay and Lesbian Liberation*. New York: Anchor, 1995.

van der Vliet, Virginia. "South Africa Divided against AIDS: A Crisis of Leadership." In *AIDS and South Africa: The Social Expression of a Pandemic*, edited by Kyle D. Kauffman and David L. Lindauer. New York: Palgrave, 2004.

Van Kessel, Ineke. *Beyond Our Wildest Dreams: The United Democratic Front and the Transformation of South Africa*. Charlottesville: University Press of Virginia, 2000.

Von Holt, Karl. *Transition from Below: Forging Trade Unionism and Workplace Change in South Africa*. Pietermaritzburg: University of Natal Press, 2003.

Warwick, Donald P. *Bitter Pills: Population Policies and Their Implementation in Eight Developing Countries*. Cambridge: Cambridge University Press, 1982.

Wat, Eric. *The Making of a Gay Asian Community: An Oral History of pre-AIDS Los Angeles*. Lanham, Md.: Rowman and Littlefield, 2002.

Watney, Simon. "Missionary Positions: AIDS, 'Africa,' and Race." *Differences* 1, no. 1 (1989): 83–100.

———. *Policing Desire: Pornography, AIDS, and the Media*. Minneapolis: University of Minnesota Press, 1996.

———. *Practices of Freedom: Selected Writings on HIV/AIDS*. Durham: Duke University Press, 1994.

Webster, Edward, and Sakhela Buhlungu. "Between Marginalisation and Revitalisation? The State of Trade Unionism in South Africa." *Review of African Political Economy* 31, no. 100 (2004): 229–45.

Weissman, Steve, ed. *The Trojan Horse: A Radical Look at Foreign Aids*. San Francisco: Ramparts Press, 1974.

White, Evelyn, ed. *The Black Women's Health Book: Speaking for Ourselves*. Seattle: Seal Press, 1990.

Whitehead, John C. *African Development: An Administration Perspective*. Washington, D.C.: U.S. Department of State, 1987.

———. *The Foreign Affairs Budget*. Washington, D.C.: U.S. Department of State, 1986.

———. *A Life in Leadership: From D-Day to Ground Zero*. New York: Basic Books, 2005.

———. *U.S. Trade Policy at the Crossroads*. Washington, D.C.: U.S. Department of State, 1987.

Wilentz, Sean. *The Age of Reagan: A History, 1974–2008*. New York: Harper, 2008.

Wilson, William Julius. *The Truly Disadvantaged: The Inner City, the Underclass, and Public Policy*. Chicago: University of Chicago Press, 1987.

Wittman, Carl. "A Gay Manifesto." In *We Are Everywhere: A Historical Sourcebook of Gay and Lesbian Politics*, edited by Mark Blasius and Shane Phelan, 380–88. New York: Routledge, 1997.

Wolfe, Maxine. "The AIDS Coalition to Unleash Power (ACT UP): A Direct Model of Community Research for AIDS Prevention." In *AIDS Prevention and Services: Community Based Research*, edited by Johannes P. Van Vugt, 217–48. Westport: Bergin and Garvey, 1994.

Wolfe, Maxine, and Laraine Sommella. "This Is about People Dying: The Tactics of Early ACT UP and Lesbian Avengers in New York City." In *Queers in Space: Communities, Public Places, Sites of Resistance*, edited by Gordon Brent Ingram, Anne-Marie Bouthillette, and Yolanda Retter, 407–37. Seattle: Bay Press, 1997.

Wood, Geoffrey. "South African Trade Unions in a Time of Adjustment." *Labour/Le Travail*, no. 47 (2001): 133–50.

Wright, Timothy. "Gay Organizations, NGOs, and the Globalization of Sexual Identity: The Case of Bolivia." *Journal of Latin American Anthropology* 5, no. 2 (2000): 89–111.

Index

"AIDSpeak," 13

AIDS Related Complex (ARC), 68, 173

AIDS service organizations (ASOs), 12, 59–61, 88, 92, 160, 203 (n. 17), 211 (n. 24). *See also* Gay Men's Health Crisis; San Francisco AIDS Foundation; Third World AIDS Advisory Task Force; *and other specific organizations*

AIDS Technical Support Program, 115

AIDS work: defined as including both activism and service, 4; in global South, 115–20 (*see also* Brazil; Ford Foundation; Haiti; Nigeria; Senegal; South Africa; Thailand); as strong challenge to 1980s conservatism, 3, 4, 5, 8–10, 43, 159. *See also* AIDS service organizations (ASOs); *and specific themes and organizations*

Alfred, Randy, 36–37

Altman, Dr. Lawrence, 20, 226 (n. 101)

Amebiasis, 31

American Association of Physicians for Human Rights (AAPHR), 25–26

American Civil Liberties Unions (ACLU), 108

American exceptionalism, 111, 230 (n. 136)

Anderson, Carl, 78, 81, 90

Andrews, Bob, 11

And the Band Played On (Shilts), 13, 79–80, 207 (n. 63), 218 (n. 6), 227 (n. 101)

Annenberg School for Communication (University of Pennsylvania), 116

Antiretroviral drugs (ARVs), 192–94; high cost of, 158, 187; and South African AIDS activism, 190, 194–200; U.S. activists and, 9, 162–68, 185–86; and U.S. trade policies, 158, 186, 187, 193–94. *See also* Azidothymidine; Food and Drug Administration; Pharmaceutical industry

Antrobus, Peggy, 128

Apuzzo, Virginia, 82–83

Armstrong, Elizabeth, 50, 204 (n. 12), 208–9 (n. 104)

Arno, Peter, 185

Artist-activists, 158–59, 160–61, 174–75

ARVs. *See* Antiretroviral drugs

Asian Americans and AIDS, 63, 65

ASOs. *See* AIDS service organizations

Asylum, political, 8, 109

Azidothymidine (AZT), 162, 180–82, 185; in South Africa, 197, 199; U.S. activists and, 180–82, 185

Ba, Edwige Bienvenue, 146

Bailey House (New York), 177

Bale, Harvey, 186, 187

Banzhaf, Marion, 171, 176, 181

Barr, David, 163, 164, 181

Bars, gay-frequented, 210 (n. 9); educational efforts focused on, 17, 47, 57–58, 70, 71; racial exclusion by some, 59; in San Francisco, 47, 49, 57–58, 59, 70, 71

Bartenders Against AIDS (San Francisco), 57–58

Barzelatto, Dr. José, 124, 125, 142–43, 144, 147–48, 153–55, 239 (n. 99); background of, 124, 142; feminism of, 124, 125, 148; reproductive health strategy of, 142–43, 149, 153; retirement of, 153–54; on sexuality, 142, 239 (n. 99)

Bastos, Cristiana, 102, 225 (n. 94)

Bathhouses, 39–40, 208 (n. 88); controversy over, 21, 35, 39–40, 83; educational efforts focused on, 17, 18, 53, 57; mainly white clientele of, 53–54; in New York, 18, 21; in San Francisco, 39–40, 53–54, 57

Bauer, Gary, 7, 87–88, 93, 120; and AIDS Commission, 93, 94, 98; on AIDS education, 7, 79, 81, 87, 90–92, 93, 99, 100–101; as conservative activist, 7, 87; on testing, 97

Bay Area Reporter (San Francisco), 16, 23, 27, 63, 204 (n. 5)

Bell, Miriam, 84

Bennett, William, 81, 87–88, 90, 93, 120

Berkowitz, Richard, 15, 30, 31. *See also* Callen, Michael: writings of, with Richard Berkowitz

Berresford, Susan, 128–29, 130, 131, 142, 153–54

Black and White Men Together (BWMT), 53–54, 63, 71, 77

Black Coalition on AIDS (San Francisco), 60

Blackwell, Morton, 83

Blaming Others (Panos Institute dossier), 113

Body Politic, The, 29

Bolan, Robert K., 16

Bordowitz, Gregg, 161, 165, 248 (n. 6)

Borovoy, Marilyn, 72

Boyd, Nan, 48–49, 210 (nn. 9, 13)

Braverman, Gedelia, 177, 178, 183

Brazil, 2, 133, 153, 193; attention to class differences in, 122–23, 140; epidemiology of AIDS in, 122–23, 132, 133, 141, 149; feminism in, 150–51; Ford Foundation grants in, 23, 133, 140–41, 149–51, 153; NGOs in, 122–23, 140–41, 150–51, 153; women's health in, 141, 149–51

Brazilian Interdisciplinary AIDS Association (ABIA, Associação Brasileira Interdisciplinar de AIDS), 123–24, 140, 150–51

Bronski, Michael, 28–29, 202 (n. 2)

Brooklyn AIDS Task Force, 170

Brotherhood, language of, 18–19, 25, 36, 39–40

Buckalew, Judi, 82–83

Burns, Richard, 30

Burroughs Wellcome, 156, 162, 193

Bush, George H. W., 115, 118

BWMT. *See* Black and White Men Together

Bye, Larry, 76, 203 (n. 18), 212 (n. 45)

Callen, Michael, 30
— writings of, with Richard Berkowitz, 30–32, 34–36; controversy over, 32–33, 208 (n. 85); influence of, 36–37, 40, 46, 52, 160, 168; and meaning of gay liberation, 30–31, 32, 34, 35; on models for sexual practice, 34–36; on multiple

causes of AIDS, 30–31; and promiscuity, 30–31, 32, 34

Campbell, Bobbi, 26

Carlomusto, Jean, 161, 171, 173–74, 184

Carmichael, William, 131, 150

Carter, George, 183

Castro neighborhood (San Francisco), 26, 45, 57, 58–59, 64

Center for Study and Research in Collective Health (Brazil), 149–50

Centers for Disease Control (CDC), 11; conferences organized by, 45, 169–70, 179; conservative attacks on, 85, 92, 100; funding of, 86, 100; San Francisco review board of, 69, 71–72, 73–74; and women with AIDS, 172, 174–75, 179

Central Intelligence Agency (CIA), 8, 81, 108, 109–10

Centre de Promotion des Femmes Ouvrières (Center for the Promotion of Women Factory Workers, or CPFO, Haiti), 137–39

Cheikh Anta Diop University (Senegal), 139

Chen, Lincoln, 128

Chesley, Robert, 20–21

Chicano gays and lesbians, 48, 50, 63. *See also* Hinojos, Ernesto; Tavera, Hank

Chou, Lei, 178, 181

Christofer, Mark, 58

Churches, 160, 170

Claro, Amparo, 143

Clinton, William J., 186–87

Cochrane, Michelle, 51

Cohen, Herman, 111

Cohen, Lizbeth, 55

Commercialization of gay sexuality, 30–31

Commercial sex workers, 133, 136, 138; feminist approaches to, 136, 140, 146, 151–52, 242 (n. 155)

Communications Technology marketing firm, 76

Community Constituency Group (CCG), 179–80, 181–82

Community Research Initiative, 163

Goodwin, Marie, 38–39
Goodwin, Ron, 83
Gordon, Kevin, 39, 40
Gould, Robert, 172
Graham, Bill, 99
Gran Fury, 174–75
Greco, Stephen, 23
Greenwich Village, 15–16, 24. *See also* Gay and Lesbian Community Center

Hafer, Dick, 84
Haiti, 31; wrongful blaming of, as source of AIDS in U.S., 31, 226 (n. 101); Ford Foundation and, 132, 133, 137–39, 238 (n. 84)
Hamilton-Houston, Amanda, 60–61
Harrington, Mark, 164, 166, 167, 183
Harvey, Philip, 56
Haslip, Katrina, 172
Heckler, Margaret, 86
Heim, Chris, 23
Heisler, Michele, 138
Helms, Jesse, 92, 107
Hempel, Margaret, 142, 143, 148
Hepatitis, 31
Hernandez, Sandra, 75
Herpes, 31
HHS. *See* U.S. Department of Health and Human Services
Hinojos, Ernesto, 63, 64–65, 74, 77
HIV-positive status, 84, 164, 172, 182–83, 195–96, 236 (n. 43); and immigration policy, 105, 108–9
Hoffman, Amy, 29–30, 38–39
Homelessness, 96, 177
Homophile activism, 49–50, 209 (n. 104), 210 (n. 9)
Horovitz, Richard, 130–31, 134, 139, 141, 146, 154
Housing, 177; ACT UP and, 168, 177–79
Housing Works (New York), 179
Howard Brown Health Center (Chicago), 17
How to Have Sex in an Epidemic (Callen and Berkowitz), 34–37, 161

Human Immunodeficiency Virus (HIV), 1, 44; testing for: *see* Testing for HIV; treatment for: *see* Antiretroviral drugs. *See also* HIV-positive status
Hunter, Nan, 108
Hyde, Sue, 38–39

Immigrants with AIDS, 79, 81–82, 104–10; differences within Reagan administration over, 8, 81–82, 108–10
Immigration and Nationality Act (McCarran-Walter Act), 104, 106, 107
Implementing Agency for Cooperation and Training (IMPACT), 137, 138–39
INS. *See* U.S. Immigration and Naturalization Service
International Federation of Pharmaceutical Manufacturers Associations, 193–94
Intravenous drug use, 31, 66, 83, 156; and definition of AIDS, 175; and educational programs, 71, 135; and people of color, 51, 60, 66

Jackman, Rich, 178
Jones, Billy S., 53–54, 65
Jones, Nicola, 140, 144–47
Journal of the American Medical Association, 24
Jurrist, Charles, 32–33, 34

Kantor, Mickey, 187
Kaolack project (Senegal), 145–46, 147
Kaplan, Amy, 82
Kaposi's sarcoma (KS), 20, 173
Kenya, 113
King, Charles, 178, 179
Kirschenbaum, David, 163, 167, 180, 183
Klenk, John, 91–92
Koop, Dr. C. Everett, 7, 81, 88–91, 107, 160, 220–21 (n. 30); Christian convictions of, 81, 88, 89, 90; surgeon general's report by, 88–91
Kramer, Larry, 12–13, 20, 160, 177, 204 (n. 6)

KS Foundation, 51. *See also* San Francisco
  AIDS Foundation
Kubisch, Anne, 144

Latino AIDS Project (San Francisco), 75
Latino Coalition on AIDS (San Fran-
  cisco), 60
Latinos, 60, 64, 72–75; high incidence of
  AIDS among, 62. *See also* Chicano gays
  and lesbians
Law, Debi, 39
Lesbians, 30, 38–39, 43, 205 (n. 17), 207
  (n. 80); in ACT UP, 161, 171, 172; over-
  looked role of, in early AIDS activism,
  11–12, 13
Levi, Jeff, 82, 97
Levine, Martin, 42
Lewis, Bill, 29
Lilly, Dr. Frank, 94
Long, Iris, 163, 183
"Lust, Wanda," 17
Lynch, Michael, 29

Madisha, Willie, 199
Majority Action Committee (MAC) of
  ACT UP, 162, 166, 168–71, 178
Mandela, Nelson, 192, 249 (n. 9)
Mann, Dr. Jonathan, 101–2
Mano a Mano (San Francisco), 75
Manoff, Richard, 56
Mason, James, 85
Mass, Dr. Lawrence (Larry), 20, 21–22,
  23, 29
Masturbation, 33, 35
Mattachine Society, 50
Mayberry, Dr. Eugene, 95
Mbeki, Thabo, 190, 196–97, 198
McCarran-Walter Act (Immigration and
  Nationality Act), 104, 106, 107
McGovern, Terry, 173, 174, 175
Medicaid, 96
Meese, Edwin, 100, 107
Men of All Colors Together (San Fran-
  cisco), 75
Meridian, 17–18, 35, 36

Mexico, 132
Michaels, Walter Benn, 3
Milk, Harvey, 50
Molaghan, J. B., 21
Montreal Manifesto, 156–57, 158, 188
Moral Majority, 83
Morgan, Tracy, 180, 181, 182
Mossinghoff, Gerald, 187
Muecke, Marjorie, 151–52
Murray, Gordon, 28
Myers, Dr. Woodrow, 95

National AIDS Vigil (1983), 36
National Association of People with AIDS
  (South Africa), 95, 194
National Coalition of Black Gays, 54.
  See also National Coalition of Black
  Lesbians and Gays
National Coalition of Black Lesbians and
  Gays, 54, 88, 89
National Coalition of Gay Sexually Trans-
  mitted Disease Services, 16
National Council of Churches, 88
National Foreign Intelligence Board, 110
National Gay and Lesbian Task Force, 82,
  115, 231 (n. 156)
National Gay Health Education Founda-
  tion, 23
National Gay Task Force (NGTF), 82.
  See also National Gay and Lesbian Task
  Force
National Institute of Allergies and Infec-
  tious Diseases (NIAID), 163–64, 165
National Institutes of Health, 162. *See also*
  National Institute of Allergies and
  Infectious Diseases
National Latino Lesbian and Gay Organi-
  zation, 184
National Minority AIDS Council, 229
  (n. 130)
National Parent Teacher Association, 90
National Security Council, 108
Native, the. See *New York Native*
Needle exchange programs, 66, 94
Negroponte, John D., 111–13, 230 (n. 139)